JUMP Math 7.1

Book 7 Part 1 of 2

Contents

JUMP Math
Toronto, Canada
www.jumpmath.org

Writers: Dr. John Mighton, Dr. Sindi Sabourin, Dr. Anna Klebanov
Contributing Writer: Margaret McClintock
Cover Design: Blakeley Words+Pictures
Text Design: Pam Lostracco
Layout: Lyubava Fartushenko, Pam Lostracco, Rita Camacho
Cover Photograph: © Gary Blakeley, Blakeley Words+Pictures

ISBN: 978-1-897120-57-6

Ninth printing July 2016

Printed and bound in Canada

A note to educators, parents, and everyone who believes that numeracy is as important as literacy for a fully functioning society

Welcome to JUMP Math

Entering the world of JUMP Math means believing that every child has the capacity to be fully numerate and to love math. Founder and mathematician John Mighton has used this premise to develop his innovative teaching method. The resulting materials isolate and describe concepts so clearly and incrementally that everyone can understand them.

JUMP Math is comprised of workbooks, teacher's guides, evaluation materials, outreach programs, tutoring support through schools and community organizations, and provincial curriculum correlations. All of this is presented on the JUMP Math website: **www.jumpmath.org**.

Teacher's guides are available on the website for free use. Read the introduction to the teacher's guides before you begin using these materials. This will ensure that you understand both the philosophy and the methodology of JUMP Math. The workbooks are designed for use by students, with adult guidance. Each student will have unique needs and it is important to provide the student with the appropriate support and encouragement as he or she works through the material.

Allow students to discover the concepts on the worksheets by themselves as much as possible. Mathematical discoveries can be made in small, incremental steps. The discovery of a new step is like untangling the parts of a puzzle. It is exciting and rewarding.

Students will need to answer the shaded questions using a notebook. Grid paper and notebooks should always be on hand for answering extra questions or when additional room for calculation is needed. Grid paper is also available in the BLM section of the Teacher's Guide.

Contents

PART 1

Unit 1: Number Sense

Unit 2: Patterns and Algebra

Unit 3: Number Sense

Unit 4: Geometry

Unit 5: Number Sense

Unit 6: Measurement

complementary

Unit 7: Probability and Data Management

NS7-1 Place Value

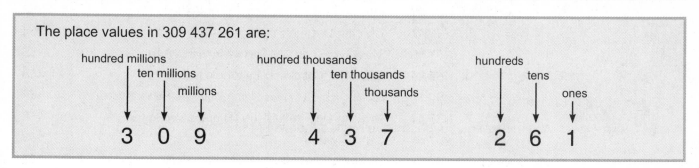

The place values in 309 437 261 are:

hundred millions	ten millions	millions	hundred thousands	ten thousands	thousands	hundreds	tens	ones
3	0	9	4	3	7	2	6	1

1. Write the next three place values greater than hundred millions, from largest to smallest.

________ ________ *billions*

2. Underline the digit with the given place value.

a) 250 329 120 ten millions

b) 791 250 329 120 ten billions

c) 791 250 329 120 hundred millions

d) 791 250 329 120 thousands

e) 791 250 329 120 billions

f) 791 250 329 120 hundred thousands

3. Write the place value of the bold digit.

a) 8**6**1 359 746 323 *ten billions*

b) 861 35**9** 746 323 *millions*

c) 861 **3**59 746 323 ________

d) **8**61 359 746 323 ________

e) 861 3**5**9 746 323 ________

f) 86**1** 359 746 323 ________

4. Write the number with the correct spacing, then write the place value of the digit 5.

a) 1405897660213 = *1* *405* *897* *660* *213* place value: *billions*

b) 76312098532 = ___ ___ ___ ___ ___ place value: ________

c) 995132498763 = ___ ___ ___ ___ ___ place value: ________

d) 3542706 = ___ ___ ___ ___ ___ place value: ________

e) 5410328 = ___ ___ ___ ___ ___ place value: ________

f) 841073521960347 = ________________ place value: ________

5. Write each number in expanded form. Example: 74 512 = 70 000 + 4 000 + 500 + 10 + 2

a) 378 403 ________________

b) 16 025 ________________

c) 721 803 ________________

6. Write the number for each expanded form. Example: 50 000 + 600 + 40 = 50 640

a) 30 000 + 4 000 + 50 + 3 ________

b) 600 000 + 30 ________

c) 40 000 + 200 + 5 ________

Done Abeka

7. Find the missing number.

a) 4 000 + 300 + ______ + 7 = 4 327 b) 2 000 000 + 30 000 + __________ + 2 = 2 035 002

8. In Japan, numbers are grouped by 4s, starting from the right.

Example: 52341 is written 5 2341 (not 5234 1)

a) Rewrite each number using Japanese spacing and then count the digits.

89034582367121 = ______________________________ ______ digits

8904358239121 = ______________________________ ______ digits

b) Does Japanese spacing make it easier to count the digits? ______________________

c) Circle the number from part a) that is larger. How do you know? ____________________

____

____

When two numbers have the same number of digits, we can compare the numbers by looking at the first digit that is different, starting from the left. Example: 764 322 769 303

this number is larger

9. Underline the left-most digits that are different and then circle the larger number in each pair.

a) 84 312 84 065

b) 74 312 908 74 314 873

c) 7 860 432 5 860 432

d) 531 658 531 662

10. Circle the larger number in each pair. First count the digits. Then, if necessary, look for the left-most digit that is different.

a) 543 806 5 412 679

b) 983 152 801 984 125 108

c) 654 009 280 654 092 800

d) 45 678 098 531 45 679 908

11. In the number 36, the 3 is worth 30 and the 6 is worth 6, so the 3 is worth 5 times as much as the 6. How many times more is the first bold digit worth than the second?

a) **84** ______ b) **84**0 ______ c) **8 4**23 ______ d) **84** 502 ______ e) **84**7 631 ______ f) **8 4**30 601 ______

g) **8**0**4** ______ h) **8** 32**4** ______ i) **8**3 20**4** ______ j) 9**8**3 20**4** ______ k) 2**8**3 651 **4**09 ______ l) 5**8**7 03**4** ______

BONUS▶ **3**7 215 48**6**

12. Write each number in words.

Example: 41 832 107 forty-one million eight hundred thirty-two thousand one hundred seven

a) 5 210 354 b) 573 312 400 c) 576 401 311 212 d) 31 485 620 417

NS7-2 Order of Operations

We add and subtract the way we read: from left to right.

1. Add or subtract from left to right.

a) $7 + 3 - 2$
$= 10 - 2$
$= 8$

b) $7 - 3 + 2$
$= 6$

c) $8 + 4 + 2$
$= 14$

d) $6 + 4 - 5$
$= 5$

2. a) Do the addition in brackets first.

i) $(4 + 6) + 5$
$=$ ____ $+ 5$
$=$ ____

ii) $4 + (6 + 5)$
$= 4 +$ ____
$=$ ____

b) Does the answer change depending on which addition you did first?

____

3. a) Do the subtraction in brackets first.

i) $(7 - 4) - 2$
$=$ ____ $-$ ____
$=$ ____

ii) $7 - (4 - 2)$
$=$ ____ $-$ ____
$=$ ____

b) Does the answer change depending on which subtraction you did first?

____

If there are brackets in an equation, do the operations in brackets first.

Example: $7 - 3 + 2 = 4 + 2 = 6$ but $7 - (3 + 2) = 7 - 5 = 2$

4. a) Calculate each expression using the correct order of operations.

i) $(15 + 7) - 3 - 1$

ii) $15 + (7 - 3) - 1$

iii) $15 + 7 - (3 - 1)$

iv) $(15 + 7 - 3) - 1$

v) $15 + (7 - 3 - 1)$

vi) $(15 + 7) - (3 - 1)$

b) How many different answers did you get in part a)? ____________

5. a) Add brackets in different ways to get as many different answers as you can.

i) $15 + 7 + 3 + 1$ ii) $15 - 7 + 3 - 1$ iii) $15 + 7 - 3 + 1$ iv) $15 - 7 - 3 - 1$

b) How many different answers did you get in part a)? i) ____ ii) ____ iii) ____ iv) ____

c) Check all that apply. The order of operations affects the answer when the expression consists of…

☐ addition only ☐ subtraction only ☐ addition and subtraction

Multiplication and division are also done from left to right. If there are brackets, do the operations in brackets first. Example: $15 \div 5 \times 3 = 3 \times 3 = 9$ but $15 \div (5 \times 3) = 15 \div 15 = 1$

6. Evaluate each expression.

a) $4 \times 3 \div 6 \times 7$ b) $6 \times 4 \div 2 \div 3$ c) $30 \div 5 \div (2 \times 3)$ d) $16 \times 2 \div (4 \times 2)$

7. a) Add brackets in different ways to get as many different answers as you can.

i) $2 \times 3 \times 2 \times 5$ ii) $64 \div 8 \div 4 \div 2$ iii) $90 \div 5 \times 6 \div 3$

b) Which expression in part a) gives the same answer, no matter where you place the brackets?

8. Do the operation in brackets first.

a) $10 + (4 \times 2)$
$= 10 + 8$
$= 18$

b) $(10 + 4) \times 2$ c) $(10 + 4) \div 2$ d) $10 + (4 \div 2)$

e) $10 - (4 \times 2)$ f) $(10 - 4) \times 2$ g) $(10 - 4) \div 2$ h) $10 - (4 \div 2)$

9. Check all that apply. The order of operations affects the answer when the expression combines…

- ☐ addition and multiplication
- ☐ addition and division
- ☐ subtraction and multiplication
- ☐ subtraction and division
- ☐ addition and subtraction
- ☐ multiplication and division

Mathematicians have ordered the operations to avoid writing brackets all the time. The order is:
1. Operations in brackets.
2. Multiplication and division, from left to right.
3. Addition and subtraction, from left to right.

Example: $3 \times 5 + 3 \times 6 = (3 \times 5) + (3 \times 6)$
$= 15 + 18$
$= 33$

but $3 \times (5 + 3) \times 6$
$= 3 \times 8 \times 6$
$= 24 \times 6$
$= 144$

10. Evaluate each expression. Use the correct order of operations.

a) $4 \times 2 - 7$ b) $2 + 4 \div 2$ c) $6 - 2 \times 3$ d) $20 \div 2 + 8$

e) $4 + 3 \times 6 - 5$ f) $6 + 6 \div 3 - 7$ g) $4 \times 3 \div 6 + 5$ h) $3 \times 7 - 6 \div 2$

i) $4 \div (2 - 1)$ j) $(5 - 1) \times 3$ k) $20 - (14 - 7)$ l) $(12 - 4) \div 4$

11. Turn the written instructions into mathematical expressions.

a) Add 8 and 3.
Then subtract 4.
Then multiply by 3.
$(8 + 3 - 4) \times 3$

b) Subtract 6 from 9.
Then multiply by 2.
Then add 4.
____

c) Multiply 6 and 5.
Then subtract from 40.
Then add 5.
____

d) Divide 4 by 2.
Then add 10.
Then subtract 4.
____

e) Divide 6 by 3.
Then add 5.
Then subtract 3.
____

BONUS▶
Divide 8 by 4 and then add 2.
Add 5 and 3 together.
Multiply the two results.
____

12. Write the mathematical expressions in words.

a) $(6 + 2) \times 3$ *Add 6 and 2. Then multiply by 3.*

b) $(6 + 1) \times 2$ ____________

c) $4 \times (3 - 1 + 5)$ ____________

d) $(5 - 2) \times (4 + 17)$ e) $(24 - 2 \times 6) \div 4$ f) $24 - 2 \times 6 \div 4$

13. a) Add brackets in different ways to get as many different answers as you can.

i) $3 + 1 \times 7 - 2$ ii) $16 - 4 \times 2 + 8$ iii) $16 \div 4 \times 2 + 8$

b) How many different answers did you get in part a)? i) ______ ii) ______ iii) ______

14. a) Calculate the expression in the box. Which expression without brackets gives the same answer?

i) $\boxed{8 - (5 + 2)} = 8 - 5 - 2$ or $8 - 5 + 2$ ii) $\boxed{7 - (3 - 2)} = 7 - 3 - 2$ or $7 - 3 + 2$

iii) $\boxed{7 + (5 - 2)} = 7 + 5 - 2$ or $7 + 5 + 2$ iv) $\boxed{6 + (2 + 4)} = 6 + 2 + 4$ or $6 + 2 - 4$

15. Rewrite each expression without brackets by changing only operations symbols.
Keep the answer the same.

a) $24 \div (6 \times 2)$ b) $5 \times 8 \div (4 \div 2)$ c) $5 \times 8 \div (4 \times 2)$

16. a) The expressions on the left have brackets and the expressions on the right do not.
Calculate the expressions, then match by the same answer.

$4 \times 6 \div (3 \times 2)$ $4 \times 6 \times 2 + 4 \times 3 \times 2$

$4 \times (6 + 3) \times 2$ $4 \times 3 + 4 \times 2 + 6 \times 3 + 6 \times 2$

$(4 + 6) \times (3 + 2)$ $4 \times 6 \div 3 \div 2$

b) Which expression with brackets from part a) needs the most writing to write without brackets and still get the same answer? ____________

NS7-3 Equations

A **numeric expression** is a combination of numbers, operation signs, and sometimes brackets, that represents a quantity. Example: These expressions all represent 10:

$7 + 3$ $\quad$ $12 - 2$ $\quad$ $100 \div 10$ $\quad$ $(4 + 1) \times 2$

1. Calculate each expression.

a) $1 + 3 + 4$ ______ b) 3×4 ______ c) $2 \times 2 \times 2$ ______ d) $5 + 2$ ______

An **equation** is a mathematical statement that has two expressions representing the same quantity separated by an equal sign. Example: $12 - 2 = 100 \div 10$

2. a) Circle two expressions in Question 1 that represent the same quantity.

b) Write an equation using those two expressions.

______________ = ______________

3. Verify that each equation is true.

a) $(4 + 3) \times 2 = 5 \times 3 - 1$ b) $3 \times 4 \times 5 = 6 \times 10$ c) $1 + 2 + 3 + 4 + 5 + 6 = 7 \times 3$

$(4 + 3) \times 2$ and $5 \times 3 - 1$

$= 7 \times 2$ $\quad$ $= 15 - 1$

$= 14$ $\quad$ $= 14$

4. Verify that each equation is true.

a) $5 + 12 = (5 + 1) + (12 - 1)$ b) $5 + 12 = (5 + 2) + (12 - 2)$ c) $5 + 12 = (5 + 3) + (12 - 3)$

5. Rewrite each pair of equations as a single equation by leaving out the number on the right.

a) $(5 + 4) + (6 - 4) = 11$ $\quad$ $5 + 6 = 11$

$(5 + 4) + (6 - 4) = 5 + 6$

b) $(7 - 2) + (4 + 2) = 11$ $\quad$ $7 + 4 = 11$

____

c) $(8 + 2) + (7 - 2) = 15$ $\quad$ $8 + 7 = 15$

____

d) $(8 - 5) + (9 + 5) = 17$ $\quad$ $8 + 9 = 17$

____

6. Write the correct number to make the equation true. Verify your answer by calculating both sides.

a) $(12 - 3) + (8 +$ *3* $) = 12 + 8$ b) $(11 + 7) + (9 -$ ____ $) = 11 + 9$ c) $(8 - 2) + (5 +$ ____ $) = 8 + 5$

$= 9 + 11$ $\quad$ $= 20$

$= 20$ ← equal →

7. Verify that each equation is true.

a) $(9 + 2) - (4 + 2) = 9 - 4$ b) $(10 - 3) - (7 - 3) = 10 - 7$ c) $(8 - 3) - (6 - 3) = 8 - 6$

8. Write the correct number to make the equation true. Verify your answers.

a) $(12 - 3) + (8 + \_\_\_\_) = 12 + 8$ b) $(12 - 5) - (8 - \_\_\_\_) = 12 - 8$

c) $(15 + 2) - (8 + \_\_\_\_) = 15 - 8$ d) $(11 + 7) + (9 - \_\_\_\_) = 11 + 9$

9. Write the correct operation to make the equation true. Verify your answers.

a) $(13 - 3) + (7 \bigcirc 3) = 13 + 7$ b) $(8 + 2) + (7 \bigcirc 2) = 8 + 7$

c) $(6 + 5) - (4 \bigcirc 5) = 6 - 4$ d) $(9 - 3) - (5 \bigcirc 3) = 9 - 5$

10. a) Write the correct operation and number to make the statement true.

i) $(26 + 3) + (35 \_\_\_\_) = 26 + 35$ ii) $(18 + 4) - (7 \_\_\_\_) = 18 - 7$

iii) $(17 - 4) + (26 \_\_\_\_) = 17 + 26$ iv) $(24 - 3) - (9 \_\_\_\_) = 24 - 9$

v) $(134 \_\_\_\_) - (38 + 7) = 134 - 38$ vi) $(287 \_\_\_\_) + (41 + 6) = 287 + 41$

b) Choose one of the equations you made and verify that it is true by calculating both sides.

BONUS▸ Add brackets where necessary to the following equations to make them true.

a) $3 + 1 \times 7 - 2 = 20$ b) $3 + 1 \times 7 - 2 = 26$ c) $3 + 1 \times 7 - 2 = 8$

d) $6 - 3 \times 2 = 6$ e) $16 \div 2 \times 2 = 4$ f) $4 + 8 \div 2 = 6$

g) $8 - 4 \times 2 + 5 = 28$ h) $8 - 4 \times 2 + 5 = 13$ i) $5 \times 4 - 3 + 2 = 7$

NS7-4 Properties of Operations

The area of a rectangle is the number of square units that cover it.

1. Find the area of each rectangle.

a) 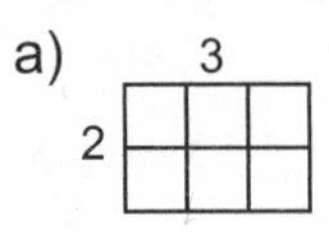

$2 \times 3 = 6$

b) 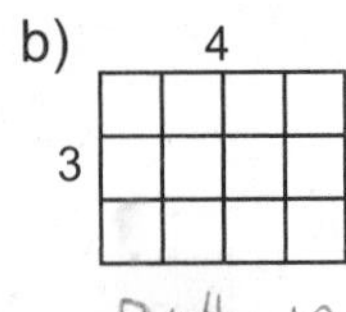

c) 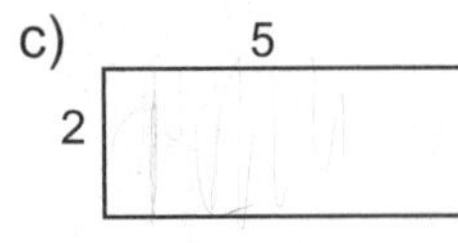

d) 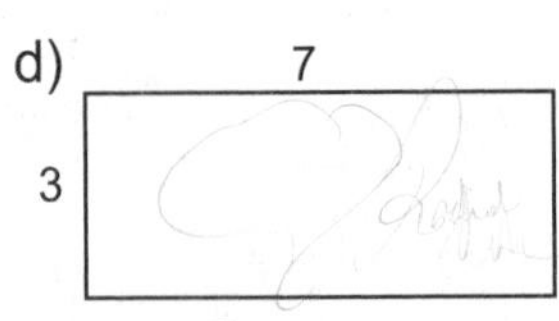

e) 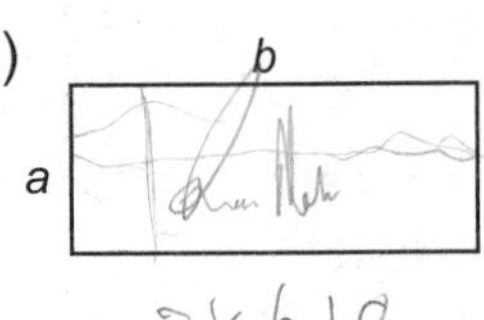

2. A rectangle is cut in half in two different ways. How long are the resulting sides?

a) 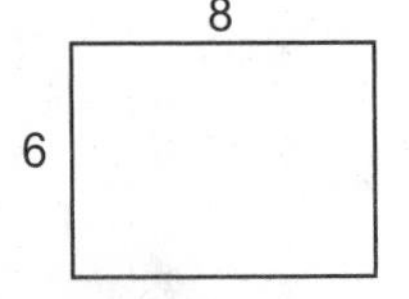 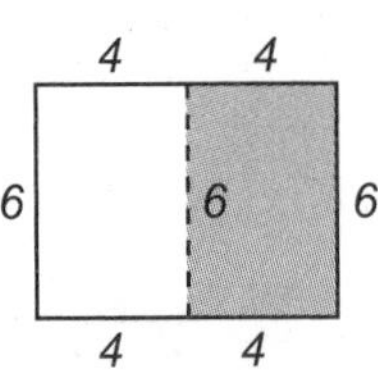 and 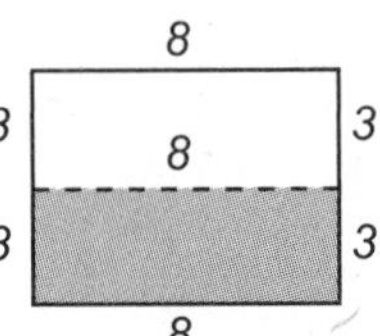

b) 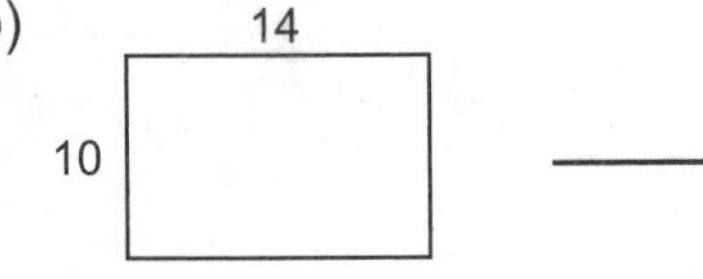 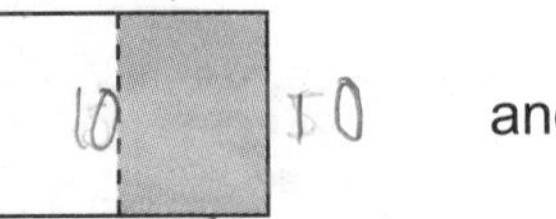 and 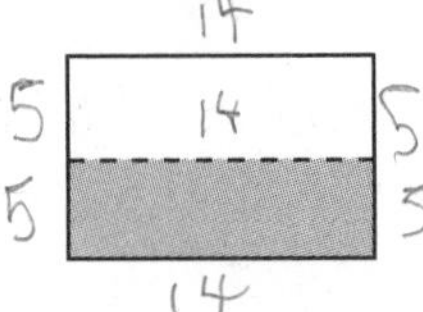

c) 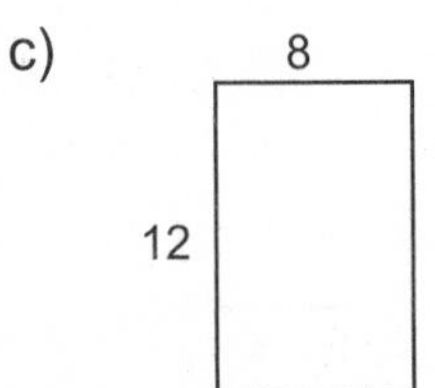 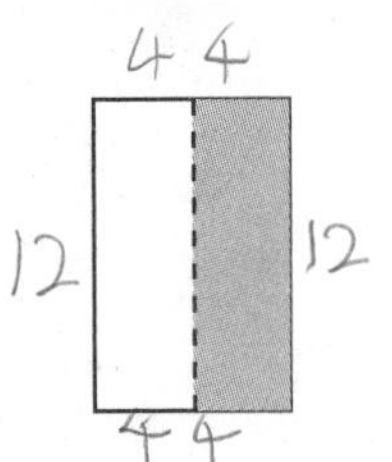 and 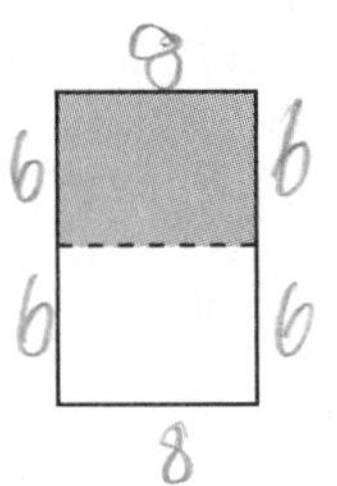

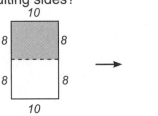

3. A rectangle is cut in half and rearranged. How long are the resulting sides?

a) 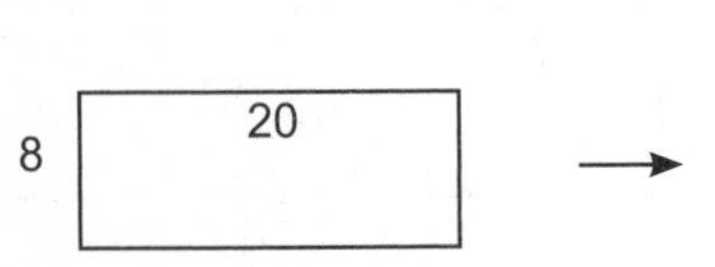 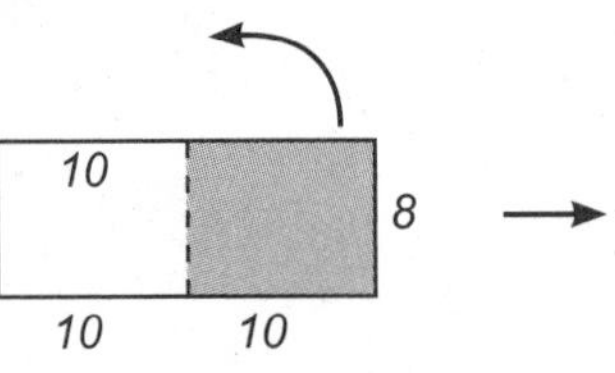 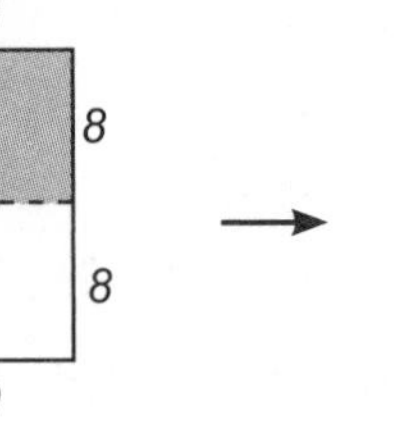 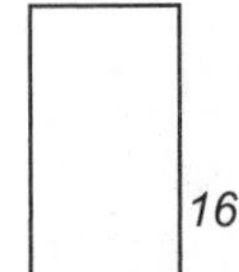

b) 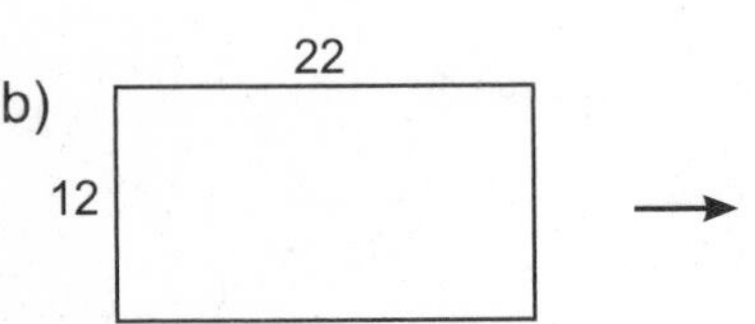 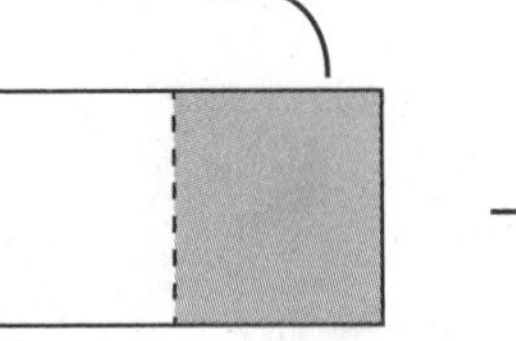 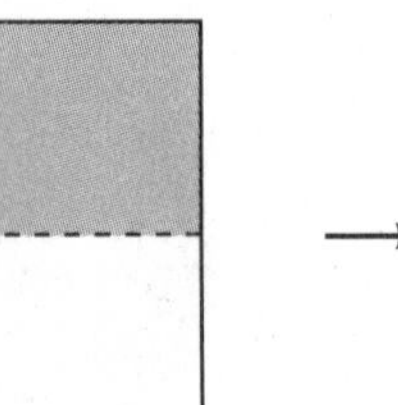 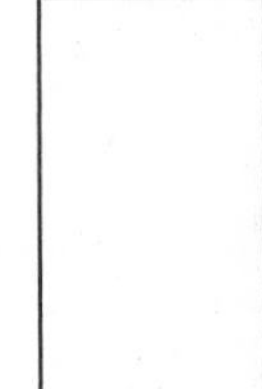 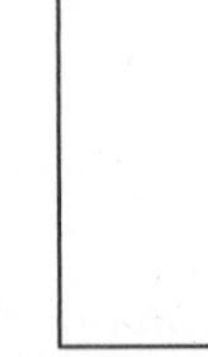

c) 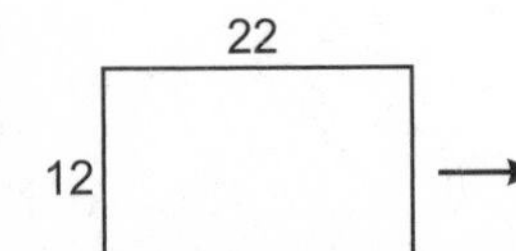 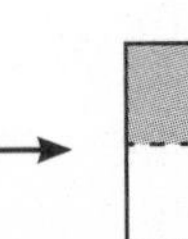 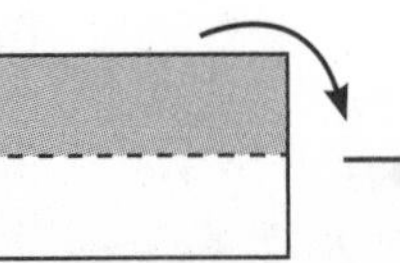 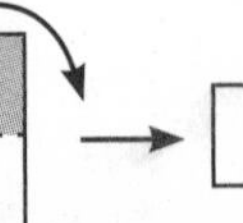 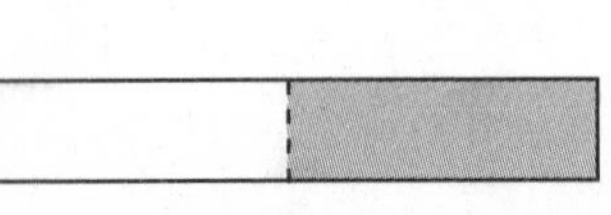

4. A rectangle is cut in half and rearranged. Make another product with the same answer to complete the equation.

a)

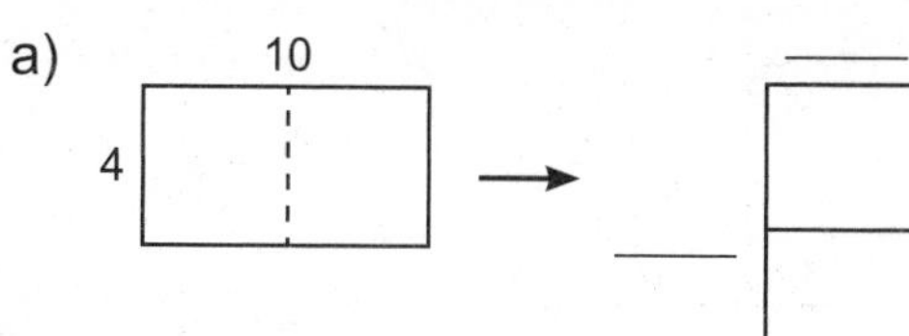

$4 \times 10 =$ ____ $\times$ ____

b)

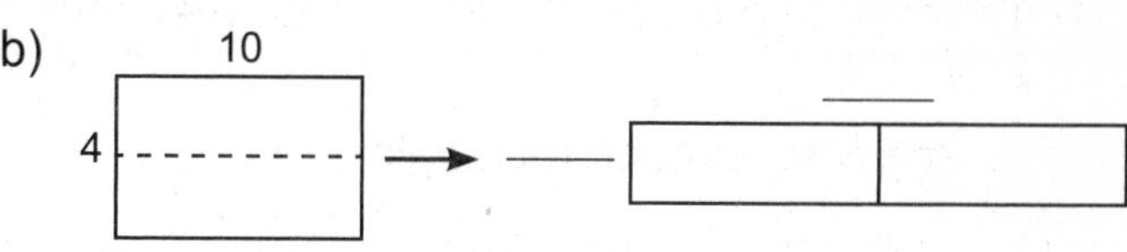

$4 \times 10 =$ ____ $\times$ ____

5. Imagine cutting the rectangle in half and rearranging. Make two more products with the same answer.

a)

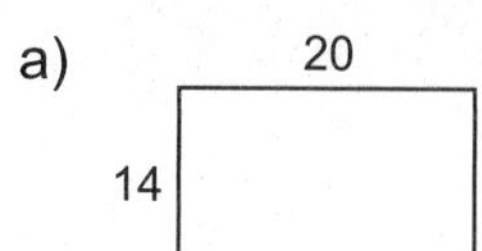

$20 \times 14 =$ ____ $\times$ ____
$=$ ____ $\times$ ____

b)
12
8

$8 \times 12 =$ ____ $\times$ ____
$=$ ____ $\times$ ____

c)

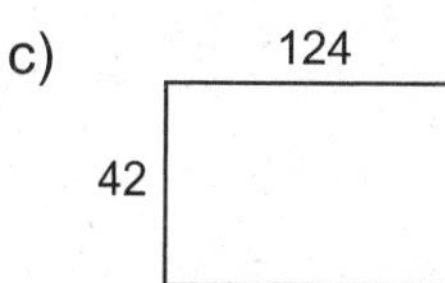

$124 \times 42 =$ ____ $\times$ ____
$=$ ____ $\times$ ____

6. Cut the rectangle in thirds and rearrange. Make two more products with the same answer.

a)

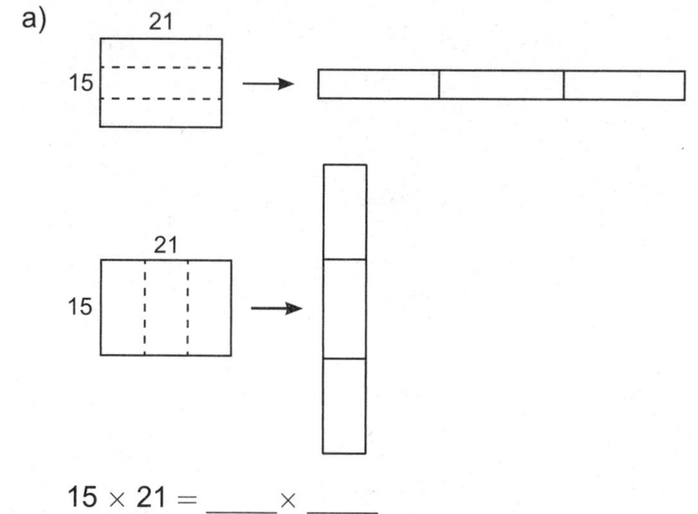

$15 \times 21 =$ ____ $\times$ ____
$=$ ____ $\times$ ____

b)
15
12
or

$12 \times 15 =$ ____ $\times$ ____
$=$ ____ $\times$ ____

c)

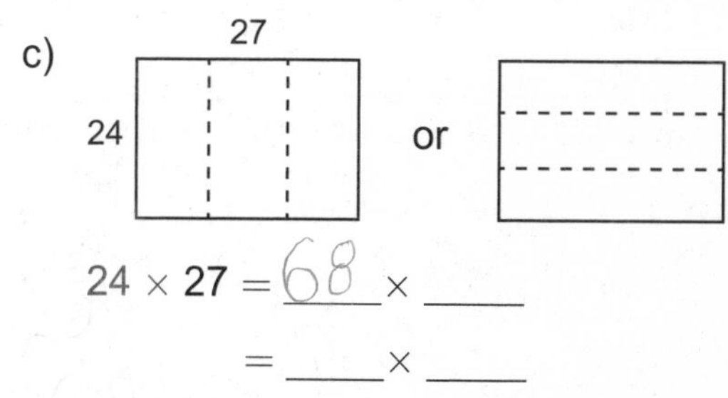

$24 \times 27 =$ 68 $\times$ ____
$=$ ____ $\times$ ____

7. Draw rectangles to show why:

a) $5 \times 6 = 10 \times 3$

b) $5 \times 9 = 15 \times 3$

c) $5 \times 12 = 20 \times 3$

8. Write the correct number to make the equation true.

a) $5 \times 6 = (5 \times 2) \times (6 \div \_\_\_)$

b) $5 \times 9 = (5 \times 3) \times (9 \div \_\_\_)$

c) $5 \times 12 = (5 \times 4) \times (12 \div \_\_\_)$

d) $4 \times 6 = (4 \times 3) \times (6 \div \_\_\_)$

e) $15 \times 16 = (15 \times 4) \times (16 \div \_\_\_)$

f) $8 \times 8 = (8 \times 2) \times (8 \div \_\_\_)$

9. Write the correct operation. Then verify your answers in your notebook, by calculating both sides.

a) $3 \times 4 = (3 \times 2) \times (4 \bigcirc 2)$ b) $4 \times 15 = (4 \times 3) \times (15 \bigcirc 3)$ c) $9 \times 21 = (9 \times 7) \times (21 \bigcirc 7)$

Start with any multiplication statement. To find another multiplication statement with the same answer **multiply one factor and divide the other by the same number**.

Example: $\mathbf{5} \times \mathbf{30} = 150$

$10 \times 15 = 150$ (**5 × 2** ↗, ↖ **30 ÷ 2**)

$50 \times 3 = 150$ (**5 × 10** ↗, ↖ **30 ÷ 10**)

10. Write the correct operation and number. Then verify your answers in your notebook.

a) $5 \times 18 = (5 \times 2) \times (18 \underline{\div 2})$ b) $7 \times 60 = (7 \times 10) \times (60 \_\_\_)$ c) $8 \times 25 = (8 \times 5) \times (25 \_\_\_)$

11. Explain why these problems have the same answer. Then choose the easiest one and solve it.

25×16 50×8 100×4

12. Multiply.

a) Since $3 \times 5 = 15$, then $6 \times 5 = \_\_\_\_\_$

b) Since $4 \times 3 = 12$, then $8 \times 3 = \_\_\_\_\_$

c) Since $9 \times 8 = 72$, then $9 \times 16 = \_\_\_\_\_$

d) Since $7 \times 9 = 63$, then $14 \times 9 = \_\_\_\_\_$

13. Multiply one factor by 5 and find the products.

factors → $3 \times 5 = 15$ ← product

a) $2 \times 3 = 6$ so $\_\_\_\_\_ \times 3 = \_\_\_\_\_$

b) $3 \times 5 = 15$ so $\_\_\_\_\_ \times 5 = \_\_\_\_\_$

c) $4 \times 5 = 20$ so $4 \times \_\_\_\_\_ = \_\_\_\_\_$

d) $2 \times 6 = 12$ so $2 \times \_\_\_\_\_ = \_\_\_\_\_$

When you multiply one factor by 5, what happens to the product? ____________________

14. Fill in the blanks with the correct operation and number.

a) $5 \times 8 = 40$
so $15 \times 8 = 40 \underline{\times 3}$

b) $5 \times 9 = 45$
so $5 \times 18 = 45 \_\_\_\_\_$

c) $3 \times 6 = 18$
so $21 \times 6 = 18 \_\_\_\_\_$

15. Write the equivalent division statement for each multiplication statement.

$6 \times 5 = 30$	so	$\underline{30} \div \underline{6} = 5$
$(6 \times 2) \times 5 = 30 \times 2$	so	$(\underline{30 \times 2}) \div (\underline{6 \times 2}) = 5$
$(6 \times 3) \times 5 = 30 \times 3$	so	$(\_\_\_\_\_\_) \div (\_\_\_\_\_\_) = 5$
$(6 \times 4) \times 5 = 30 \times 4$	so	$(\_\_\_\_\_\_) \div (\_\_\_\_\_\_) = 5$

16. Write the correct operation and number.

$30 \div 6 = (30 \times 2) \div (6$ ______ $)$

$= (30 \times 3) \div (6$ ______ $)$

$= (30 \times 4) \div (6$ ______ $)$

17. Fill in the blanks with the correct operation and number. Verify your answers in your notebook.

a) $12 \div 3 = (12 \times 2) \div (3$ _____ $)$ b) $20 \div 5 = (20 \times 2) \div (5$ _____ $)$ c) $90 \div 6 = (90 \times 5) \div (6$ _____ $)$

18. Explain why these problems have the same answer. Then choose the easiest one and solve it.

$35 \div 5$ $70 \div 10$ $105 \div 15$

19. Fill in the blanks to solve the problems.

a) $135 \div 5 =$ *270* $\div 10$ $=$ ______

b) $120 \div 5 =$ ______ $\div 10$ $=$ ______

c) $65 \div 5 =$ ______ $\div 10$ $=$ ______

Start with any division statement. To find another division statement with the same answer, **multiply both terms (the dividend and the divisor) by the same number**.

Example: $\mathbf{6} \div \mathbf{2} = 3$ $12 \div 4 = 3$ ($\mathbf{6} \times 2$, $\mathbf{2} \times 2$) $18 \div 6 = 3$ ($\mathbf{6} \times 3$, $\mathbf{2} \times 3$) $24 \div 8 = 3$ ($\mathbf{6} \times 4$, $\mathbf{2} \times 4$)

20. Write the equivalent division statement for each multiplication statement.

$12 \times 5 = 60$ so *60* $\div$ *12* $= 5$

$(12 \div 2) \times 5 = 60 \div 2$ so (*60 ÷ 2*) $\div$ (*12 ÷ 2*) $= 5$

$(12 \div 3) \times 5 = 60 \div 3$ so (__________) $\div$ (__________) $= 5$

$(12 \div 4) \times 5 = 60 \div 4$ so (__________) $\div$ (__________) $= 5$

21. Write the correct operation and number.

$60 \div 12 = (60 \div 2) \div (12$ ______ $)$

$= (60 \div 3) \div (12$ ______ $)$

$= (60 \div 4) \div (12$ ______ $)$

22. Write the correct operation and number. Verify your answers in your notebook.

a) $20 \div 4 = (20 \div 2) \div (4$ ______ $)$ b) $24 \div 6 = (24 \div 3) \div (6$ ______ $)$

23. Write an operation and a number to make the equation true.

a) $9 - 5 = (9 + 2) - (5$ _____ $)$ b) $9 + 5 = (9 + 2) + (5$ _____ $)$ c) $18 \times 6 = (18 \times 3) \times (6$ _____ $)$

d) $18 \div 6 = (18 \times 3) \div (6$ _____ $)$ e) $5 \times 12 = (5 \times 3) \times (12$ _____ $)$ f) $7 \times 9 = ($ _____ $3) \times (9 \div 3)$

g) $8 + 7 = (8 - 4) + (7$ _____ $)$ h) $30 \div 6 = (30 \div 2) \div (6$ _____ $)$ i) $12 \times 10 = (12 \div 2) \times (10$ _____ $)$

BONUS▶

j) $m \div n = (m \times p) \div (n$ _____ $)$ k) $a \times d = (a \div m) \times (d$ _____ $)$ l) $r + s = (r - t) + (s$ _____ $)$

NS7-5 Multiplication and Division with 0 and 1

1. Draw arrays to show the products and multiply.

   a) $1 \times 3 =$ 3 b) $1 \times 7 =$ 7

   c) $2 \times 1 =$ 2 d) $5 \times 1 =$ 5

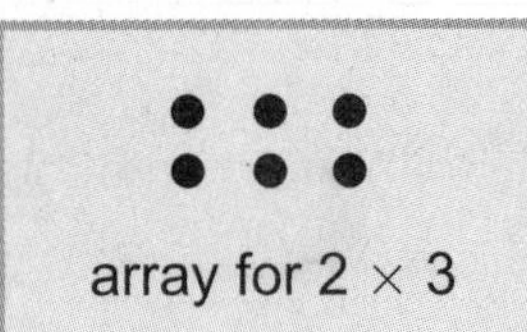

array for 2×3

2. What is $1 \times 34\ 716$? 34 716 What is $34\ 716 \times 1$? 34 716

   How do you know? The anser is the Same

3. Divide.

   a) $4 \div 4 =$ 1 b) $7 \div 7 =$ 1 c) $6 \div 1 =$ 6 d) $12 \div 1 =$ 12

4. a) $854\ 302 \div 854\ 302 =$ 1 b) $854\ 302 \div 1 =$ 854 302

5. a) $7 \times 0 = 0 + 0 + 0 + 0 + 0 + 0 + 0 =$ 7

   b) $5 \times 0 = 0 + 0 + 0 + 0 + 0 =$ 5

   c) $974 \times 0 =$ 974

6. Extend the pattern in the factors and the products to find 0×5. ✓ Done abecka

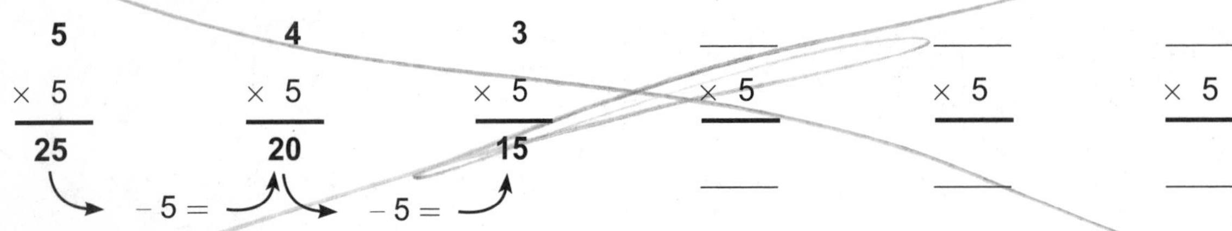

7. Extend the pattern in the factors and the products to find 0×3.

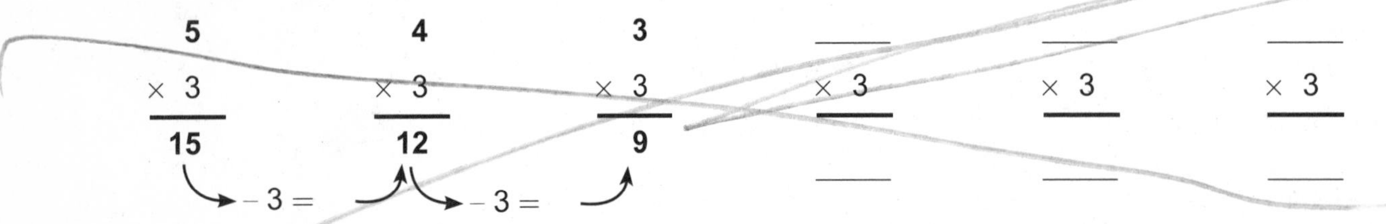

8. Multiply.

   a) $0 \times 7 =$ 0 b) $0 \times 2 =$ 0 c) $0 \times 0 =$ 0 d) $0 \times 1 =$ 0

9. What is $0 \times 34\ 716$? 34 716

   How do you know? The anser is the Same

The multiplication statement $2 \times 4 = 8$ can be written in terms of division: $8 \div 4 = 2$.

If you start with 2 and multiply by 4, then to get back to where you started, you divide by 4.

10. Write each multiplication in terms of division.

a) Since $1 \times 0 = 0$, then $0 \div 0 =$ 0 .

b) Since $2 \times 0 = 0$, then $0 \div 0 =$ 0 .

c) Since $3 \times 0 = 0$, then $0 \div 0 =$ 0 .

d) Since $4 \times 0 = 0$, then $0 \div 0 =$ 0 .

The result of an operation needs to have **exactly one answer**. Example: $15 \div 3 = 5$

Since $0 \div 0$ can have many answers, mathematicians have decided not to define it at all!

11. a) What answer will ☐ $\times$ 0 always have? 0

b) Can you find a number ☐ that makes ☐ $\times 0 = 7$? No.

c) Does $7 \div 0$ have an answer? Explain. 0 Becuse if u have 0 Cookies and 7 friends you still have 0 cookies.

12. Write "no answer" or "too many answers."

a) $0 \div 0$ does not make sense because it has no awnser .

b) $9 \div 0$ does not make sense because it has no awnser .

13. Either write **the unique answer** or explain why you cannot.

a) $5 \times$ *0* $= 0$

b) $0 \times$ 5 $= 5$

no answer

c) $0 \times$ 9 $= 0$

too many answers

d) $0 \times 5 =$ 5

e) $5 \times$ 5 $= 5$

f) $3 \div 0 =$ 0

g) $0 \div 3 =$ ______

h) $0 \div 0 =$ ______

i) $3 \div 3 =$ ______

j) $3 \div$ ______ $= 0$

k) ______ $\times 0 = 10$

l) ______ $\times 0 = 0$

NS7-6 The Area Model for Multiplication

1. a) Write 7 as a sum of two smaller numbers in different ways.

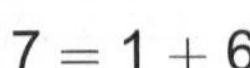

7 = 1 + 6 

7 = 2 + 6

7 = 3 + 4

7 = 4 + 3

7 = 5 + 2

7 = 6 + 1

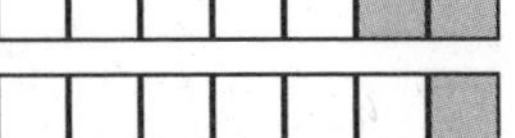

b) How are the sums on the left the same as the sums on the right?

____

____

2. a) Write 3 × 7 as a sum of two smaller multiples of 3 in different ways.

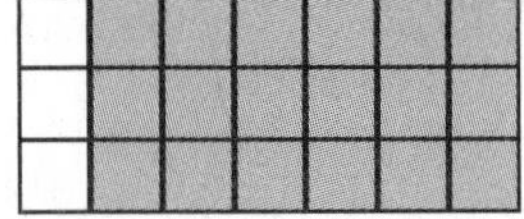

3 × 7 = 3 × 1 + 3 × 6

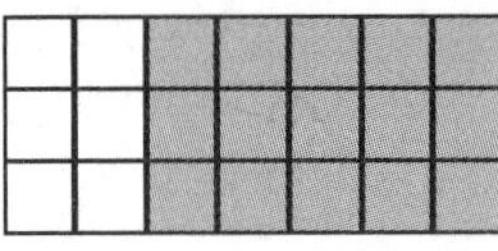

____

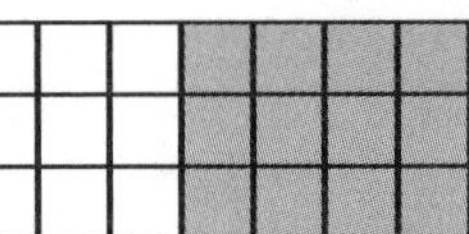

____

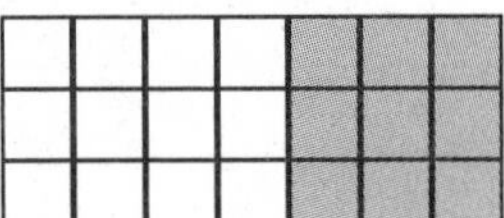

____

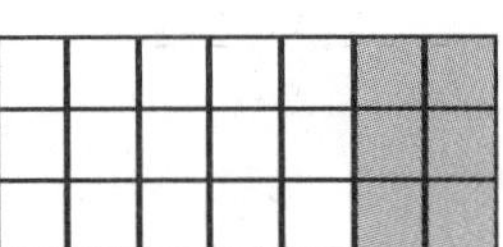

____

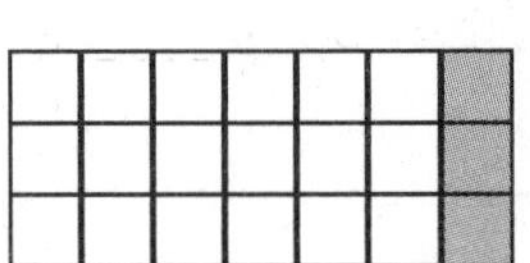

____

b) How are the sums in the first row the same as the sums in the second row?

____

____

3. a) Write **4** × **13** as a sum of two smaller multiples of 4 in all the ways possible.

4 × **1** + 4 × 12 = 4 + ____

4 × **2** + 4 × 11 = 8 + ____

4 × **3** + 4 × ____ = ____ + ____

4 × **4** + 4 × ____ = ____ + ____

4 × **5** + 4 × ____ = ____ + ____

4 × **6** + 4 × ____ = ____ + ____

We can stop at 4 × 6 + 4 × 7 because ______________________________.

b) What is 4 × 13? ____

Which of the sums did you use to find it? Why? ______________________________.

c) Write 4 × 13 as a sum of three smaller products.

4 × 13 = 4 × ____ + 4 × ____ + 4 × ____

4. Are the two expressions equal (=) or not equal (≠)? Show your work.

a) $4 \times (8 + 2)$ ☐ $(4 \times 8) + (4 \times 2)$

b) $4 \times (8 - 2)$ ☐ $(4 \times 8) - (4 \times 2)$

c) $4 + (8 \times 2)$ ☐ $(4 + 8) \times (4 + 2)$

d) $4 + (8 \div 2)$ ☐ $(4 + 8) \div (4 + 2)$

5. Write the dimensions of the two smaller rectangles.

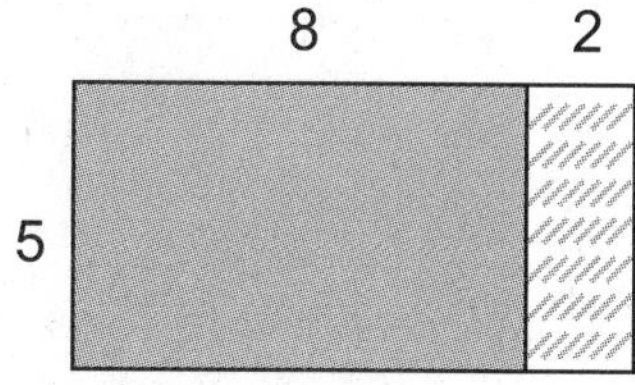

= ____ 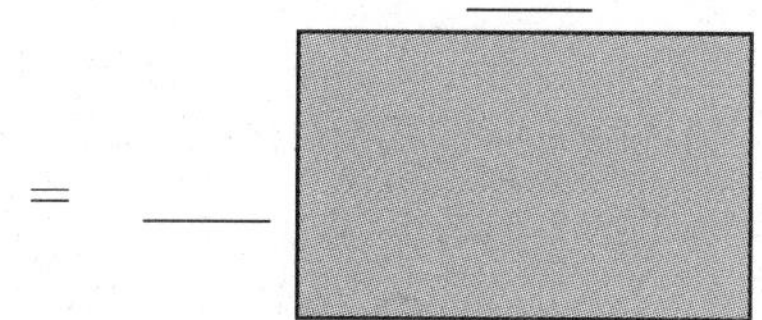 (top: ____) + ____ 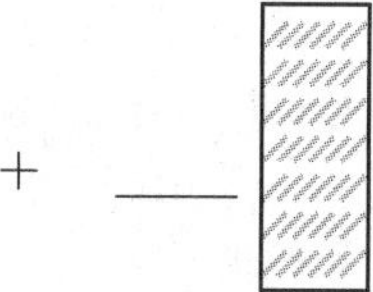 (top: ____)

Now find the area of the large rectangle in two ways. Then write an equation.

Area = $5 \times$ (____ + ____) and Area = ____ × ____ + ____ × ____

So $5 \times$ (____ + ____) = ____ × ____ + ____ × ____

6. Find the dimensions of the shaded part in two ways. Then write an equation.

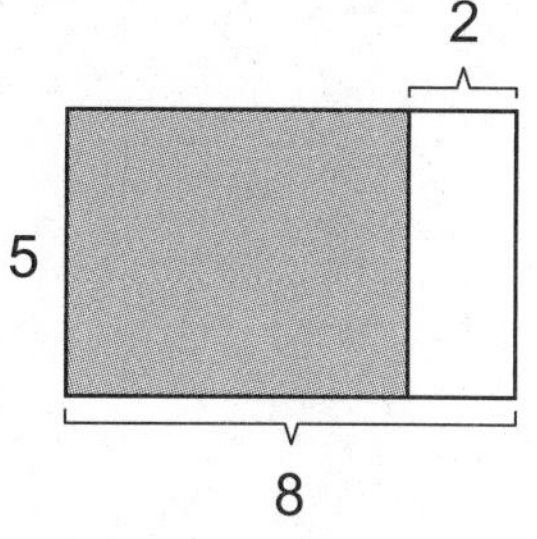

= 5 (top: ____) − 5 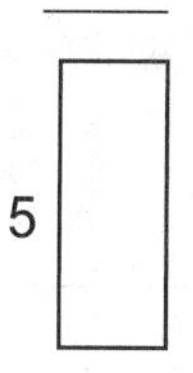 (top: ____)

Area = $5 \times$ (____ − ____) and Area = $5 \times$ ____ − $5 \times$ ____

So ______________________ = ______________________

7. Draw an area model to show that $7 \times 12 = 7 \times 10 + 7 \times 2$.

8. Write the dimensions of the four smaller rectangles.
Then find the area of the large rectangle in two ways.
Then write an equation.

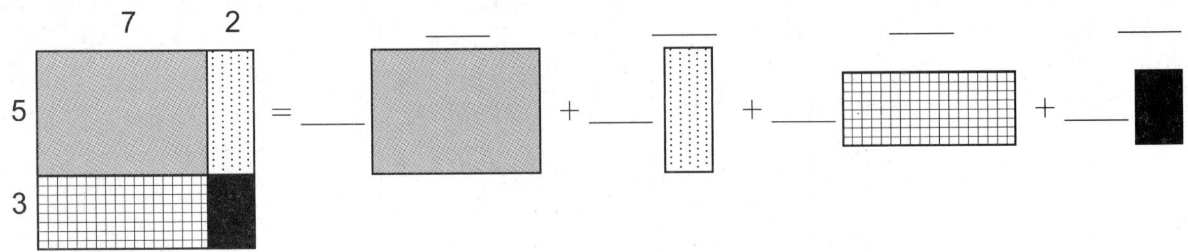

Area = (5 + 3) × (____ + ____)   and

Area = 5 × 7 + ____ × ____ + ____ × ____ + ____ × ____

So ______________________ = ______________________________

9. Use these pictures to write 12 × 13 as a sum of four smaller products.

a)

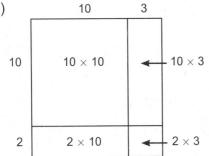

	10	3
10	10 × 10	← 10 × 3
2	2 × 10	← 2 × 3

12 × 13 = (10 + 2) × (10 + 3)

= ____ × ____ + ____ × ____

+ ____ × ____ + ____ × ____

= ____ + ____ + ____ + ____

= ____

b)

	7	6
4	4 × 7	____
8	____	____

12 × 13 = (4 + 8) × (7 + 6)

= ____ × ____ + ____ × ____

+ ____ × ____ + ____ × ____

= ____ + ____ + ____ + ____

= ____

c) Did you get the same answer both ways? ________

d) Which way made it easier to find 12 × 13? Explain. ______________________________

____

NS7-7 Breaking Multiplication into Simpler Problems

Mathematicians often break problems into simpler problems.
In multiplication, this often means using multiplication by 10, 100, or 1 000.

1. Find each product.

a) $3 \times 20 = 3 \times$ ____ tens
$=$ ____ tens
$=$ ____

b) $3 \times 200 = 3 \times$ ____ hundreds
$=$ ____ hundreds
$=$ ____

c) $3 \times 2\,000 =$ ______
d) $3 \times 20\,000 =$ ______
e) $3 \times 200\,000 =$ ______

f) $3 \times 700 =$ ______
g) $5 \times 4\,000 =$ ______
h) $15 \times 40\,000 =$ ______

2. Use multiples of 10 or 100 to break each problem into simpler problems.

a) $5 \times 23 = 5 \times 20 + 5 \times$ ______
$=$ ______ $+$ ______
$=$ ______

b) $2 \times 432 = 2 \times$ ______ $+ 2 \times$ ______ $+ 2 \times$ ______
$=$ ______ $+$ ______ $+$ ______
$=$ ______

c) $3 \times 312 =$ ________________ $+$ ________________ $+$ ________________
$=$ ______ $+$ ______ $+$ ______
$=$ ______

3. Multiply in your head.

a) $3 \times 12 =$ ______
b) $3 \times 52 =$ ______
c) $6 \times 31 =$ ______
d) $7 \times 21 =$ ______

e) $5 \times 31 =$ ______
f) $3 \times 621 =$ ______
g) $5 \times 411 =$ ______
h) $3 \times 632 =$ ______

4. Use the 2 times table and the 10 times table to write the 12 times table.

	1	**2**	**3**	**4**	**5**	**6**	**7**	**8**	**9**	**10**
× 2	2	4	6							
× 10	10	20	30							
× 12	12	24	36							

5. Use the 3 times table and the 20 times table to write the 23 times table.

	1	**2**	**3**	**4**	**5**	**6**	**7**	**8**	**9**	**10**
× 3	3	6	9							
× 20	20	40	60							
× 23	23	46								

Long Multiplication

How to solve $3 \times 42 = 3 \times 40 + 3 \times 2$

$= 3 \times 4 \text{ tens} + 3 \times 2 \text{ ones}$

Step 1:

Multiply the ones digit by 3 (3×2 ones $= 6$ ones).

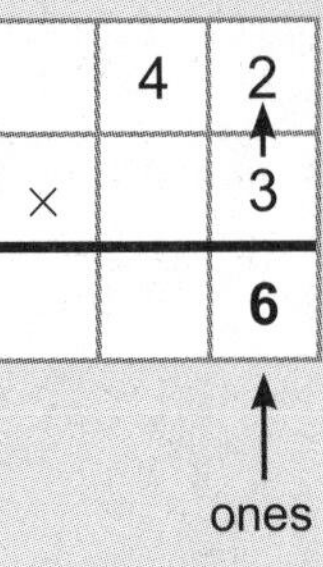

Step 2:

Multiply the tens digit by 3 (3×4 tens $= 12$ tens).

Regroup 10 tens as 1 hundred.

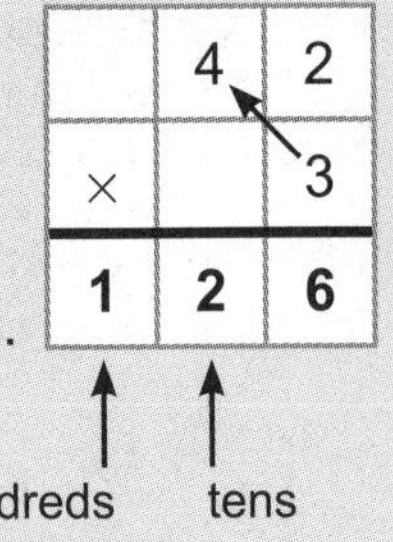

1. Use Steps 1 and 2 to find the products.

a)

	9	4
×		2

b)

	8	3
×		3

c)

	7	4
×		2

d)

	9	4
×		2

e)

	9	2
×		3

How to solve $7 \times 43 = 7 \times 40 + 7 \times 3$

$= 7 \times 4 \text{ tens} + 7 \times 3 \text{ ones}$

Step 1:

Multiply 3 ones by 7 ($7 \times 3 = 21$).

Step 2:

Regroup 20 ones as 2 tens.

2. Complete **Steps 1** and **2** of the multiplication.

a)

	3	
	2	7
×		5
		5

b)

	1	5
×		6

c)

	2	5
×		3

d)

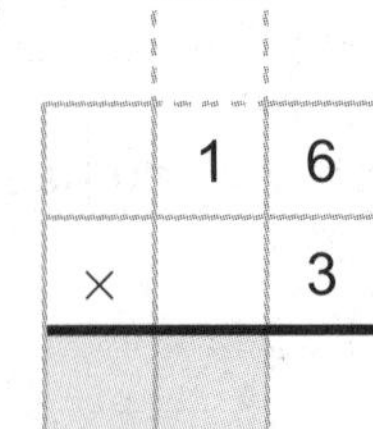

e)

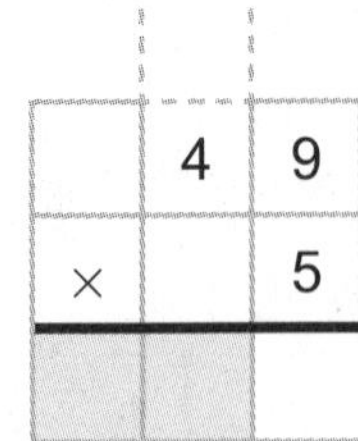

Step 3:

Multiply 4 tens by 7
(7×4 tens $= 28$ tens).

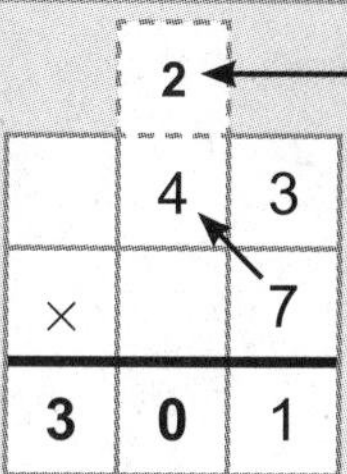

Step 4:

Add 2 tens to the result
($28 + 2 = 30$ tens).

3. Complete **Steps 3** and **4** of the multiplication.

a) carry: *1*; 2 4 × 3; result: *7 2*

b) carry: *4*; 3 5 × 9; result: *5*

c) carry: *2*; 1 5 × 5; result: *5*

d)

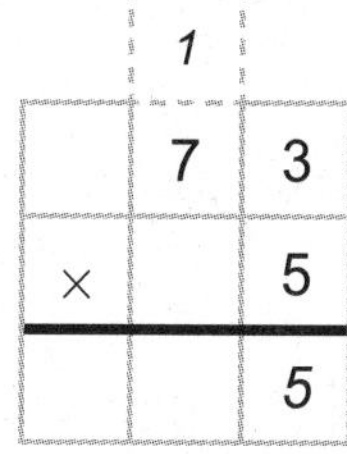

e) carry: *4*; 8 9 × 5; result: *5*

4. Complete **all steps** of the multiplication.

a) 3 5 × 8

b) 3 5 × 6

c) 1 5 × 7; result: 5

d) 2 5 × 8

e) 2 4 × 5

5. Multiply.

a) 4 1 × 5

b) 4 3 4 × 2

c) 3 1 2 × 3

d) 1 2 4 × 2

e) 3 2 3 × 3

6. Multiply by regrouping ones as tens.

a) 2 2 7 × 3

b) 1 1 6 × 5

c) 2 2 4 × 3

d) 1 1 9 × 5

e) 3 2 8 × 3

7. Multiply by regrouping when you need to.

a) 2 3 7 × 5

b) 7 5 6 × 3

c) 5 2 8 × 2

d)

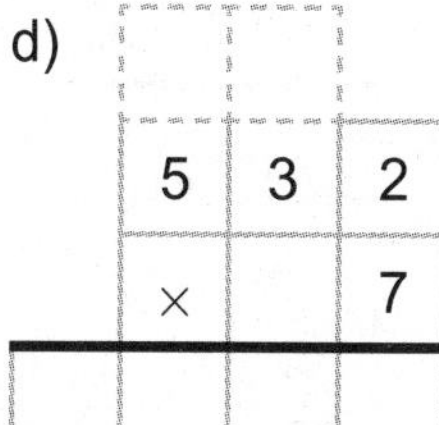

e)

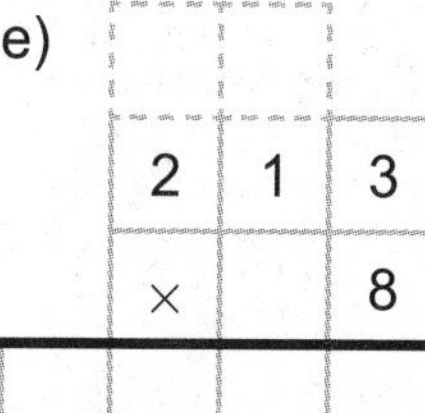

f) 5×174

g) 7×321

h) 6×132

i) 9×532

BONUS▶ $8 \times 31\ 245$

To multiply a 2-digit number by any multiple of ten, first multiply by the number of tens, then multiply by 10. Example: to find 37 × 20, find 37 × 2, then multiply by 10.

	1	
	3	7
×		2
	7	4

→ × 10 →

	1	
	3	7
×	2	0
7	4	0

8. Multiply.

a)

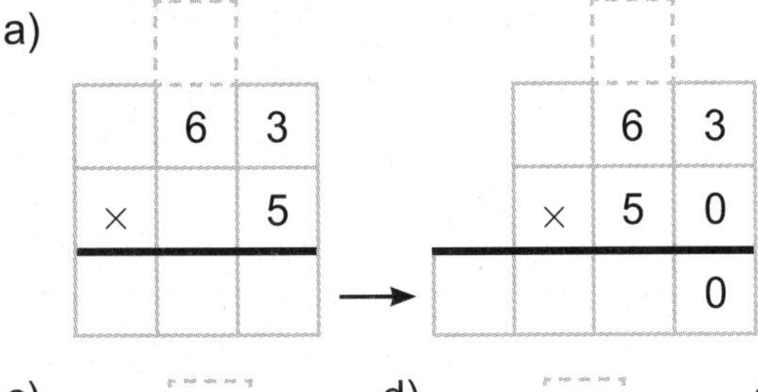

b)

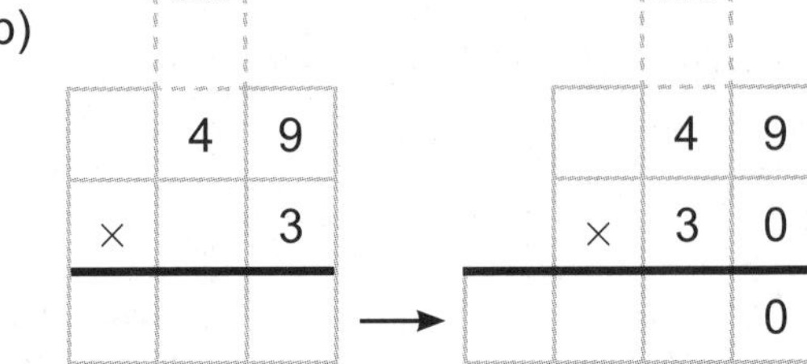

c)

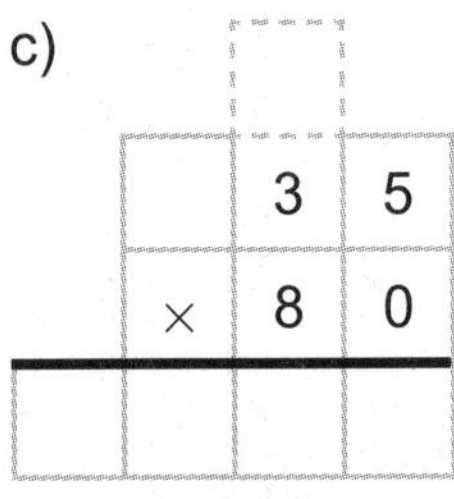

d)

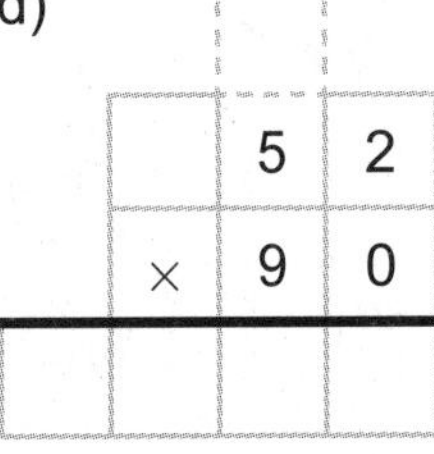

e)

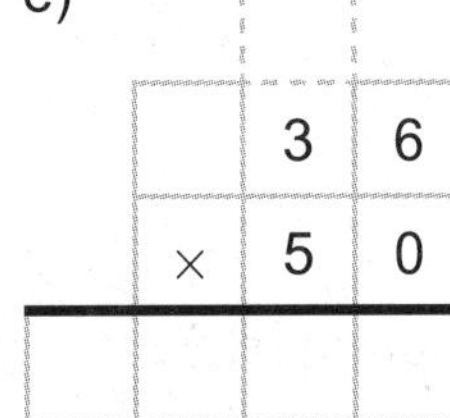

f)

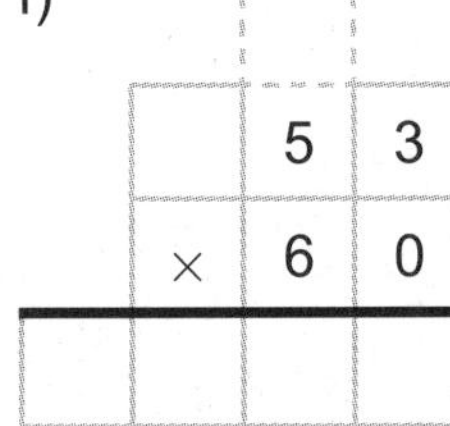

g)

		7	9
	×	3	0

To multiply 2-digit numbers, split the product into a sum of two easier products.

Example: 37 × 25 = 37 × a multiple of ten + 37 × a 1-digit number

37 × **25** = 37 × **20** + 37 × **5**

= 740 + 185

= 925

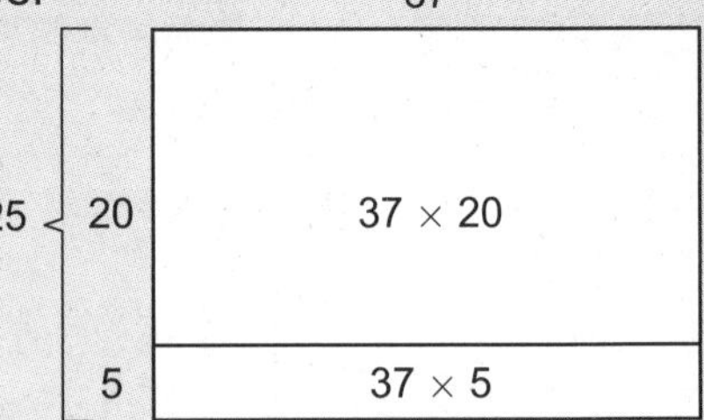

Keep track using a grid:

	1	*3*	
		3	7
	×	2	5
	1	*8*	*5* ← 37 × 5
+	*7*	*4*	*0* ← 37 × 20
	9	*2*	*5*

Step 1: Calculate 37 × 5

Step 2: Calculate 37 × 20

Step 3: Add the results

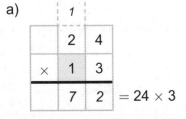

9. Practise Step 1.

a)

	1	
	2	4
×	1	3
	7	2

= 24 × 3

b)

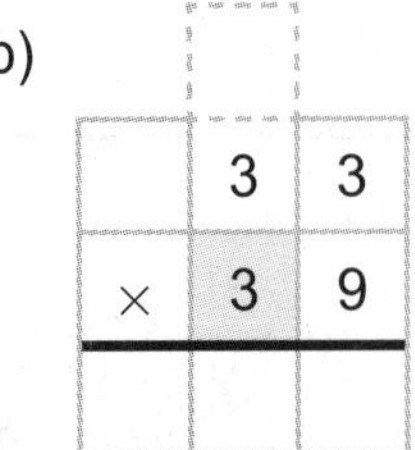

c)

	5	2
×	4	4

d)

	1	6
×	3	5

10. Practise Step 2.

a)
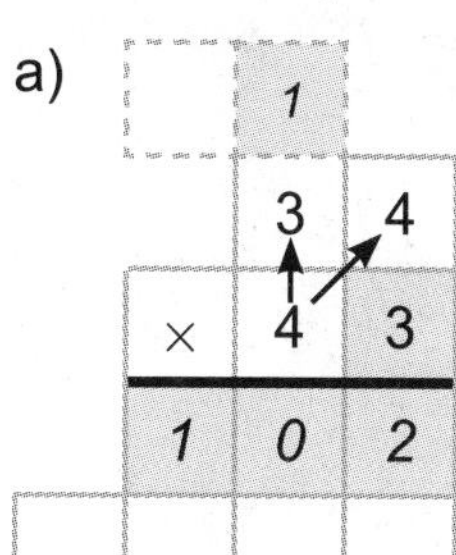
= 34 × 40

b)
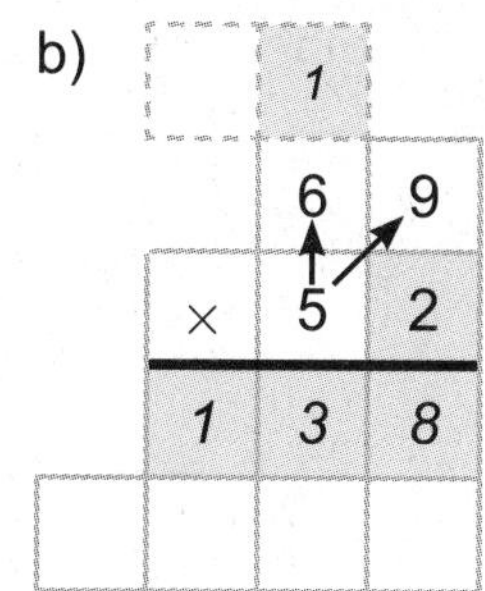

c)

	1	
	5	2
×	3	6
3	1	2

d)

	3	
	6	7
×	2	5
3	3	5

11. Practise Steps 1 and 2.

a)
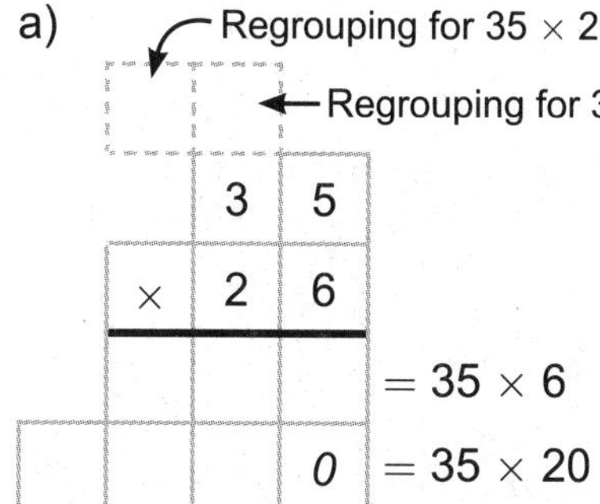

b)
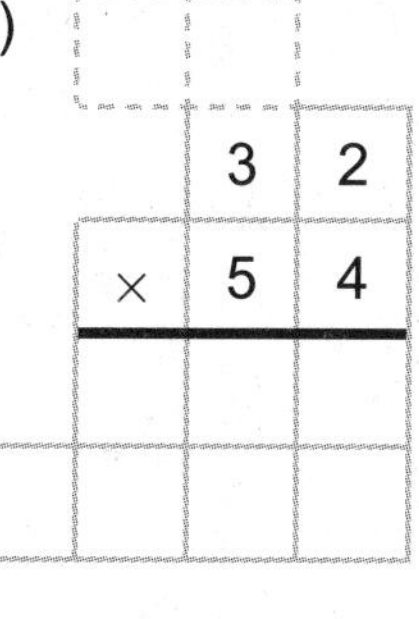

c)
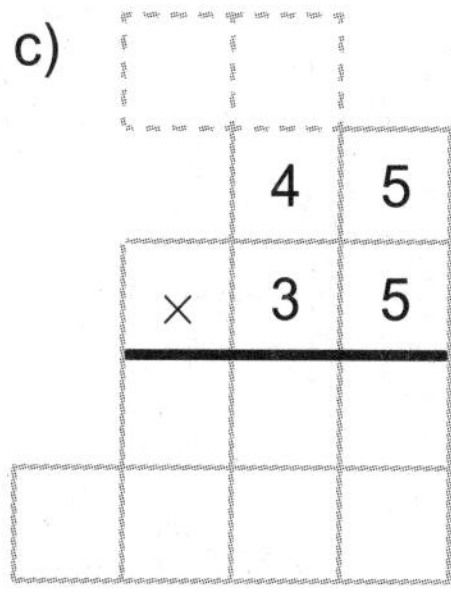

d)
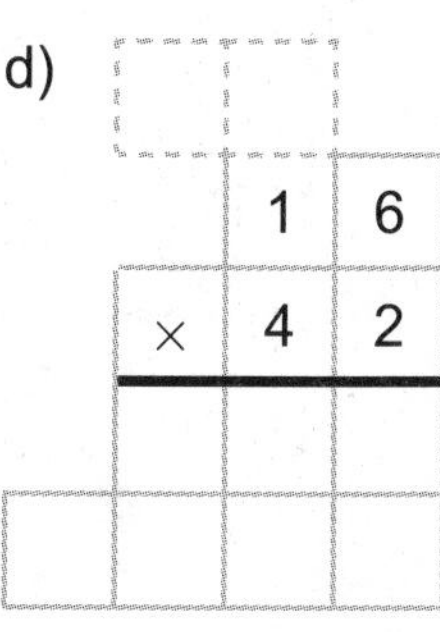

12. Complete the multiplication by adding the numbers in the last two rows of the chart.

a)

	1	2		
		4	8	
	×	2	3	
	1	4	4	48 × 3
+	9	6	0	+ 48 × 20
1	1	0	4	48 × 23

b)

		3	1	
			7	6
		×	5	3
		2	2	8
+	3	8	0	0

c)

		3	4	
			2	5
		×	7	9
		2	2	5
+	1	7	5	0

d)

	4	1	
		1	9
	×	5	2
		3	8
+	9	5	0

13. Multiply.

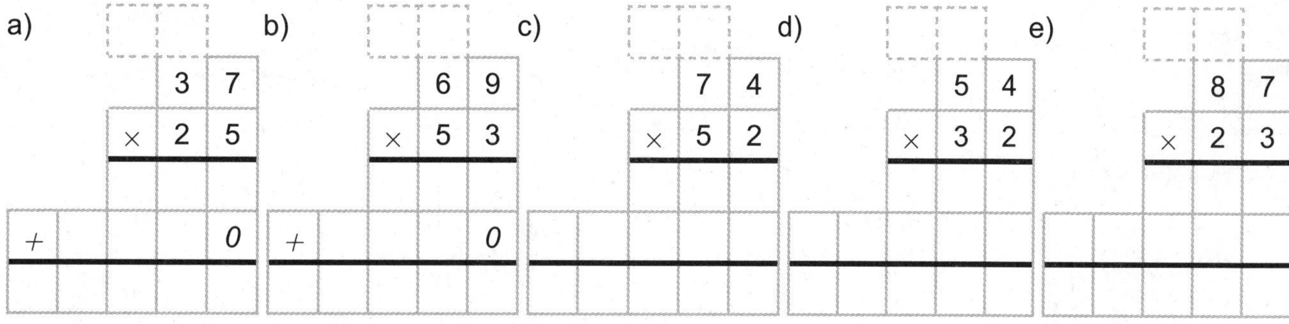

f) 35 × 23   g) 64 × 51   h) 25 × 43   i) 12 × 87   **BONUS ▶** 652 × 473

PA7-1 Extending Patterns

1. These sequences were made by adding the same number to each term.
Find the number, then extend the pattern.

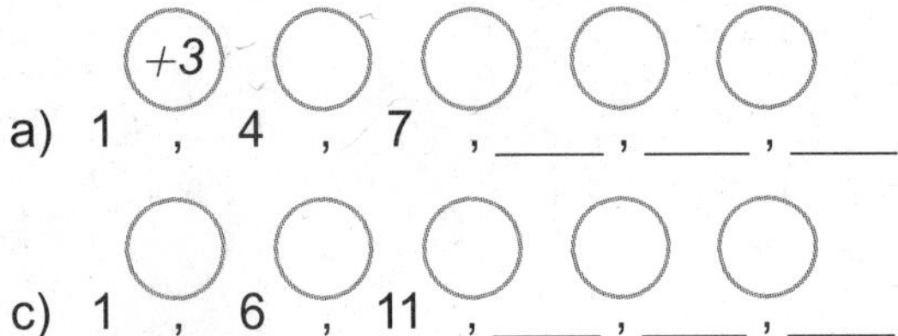

a) 1 , 4 , 7 , ____ , ____ , ____

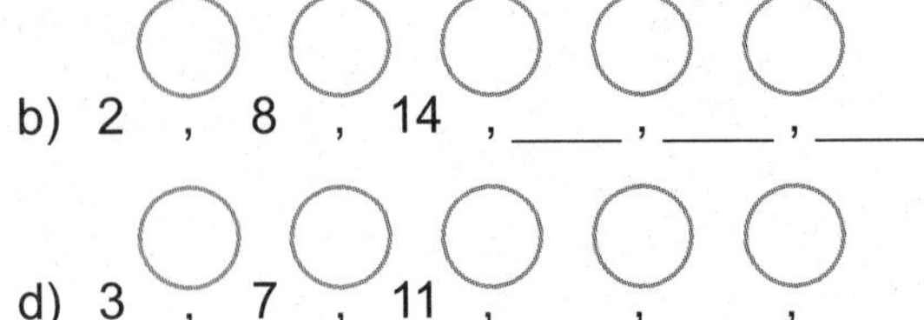

b) 2 , 8 , 14 , ____ , ____ , ____

c) 1 , 6 , 11 , ____ , ____ , ____

d) 3 , 7 , 11 , ____ , ____ , ____

2. These sequences were made by subtracting the same number from each term.
Find the number, then extend the pattern.

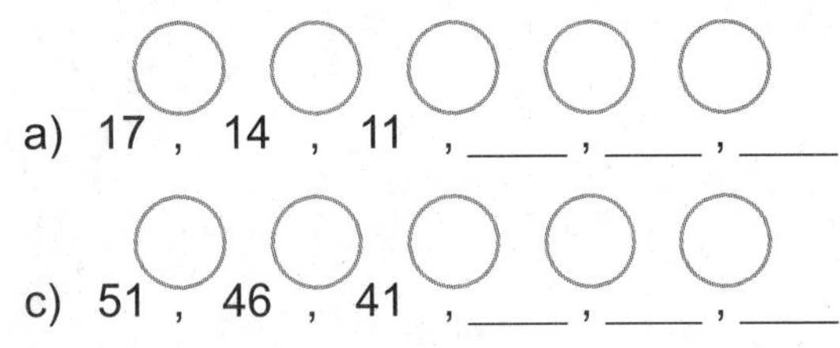

a) 17 , 14 , 11 , ____ , ____ , ____

c) 51 , 46 , 41 , ____ , ____ , ____

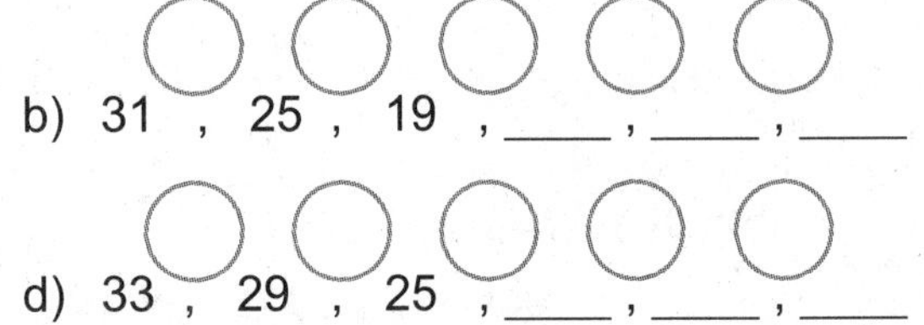

b) 31 , 25 , 19 , ____ , ____ , ____

d) 33 , 29 , 25 , ____ , ____ , ____

3. Find the numbers that are added or subtracted, then extend the pattern. Write a plus sign (+) if you add the number and a minus sign (–) if you subtract the number.

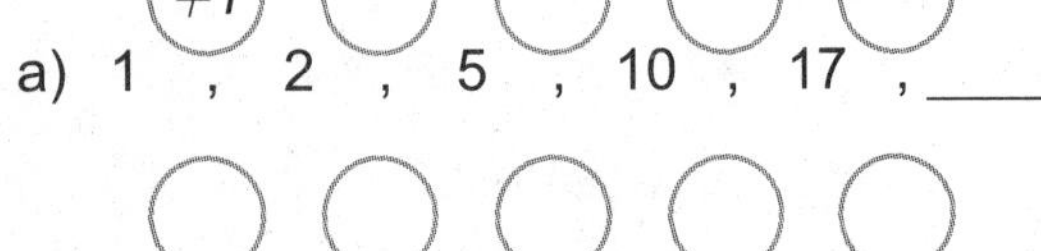

a) 1 , 2 , 5 , 10 , 17 , ____

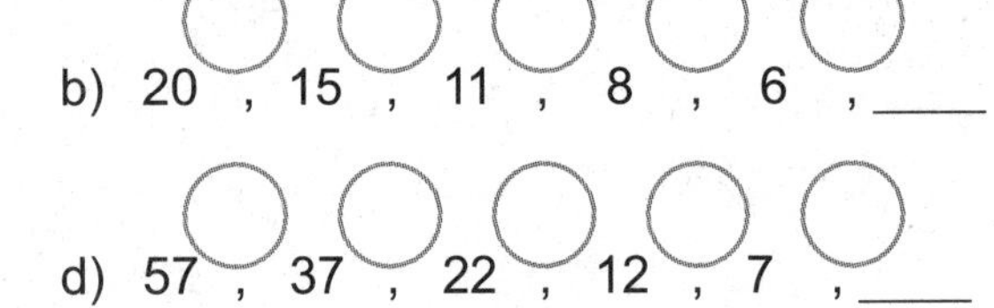

b) 20 , 15 , 11 , 8 , 6 , ____

c) 1 , 2 , 4 , 8 , 16 , ____

d) 57 , 37 , 22 , 12 , 7 , ____

e) 1 , 1 , 2 , 3 , 5 , 8 , 13 , 21 , 34 , ____ , ____ , ____

4. The sequence in Question 3e) is called the **Fibonacci sequence**.

How can you get each term from the previous two terms? ______________________________

____.

5. Find the gaps between the gaps and extend the patterns.

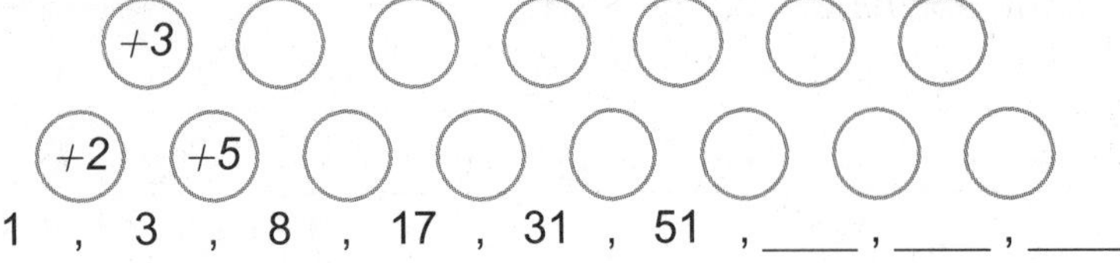

1 , 3 , 8 , 17 , 31 , 51 , ____ , ____ , ____

PA7-2 Describing Patterns

1. Write the amount by which each term in the sequence increases (goes up) or decreases (goes down). Use a plus sign (+) if the sequence increases and a minus sign (–) if it decreases.

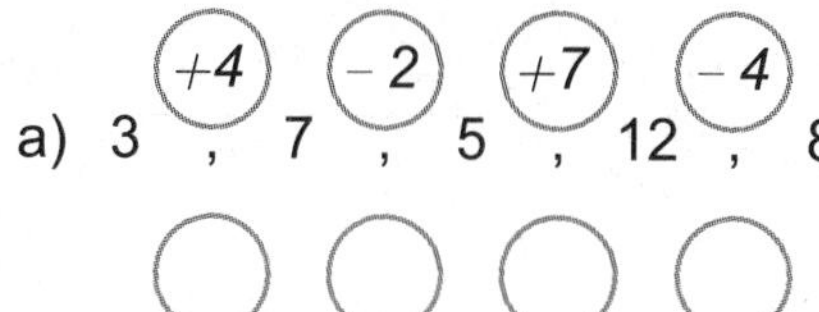

a) 3 , 7 , 5 , 12 , 8

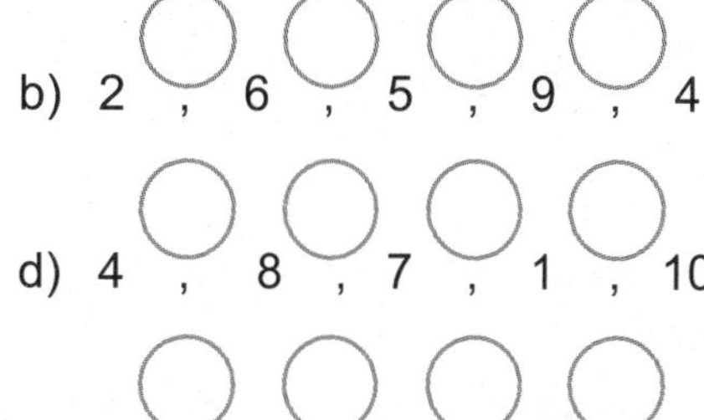

b) 2 , 6 , 5 , 9 , 4

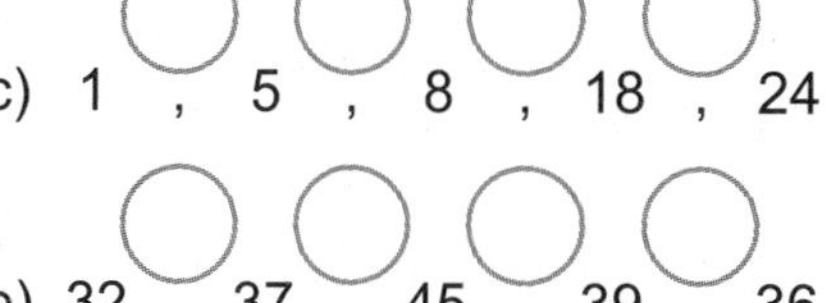

c) 1 , 5 , 8 , 18 , 24

d) 4 , 8 , 7 , 1 , 10

e) 32 , 37 , 45 , 39 , 36

f) 58 , 61 , 54 , 62 , 57

2. Match each sequence (A, B, C, and D) with the correct description.

a) A. increases by 5 each time
B. increases by different amounts

B 8 , 12 , 18 , 22 , 24

A 7 , 12 , 17 , 22 , 27

b) A. increases by 9 each time
B. increases by different amounts

____ 10 , 19 , 28 , 37 , 46

____ 6 , 13 , 18 , 26 , 31

c) A. decreases by different amounts
B. decreases by the same amount

____ 21 , 20 , 18 , 15 , 11

____ 13 , 10 , 7 , 4 , 1

d) A. decreases by 11 each time
B. decreases by different amounts

____ 51 , 40 , 29 , 18 , 7

____ 48 , 35 , 22 , 15 , 3

e) A. increases by 5 each time
B. decreases by different amounts
C. increases by different amounts

____ 18 , 23 , 29 , 33 , 35

____ 27 , 24 , 20 , 19 , 16

____ 24 , 29 , 34 , 39 , 44

f) A. increases and decreases
B. increases by the same amount
C. decreases by different amounts
D. decreases by the same amount

____ 31 , 29 , 25 , 13 , 9

____ 10 , 14 , 9 , 6 , 5

____ 18 , 16 , 14 , 12 , 10

____ 8 , 11 , 14 , 17 , 20

3. Make 3 sequences that match the descriptions. Ask a partner to match each sequence with the correct description. (Write the sequences out of order!)

A. increases by 4 each time ____ ______________________

B. decreases by different amounts ____ ______________________

C. increases and decreases ____ ______________________

4. These sequences were made by multiplying each term by the same number. Find the number, then extend the pattern.

a) 1 , 2 , 4 , ____ , ____

b) 5 , 10 , 20 , ____ , ____

c) 2 , 6 , 18 , ____ , ____

d) 7 , 70 , 700 , ____ , ____

5. These sequences were made by dividing each term by the same number. Find the number, then extend the pattern.

a) 400 , 200 , 100 , ____ , ____

b) 96 , 48 , 24 , ____ , ____

c) 500 , 100 , 20 , ____ , ____

d) 1 600 , 400 , 100 , ____ , ____

6. Write a rule for each pattern. Use the words **add**, **subtract**, **multiply**, or **divide**.

a) 3 , 6 , 12 , 24 (×2, ×2, ×2) *Start at 3 and multiply by 2*

b) 4 , 7 , 10 , 13 ____________________

c) 28 , 25 , 22 , 19 ____________________

d) 27 , 9 , 3 , 1 ____________________

e) 2, 10, 50, 250

f) 32, 16, 8, 4

g) 30 000, 3 000, 300, 30

h) 10, 200, 4 000, 80 000

7. Describe each pattern as **increasing, decreasing,** or **repeating**.

a) 2 , 4 , 8 , 16 , 32 , 64 ____________

b) 3 , 7 , 1 , 3 , 7 , 1 ____________

c) 29 , 27 , 25 , 23 , 22 ____________

d) 2 , 6 , 10 , 14 , 17 ____________

e) 11 , 9 , 6 , 11 , 9 , 6 ____________

f) 61 , 56 , 51 , 46 , 41 ____________

8. Write the rule for each repeating pattern.

a) 3, 7, 1, 3, 7, 1 *3, 7, 1, then repeat*

b) 0, 5, 0, 5, 0, 5 ____________

c) 11, 9, 6, 11, 9, 6 ____________

d) M, M, N, M, M, N ____________

PA7-3 T-tables

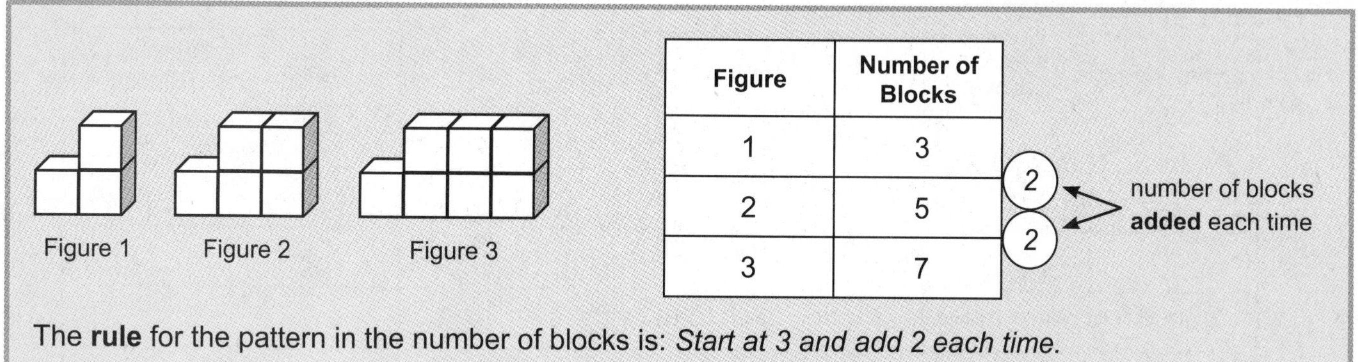

Figure	Number of Blocks
1	3
2	5
3	7

The **rule** for the pattern in the number of blocks is: *Start at 3 and add 2 each time.*

1. Here are more patterns with blocks. How many blocks do you add to make each new figure? Write your answer in the circles. Then write a rule for the pattern.

a)

Figure	Number of Blocks
1	3
2	7
3	11

Rule: *Start at* ____ *and add* ____.

b)

Figure	Number of Blocks
1	2
2	6
3	10

Rule:

c)

Figure	Number of Blocks
1	2
2	4
3	6

Rule:

d)

Figure	Number of Blocks
1	1
2	6
3	11

Rule:

e)

Figure	Number of Blocks
1	5
2	9
3	13

Rule:

f)

Figure	Number of Blocks
1	12
2	18
3	24

Rule:

2. Extend the pattern. How many blocks would be used in Figure 6?

a)

Figure	Number of Blocks
1	2
2	7
3	12

b)

Figure	Number of Blocks
1	4
2	7
3	10

c)

Figure	Number of Blocks
1	3
2	8
3	13

3. Amy makes an increasing pattern with blocks. After making the 3rd figure, she has only 14 blocks left. Does she have enough blocks to complete the 4th figure?

a)

Figure	Number of Blocks
1	8
2	10
3	12

Yes No

b)

Figure	Number of Blocks
1	7
2	10
3	13

Yes No

c)

Figure	Number of Blocks
1	1
2	5
3	9

Yes No

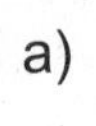

4. Make a table to show how many squares are needed to make the 5th figure in each pattern.

a) 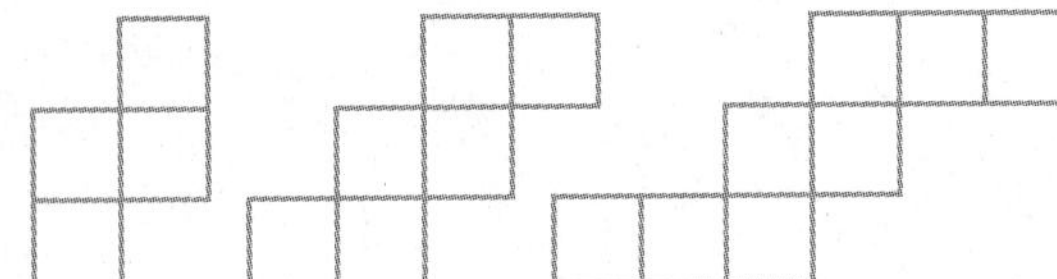

b) 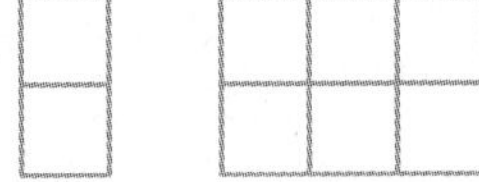 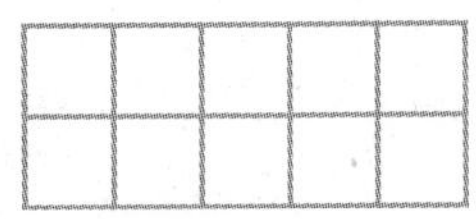

5. Claude buys a plant that is 12 cm high. After 1 week, it is 17 cm high. After 2 weeks it is 22 cm high.

a) How much does the plant grow each week?

____

b) How high will it be after 3 weeks?

____

c) After how many weeks will the plant be 42 cm high?

____

Weeks	Height of Plant (cm)
0	12
1	17
2	22

6. Claude's fish tank is leaking. At 6 p.m., there are 24 L of water in the tank. At 7 p.m., there are 20 L and at 8 p.m. there are 16 L.

Time	Amount of Water in the Tank (L)
6 p.m.	24
7 p.m.	20
8 p.m.	16
9 p.m.	
10 p.m.	

a) How many litres of water leak out each hour?

____

b) How many litres will be left in the tank at 10 p.m.?

____

c) How many hours will it take for all the water to leak out?

____

7. The snow is 19 cm deep at 4 p.m. Snow falls at a rate of 5 cm per hour. How deep is the snow at 8 p.m.?

8. A marina rents sailboats at a rate of $8 for the first hour and $4 for every hour after that. How much does it cost to rent a sailboat for 5 hours?

9. Use a table of values to find out how many toothpicks will be required to make the 5th figure in each pattern.

a) 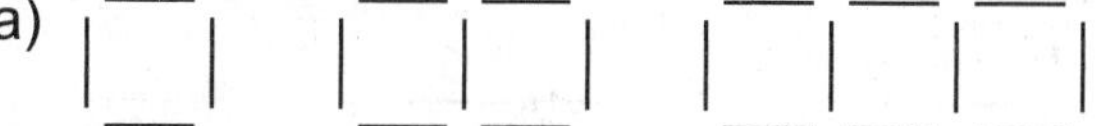

b)  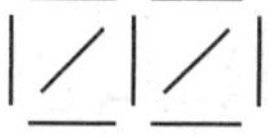 

10. Sue makes an ornament using a hexagon (the white figure), rhombuses (the striped figures), triangles, and squares.

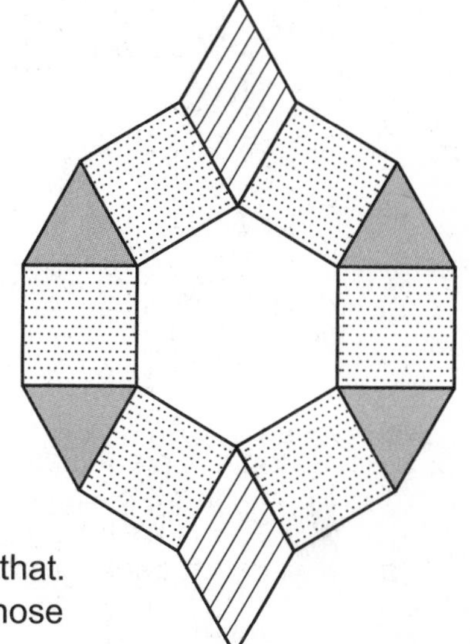

a) How many triangles would Sue need to make 9 ornaments?

b) How many squares would Sue need to make 6 ornaments?

c) Sue used 4 hexagons to make ornaments. How many rhombuses and how many triangles did she use?

d) How many triangles would Sue need to make ornaments with 12 rhombuses?

11. Edith's maple sapling grows 5 cm in July. It grows 7 cm each month after that. Ron's sapling grows 7 cm in July. It grows 3 cm each month after that. Whose sapling is higher by the end of September?

12. Wang has $79 and spends $3 per week. Kam has $84 and spends $4 per week. How many weeks will it take for them to have the same amount left?

PA7-4 Patterns (Advanced)

1. Draw a T-table to predict the number of shaded parts in Figure 5 of each pattern.

a)

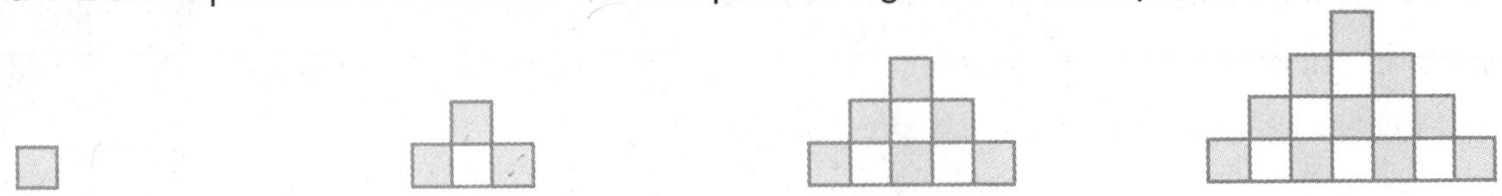

Figure 1 Figure 2 Figure 3 Figure 4

b)

Figure 1 Figure 2 Figure 3 Figure 4

2. One of the most famous sequences in mathematics is the **Fibonacci sequence**.

a) In the circles, write the amount added between the terms of the Fibonacci sequence. Then use the pattern in the steps to continue the sequence.

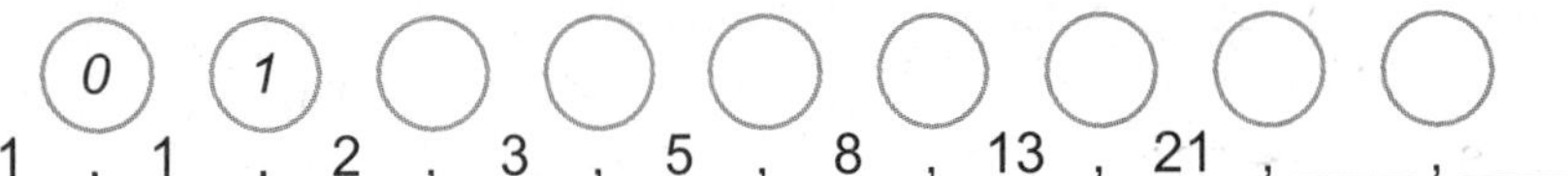

1 , 1 , 2 , 3 , 5 , 8 , 13 , 21 , ____ , ____

b) Complete the table by writing whether each number in the sequence is even (E) or odd (O).

Number	1	1	2	3	5	8	13	21		
Even or Odd	O	O	E	O						

c) Describe the odd-even pattern in the Fibonacci sequence.

d) Is the 38th term in the Fibonacci sequence even or odd? Explain.

e) Add the first four odd Fibonacci numbers. Then add the first two even Fibonacci numbers. What do you notice?

f) Add the first six odd Fibonacci numbers. Then add the first three even Fibonacci numbers. What do you notice?

3. a) Pick any number greater than 1 on **Pascal's Triangle**. Add the two numbers directly above it. (Example: for 6, add 3 + 3.) Repeat several times. Do you see a pattern?

b) Create Pascal's Triangle up to 7 rows. Use the pattern you found in part a).

c) What is the third number in the 9th row of Pascal's Triangle? Hint: Extend the pattern in the 3rd diagonal.

d) Describe any other patterns you see in the triangle.

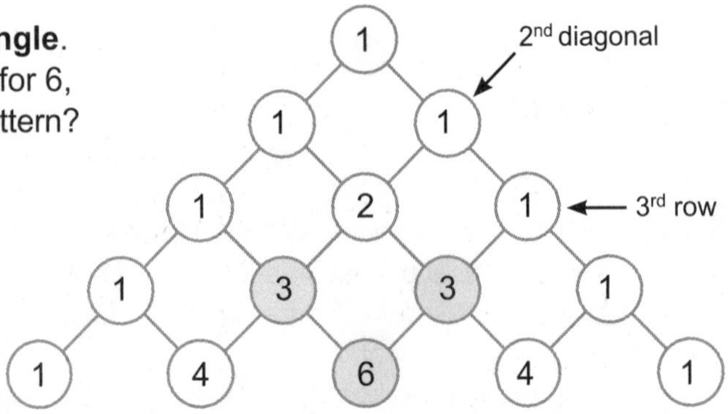

1
1 1
1 2 1
1 3 3 1
1 4 6 4 1

2nd diagonal
3rd row

INVESTIGATION ▶ There are 8 dots in the figure at right.

Each pair of dots is joined by exactly 1 line segment (●——●).

How can you find out how many line segments there are without counting every line?

Start with fewer dots and use a pattern to make a prediction.

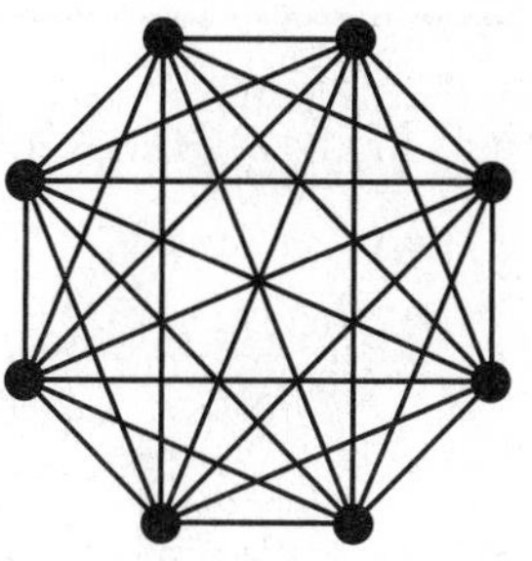

A. For each set of dots, use a ruler to join every pair of dots with a straight line. Write the number of lines in the blank.

a) ●

1 dot

____ lines

b) ● ●

2 dots

____ lines

c) ● ● ●

3 dots

____ lines

d) ● ● ● ●

4 dots

____ lines

B. Write the numbers of lines from Question A on the blanks. Find the gaps between the numbers and write your answers in the circles.

a) ____ ◯ b) ____ ◯ c) ____ ◯ d) ____

1 dot 2 dots 3 dots 4 dots

C. Predict the gaps and numbers in the sequence. Write your predictions below.

____ ◯ ____ ◯ ____ ◯ ____ ◯ ____ ◯ ____

1 dot 2 dots 3 dots 4 dots 5 dots 6 dots

D. Test your predictions by joining the dots in each figure. Were you right?

● ● ● ● ●

5 dots

● ● ● ● ● ●

6 dots

E. a) Extend the pattern to calculate the number of line segments in the figure at the top of the page (8 dots).

b) How many lines would you need to join every pair of dots in a set of 10 dots?

PA7-5 Constant Rates

A **variable** is a letter or symbol (such as x, n, or h) that represents a number. An **algebraic expression** is a combination of one or more variables that may include numbers and operation signs.

Examples of algebraic expressions: $5 \times t + 7$ $n \div 5$ $3 + z + 5y$

1. Make your own example of an algebraic expression. 11 − 8 = 3

In the product of a number and a variable, the multiplication sign is usually dropped.

Example: $3 \times t$ and $t \times 3$ are both written as $3t$.

2. Write these expressions without multiplication signs.

a) $3 \times s =$ $3s$ b) $n \times 5 + 2 =$ $5n + 2$ c) $12 - 4 \times r =$ 12−4r

d) $7 \times a - 3 =$ 7a−3 e) $b \times 4 - 3 =$ b4−3 f) $5 + 6 \times w =$ 5+6w

3. Write these expressions with multiplication signs.

a) $3h =$ $3 \times h$ b) $2 - 3g =$ 2−3xg c) $3f + 4 =$ 3xf+4

d) $5 + 7t =$ 5+7xt e) $7a - 4 =$ 7xa−4 f) $3x + 4y =$ 3xX+4xy

4. It costs \$3 per hour to rent a pair of skates. Write a numeric expression for the cost of renting skates for…

a) 2 hours: 3×2 b) 5 hours: 5x3 c) 6 hours: 3x6

5. It costs \$5 per hour to rent a pair of skis. Write an algebraic expression for the cost of renting skis for…

a) h hours: $5 \times h$ or $5h$ b) t hours: ________ or ______ c) x hours: ________ or ______

6. Write an expression for the distance a car would travel at…

a) Speed: 60 km per hour
Time: 2 hours
Distance: 60×2 km

b) Speed: 80 km per hour
Time: 3 hours
Distance: __________ km

c) Speed: 70 km per hour
Time: 5 hours
Distance: __________ km

7. A car is travelling at a speed of 70 km per hour. Write an algebraic expression for the distance it would travel in...

a) h hours: $70h$ km b) t hours: __________ km c) z hours: __________ km

A **flat fee** is a fixed charge that does not depend on how long you rent an item.

Example: It costs a flat fee of \$7 to rent a boat, plus \$3 for each hour you use the boat.

8. Write an expression for the amount you would pay to rent a boat for…

a) 2 hours
Flat fee: \$9
Hourly rate: \$5 per hour
$2 \times 5 + 9$

b) 3 hours
Flat fee: \$4
Hourly rate: \$6 per hour
6x3+4

c) 7 hours
Flat fee: \$5
Hourly rate: \$4 per hour
4x7+5

d) h hours
Flat fee: \$5
Hourly rate: \$4
$4h + 5$

e) t hours
Flat fee: \$8
Hourly rate: \$3
3t+8

f) w hours
Flat fee: \$6
Hourly rate: \$5
5w+6

9. Match the fee for renting a windsurf board (left) to the correct algebraic expression (right).

A \$15 flat fee and \$7 for each hour	$15h + 7$
\$15 for each hour, no flat fee	$7h + 15$
A \$7 flat fee and \$15 for each hour	$15h$

10. Underline the variable — the quantity that changes. Then write an expression for each cost. Use n for the variable.

	Cost (\$)
a) Umbrellas are on sale for \$2 each.	$2n$
b) A copy shop charges \$0.79 for each copy.	0.79n
c) A bus company charges a \$10 flat fee plus \$5 per passenger.	5n+10
d) A boat company charges a \$20 flat fee plus \$7 per passenger.	7n+20

11. Sara has \$$n$. How much money, in dollars, will she have if her mother gives her…

a) \$7 $n + 7$ b) \$5 n+5 c) \$12 n+12 d) \$31 N+31

12. Sara has \$5 (n = \$5). Replace n with 5 in Question 11 to calculate Sara's money in dollars.

a) $5 + 7 = 12$ b) 5+5=10 c) 5+12=17 d) 5+31=36

13. Socks cost \$2 per pair. The cost of n pairs is \$2n.

John says that the cost of 6 pairs is \$26 and the cost of 7 pairs is \$27.

Is this correct? _______ What did John do wrong? ____________________

____

> When replacing a variable with a number, we use brackets.
>
> Example: 3(7) is another way to write 3×7.

14. Write the number 2 in the brackets and evaluate.

a) $5(\ 2\ ) = \underline{\ 5 \times 2\ } = \underline{\ 10\ }$ b) $3(2) = \underline{3 \times 2} = \underline{6}$ c) $4(2) = \underline{4 \times 2} = \underline{8}$

d) $2(2) + 5$ $= \underline{2 \times 2 + 5} = \underline{9}$ e) $4(2) - 2$ $= \underline{4 \times 2 - 2} = \underline{6}$ f) $6(2) + 3$ $= \underline{6 \times 2 + 3} = \underline{15}$

15. Replace n with 2 in each expression.

a) $4n + 3$
$4(2) + 3$
$= 8 + 3$
$= 11$

b) $5n + 1$
$5(2) + 1$
$= 10 + 1$
$= 11$

c) $3n - 2$
$3(2) + 2$
$= 6 + 2$
$= 8$

d) $2n + 3$
$2(2) + 3$
$= 4 + 3$
$= 7$

16. A company charges a \$6 flat fee to rent a pair of skis plus \$3 for each hour you use the skis. The total is given by the expression $3h + 6$. Find the cost of renting a pair of skis for…

a) 4 hours
$3(4) + 6$
$= 12 + 6$
$= 18$

b) 2 hours

c) 5 hours

d) 7 hours

17. Replace the variable with the given value and evaluate — this is called **substitution**.

a) $5h + 2, \quad h = 3$
$5(3) + 2$
$= 15 + 2$
$= 17$

b) $2n + 3, \quad n = 6$

c) $5t - 2, \quad t = 4$

d) $3m + 9, \quad m = 8$

e) $9 - 2z, \quad z = 4$

f) $3n + 2, \quad n = 5$

18. Evaluate each expression.

a) $2n + 3, \quad n = 5$

$2(5) + 3$

$= 10 + 3 = 13$

b) $2t + 3, \quad t = 5$

c) $2w + 3, \quad w = 5$

19. What do you notice about your answers to Question 18? ______________________

Why is that so? ______________________

20. Evaluate each expression.

a) $2x + 7, \quad x = 6$

b) $7 + 2x, \quad x = 6$

21. What do you notice about your answers to Question 20? ______________________

Why is that so? ______________________

22. Circle all the expressions that mean the same thing as $4n + 7$.

$7 + 4n$ $\quad$ $7n + 4$ $\quad$ $4m + 7$ $\quad$ $7t + 4$

$7 + 4w$ $\quad$ $7 + 4 \times p$ $\quad$ $4 + 7s$ $\quad$ $n \times 4 + 7$

23. Sandwiches cost \$3 and drinks \$2. The cost of *s* sandwiches and *d* drinks is: $3s + 2d$.

Find the cost of the following items.

a) 5 sandwiches and 4 drinks

$3s + 2d = 3(5) + 2(4)$

$= 15 + 8$

$= 23$

The cost is *\$23*

b) 6 sandwiches and 6 drinks

The cost is ______

c) 2 sandwiches and 7 drinks

The cost is ______

24. A company charges a \$5 flat fee to rent a bike plus \$8 for each hour you use the bike.

a) Write an expression for the cost of renting a bike for *h* hours.

b) Sara has \$61. How many hours can she rent the bike for? (Can you write an equation to help you solve the problem?)

PA7-6 Solving Equations — Guess and Check

1. a) Calculate $x + 3$ for each value of x.

x	0	1	2	3	4	5	6	7	8	9	10
$x + 3$	3	4									

b) In each equation below, only one value of x will make the equation true. Find the value of x that will make the equation true.

i) $x + 3 = 10$ $x =$ 7
ii) $x + 3 = 4$ $x =$ ______
iii) $x + 3 = 12$ $x =$ ______
iv) $x + 3 = 7$ $x =$ ______
v) $x + 3 = 3$ $x =$ ______

Finding the value of a variable that makes an equation true is called **solving for the variable.** In Question 1, you **solved for *x*.**

2. a) Calculate $3n$ ($= 3 \times n$) and $3n - 5$ for each value of n.

n	2	3	4	5	6	7	8	9	10	11	12
$3n$	6	9	12								
$3n - 5$	1	4	7								

b) Solve for n.

i) $3n - 5 = 16$ $n =$ ______
ii) $3n - 5 = 25$ $n =$ ______
iii) $3n - 5 = 10$ $n =$ ______
iv) $3n - 5 = 31$ $n =$ ______

3. Substitute $n = 5$ into the expression on the left side of the equation. Does n need to be **greater than**, **less than**, or **equal to** 5 to make the equation true?

a) $3n + 2 = 20$
$3(5) + 2 =$ 17 is less than 20.
So n should be greater than 5.

b) $5n + 6 = 26$
$5(5) + 6 =$ ______ is ______ 26.
So n should be ______ 5.

c) $2n + 3 = 13$
$2(5) + 3 =$ ______ is ______ 13.
So n should be ______ 5.

d) $4n + 3 = 27$
$4(5) + 3 =$ ______ is ______ 27.
So n should be ______ 5.

4. Solve for n by guessing small values for n, checking, and revising. Do your rough work in your notebook.

a) $3n + 2 = 8$ $n =$ ______
b) $5n - 2 = 13$ $n =$ ______
c) $4n - 1 = 15$ $n =$ ______
d) $6n - 5 = 31$ $n =$ ______

e) $7n - 2 = 19$ $n =$ ______
f) $2n + 3 = 9$ $n =$ ______
g) $3n + 5 = 14$ $n =$ ______
h) $2n - 5 = 3$ $n =$ ______

5. Sara solves $7x + 11 = 67$ and gets $x = 8$.

a) Verify Sara's answer.

b) What value for t solves $7t + 11 = 67$? _______

c) What value for x solves $11 + 7x = 67$?

How do you know? ______________________________

d) What value for x solves $67 = 7x + 11$? _______

How do you know? ______________________________

6. Circle the equations that mean the same thing as $8x + 3 = 51$.

$3 + 8x = 51$	$8t + 3 = 51$	$3w + 8 = 51$	$8 + 3x = 51$
$51 = 3 + 8x$	$51 = 8w + 3$	$r \times 8 + 3 = 51$	$51 = 3 + 8t$
$3 + 8r = 51$	$51 + 8r = 3$	$8z + 3 = 51$	$8z + 51 = 3$

7. Solve these equations by guessing, checking, and revising. Do your rough work in your notebook.

a) $3t + 4 = 13$ $t =$ _______	b) $4h + 5 = 13$ $h =$ _______	c) $2w + 9 = 17$ $w =$ _______	d) $10p = 30$ $p =$ _______
e) $2 + 7x = 23$ $x =$ _______	f) $3 + 5x = 38$ $x =$ _______	g) $8 + 2x = 26$ $x =$ _______	h) $5 + 3n = 20$ $n =$ _______
i) $10 = 3x + 1$ $x =$ _______	j) $15 = 4x - 1$ $x =$ _______	k) $20 = 4x$ $x =$ _______	l) $32 = 5w + 2$ $w =$ _______
m) $3 + 5x = 18$ $x =$ _______	n) $23 = 7u + 2$ $u =$ _______	o) $7u + 5 = 40$ $u =$ _______	p) $30 = 3 + 9n$ $n =$ _______

8. Find another equation from Question 7 that means the same thing as the equation in part e). ______________________

BONUS▶ Solve for x and y: $2x + 1 = 7 = 4y - 1$

PA7-7 Modelling Equations

1. Each bag contains the same unknown number of apples. Let x stand for the number of apples in one bag. Write a mathematical expression for the total number of apples.

a) 

$x + 2$

b) 

______

c) 

______

2. Write an **expression** for the total number of apples. Write an **equation** by making the expression equal to the total number of apples.

a) There are **7 apples** in total.

Expression $x + 2$

Equation $x + 2 = 7$

b) There are **10 apples** in total.

Expression ______

Equation ______

c) There are **15 apples** in total.

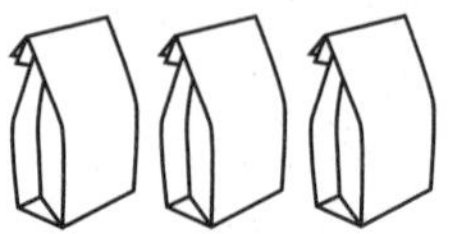

Expression ______

Equation ______

3. Write an equation and find the number of apples in each bag.

a) 10 apples in total

b) 13 apples in total

c) 17 apples in total

d) 11 apples in total

e) 14 apples in total

f) 31 apples in total

4. Solve each equation for x by guessing and checking, then draw a model to verify your answer.

a) $3x + 4 = 19$

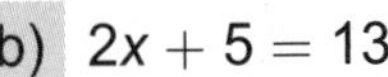

b) $2x + 5 = 13$ c) $4x + 2 = 14$ d) $3x + 8 = 14$ e) $5x + 2 = 27$ f) $4x + 3 = 15$

5. Does this type of model work for the equation $3x - 4 = 14$? ______. Explain in your notebook.

PA7-8 Solving Equations — Preserving Equality

1. Write the number that makes each equation true.

a) $8 + 4 - \square = 8$ b) $8 \times 3 \div \square = 8$ c) $8 \div 2 \times \square = 8$ d) $8 - 5 + \square = 8$

e) $12 \div 4 \times \square = 12$ f) $13 - 6 + \square = 13$ g) $3 \times 5 \div \square = 3$ h) $19 + 3 - \square = 19$

2. Write the operation that makes each equation true.

a) $7 + 2 \bigcirc 2 = 7$ b) $8 \times 3 \bigcirc 3 = 8$ c) $12 \div 2 \bigcirc 2 = 12$ d) $15 - 4 \bigcirc 4 = 15$

e) $18 \div 3 \bigcirc 3 = 18$ f) $8 - 2 \bigcirc 2 = 8$ g) $5 \times 3 \bigcirc 3 = 5$ h) $6 + 4 \bigcirc 4 = 6$

3. Write the operation and number that make each equation true.

a) $17 + 3$ *− 3* $= 17$ b) $20 \div 4$ ______ $= 20$ c) 18×2 ______ $= 18$

d) $11 - 4$ ______ $= 11$ e) 4×3 ______ $= 4$ f) $15 + 2$ ______ $= 15$

g) 15×2 ______ $= 15$ h) $5 + 3$ ______ $= 5$ i) 5×3 ______ $= 5$

j) $6 \div 2$ ______ $= 6$ k) 6×2 ______ $= 6$ l) $6 - 2$ ______ $= 6$

4. How could you undo each operation and get back to the number you started with?

a) add 4 *subtract 4* b) multiply by 3 ______

c) divide by 2 ______ d) subtract 7 ______

5. Start with the number 3. Do the operations and then undo them in backwards order.

Add 7.	*10*	Subtract 7.	______
Multiply by 2.	*20*	Divide by 2.	______
Subtract 5.	______	Add 5.	______
Divide by 3.	______ →	Multiply by 3.	______

Did you finish with the number you started with? ______

6. Start with the number 11. Do the operations and then undo them in backwards order.

Add 4.	*15*	______	______
Divide by 3.	______	______	______
Subtract 1.	______	______	______
Multiply by 4.	______ →	*Divide by 4.*	______

Did you finish with the number you started with? ______

Remember: The variable x represents a number, so you can treat it like a number.

Operation	Result	Operation	Result
Add 3 to x	$x + 3$	Multiply 3 by x	$3 \times x = 3x$
Add x to 3	$3 + x$	Multiply x by 3	$x \times 3 = 3x$
Subtract 3 from x	$x - 3$	Divide x by 3	$x \div 3$
Subtract x from 3	$3 - x$	Divide 3 by x	$3 \div x$

7. Show the result of each operation.

a) Multiply x by 7 ___*7x*___ b) Add 4 to x ___*x + 4*___ c) Subtract 5 from x ______

d) Subtract x from 5 ______ e) Divide x by 10 ______ f) Divide 9 by x ______

g) Multiply 8 by x ______ h) Add x to 9 ______ **BONUS▶** Add x to y ______

8. What happens to the variable x?

a) $2x$ ___*Multiply by 2.*___ b) $3x$ ______ c) $x + 4$ ______

d) $x - 5$ ______ e) $x \div 3$ ______ f) $6 \div x$ ______

g) $4 - x$ ______ **BONUS▶** $x + x$ ______

9. Start with the variable. Write the correct operation and number to get back where you started.

a) $n + 3$ ___*− 3*___ $= n$ b) $n \times 3$ ______ $= n$ c) $5m$ ______ $= m$

d) $x - 5$ ______ $= x$ e) $x + 7$ ______ $= x$ f) $x - 14$ ______ $= x$

g) $z \div 5$ ______ $= z$ h) $7y$ ______ $= y$ i) $r + 8$ ______ $= r$

j) $x + 4$ ______ $= x$ k) $6x$ ______ $= x$ l) $x + 7 - 3$ ______ $= x$

10. Circle the expressions that get you back to m.

$7m - 7$ $7m \div 7$ $m \div 7 \times 7$ $7 \div m \times 7$ $7 + m - 7$ $7 - m + 7$

11. Solve for x by doing the same thing to both sides of the equation. Check your answer.

a) $3x = \mathbf{12}$

$3x \div 3 = 12 \div 3$

$x = 4$

Check by replacing x with your answer:
$3(4) = 12$ ✓

b) $x - 4 = \mathbf{11}$

c) $4x = 20$ d) $3 + x = 9$ e) $x + 5 = 8$

f) $x \div 6 = 3$ g) $5x = 15$ h) $x - 7 = 10$

i) $2x = 18$ j) $x \div 2 = 3$ k) $x + 1 = 20$

l) $10x = 90$ m) $9x = 54$ n) $x + 26 = 53$

PA7-9 Solving Equations — Two Operations

1. Jason does some operations to the secret number x. He gets 37 every time. Write an equation and then work backwards to find x.

a) **Jason's operations**

Start with x. x

Multiply by 5. $5x$

Add 7. $5x + 7$

The answer is 37. $5x + 7 = 37$

Work backwards to find x

Write the equation again. $5x + 7 = 37$

Undo adding 7 by subtracting 7. $5x + 7 - 7 = 37 - 7$

Write the new equation. $5x = 30$

Undo multiplying by 5 by dividing by 5. $5x \div 5 = 30 \div 5$

Write the new equation. $x = 6$

You solved for x!

Check your answer by doing the operations in order, the way Jason did them.

Start with your answer: 6 Multiply by 5: 30 Add 7: 37 Do you get 37? Yes

b) **Jason's operations**

Start with x. x

Multiply by 8. ______

Add 5. ______

The answer is 37. ______

Work backwards to find x

Write the equation again. ______

Undo adding 5 by subtracting 5. ______

Write the new equation. ______

Undo multiplying by 8 by dividing by 8. ______

Write the new equation. ______

You solved for x!

Check your answer by doing the operations in order, the way Jason did them.

Start with your answer: ______ Multiply by 8: ______ Add 5: ______ Do you get 37? ______

c) **Jason's operations**

Start with x. x

Multiply by 4. ______

Subtract 3. ______

The answer is 37. ______

Work backwards to find x

Write the equation again. ______

Undo subtracting 3 by adding 3. ______

Write the new equation. ______

Undo multiplying by 4 by dividing by 4. ______

Write the new equation. ______

You solved for x!

Check your answer by doing the operations in order, the way Jason did them.

Start with your answer: ______ Multiply by 4: ______ Subtract 3: ______ Do you get 37? ______

2. Solve for the variable by undoing each operation in the equation.

a) $8x + 3 = 27$

$8x + 3 - 3 = \underline{\ 27\ } - \underline{\ 3\ }$

$8x = \underline{\qquad}$

$8x \div 8 = \underline{\qquad} \div \underline{\qquad}$

$x = \underline{\qquad}$

b) $4h - 3 = 37$

$4h - 3 + 3 = 37 + \underline{\qquad}$

$4h = \underline{\qquad}$

$4h \div 4 = \underline{\qquad} \div \underline{\qquad}$

$h = \underline{\qquad}$

c) $3s - 4 = 29$ d) $2t + 3 = 11$ e) $2m - 7 = 13$ f) $5a + 2 = 47$

g) $4z + 3 = 19$ h) $7w - 2 = 26$ i) $8x + 3 = 3$ j) $9r - 3 = 6$

3. A store charges you $3 per hour to rent a pair of roller blades.

a) Write an expression for the cost of renting the roller blades. Use *h* for hours. _______

b) Mary rented the roller blades for 4 hours. How much did she pay? _______

c) Sue paid $15 to rent the roller blades. How many hours did she rent the roller blades for? _______

4. Kim has $36 in savings. She earns $9 an hour. She saves all the money she makes.

a) Write an expression for the amount Kim will have saved after working *h* hours.

b) How much will she have saved after working 3 hours?

c) How many hours does she have to work to buy a shirt that costs $90?

5. a) In which part of Question 4 did you **substitute** for *h*? _______

b) In which part of Question 4 did you **solve** for *h*? _______

6.

	Company A	**Company B**	**Company C**
Rental fee for boat	$100	$120	$70
Fee for each person	$3	$5	$7

a) Write an expression that gives the total amount each company would charge for a boat carrying *n* people.

b) A group chose Company C and paid $126. How many people were in the group?

c) How much would the group have paid with Companies A and B?

d) Was Company C the best choice for the group? Why or why not?

PA7-10 Modelling Equations — Advanced

Scale A is balanced. A triangle has mass x kg and a circle has mass 1 kg. 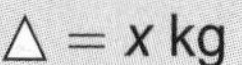 $\triangle = x$ kg $\bigcirc = 1$ kg

1. Write the equation for each balance.

a) 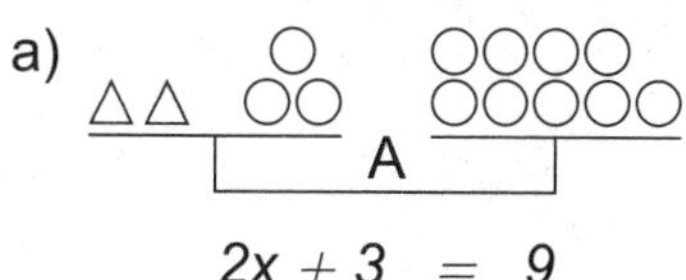

$2x + 3 = 9$

b) 

c) 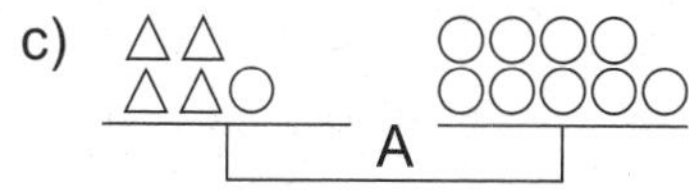

2. Write the equation that Scale A shows. Draw Scale B so that it balances only the triangles from Scale A, and write the new equation.

a) 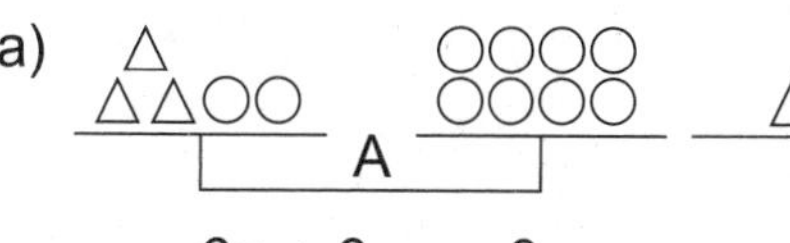

$3x + 2 = 8$

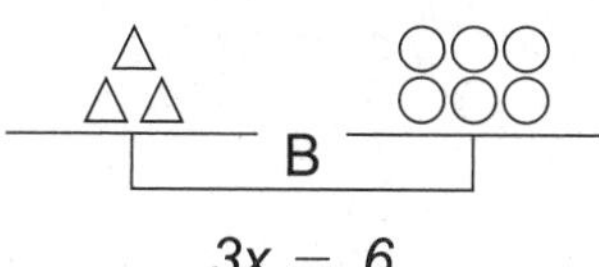

$3x = 6$

b) 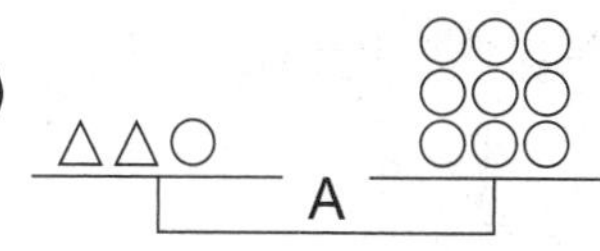

B

3. Scale B is balanced and has only triangles on one side and only circles on the other. Put the circles into the number of groups given by the number of triangles. Show on Scale C what balances 1 triangle.

a) 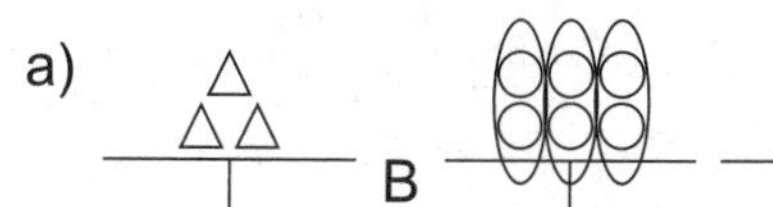

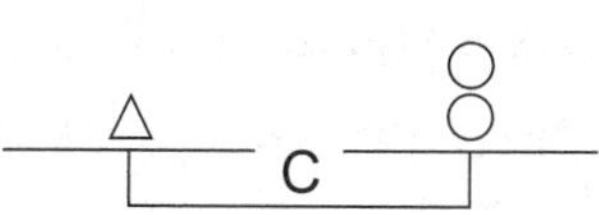

b) 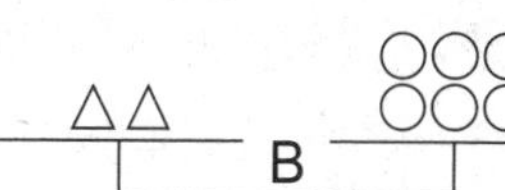

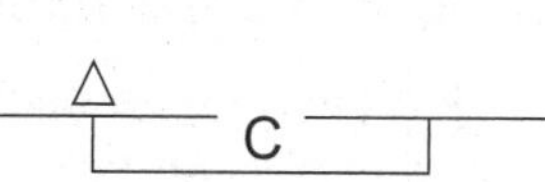

c) B

C

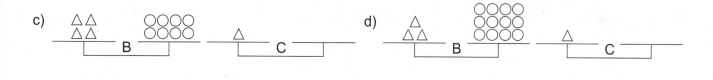

d) 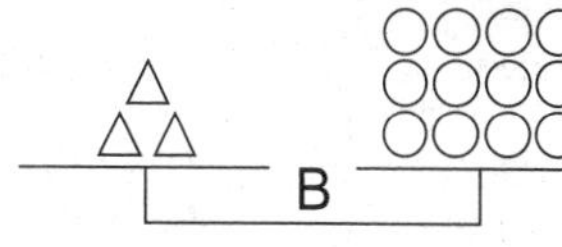

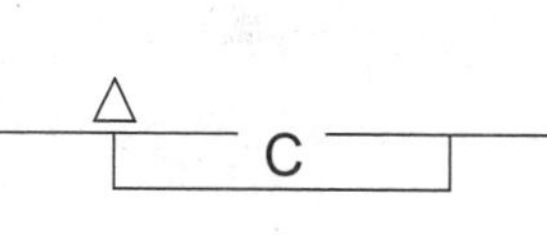

4. Scale A is balanced perfectly. Draw scales B and C as in Questions 2 and 3. Write the new equations.

a) 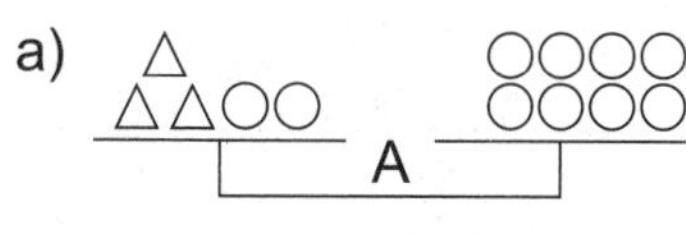

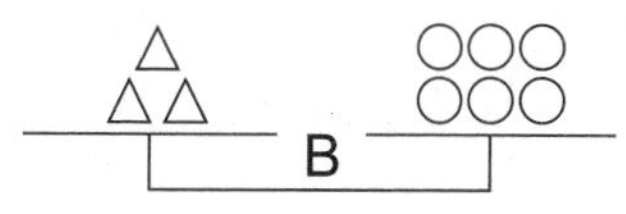

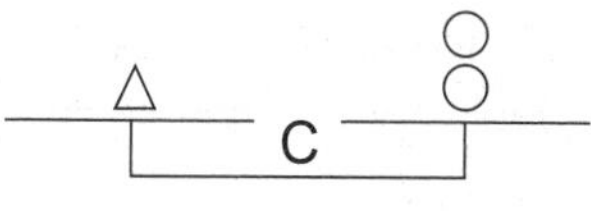

b) 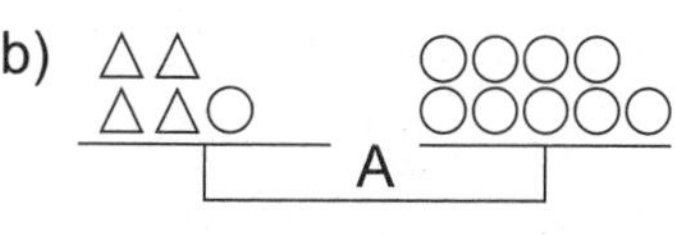

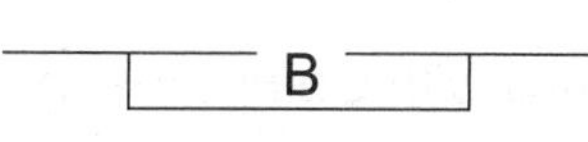

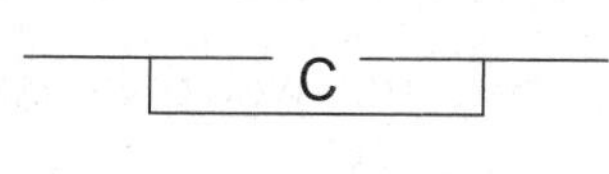

5. Draw Scales A, B, and C to model the process of solving the equation $3x + 5 = 11$.

Solving Equations — Advanced

The expression 3×2 is short for $2 + 2 + 2$. Similarly, the expression $3x$ is short for $x + x + x$.

1. Write $6x$ in three ways.

a) $6x = \underbrace{x + x + x}_{} + \underbrace{x + x + x}_{}$
$6x = 3x + 3x$

b) $6x = \underbrace{x + x}_{} + \underbrace{x + x + x + x}_{}$
$6x = \quad + \quad$

c) $6x = \underbrace{x}_{} + \underbrace{x + x + x + x + x}_{}$
$6x = \quad + \quad$

2. Add.

a) $3x + x =$ <u>$4x$</u> b) $5x + 2x =$ ____ c) $7x + x =$ ____ d) $4x + 2x + 3x =$ ____

3. Group the x's together, then solve the equation for x.

a) $2x + 5x = 21$ b) $5x + 4x + 2 = 20$ c) $6x + x + 4 = 32$ d) $3x + 2x + 2 = 22$

4. Fill in the blanks.

a) $3 - 3 =$ ____ b) $8 - 8 =$ ____ c) $132 - 132 =$ ____ d) $x - x =$ ____

e) $3 + 3 - 3 =$ ____ f) $7 + 7 - 7 =$ ____ g) $5 + 5 - 5 =$ ____ h) $x + x - x =$ ____

Every time you see a number or variable subtracted by itself in an equation (Examples: $3 - 3$, $5 - 5$, $8 - 8$, $x - x$), you can cross out both numbers or variables because they will add to 0. Crossing out parts of an equation that make 0 is called **cancelling**.

5. Fill in the blanks by crossing out numbers or variables that add to 0.

a) $4 + \cancel{3} - \cancel{3} =$ <u>4</u> b) $5 + 2 - 2 =$ ____ c) $7 + 1 - 1 =$ ____

d) $8 + 6 - 6 =$ ____ e) $3 + 7 - 3 =$ ____ f) $2 + 9 - 2 =$ ____

g) $4 + 3 - 3 + 7 - 7 + 6 - 6 =$ ____ h) $5 + 2 - 2 + 4 - 5 =$ ____ i) $7 + x - x =$ ____

j) $x + 12 - x =$ ____ k) $x + x - x =$ ____ l) $x + x + x - x =$ ____

m) $x + x - x + x + x + x - x - x =$ ____

6. Rewrite these expressions as sums of individual variables and then cancel. Write what's left.

a) $5x - 2x =$ ____
$x + x + x + \cancel{x} + \cancel{x} - \cancel{x} - \cancel{x}$

b) $4x - x =$ ____ c) $5x - x + 2x =$ ____

7. Add or subtract without writing the expressions as sums of individual x's.

a) $7x - 5x =$ <u>$2x$</u> b) $8x - 4x =$ ____ c) $4x - 2x + 3x =$ ____ d) $9x - 3x + 4x =$ ____

8. Group the x's together, then solve for x.

a) $8x - 3x + x - 2 = 28$ b) $5x + x - x - 2x + 4 = 19$ c) $7x + 4 - 2x - 3 = 26$

PA7-12 Equations and Expressions

1. Circle the equations and underline the expressions.

$5n - 3$ $\quad$ $n + 6 = 7$ $\quad$ $7 + 3n$ $\quad$ $7 + 3n = 5 + 2n$ $\quad$ $a + b$

$a + b = b + a$ $\quad$ $8 - 3n = 5$ $\quad$ $a \times b = b \times a$ $\quad$ $4 + 6n - 5m$

2. What is the difference between an expression and an equation? ____________________

____

3. How are an equation and an expression the same? ____________________

____

4. Write an equation that contains the expression $5n + 3$. ____________________

5. In the expression $5n + 3$, which quantity is changing, $5n$ or 3?

How do you know? ____________________

In an expression, the number that is multiplied by the variable is called the **coefficient**.

Examples: $\quad 5x + 2 \quad\quad x - 7 = 1x - 7$

coefficient = 5 $\quad$ coefficient = 1

6. Write the coefficient in each expression.

a) $2x - 7$ ______ b) $m + 3$ ______ c) $4n + 5$ ______ d) $6 + 7w$ ______

Some expressions have more than one variable. Each variable has its own coefficient. In the expression $3a + 7b + 5$, the coefficient of a is 3 and the coefficient of b is 7.

7. Write the coefficient of x in each expression.

a) $3x + 4y + 7$ ___*3*___ b) $2u + 5x + 4w + 6$ ______ c) $3 + 4x + w$ ______ d) $3w + x$ ______

In an expression, the quantity without the variable is called the **constant term** because it does not change.

Examples: $\quad 3x + 4 \quad\quad 5x = 5x + 0$

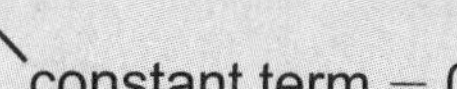

constant term = 4 $\quad$ constant term = 0

8. Write the constant term in each expression.

a) $4x + 7$ ______ b) $8r$ ______ c) $7u + 9$ ______ d) $5 + 3x$ ______

9. It costs $3 per hour to use the ski hill and $10 to rent the skis.

a) Write an expression for the cost of renting skis to go skiing for h hours. ______________

b) What is the coefficient in your expression? _______

c) What is the constant term in your expression? _______

10. A car is travelling at a speed of 50 km per hour.

a) Write an expression for the distance the car travels in h hours. ______________

b) What is the constant term? _______

c) What is the coefficient? _______

d) What does the variable in your expression represent? Circle the correct answer.

The speed at which the car is travelling

The number of hours the car travels

The distance the car travels.

11. Ron models the equation $3x + 4 = 13$ by drawing bags with the same number of apples in each and then some apples outside the bags.

a) Draw Ron's model.

Circle the correct answer.

b) What is the number of bags?	coefficient	constant term	variable
c) What is the number of apples in each bag?	coefficient	constant term	variable
d) What is the number of apples outside the bags?	coefficient	constant term	variable

e) Which number in the equation shows the total number of apples? _______

12. A company charges a flat fee and an hourly rate to rent a bike. Draw a line to match the coefficient, the constant term, and the variable with the correct quantity.

coefficient	the flat fee
constant term	the hourly rate
variable	the number of hours rented

PA7-13 Dividing by a Constant

Division is often written in fractional form:

$12 \div 4 = \frac{12}{4}$ $15 \div 5 = \frac{15}{5}$ $x \div 3 = \frac{x}{3}$ $w \div 7 = \frac{w}{7}$

1. Solve these division problems.

a) $\frac{6}{3} = $ 2 b) $\frac{12}{6} = $ ____ c) $\frac{12}{4} = $ ____ d) $\frac{15}{5} = $ ____ e) $\frac{20}{2} = $ ____

To solve the equation $3x = 12$, Jill thinks:

"If $3x = 12$, I can multiply x by 3 to get 12. But then I can divide 12 by 3 to find x."

If $3x = 12$ then $x = \frac{12}{3}$

2. Solve the following equations by working backwards.

a) $3x = 12$

$x = \frac{12}{3}$

$x = 4$

b) $2x = 10$ c) $4x = 12$ d) $2x = 14$ e) $3x = 21$

f) $7x = 28$ g) $6x = 18$ h) $7x = 49$ i) $8x = 48$ j) $9x = 72$

To solve the equation $\frac{x}{3} = 5$, Jill thinks:

"If $\frac{x}{3} = 5$, I can divide x by 3 to get 5. But then I can multiply 5 by 3 to get x."

If $\frac{x}{3} = 5$ then $x = 5 \times 3 = 5(3)$ so $x = 15$.

3. Solve each equation by working backwards.

a) $\frac{x}{3} = 4$

$x = 4(3)$

$x = 12$

b) $\frac{x}{5} = 2$ c) $\frac{x}{3} = 3$ d) $\frac{x}{2} = 7$ e) $\frac{x}{9} = 4$

4. Solve each equation by working backwards.

a) $\frac{x}{2} = 3$

$x = 3(2)$

$x = 6$

b) $2x = 8$ c) $\frac{x}{4} = 5$ d) $3 + x = 8$ e) $x - 5 = 6$

f) $\frac{x}{3} = 4$ g) $5 - x = 2$ h) $12 = 2x$ i) $16 = 3x + 1$ j) $5 = \frac{x}{3} + 1$

PA7-14 Word Problems

To solve word problems, you turn the words into algebraic expressions. The words give clues to the operations you need to use. Here are some of the clues for different operations.

Add	Subtract	Multiply	Divide
increased by	less than	product	divided by
sum	difference	times	divided into
more than	decreased by	twice as many	quotient
	reduced by		

1. Match each algebraic expression with the correct description.

a)

2 more than a number	$4x$
a number divided by 3	$x - 2$
2 less than a number	$x + 2$
the product of a number and 4	$x - 3$
a number decreased by 3	$x \div 3$

b)

2 divided into a number	$3x$
a number reduced by 4	$x \div 2$
a number times 3	$x + 3$
twice as many as a number	$x - 4$
a number increased by 3	$2x$

2. Write an algebraic expression for each description.

a) Four more than a number.
b) A number decreased by 10.
c) The product of 7 and a number.
d) A number divided by 8.
e) Two less than a number.
f) The sum of a number and 7.
g) A number increased by 9.
h) A number reduced by 4.
i) The product of a number and 3.
j) Five times a number.
k) 6 divided into a number.
l) Twice as many as a number.

When solving word problems, the word "is" translates to the equal sign, $=$.

Example: "Two more than a number is seven" can be written $x + 2 = 7$.

3. Solve the following problems by first writing an equation.

a) Four more than a number is eighteen.
b) Five less than a number is 12.
c) Five times a number is thirty.
d) Six times a number is forty-two.
e) Six divided into a number is four.
f) The product of a number and 5 is forty.
g) A number multiplied by two then increased by five is thirty-five.
h) A number multiplied by three then decreased by four is seventeen.
i) Two more than 3 divided into a number is 8.
j) Twice a number is 4 more than 10.
k) Three times a number is 4 less than 28.

BONUS▶ Half of a number is 5 more than 3.

Two numbers are **consecutive** if one is the next number after the other.

Examples: 6 and 7 are consecutive numbers because 7 is the next number after 6
6 and 8 are consecutive even numbers because 8 is the next even number after 6

4. Fill in the blanks.

a) 4 and ____ are consecutive.

b) 7 and ____ are consecutive.

c) 36, 37, 38, and ____ are consecutive.

d) x, $x + 1$, and ____ are consecutive.

5. Fill in the blanks.

a) 4 and ____ are consecutive even numbers.

b) 7 and ____ are consecutive odd numbers.

c) 16, 18, 20, and ____ are consecutive even numbers.

d) 35, ____ , 39, and 41 are consecutive odd numbers.

e) x is even. x, ____ , and ____ are consecutive even numbers.

f) x is odd. x, ____ , and ____ are consecutive odd numbers.

6. Problem: The sum of two consecutive numbers is 35. What are the numbers?
Do this problem in two ways.

a) Use a T-table to list all possible pairs of consecutive numbers, in order, and find the sums. Stop when you reach 35.

b) Use algebra.

i) If the smaller of the consecutive numbers is x, write a formula for the other number.

Smaller Number $= x$

Next Number = ______________________

ii) Write an equation using the given information:
The sum of the two consecutive numbers is 35.

______________________ $= 35$

iii) Solve your equation. What are the two numbers?

2 Consecutive Numbers	**Their Sum**
1, 2	$1 + 2 = 3$
2, 3	$2 + 3 = 5$
3, 4	$3 + 4 = 7$
4, 5	
5, 6	

7. The sum of two consecutive odd numbers is 32. What are the two numbers?

a) Let the smaller number be x and solve the problem.

b) Let the larger number be x and solve the problem.

c) Did you get the same answer both ways?

8. a) Do Question 7 by using T-tables.

b) Did you get the same answer using T-tables as you did using algebra?

c) Which method do you like better, T-tables or algebra? Explain.

9. The sum of three consecutive even numbers is 42. What are the three numbers?

10. a) The area (A) of a rectangle is given by $A = l \times w$ (also written $A = lw$), where l = length and w = width. Evaluate the expression for the area of a rectangle with...

i) $l = 2$ $w = 5$ ii) $l = 7$ $w = 9$ iii) $l = 15$ $w = 10$

b) A rectangle has area 56 and length 8. Write an equation for the width w and solve your equation.

REMINDER▸ The perimeter of a shape is the distance around the shape.

11. a) Write an expression for the perimeter of each shape (x stands for the length of the unknown sides).

i)

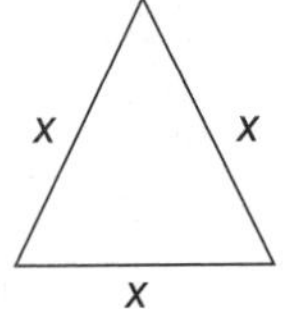

ii)

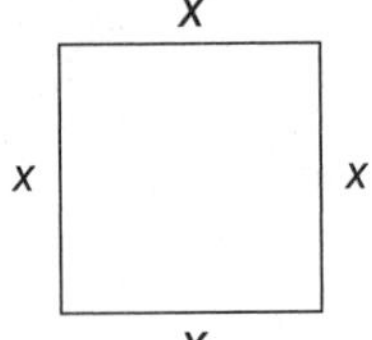

iii)

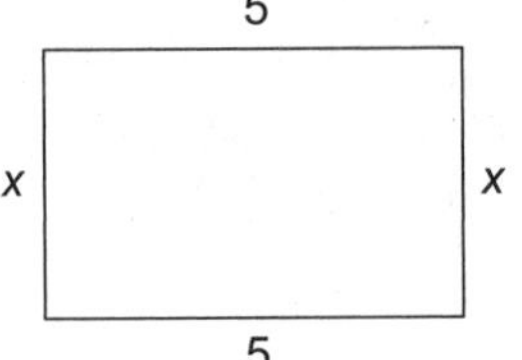

iv)

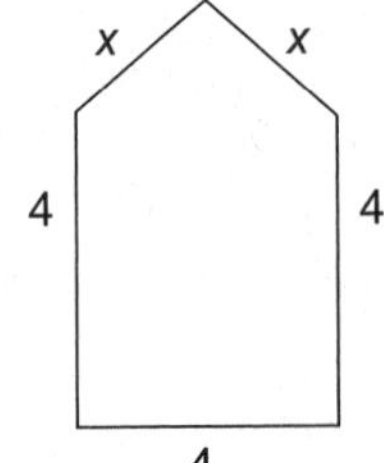

b) The perimeter of each shape in part a) is 24. Find the unknown side lengths.

12. Anna is 5 years older than Rita. The sum of their ages is 31. How old are they?

13. Mark's dad is three times as old as Mark. The sum of their ages is 48. How old is Mark?

BONUS▸ Bilal's sister is 3 years younger than Bilal.
Bilal's mother is three times Bilal's age.
Bilal's father is 4 years older than Bilal's mother.
The sum of all four ages is 89.
How old was Bilal's mother when Bilal was born?

PA7-15 Investigating Equations

Look at these equations: $2 \times 3 = 3 + 3$ $2 \times 0 = 0 + 0$ $2 \times 7 = 7 + 7$ $2 \times 26 = 26 + 26$

The equations are all different, but they have the same form. They all look like this: $2 \times a = a + a$ for some number a. The letter a is a **variable** — it represents a number.

1. Replace the number that changes in each group of equations with the variable m.

a) $5 \times 3 \div 3 = 5$
$7 \times 3 \div 3 = 7$
$12 \times 3 \div 3 = 12$
$m \times 3 \div 3 = m$

b) $7 + 3 - 3 = 7$
$18 + 3 - 3 = 18$
$25 + 3 - 3 = 25$
____

c) $7 + 3 - 3 = 7$
$7 + 4 - 4 = 7$
$7 + 12 - 12 = 7$
____

d) $16 \div 2 \times 2 = 16$
$12 \div 2 \times 2 = 12$
$7 \div 2 \times 2 = 7$
____

e) $9 - 5 + 5 = 9$
$15 - 5 + 5 = 15$
$21 - 5 + 5 = 21$
____

f) $9 - 5 + 5 = 9$
$9 - 0 + 0 = 9$
$9 - 7 + 7 = 9$
____

2. Sara notices that these equations have the same right side:

$7 \times 3 \div 3 = 7$
$7 \times 5 \div 5 = 7$
$7 \times 200 \div 200 = 7$

a) Sara thinks that $7 \times a \div a = 7$ will be true for any number a. Is she correct?
Hint: Are there any numbers that you are not allowed to divide by?

b) Choose a number a that you think will make $7 \times a \div a = 7$ true.

$a =$ ______ Check your answer.

3. Calculate each expression if $a = 12$ and $b = 3$.

a) $a - b = 12 - 3$
$= 9$

b) $a + b = 12 + 3$
$=$ ______

c) $a \times b =$ ______ $\times$ ______
$=$ ______

d) $a \div b =$ ______ $\div$ ______
$=$ ______

e) $b \times a =$ ______ $\times$ ______
$=$ ______

f) $b \div a =$ ______ $\div$ ______
$=$ ______

4. Circle two expressions from Question 3 that have the same answer.
Check in your notebook whether they will also have the same answer when...

a) $a = 4$ and $b = 7$

b) your choice: $a =$ ______ and $b =$ ______

5. Write an equation to show that the two expressions you circled in Question 4 always have the same answer. ________ = ________

To **verify** that an equation is true, calculate both sides and make sure they both equal the same number.

6. Verify that each equation is true for $a = 3$ and $b = 5$.

a) $a \times (b + 2) = a \times b + a \times 2$

$3 \times (5 + 2)$ $\quad$ $3 \times 5 + 3 \times 2$

$= 3 \times 7$ $\quad$ $= 15 + 6$

$= 21$ $\quad$ $= 21$

equal

b) $a \times (b + 3) = a \times b + a \times 3$

$\_\_\_\_ \times (\_\_\_\_ + \_\_\_\_)$ $\quad$ $\_\_\_\_ \times \_\_\_\_ + \_\_\_\_ \times \_\_\_\_$

$= \_\_\_\_ \times \_\_\_\_$ $\quad$ $= \_\_\_\_ + \_\_\_\_$

$= \_\_\_\_$ $\quad$ $= \_\_\_\_$

c) $a \times (b + 4) = a \times b + a \times 4$ $\quad$ d) $a \times (b + 5) = a \times b + a \times 5$ $\quad$ e) $a \times (b + 6) = a \times b + a \times 6$

7. All equations in Question 6 look like this: $a \times (b + c) = a \times b + a \times c$.
This is an equation in 3 variables.

a) In Question 6 c), you used: $a =$ 3, $b =$ 5, and $c =$ 4.

b) In Question 6 d), you used: $a =$ ____, $b =$ ____, and $c =$ ____.

c) In Question 6 e), you used: $a =$ ____, $b =$ ____, and $c =$ ____.

8. Use $a \times (b + c) = a \times b + a \times c$ to find what values a, b, and c have in these equations.

a) $5 \times (2 + 7) = 5 \times 2 + 5 \times 7$ $\quad$ $a =$ ____ $b =$ ____ $c =$ ____

b) $3 \times (2 + 5) = 3 \times 2 + 3 \times 5$ $\quad$ $a =$ ____ $b =$ ____ $c =$ ____

c) $2 \times (6 + 7) = 2 \times 6 + 2 \times 7$ $\quad$ $a =$ ____ $b =$ ____ $c =$ ____

d) $4 \times (12 + 83) = 4 \times 12 + 4 \times 83$ $\quad$ $a =$ ____ $b =$ ____ $c =$ ____

9. Use $a \times (b + c) = a \times b + a \times c$ to finish writing the equations.

a) $3 \times (5 + 1) = 3 \times \_\_\_\_ + 3 \times \_\_\_\_$ $\quad$ b) $4 \times (2 + 6) = \_\_\_\_ \times 2 + \_\_\_\_ \times 6$

c) $7 \times (0 + 3) = \_\_\_\_ \times \_\_\_\_ + \_\_\_\_ \times \_\_\_\_$ $\quad$ d) $0 \times (3 + 4) = \_\_\_\_\_\_\_\_$

e) $9 \times (2 + 7) = \_\_\_\_\_\_\_\_$ $\quad$ f) $10 \times (1 + 1) = \_\_\_\_\_\_\_\_$

10. Calculate $(a + b) \times c$ and $a \times c + b \times c$ for the values of a, b, and c given.

a) $a = 3, b = 5, c = 4$ $\quad$ b) $a = 2, b = 3, c = 1$ $\quad$ c) $a = 5, b = 2, c = 10$

What do you notice about your answers? Write an equation using the variables a, b, and c.

11. Use the equation from Question 10 to fill in the blanks.

a) In the expression $(5 + 3) \times 6$

$a =$ 5 $\quad b =$ 3 $\quad c =$ 6

So $(5 + 3) \times 6 = \_\_\_\_ \times 6 + \_\_\_\_ \times 6$

b) In the expression, $(8 + 5) \times 3$

$a =$ ____ $\quad b =$ ____ $\quad c =$ ____

So $(8 + 5) \times 3 = 8 \times \_\_\_\_ + 5 \times \_\_\_\_$

c) In the expression $(7 + 2) \times 9$

$a =$ ____ $\quad b =$ ____ $\quad c =$ ____

So $(7 + 2) \times 9 = \_\_\_\_ \times \_\_\_\_ + \_\_\_\_ \times \_\_\_\_$

d) In the expression, $(3 + 2) \times 0$

$a =$ ____ $\quad b =$ ____ $\quad c =$ ____

So $(3 + 2) \times 0 = \_\_\_\_\_\_\_\_$

NS7-9 Factors and Multiples

The **multiples** of a number are the numbers you say when counting by that number.

$3 \times 5 = 15$ ← 15 is a **multiple** of both 3 and 5
3 and 5 are both **factors** of 15

$0 \times 4 = 0$ ← 0 is a **multiple** of both 0 and 4
0 and 4 are both **factors** of 0

1. List the first few multiples of these numbers.

   a) 3: _0_, _3_, _6_, _9_, ____, ____, ____.
   b) 4: ____, ____, ____, ____, ____, ____, ____.
   c) 5: ____, ____, ____, ____, ____, ____, ____.

2. Look at the lists you made in Question 1.

   a) Is 12 a multiple of 4? ____
   b) Is 17 a multiple of 5? ____
   c) Is 0 a multiple of 3? ____ Of 4? ____ Of 5? ____

3. a) Write 0 as a multiple of 17. $0 = 17 \times$ ______

   b) Which whole numbers is 0 a multiple of? Explain. ______________________

   ____

4. Rewrite each statement in a way that means the same thing but uses the word "factor."

   a) 20 is a multiple of 5. _5 is a factor of 20._
   b) 9 is a multiple of 1. ______________________
   c) 0 is a multiple of 8. ______________________
   d) 11 is not a multiple of 4. ______________________

INVESTIGATION 1 ▶ What are the factors of 12?

A. Count by each number until you either reach 12 or pass it.

a) by 1s: 0, 1, 2, 3, 4, 5, 6, 7, 8, _9, 10, 11, 12_
b) by 2s: 0, 2, 4, ______________________
c) by 3s: 0, 3, 6, ______________________
d) by 4s: 0, 4, ______________________
e) by 5s: 0, 5, ______________________
f) by 6s: 0, 6, ______________________
g) by 7s: 0, 7, ______________________
h) by 8s: 0, 8, ______________________
i) by 9s: 0, 9, ______________________
j) by 10s: 0, 10, ______________________
k) by 11s: 0, 11, ______________________
l) by 12s: 0, 12, ______________________
m) by 13s: 0, ______________________

B. How do you know that any number greater than 12 cannot be a factor of 12?

____

C. a) List all the factors of 12. ______________________
b) Is 12 a factor of 12? ______________________

5. a) Count by 0s from 0. 0, 0, 0, ____, ____, ____.

   b) Is 8 a multiple of 0? ______

   c) Is 0 a factor of 8? ______

   d) What is the only number that is a multiple of 0? ______

   e) What is the only number that has 0 as a factor? ______

6. a) Show that 13 is a factor of 13 by counting by 13s starting at 0.

   b) Which whole numbers are factors of themselves? Explain. ______

7. a) Show that 1 is a factor of 8 by counting by 1s starting at 0.

   b) Which whole numbers have 1 as a factor? Explain. ______

8. a) Fill in the blanks:

   $0 \times 1 =$ ______ $0 \times 2 =$ ______ $0 \times 3 =$ ______ $0 \times 4 =$ ______

   b) What numbers will fit in the blank here: $0 \times$ ______ $= 0$?

   Can you find a number that does not fit? ______

   c) We know that 0 is a factor of 0. What are the other factors of 0? Explain. ______

9. Rewrite each statement in a way that means the same thing but uses the word "factor."

   a) 5 is a multiple of 1. ______

   b) Every number is a multiple of 1. ______

   c) 8 is a multiple of 8. ______

   d) Every number is a multiple of itself. ______

   e) 0 is a multiple of 7. ______

   f) 0 is a multiple of any number. ______

10. Rewrite each statement in a way that means the same thing but uses the word "multiple."

   a) 5 is a factor of 15.

   b) 3 is a factor of 0.

   c) Any factor of 12 is at most 12.

   d) Any factor of a number (except 0) is at most the number.

   e) 6 is a factor of 6.

   f) Any number is a factor of itself.

NS7-10 Organized Search

1. Alana uses a chart to find all the factors of 10 by pairing up numbers that multiply to give 10. She lists numbers 1 to 10 in the 1st column, and the number you multiply each one by to get 10 in the 2nd column. If there is no number that multiplies to 10, she leaves the box in the 2nd column blank.

1st	2nd
1	10
2	5
3	
4	
5	2
6	
7	
8	
9	
10	1

   a) Why did Alana not list any 1st number greater than 10?

   ____

   b) Why did Alana not list 0 as a 1st number?

   ____

2. Use Alana's method to find all the pairs of numbers that multiply to give the number in bold.

   a) **6**

1st	2nd
1	
2	
3	
4	
5	
6	

   b) **8**

1st	2nd
1	
2	
3	
4	
5	
6	
7	
8	

   c) **9**

1st	2nd
1	
2	
3	
4	
5	
6	
7	
8	
9	

3. Cross out the pairs of numbers that are repeated in Question 2.

4. Connor makes a chart to list all the factors of 24. He does not want to write and check all the numbers from 1 to 24. He starts his list as shown.

1st	2nd
1	24
2	12
3	8
4	6
5	
6	4

   a) Connor knows that $6 \times 4 = 24$. He thinks that if $7 \times \square = 24$, then $\square$ must be less than 4. Explain his thinking.

   b) Explain why Connor's list is complete.

5. Connor used this chart to help him identify pairs that multiply to 16. Why did he know that his search was complete as soon as he found a pair with both numbers the same?

1st	2nd
1	16
2	8
3	
4	4

To list all the factors of a given number (the pairs of numbers that multiply to give that number), stop when you get a number that is already part of a pair.

6. Make a chart to find all the pairs of numbers that multiply to give each number.

a) 20 b) 12 c) 15 d) 14 e) 25 f) 5
g) 26 h) 30 i) 42 j) 72
k) 63 l) 100 m) 64 n) 91

A **factor rainbow** for a number, such as 9 or 10, pairs the factors that multiply to give that number.

Factor rainbow for 9

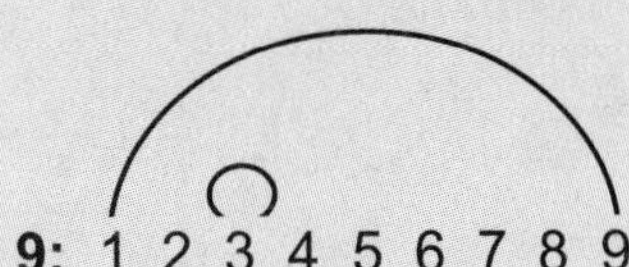

9: 1 2 3 4 5 6 7 8 9

Factor rainbow for 10

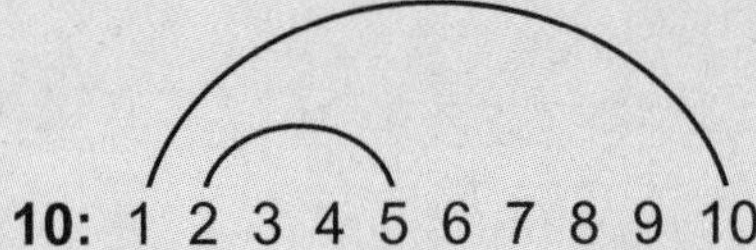

10: 1 2 3 4 5 6 7 8 9 10

7. Finish the factor rainbow for each number.

6: 1 2 3 4 5 6 **8:** 1 2 3 4 5 6 7 8 **12:** 1 2 3 4 5 6 7 8 9 10 11 12

8. As a shortcut to making a factor rainbow, we can leave out all numbers that are not factors. Using this shortcut, make a factor rainbow for each number.

Example: **6:** 1 2 3 6

a) 4 b) 8 c) 12 d) 15 e) 7 f) 24 g) 42

9. a) Tom knows that 3 is a factor of 144. Is 144 ÷ 3 also a factor of 144? _______

b) Tom's teacher tells him that 1, 2, 3, 4, 6, and 12 are all factors of 144. Find 6 more factors of 144 by division.

144 ÷ 1 = _______ 144 ÷ 2 = _______ 144 ÷ 3 = _______

144 ÷ 4 = _______ 144 ÷ 6 = _______ 144 ÷ 12 = _______

c) As n gets larger, what happens to 144 ÷ n? _______________

d) List the factors of 144 you found so far in order. Have you found all of them? How do you know?

10. 1 is a factor of every number. What is the next smallest factor of 3 256? What is the largest factor of 3 256, other than 3 256? How do you know?

NS7-11 LCMs and GCFs

The multiples of 2 and 3 are marked with X on the number lines.

multiples of 2: 0 1 2 3 4 5 6 7 8 9 10 11 12 13 14 15 16

multiples of 3: 0 1 2 3 4 5 6 7 8 9 10 11 12 13 14 15 16

The numbers marked with X on both number lines are 0, 6, and 12. These numbers are called **common multiples** of 2 and 3.

1. Predict the next common multiple of 2 and 3, then check by extending the number sequences.

2. Mark the multiples of each number on the number lines.

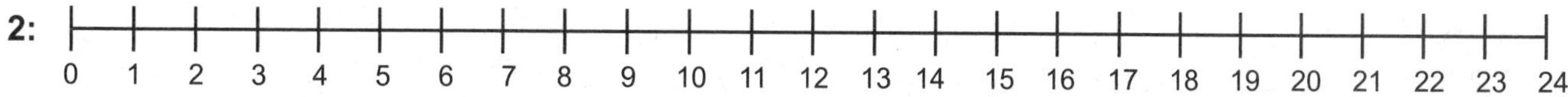

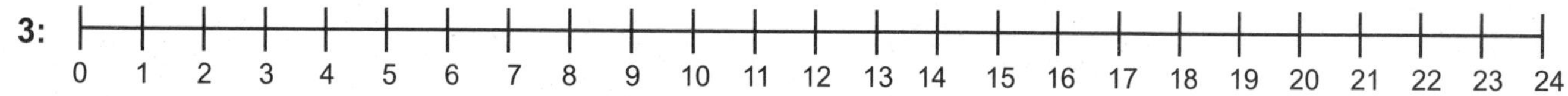

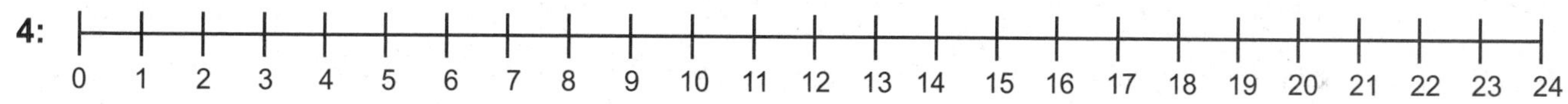

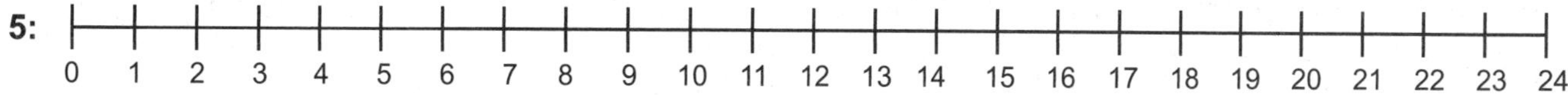

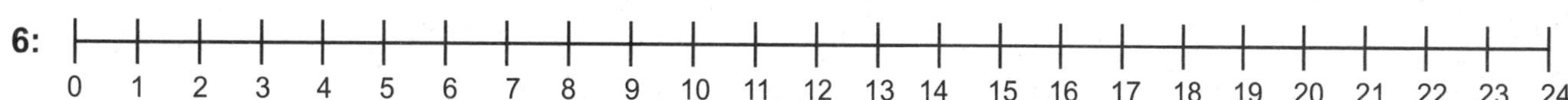

3. Find the first 2 common multiples (after 0) of…

a) 2 and 5: ______, ______ b) 3 and 6: ______, ______ c) 2 and 4: ______, ______

d) 3 and 4: ______, ______ e) 4 and 6: ______, ______ f) 3, 4, and 6: ______, ______

4. a) How can you find the second common multiple of two numbers from the first?

b) The first common multiple of 18 and 42 is 126. What is the second common multiple?

5. a) Write the first 4 common multiples of 2 and 3, after 0. ______ ______ ______ ______.

b) Extend the pattern from part a). Predict the fifth common multiple of 2 and 3. ______

The **lowest common multiple (LCM)** of two numbers is the smallest number (not 0) that is a multiple of both numbers.

6. Look at your answers to Question 3. What is the LCM of…

a) 2 and 5 b) 3 and 6 c) 2 and 4 d) 3 and 4 e) 4 and 6

7. Find the lowest common multiple of each pair of numbers.

a) 3 and 5
*3: 3, 6, 9, 12, **15**, 18*
*5: 5, 10, **15**, 20*
LCM = ***15***

b) 4 and 10
LCM = ______

c) 3 and 9
LCM = ______

d) 2 and 6
LCM = ______

e) 2 and 10 f) 2 and 7 g) 3 and 12 h) 4 and 8

i) 8 and 10 j) 5 and 15 k) 6 and 10 l) 3 and 10

m) 6 and 8 n) 6 and 9

REMINDER▶ The **factors** of 24 are 1, 2, 3, 4, 6, 8, 12, and 24, since:

1 × 24 = 24 **2 × 12 = 24** **3 × 8 = 24** **4 × 6 = 24**

8. Find all the factors of each number below by dividing the number by the whole numbers in increasing order—divide by 1, 2, 3, 4, 5, and so on. How do you know when to stop dividing?

a) 20 b) 22 c) 26 d) 65 e) 66

The greatest number that is a factor of two or more numbers is called the **greatest common factor (GCF)** of the numbers.

9. Use your answers to Question 8. Find the greatest common factor of…

a) 20 and 22 b) 22 and 66 c) 20 and 65 d) 65 and 66

e) 26 and 65 f) 22 and 65 g) 20, 26, and 65 h) 20, 22, and 66

10. i) List the factors of each number below in order from least to greatest.
ii) Circle all the **common factors** for each pair.
iii) Put a double circle around the **GCF** of the pair.

a) 10 and 15 b) 18 and 24 c) 20 and 30 d) 28 and 42

11. a) Find the factors of each number and then the greatest common factor (GCF) of each pair.

i) 2 and 10
2: *1, 2*
10: *1, 2, 5, 10*
GCF = *2*

ii) 5 and 15
5:
15:
GCF = ______

iii) 6 and 30
6:
30:
GCF = ______

iv) 10 and 50
10:
50:
GCF = ______

b) If *a* is a factor of *b*, what is the **GCF** of *a* and *b*? ______

Two numbers are called **consecutive** if one number is the next number after the other.
Example: 13 and 14 are consecutive because 14 is the next number after 13.

INVESTIGATION 1 ▶ What is the GCF of two consecutive numbers?

A. Find the factors of each number and then the GCF of each pair.

a) 14 and 15
14: *1, 2, 7, 14*
15: *1, 3, 5, 15*
GCF = *1*

b) 20 and 21
20:
21:
GCF = ______

c) 15 and 16
15:
16:
GCF = ______

d) 35 and 36
35:
36:
GCF = ______

B. Make a conjecture about the GCF of any two consecutive numbers.

____

C. Test your conjecture on two more consecutive numbers of your choice: ______ and ______

INVESTIGATION 2 ▶ How are the GCF, the LCM, and the product of two numbers related?

A. Find the **GCF**, the **LCM**, and the **product** of each pair of numbers. Do rough work in your notebook.

a) 3 and 4
GCF = ______
LCM = ______
$3 \times 4 =$ ______

b) 2 and 5
GCF = ______
LCM = ______
$2 \times 5 =$ ______

c) 4 and 6
GCF = ______
LCM = ______
$4 \times 6 =$ ______

d) 10 and 15
GCF = ______
LCM = ______
$10 \times 15 =$ ______

e) 5 and 10
GCF = ______
LCM = ______
$5 \times 10 =$ ______

f) 3 and 5
GCF = ______
LCM = ______
$3 \times 5 =$ ______

g) 4 and 5
GCF = ______
LCM = ______
$4 \times 5 =$ ______

h) 6 and 9
GCF = ______
LCM = ______
$6 \times 9 =$ ______

B. Circle the questions from part A where the LCM is the product of the two numbers.

C. Make a conjecture: When the LCM is the product of the two numbers, the GCF is ______.

NS7-12 Perfect Squares and Square Roots

1. Find the factors of each number by drawing all different rectangles (with whole-number sides) that have an area equal to the number.

Example:

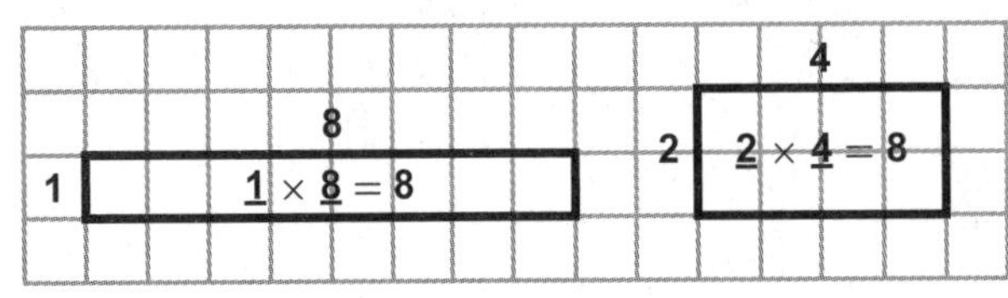

So the factors of 8 are 1, 2, 4, and 8.

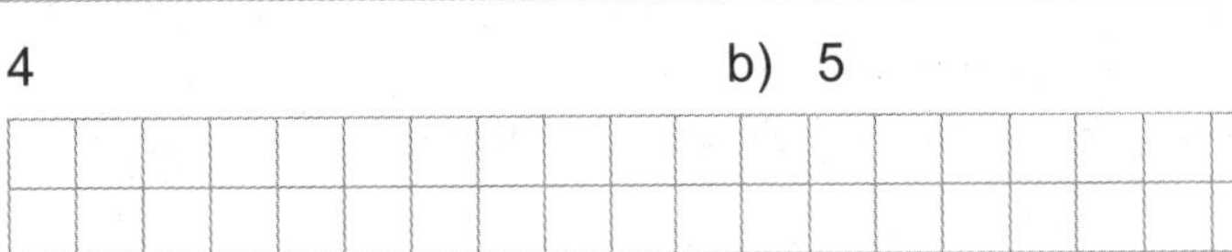

a) 4 b) 5 c) 6

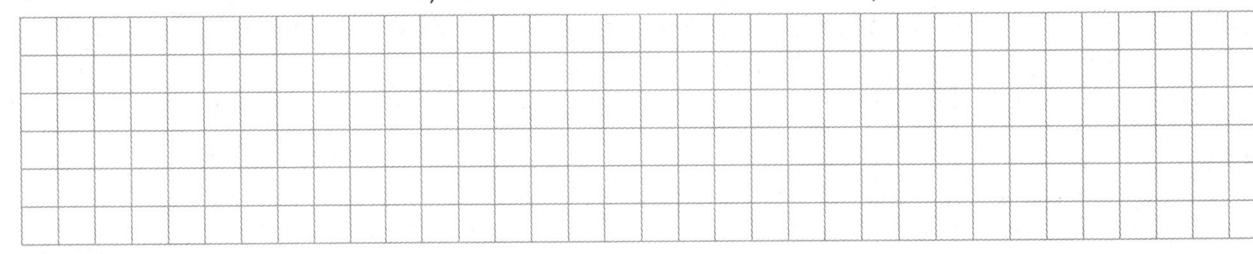

d) 7 e) 8 f) 9

A number larger than 1 is called a **prime number** if you can draw only 1 rectangle with an area equal to that number.

A number larger than 0 is called a **perfect square** if you can draw a square with whole-number side lengths having that area.

2. Which numbers from Question 1 are prime numbers? ____________________

3. Which numbers from Question 1 are perfect squares? ____________________

4. Can a prime number be a perfect square? Explain. ____________________

____

5. a) Draw squares with side lengths 1, 2, 3, 4, and 5 on the grid below.

b) Write the first 5 perfect squares larger than 0. ______ ______ ______ ______ ______

6. Show that 36 is a perfect square by drawing a square with area 36.

7. Show that 10 is not a perfect square by drawing all non-congruent rectangles with area 10.

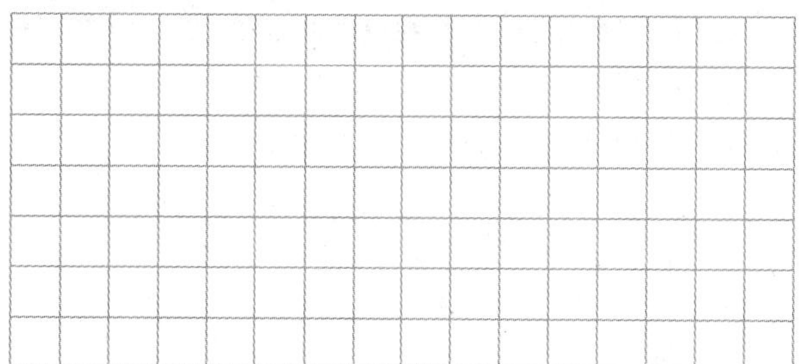

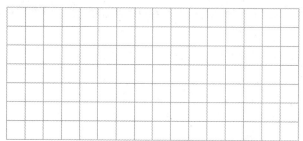

Any perfect square can be written as a product of a whole number with itself.

Example: $25 = 5 \times 5$ 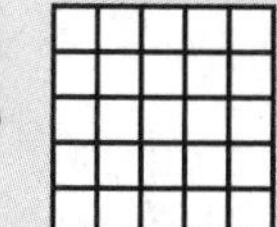 Area $= 5 \times 5 = 25$ squares

Note: Since $0 = 0 \times 0$, we say that 0 is a perfect square even though you cannot draw a square with area 0.

8. Write down the first 10 perfect squares larger than 0.

$1 \times 1 =$ ______ $2 \times 2 =$ ______ $3 \times 3 =$ ______ $4 \times 4 =$ ______ $5 \times 5 =$ ______

$6 \times 6 =$ ______ $7 \times 7 =$ ______ $8 \times 8 =$ ______ $9 \times 9 =$ ______ $10 \times 10 =$ ______

When we multiply a number by itself, we get a perfect square. This process is called **squaring the number.** Example: 6 squared is $6 \times 6 = 36$. We write $6^2 = 36$. (The 2 is because we multiplied 2 sixes.)

9. Write each perfect square as a product and evaluate it.

a) $5^2 = 5 \times 5$
$= 25$

b) $3^2 =$

c) $8^2 =$

d) $0^2 =$

e) $7^2 =$

10. a) Will a square of side length 131 cm fit into a square of side length 132 cm? ______

b) Explain how you know that $131^2 < 132^2$. ______

______

11. Write the numbers from smallest to largest without calculating the perfect squares.

a) 3^2 5^2 4^2

____ ____ ____

b) 10^2 8^2 9^2

____ ____ ____

c) 5^2 12^2 7^2

____ ____ ____

12. Write the numbers from largest to smallest. You will need to calculate the perfect squares.

a) 3^2 5 10 4^2 2^2

____ ____ ____ ____ ____

b) 50 7^2 9^2 8^2 85

____ ____ ____ ____ ____

5 is called the **square root** of 25 because 25 is the **square** of 5.

We write $\sqrt{25} = 5$ because $25 = 5^2 = 5 \times 5$.

13. Write the same number in each box.

a) $9 = \square \times \square$ b) $49 = \square \times \square$ c) $0 = \square \times \square$ d) $25 = \square \times \square$

14. Evaluate.

a) $\sqrt{49}$ $= 7$ b) $\sqrt{16}$ c) $\sqrt{9}$ d) $\sqrt{36}$ e) $\sqrt{1}$ f) $\sqrt{100}$ g) $\sqrt{81}$ h) $\sqrt{64}$

15. Square roots are numbers, so you can add, subtract, multiply, and divide them. Evaluate.

a) $\sqrt{25} + \sqrt{4}$ $= 5 + 2 = 7$ b) $\sqrt{36} \times \sqrt{25}$ c) $\sqrt{64} - \sqrt{9}$ d) $\sqrt{100} \div \sqrt{4}$ e) $\sqrt{49} + \sqrt{64}$

f) $\sqrt{36} - \sqrt{25}$ g) $\sqrt{36} \div \sqrt{4}$ h) $\sqrt{36} + \sqrt{25} - \sqrt{1}$ **BONUS▶** $\sqrt{25} + \sqrt{16} \times \sqrt{9}$

16. Evaluate.

a) $\sqrt{3^2}$ $= \sqrt{3 \times 3} = \sqrt{9} = 3$ b) $\sqrt{5^2}$ c) $\sqrt{9^2}$ d) $\sqrt{4105^2}$ e) $\sqrt{n^2}$

17. The side length of a square is the square root of the area. Find the side lengths.

a)

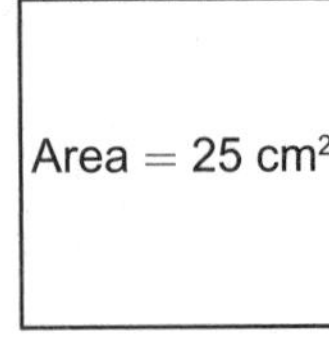

_______ cm

b)

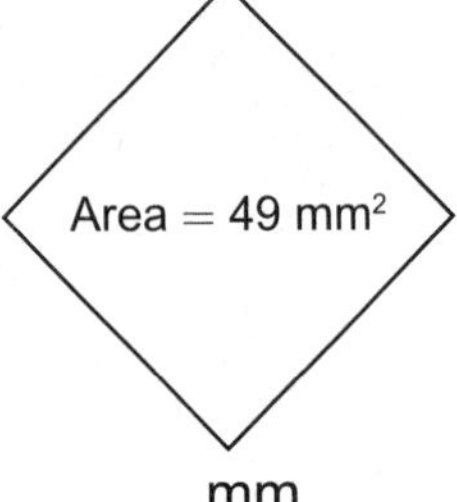

_______ mm

c)

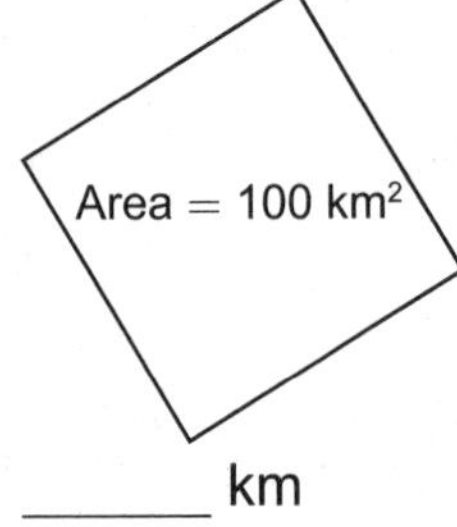

_______ km

18. One square has area 64 cm² and another square has area 36 cm².

a) Which square has a larger side length? How do you know?

b) Write > or <. $\sqrt{64}$ _______ $\sqrt{36}$

19. Order these numbers from smallest to largest.

a) $\sqrt{49}$ $\sqrt{64}$ $\sqrt{25}$ $\sqrt{9}$ $\sqrt{16}$

b) $\sqrt{100}$ 3^2 5 4^2 $\sqrt{4}$ $\sqrt{8^2}$

c) $\sqrt{100} \div \sqrt{4}$ $\sqrt{16}$ $\sqrt{4} \times \sqrt{9}$ 3^2 $\sqrt{100}$ $\sqrt{36} + \sqrt{4}$ $\sqrt{81} - \sqrt{49}$

20. How is the notation for units of area similar to the notation for square numbers?

NS7-13 Counter-Examples

To prove that a statement is false, all you need is one **counter-example.** Example: To prove that the statement "All girls wear glasses" is false, you just need to find one girl who does **not** wear glasses.

1. For each statement, circle the counter-example.

   a) All circles in the set are shaded.

   b) All triangles in the set are white.

   c) All striped shapes in the set are circles.

   d) All white shapes in the set are circles.

2. Circle the counter-examples. Some questions will have more than one counter-example.

   a) All balls are spheres.

   b) All vehicles have four wheels.

   TAXI

   c) All words have an "e."

   person place thing object bcjxp bcjxe

   d) All English sentences end with a period.

   Who's there? No way! ¿Cual es tu nombre? My name is Ahmed.

3. In Question 2b), why is the banana not a counter-example? ____________________

4. Ms. K gives each student a card with both a number and a letter. She says that all cards with an even number (0, 2, 4, 6,...) should have a vowel (A, E, I, O, or U).

   a) 3 is not an even number. Can the card | 3 | J | be a counter-example? ____________

      Why or why not? ____

   b) Find all the cards that are wrong.

3	J

6	A

5	E

12	R

24	U

7	O

19	X

E	19

J	16

H	13

A	14

C	28

To prove a statement false, you need to **find only one counter-example**.

To prove a statement true, you need to **make sure it is true for all examples**.

5. Each card below has a letter and a number. Decide whether each statement is true or false for the cards shown. A statement will be true if it is true for all the cards. A statement will be false if you find a counter-example. For the statements that are false, write the first counter-example you find.

r	15

E	13

U	3

B	4

D	7

M	6

j	3

e	5

F	8

H	10

   a) All cards with capital letters have even numbers.
   b) All cards with vowels have odd numbers.
   c) All cards with capital letter vowels have odd numbers.
   d) All cards with odd numbers have capital letters.
   e) All cards with even numbers have capital letters.
   f) All cards with odd numbers have vowels.
   g) All cards with even numbers have a consonant.
   h) All cards with small letters have odd numbers.
   i) All cards with odd numbers have small letters.
   j) All cards with small letter consonants have odd numbers.

6. Was it easier to prove a statement true or false? Explain.

The two statements below are **the reverse** of each other.

"All girls in the class are wearing glasses." "All people wearing glasses in the class are girls."

7. A counter-example for a statement will be different from a counter-example for its reverse. Find a counter-example for each statement and for its reverse.

A. □ B. ○ C. ■ D. ● E. □ F. ●

a) All dark shapes are circles. Counter-example: *C*

All circles are dark. Counter-example: ______

b) All white shapes are big. Counter-example: ______

All big shapes are white. Counter-example: ______

c) All circles are big. Counter-example: ______

All big shapes are circles. Counter-example: ______

8. Sometimes a statement is true but its reverse is not. Find the reverse of each statement and then find a counter-example for the reverse.

a) All boys are people.

Reverse: All ______ are ______.

Counter-example: ______.

b) All bananas are fruit.

Reverse: All ______ are ______.

Counter-example: ______.

c) All fish are animals that live in water.

Reverse: All ______ are ______.

Counter-example: ______.

d) Any sequence of words that form a sentence must start with a capital letter.

Reverse: Any sequence of words that ______ must ______.

Counter-example: ______.

9. Write the reverse of each statement and whether or not the statements are true or false.

a) All vehicles with wheels are cars. *False*.

Reverse: *All cars are vehicles with wheels.* *True*.

b) All apples are red fruits. ______.

Reverse: ______ ______.

c) All girls are soccer players. d) All circles are shapes. e) All Canadian coins worth $2 are toonies.

NS7-14 Divisibility by 2, 5, and 10

In math, there are sometimes many ways to say the same thing. Example: These statements all mean the same thing:

8 is a multiple of 2   2 is a factor of 8   2 divides 8   8 is divisible by 2

8 leaves no remainder when divided by 2   You say 8 when counting by 2s from 0

INVESTIGATION 1 ▶ Are all whole numbers with ones digit 0 multiples of 10?

A. Rewrite the question using the word "divisible."

____

B. Choose 3 numbers with ones digit 0 and write them as multiples of 10.
Example: 4 700 = 470 × 10

_______ = _______ × 10   _______ = _______ × 10   _______ = _______ × 10

C. In the first row of the chart, write the first 15 whole numbers greater than 0 that have ones digit 0. Then write each number as a multiple of 10.

	10	**20**	**30**												
= _____ × 10	*1*	*2*	*3*												

D. Look for a pattern. The 1st number with ones digit 0 is _______ × 10.

The 2nd number with ones digit 0 is _______ × 10.

The 3rd number with ones digit 0 is _______ × 10.

The 12th number with ones digit 0 is _______ × 10.

The nth number with ones digit 0 is _______ × 10.

E. Are all whole numbers with ones digit 0 divisible by 10? __________

INVESTIGATION 2 ▶ Is any number with ones digit divisible by 2 also divisible by 2?

A. Write the first 15 numbers larger than 0 with ones digit divisible by 2 and complete the chart. Then look for a pattern.

	2	**4**	**6**	**8**	**10**	**12**	**14**			**20**					
= _____ × 2	*1*	*2*	*3*												

B. The nth number with ones digit divisible by 2 is _______ × 2.

INVESTIGATION 3 ▶ Is any number with ones digit divisible by 3 also divisible by 3?

A. Write down the first 10 numbers larger than 0 with ones digit divisible by 3.
Then divide each number by 3. Do you get a remainder?

	3	**6**	**9**	**10**	**13**					
÷ 3	*1*	2	3	3R___	4R___					

B. Write the smallest counter-example to this statement: Any number with ones digit divisible by 3 is also divisible by 3. ______________________

---

1. The statement "Any number that has ones digit divisible by 2 is also divisible by 2" is true.

a) Write the reverse.

Any number that is ____________________ has ______________________.

b) Write the first fifteen numbers that are divisible by 2 (the multiples of 2) and then their ones digits.

divisible by 2	**0**	**2**	**4**	**6**	**8**	**10**	**12**								
ones digit	*0*	*2*	*4*												

c) What type of pattern do you see in the ones digits — increasing, decreasing, or repeating? Describe it.

____

d) Is the statement in part a) true? ____________________

2. The statement "Any number with ones digit divisible by 3 is also divisible by 3" is false.

a) Write the reverse.

Any number that is ____________________ has ______________________.

b) Is the reverse statement true? _______ In your notebook, describe the pattern or the counter-example.

3. Write the reverse of each statement, then decide whether the statements are true or false.

a) Any number whose ones digit is divisible by 4 is also divisible by 4.
b) Any number whose ones digit is divisible by 5 is also divisible by 5.

4. How can looking at the ones digit of a number tell you if the number is...

a) divisible by 2? ______________________________

b) divisible by 5? ______________________________

c) divisible by 10? ______________________________

5. Circle the numbers that are divisible by 2.

17 3 418 312 64 76 234 89 94 167 560

6. Circle the numbers that are multiples of 5.

83 17 45 37 150 64 190 65 71 235 618 1 645

7. Underline the numbers in Question 6 that are divisible by 10.

NS7-15 Divisibility by 3, 6, and 9

A number is divisible by 3 if it can be divided into equal groups of three. For instance, 12 is divisible by 3 because it can be divided into four groups of three.

12 = 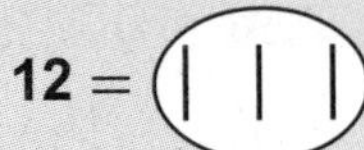 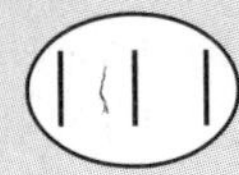  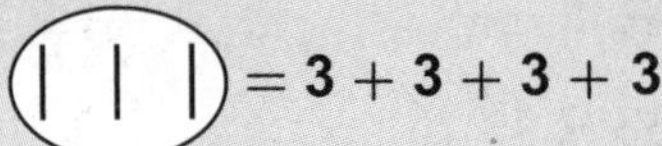

1. Group lines into sets of 3 to show that each number is divisible by 3.

6: 

12: | | | | | | | | | | | |

9: | | | | | | | | |

2. Group lines into sets of 3 to find the remainder.

a) 

$7 \div 3$: Remainder *1*

b) | | | | |

$5 \div 3$: Remainder ______

c) 

$11 \div 3$: Remainder ______

3. 6 and 9 are both divisible by 3. Miki draws a picture to show that $6 + 9$ is divisible by 3.

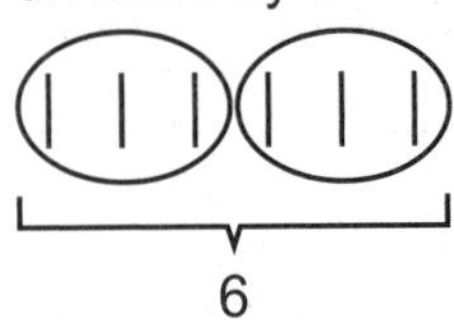

+

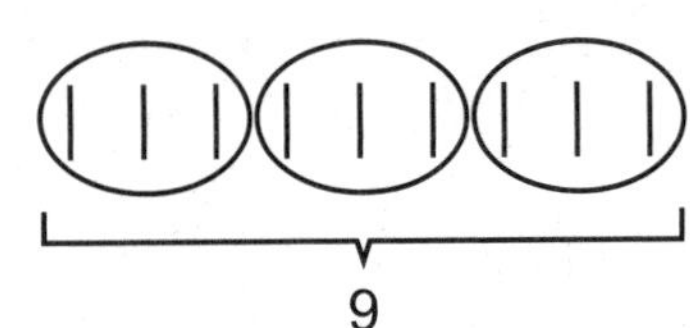

Draw a picture to show that $6 + 12$ is divisible by 3.

4. a) 6 is a multiple of 3. Is $5 \times 6 = 6 + 6 + 6 + 6 + 6$ also a multiple of 3? Explain.

b) Is any multiple of a multiple of 3 also a multiple of 3? ______

5. 12 is divisible by 3 but 5 is not. Ron draws a picture to show that $12 + 5$ is not divisible by 3.

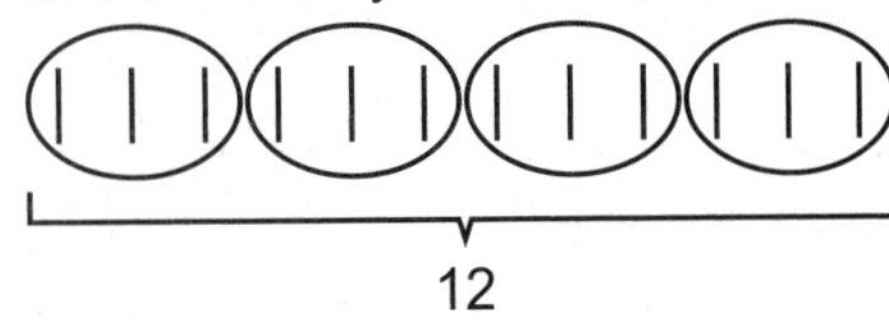

+

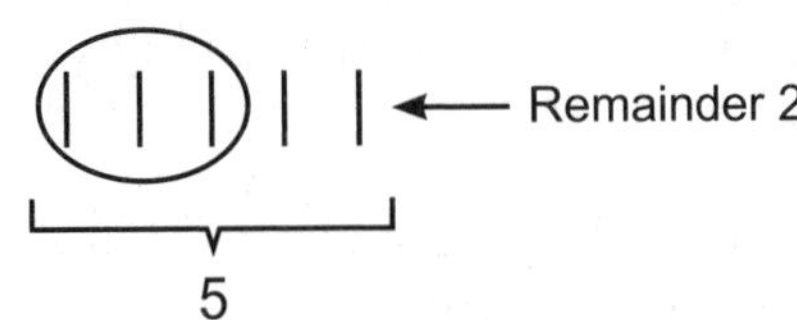

a) Draw a picture to show that $9 + 7$ is not divisible by 3.

b) What is the remainder of $(9 + 7) \div 3$?

c) Explain why the remainder of $(9 + 7) \div 3$ is the same as the remainder of $7 \div 3$.

d) Predict the remainder when each sum is divided by 3. Check your prediction.

i) $12 + 7$ ii) $9 + 5$ iii) $15 + 7$ iv) $33 + 7$ v) $27 + 8$ vi) $33 + 3$

6. Explain why $(12 + 5 + 15 + 2) \div 3$ has the same remainder as $(5 + 2) \div 3$.

7. Follow the pattern to predict the answers. Then check your answers by long division in your notebook.

a) $7 \div 3 = 2$ R 1

$70 \div 3 = 23$ R 1

$700 \div 3 = 233$ R 1

$7\,000 \div 3 =$ _____ R _____

b) $5 \div 3 = 1$ R 2

$50 \div 3 = 16$ R 2

$500 \div 3 = 166$ R 2

$5\,000 \div 3 =$ _____ R _____

c) $8 \div 3 = 2$ R 2

$80 \div 3 = 26$ R 2

$800 \div 3 = 266$ R 2

$8\,000 \div 3 =$ _____ R _____

d) $2 \div 3 = 0$ R 2

$20 \div 3 = 6$ R 2

$200 \div 3 = 66$ R 2

$2\,000 \div 3 =$ _____ R _____

e) $9 \div 3 = 3$ R 0

$90 \div 3 = 30$ R 0

$900 \div 3 = 300$ R 0

$9\,000 \div 3 =$ _____ R _____

f) $4 \div 3 = 1$ R 1

$40 \div 3 = 13$ R 1

$400 \div 3 = 133$ R 1

$4\,000 \div 3 =$ _____ R _____

8. Predict the remainder when dividing by 3. Check your prediction in your notebook by long division.

a) $20\,000 \div 3$ has remainder _____

b) $4\,000\,000 \div 3$ has remainder _____

9. a) Is 999×8 a multiple of 3? _____ How do you know? _____________________

____

b) $8\,000 = 1\,000 \times 8$

$= 999 \times 8 +$ _____

c) Explain why 8 000 has the same remainder as 8 when you divide both by 3.

d) Explain why 800 and 80 both have the same remainder as 8 when you divide both by 3. Hint: $800 = 99 \times 8 + 8$.

REMINDER▶ A number is divisible by 3 if the remainder is 0 when you divide by 3.

10. Look at your answer to Question 9c). Is 8 000 divisible by 3? How do you know?

11. Use expanded form and the pattern from Question 7 to find the remainder when dividing by 3. Check your answer by dividing.

a) $52 = 50 + 2$, so $52 \div 3$ has the same remainder as (_5_ + _2_) $\div 3 =$ _7_ $\div 3 =$ _2_ R _1_

Check: $52 \div 3 =$ _17_ R _1_

b) $84 = 80 + 4$ has the same remainder as _____ + _____ = _____ which is _____.

Check: $84 \div 3 =$ _____ R _____

c) $47 = 40 + 7$ has the same remainder as _____ + _____ = _____ which is _____.

Check: $47 \div 3 =$ _____ R _____

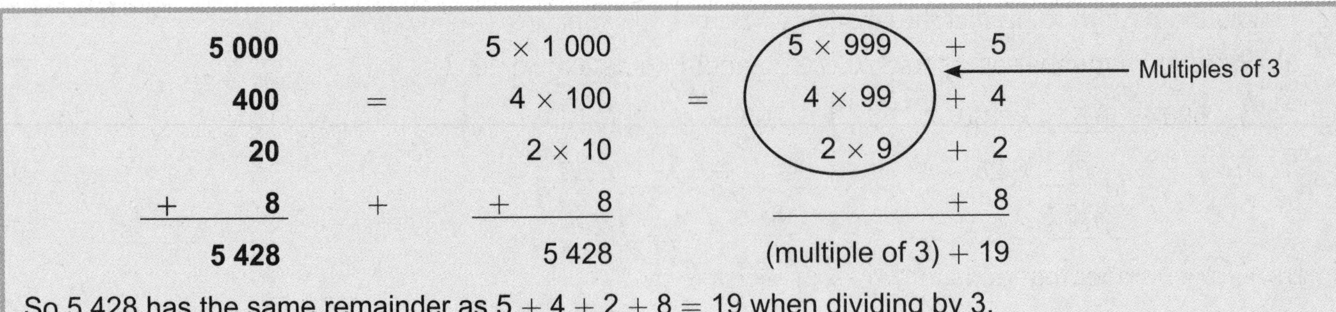

So 5 428 has the same remainder as $5 + 4 + 2 + 8 = 19$ when dividing by 3.

12. a) When dividing by 3,

5 428 has the same remainder as: _____ + _____ + _____ + _____ = _____ which is _____.

5 482 has the same remainder as: _____ + _____ + _____ + _____ = _____ which is _____.

2 485 has the same remainder as: _____ + _____ + _____ + _____ = _____ which is _____.

b) Can you rearrange the digits of 5 482 to make a number that is divisible by 3? Explain.

13. Write a rule to determine if a number is divisible by 3, by using the sum of its digits.

14. a) Explain why 5 428 has the same remainder as $5 + 4 + 2 + 8$ when dividing by 9.

b) Write a rule to determine if a number is divisible by 9, by using the sum of its digits.

15. a) Find the sum of the digits for each number below.

Number	28	37	42	61	63	87	93	123
Sum of Digits								

b) Sort the numbers in this Venn diagram, using the attributes "divisible by 3" and "divisible by 9."

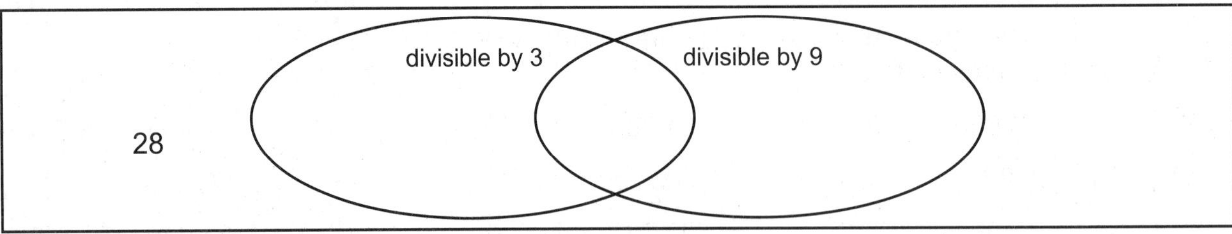

c) Which part of the Venn diagram is empty? Why is it empty?

16. a) Sort the numbers from 0 to 30 in a Venn diagram in your notebook, using the following attributes: divisible by 2; divisible by 3.

b) Where, in the Venn diagram, are the numbers that are divisible by 6? Why did that happen?

c) Use the tests for divisibility by 2 and 3 to make a test for divisibility by 6.

d) Circle the numbers that are divisible by 6. 3 471 3 174 7 314 7 413 3 741

NS7-16 Divisibility by 2, 4, and 8

1. a) Write each number as a multiple of 100 and then as a multiple of 4.

i) 600 = _6_ × 100
= _6_ × 25 × 4
= _150_ × 4

ii) 700 = ____ × 100
= ____ × 25 × 4
= ____ × 4

iii) 3 000 = ____ × 100
= ____ × 25 × 4
= ____ × 4

b) Is any number that ends in two zeros divisible by 4? ________

If two numbers are divisible by 4, so is their sum. If one number is divisible by 4 and the other is not, their sum is not divisible by 4.

2. Split each number into a number ending in two zeros and another number.
Decide if the number is divisible by 4. Divide the 2-digit number in your notebook.

a) 3 464 = 3 400 + _64_
Divisible by 4? _Yes_

b) 782 = 700 + ____
Divisible by 4? ____

c) 560 = 500 + ____
Divisible by 4? ____

d) 32 546 = 32 500 + ____
Divisible by 4? ____

e) 667 = 600 + ____
Divisible by 4? ____

f) 1 984 = 1 900 + ____
Divisible by 4? ____

g) 74 326 = 74 300 + ____
Divisible by 4? ____

h) 43 206 609 841 322 = 43 206 609 841 300 + ____
Divisible by 4? ____

3. Explain why a number is divisible by 4 if its last 2 digits form a number that is divisible by 4.

4. a) 1 000 is divisible by 8. Is any number that ends in 3 zeros divisible by 8? Explain.

b) Explain why a number is divisible by 8 if its last 3 digits form a number that is divisible by 8.

5. Split each number into a number ending in three zeros and another number.
Decide if the number is divisible by 8.

a) 34 364 = 34 000 + _364_
Divisible by 8? _No_

b) 54 688 = 54 000 + ____
Divisible by 8? ____

c) 32 408 = 32 000 + ____
Divisible by 8? ____

d) 41 546 = 41 000 + ____
Divisible by 8? ____

e) 58 767 = 58 000 + ____
Divisible by 8? ____

f) 21 936 = 21 000 + ____
Divisible by 8? ____

6. We know that 200 = 8 × 25 is a multiple of 8. Write each number as the sum of a multiple of 200 and a smaller number. Then decide if the number is a multiple of 8.

a) 732 = 600 + _132_ Divisible by 8? _No_

b) 432 = 400 + _32_ Divisible by 8? _Yes_

c) 236 = 200 + ____ Divisible by 8? ____

d) 746 = ____ + ____ Divisible by 8? ____

e) 976 = ____ + ____ Divisible by 8? ____

f) 672 = ____ + ____ Divisible by 8? ____

Problems and Puzzles

1. a) Find the factors of the numbers from 1 to 20.

   b) Which numbers have exactly two factors?

   What are those numbers called? (see p.58)

   c) Find the next number after 20 that has exactly two factors.

   d) Which numbers have an odd number of factors?

   e) Extend the sequence of numbers you found in part d) by using the gaps between the numbers.

   (+3) ◯ ◯ ◯ ◯

   1, 4, ___, ___, ___, ___

   f) Do you recognize the numbers from part e)? What are they called?

   g) Find the first number greater than 100 that has an odd number of factors. How did you find it?

Number	Factors
1	*1*
2	*1, 2*
3	*1, 3*
4	*1, 2, 4*
5	
6	
7	
8	
9	
10	
11	
12	
13	
14	
15	
16	
17	
18	
19	
20	

2. 32 ☐74 is divisible by 3. What are some possible values for the missing digit?

3. Circle the numbers which will divide evenly into 6 213 400.

   2 3 4 5 6 8 9 10

4. a) Is 3 a common factor of 144 and 240? How do you know?

   b) Is 3 a common factor of 134 742 and 1 234 698? How do you know?

5. a) A number between 113 and 130 has 3 and 5 as factors. What is the number?

   b) A number between 264 713 and 264 732 has 3 and 5 as factors. What is the number?

6. a) Is 532 divisible by 2? How do you know?

   b) Is 532 divisible by 5? How do you know?

   c) Rearrange the digits in 532 to make a number that is divisible by 5.

   d) Is 532 divisible by 10? How do you know?

   e) Can you rearrange the digits in 532 to make a number that is divisible by 10? Explain.

7. Write 9 as both the square of a number and the square root of another number.

8. a) For which of these statements is 10 a counter-example?

      i) Every even number is a perfect square.
      ii) Every odd number is prime.
      iii) Every prime number is odd.
      iv) Every multiple of 5 has ones digit 5.
      v) Every even number has ones digit 0.

   b) All the statements above are false. Find a counter-example (not 10!) for each statement.

9. Rearrange the digits of 30 780 to make the largest number you can that is divisible by 2 but not 5.

10. a) Write 27 as a sum of 5 different digits. Then make a 5-digit number divisible by 9.
    b) Make a 6-digit number divisible by 5 and 6.

11. Dale has guitar lessons every third day. Bill has guitar lessons every fourth day. They both have guitar lessons today. In how many days will they next have guitar lessons on the same day?

12. Jacob makes $12 an hour delivering newspapers. He made enough money to buy some books that cost $30 each. If he did not have any money left over, what is the smallest number of books he could have bought?

13. Tegan wants to make a quilt blanket for her baby brother's doll. She will place small square pieces side by side in rows and columns to make her quilt. She wants her quilt to be 144 mm by 252 mm. What is the largest sized square she can use?

14. Decide whether each statement is true or false by looking for a pattern or a counter-example.

    a) Any number that is divisible by 2 and 5 is also divisible by $2 \times 5 = 10$.
    b) Any number that is divisible by 4 and 6 is also divisible by $4 \times 6 = 24$.

NS7-18 Fractions

Fractions name equal parts of a whole.

This pie is cut into 4 equal parts, and 3 of the parts are shaded.

So $\frac{3}{4}$ of the pie is shaded.

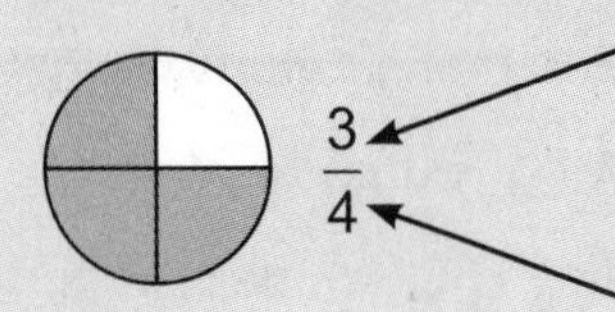

The **numerator** tells you how many parts are counted.

The **denominator** tells you how many equal parts are in a whole.

1. How much of each shape is shaded? Write the fraction.

a) 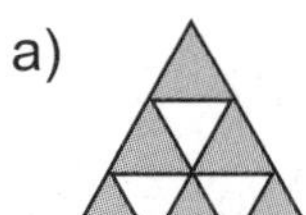

b) 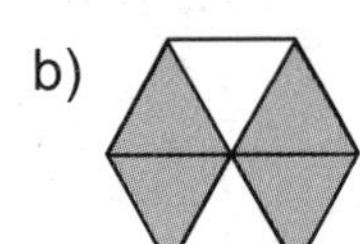

c) 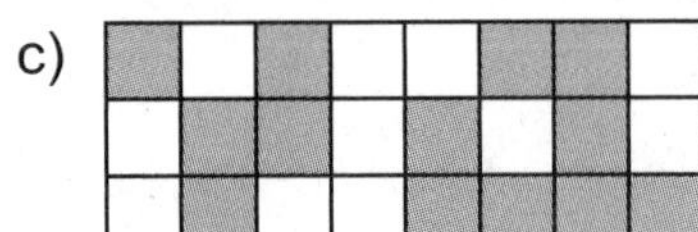

2. Draw lines to divide each figure into equal parts. Then write what fraction of each figure is shaded.

a) 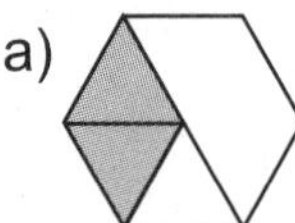

b) 

c) 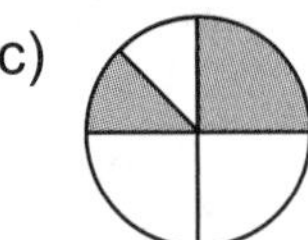

d) 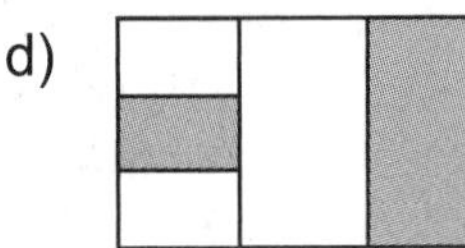

3. Use a ruler to divide each box into...

a) 3 equal parts. 

b) 10 equal parts. 

4. This figure represents $\frac{3}{7}$ of a whole. Use a ruler to turn it into a whole. Then fill in the blanks.

$\frac{3}{7}$ is _______ out of _______ parts. _______ more parts make a whole.

5. Divide each line into the given parts.

a) Thirds

b) Halves

c) Quarters

6. You have $\frac{5}{8}$ of a pie.

a) What does the bottom (denominator) of the fraction tell you?

b) What does the top (numerator) of the fraction tell you?

7. Rectangle A has 5 out of 6 parts shaded.
Rectangle B has 3 out of 4 parts shaded.

A 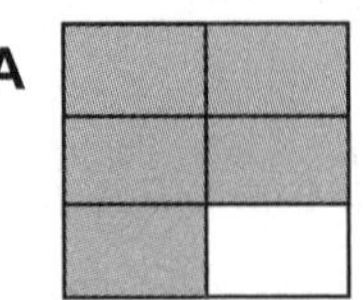

B 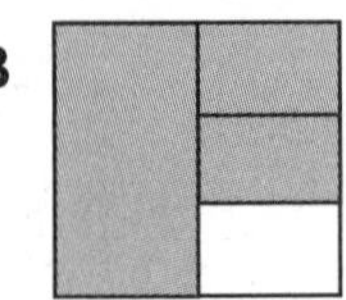

a) Do rectangles A and B have the same amount shaded?

b) What fraction is shaded in each rectangle, $\frac{5}{6}$ or $\frac{3}{4}$? How do you know?

Fractions can name parts of a set. In this set, $\frac{3}{5}$ of the figures are pentagons, $\frac{1}{5}$ are squares, and $\frac{1}{5}$ are circles.

8. Fill in the blanks for this set.

a) $\frac{4}{10}$ of the figures are ______________.

b) ______ of the figures are circles.

c) ______ of the figures are squares.

d) $\frac{1}{10}$ of the figures are ______________.

e) ______ of the figures are shaded.

f) ______ of the figures are unshaded.

9. A hockey team wins 6 games, loses 4 games, and ties 1 game. What fraction of the games did the team…

a) win? ______ b) lose? ______ c) tie? ______

10. A box contains 2 blue marbles, 3 red marbles, and 4 yellow marbles.

What fraction of the marbles are blue? ______

What fraction of the marbles are **not** blue? ______

11. There are 23 students in a class. Each student chose to do a science project on either animals or plants. The chart shows the number of students who chose each topic.

a) Fill in the missing numbers in the chart.

b) What fraction of the children chose to study…

animals? ☐ plants? ☐

c) What fraction of the girls chose to study…

animals? ☐ plants? ☐

	Animals	**Plants**
Boys	7	4
Girls		
Students	12	

12. Draw a picture to solve this puzzle: There are 5 shapes (circles and squares).

$\frac{3}{5}$ of the figures are squares. $\frac{3}{5}$ of the figures are shaded. One square is **not** shaded.

NS7-19 Mixed Numbers

Mattias and his friends ate the amount of pie shown.

They ate three and three quarter pies altogether (or $3\frac{3}{4}$ pies).

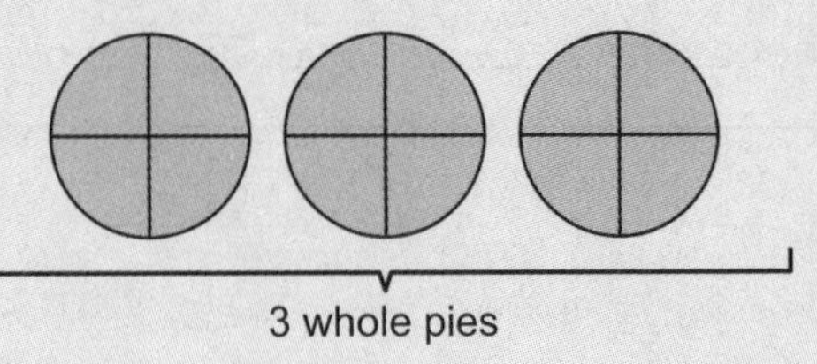

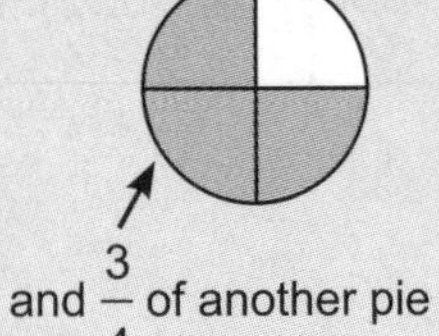

$3\frac{3}{4}$ is called a **mixed number** because it is a mixture of a whole number and a fraction.

1. Find the mixed number for each picture.

a) 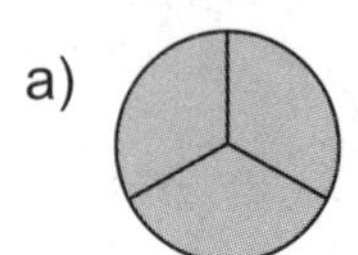 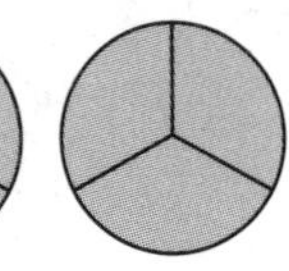 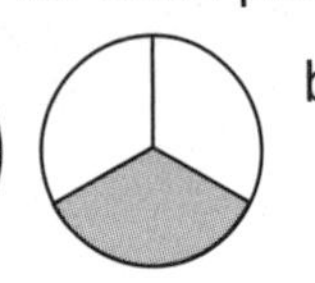 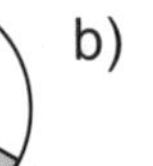

_2_ whole pies and $\frac{1}{3}$ of another pie = $2\frac{1}{3}$ pies

b) 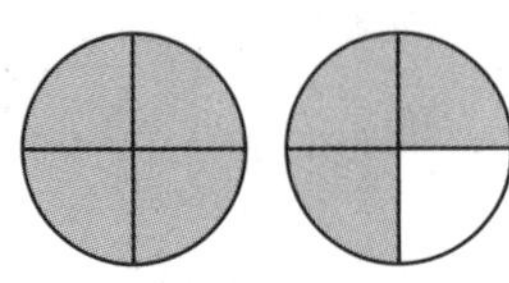

_____ whole pies and _____ of another pie = _____ pies

c) 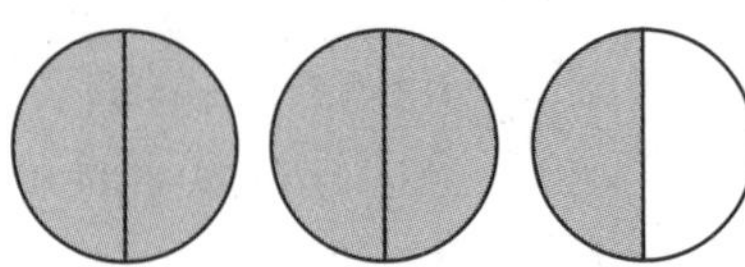

_____ whole pies and _____ of another pie = _____ pies

2. Write the fraction of the shapes that is shaded as a mixed number.

a) 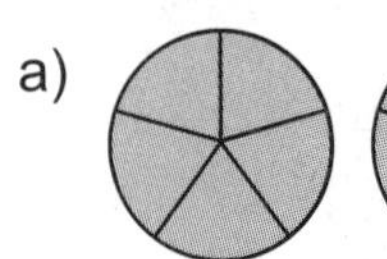 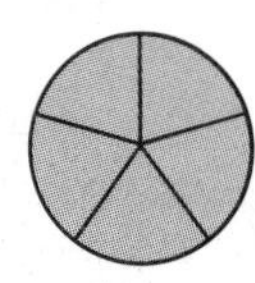 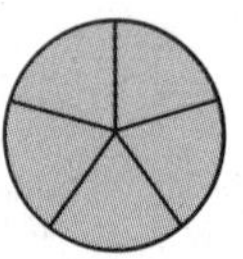 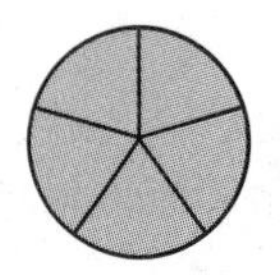 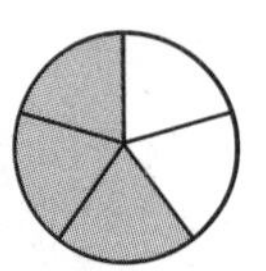

b) 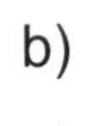 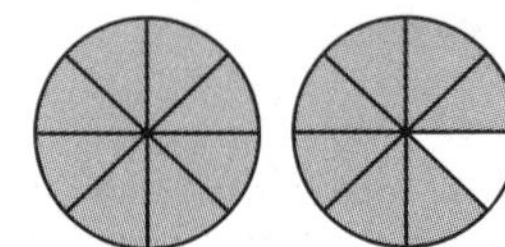

c) 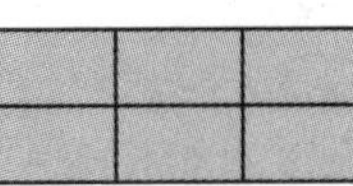 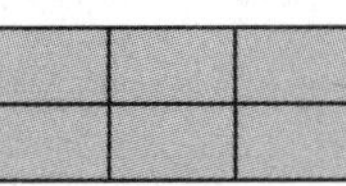 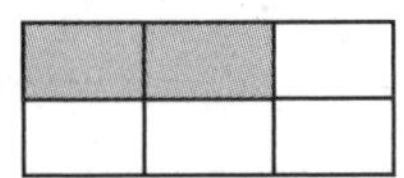

d) 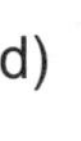 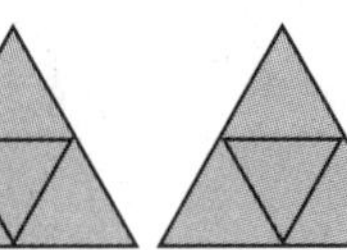 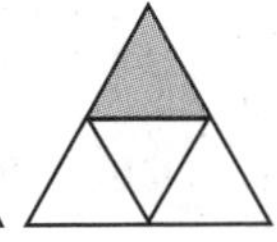

3. Shade the area given by the mixed number. Note: There may be more figures than you need.

a) $2\frac{2}{3}$  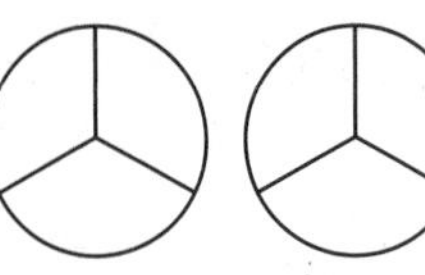

b) $3\frac{1}{4}$ 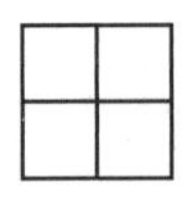 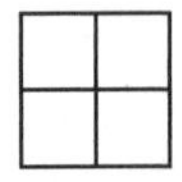

c) $1\frac{5}{6}$ 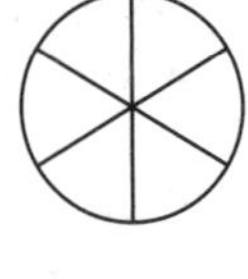

d) $2\frac{4}{5}$ 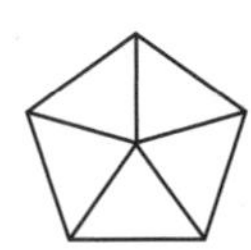  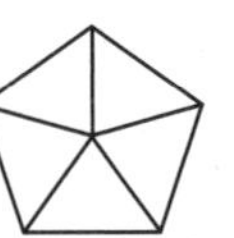 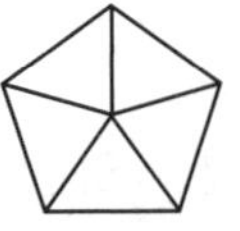

4. Sketch.

a) $3\frac{3}{4}$ pies b) $2\frac{1}{3}$ pies c) $1\frac{3}{5}$ pies d) $2\frac{5}{6}$ pies e) $3\frac{7}{8}$ pies

5. Which fraction represents more pie: $3\frac{2}{3}$, $4\frac{1}{4}$, or $4\frac{3}{4}$? How do you know?

6. Is $5\frac{3}{4}$ closer to 5 or 6?

NS7-20 Improper Fractions

Huan-Yue and her friends ate 9 quarter-sized pieces of pizza.

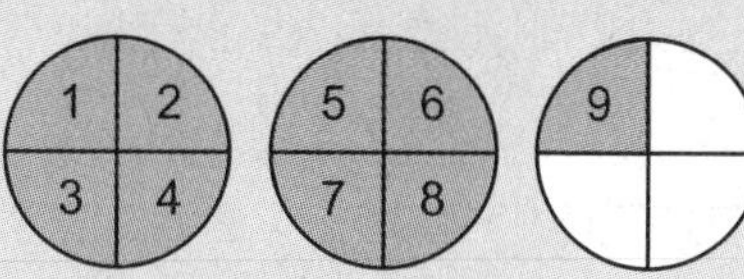

$\frac{9}{4} = 2\frac{1}{4}$

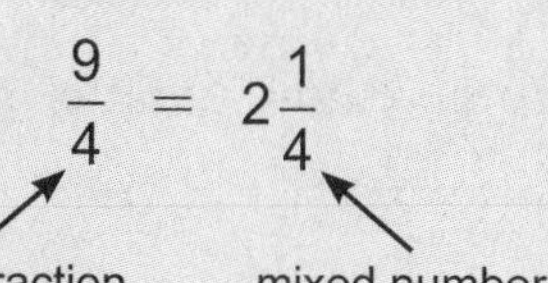

Altogether, they ate $\frac{9}{4}$ pizzas.

When the numerator of a fraction is larger than the denominator, the fraction represents **more than a whole**. Such fractions are called **improper fractions**.

1. Write these fractions as improper fractions.

a) 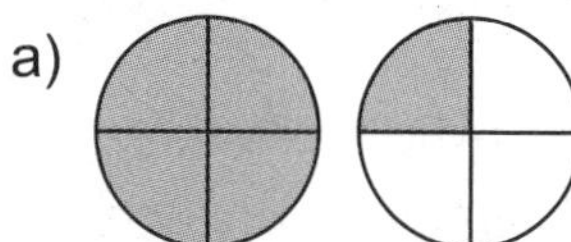

b) 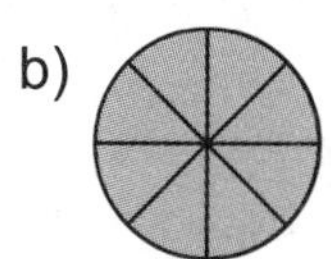 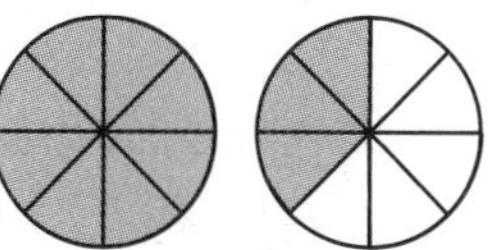

c) 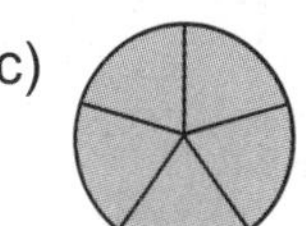 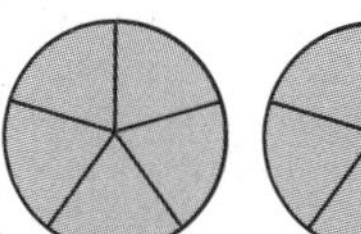

d) 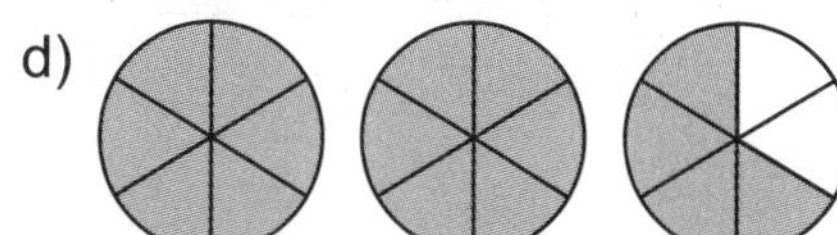

e) 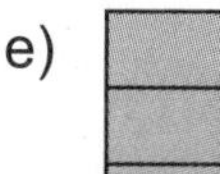 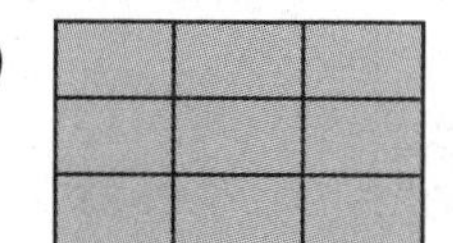 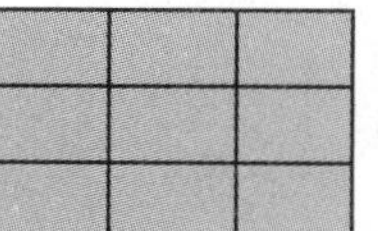 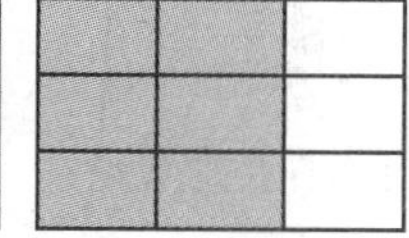

f) 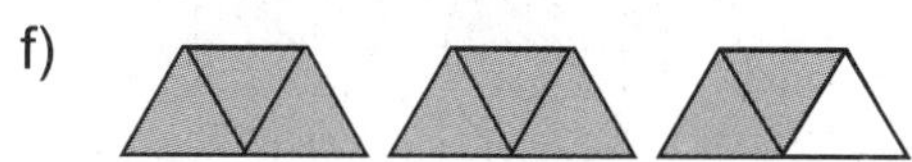

g) 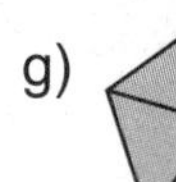 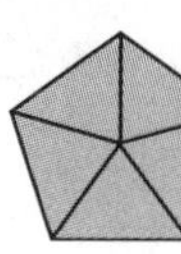 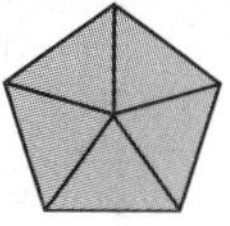 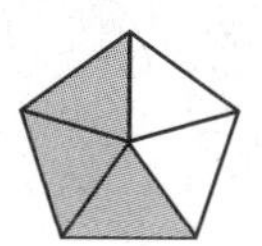

2. Shade one piece at a time until you have shaded the amount of pie given by the improper fraction.

a) $\frac{7}{2}$ 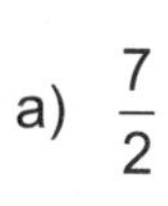 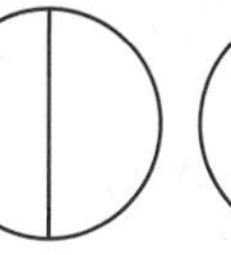 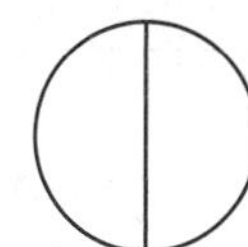 

b) $\frac{9}{4}$ 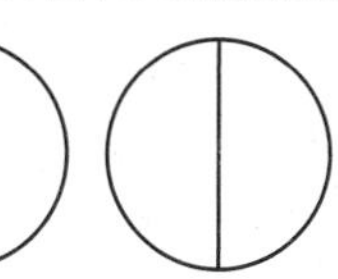 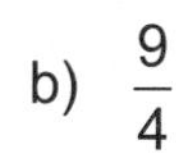 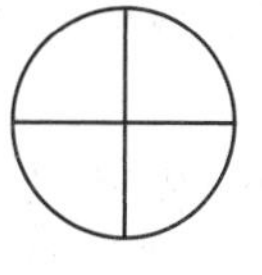 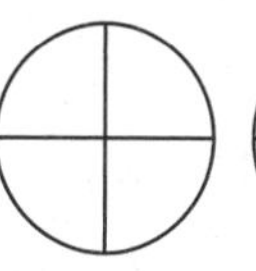 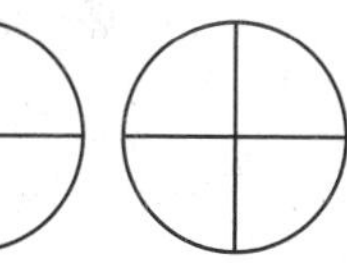

c) $\frac{8}{3}$  

d) $\frac{15}{5}$   

3. Sketch.

a) $\frac{13}{4}$ pies b) $\frac{7}{3}$ pies c) $\frac{9}{2}$ pies d) $\frac{11}{6}$ pies e) $\frac{17}{8}$ pies

4. Which fraction represents more pie: $\frac{7}{4}$, $\frac{9}{4}$, or $\frac{9}{3}$? How do you know?

5. Which fractions are improper fractions? How do you know?

a) $\frac{5}{7}$ b) $\frac{9}{8}$ c) $\frac{13}{11}$

NS7-21 Mixed Numbers and Improper Fractions

1. Write these fractions as mixed numbers and as improper fractions.

a) 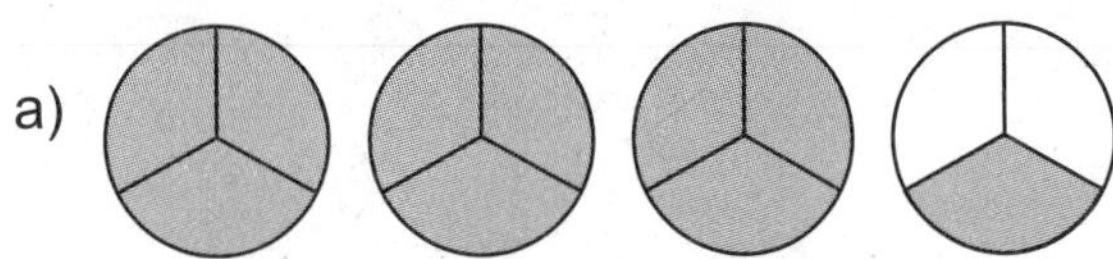

b) 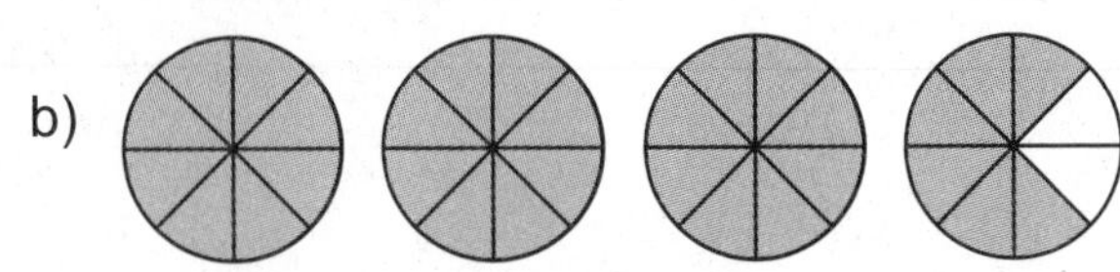

c) 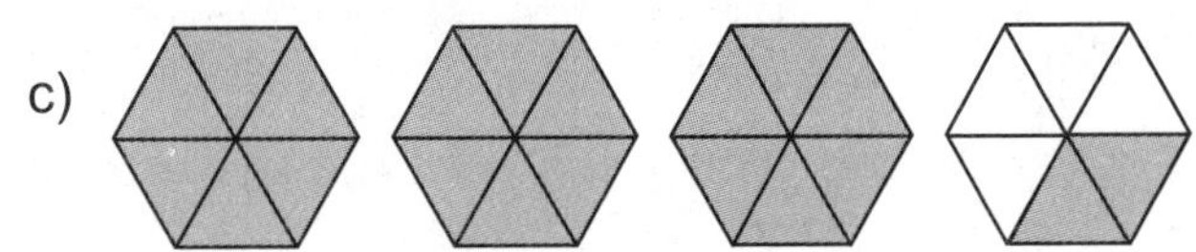

d) 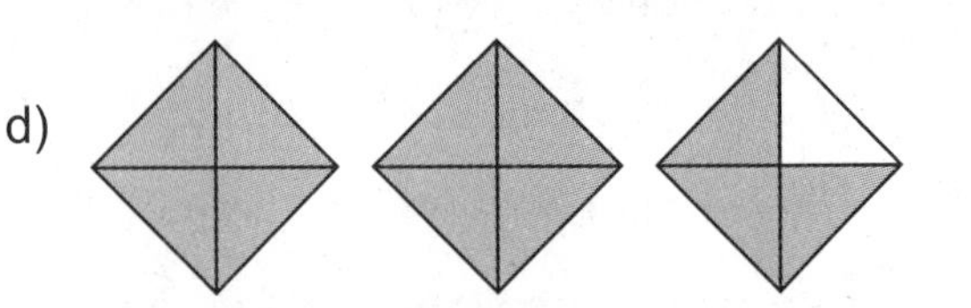

e) 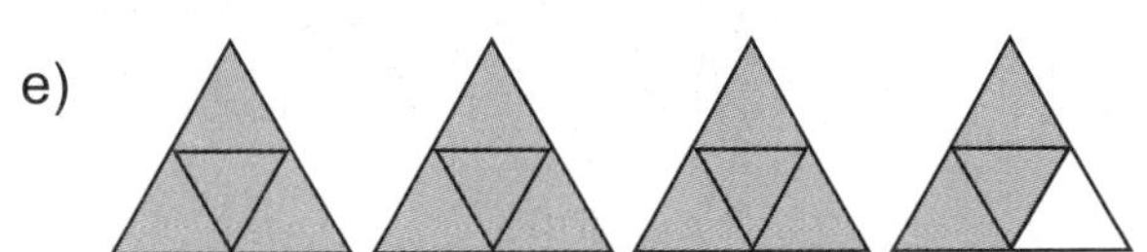

f) 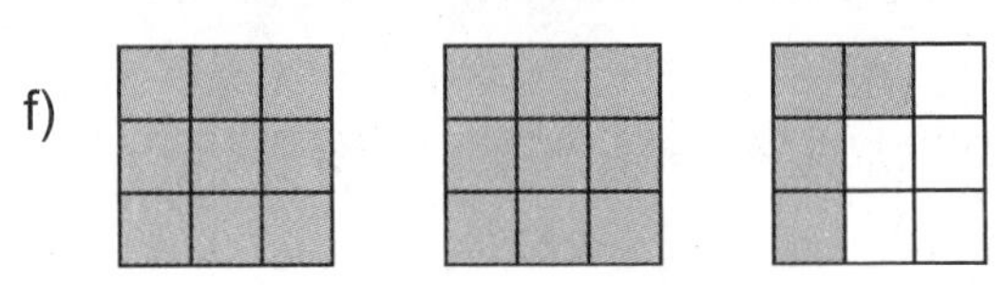

2. Shade the amount of pie given by the mixed number. Then write an improper fraction for the amount.

a) $3\frac{1}{2}$ 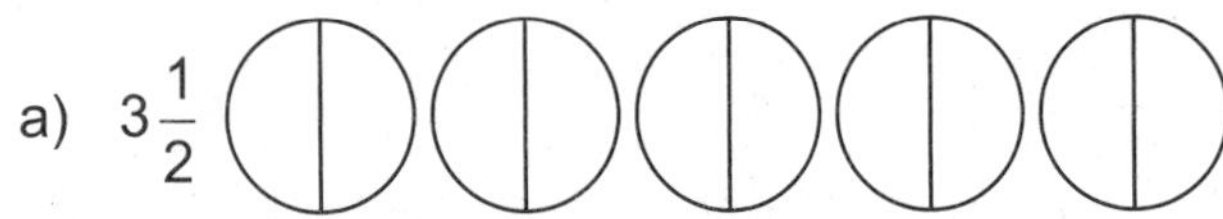

Improper fraction: ______________

b) $4\frac{3}{4}$ 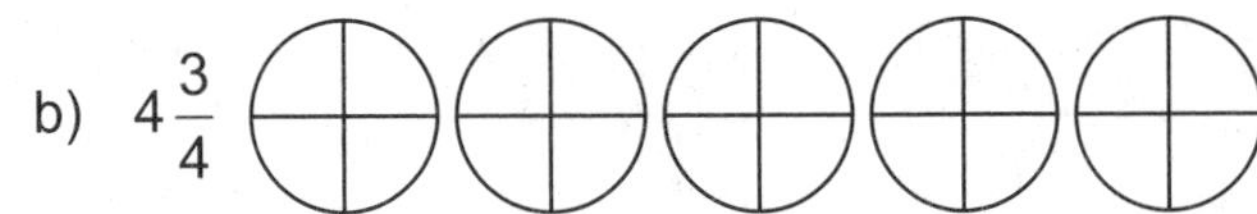

Improper fraction: ______________

3. Shade the area given by the improper fraction. Then write a mixed number for the amount of area shaded.

a) $\frac{7}{3}$ 

Mixed number: ______________

b) $\frac{17}{6}$ 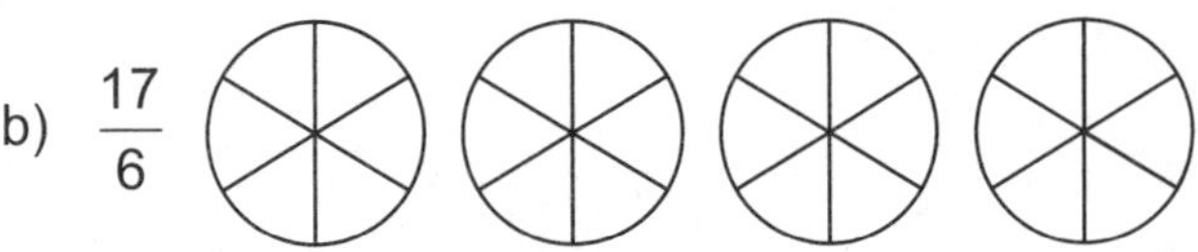

Mixed number: ______________

c) $\frac{13}{5}$ 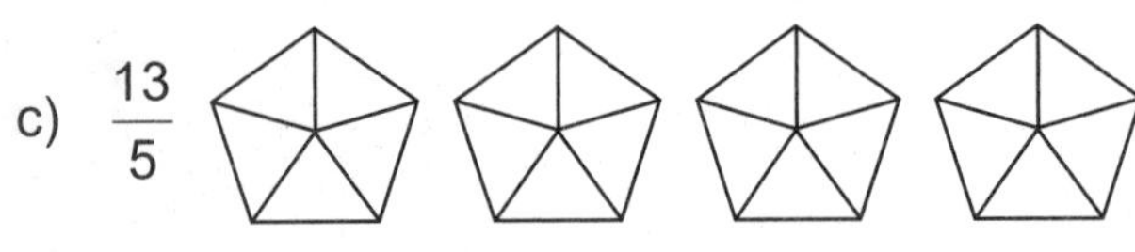

Mixed number: ______________

d) $\frac{21}{8}$ 

Mixed number: ______________

4. Draw a picture to find out which fraction is greater.

a) $3\frac{1}{2}$ or $\frac{5}{3}$ b) $1\frac{4}{5}$ or $\frac{11}{5}$ c) $\frac{15}{8}$ or $\frac{7}{3}$ d) $\frac{13}{4}$ or $2\frac{2}{3}$

5. How could you use division to find out how many **whole** pies are in $\frac{13}{5}$ of a pie? Explain.

How many quarter pieces are in $2\frac{3}{4}$ pies?

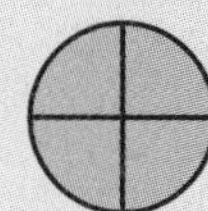

There are 4 quarter pieces in 1 pie.

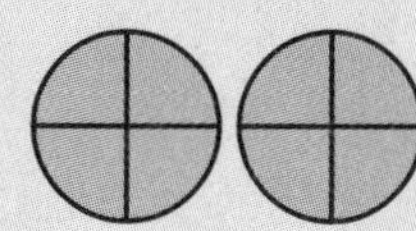

There are 8 (2 × 4) quarters in 2 pies.

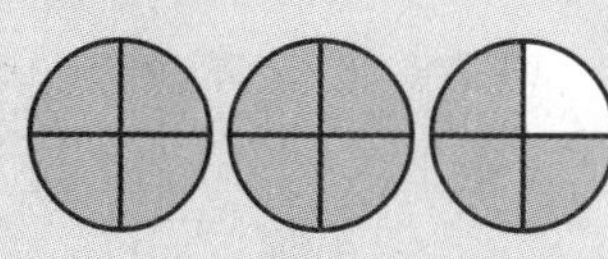

8 pieces (2 × 4) + 3 extra pieces = 11

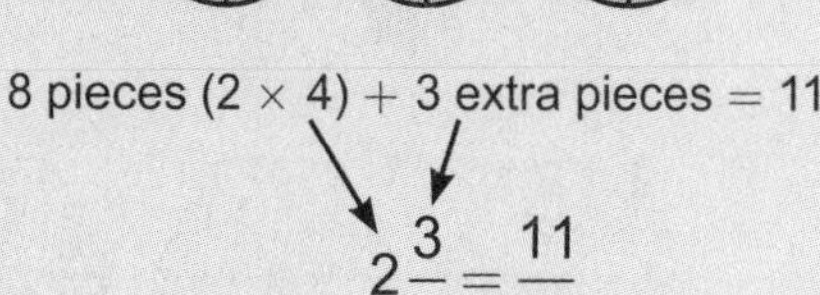

$2\frac{3}{4} = \frac{11}{4}$

So there are 11 quarter pieces altogether.

6. Find the number of **halves** in each amount.

a) 1 pie = ______ halves   b) 2 pies = ______ halves   c) 4 pies = ______ halves

d) $3\frac{1}{2}$ pies = ______ halves   e) $4\frac{1}{2}$ pies = ______ halves   f) $5\frac{1}{2}$ pies = ____________

7. Each pie has 3 pieces, so each piece is a third. Find the number of **thirds** in each amount.

a) 1 pie = ___3___ thirds   b) 2 pies = ______ thirds   c) 4 pies = ______ thirds

d) $1\frac{1}{3}$ pies = ______ thirds   e) $2\frac{2}{3}$ pies = ____________   f) $5\frac{2}{3}$ pies = ____________

8. A box holds 4 cans, so each can is a fourth. Find the number of **cans** each amount holds.

a) 2 boxes hold ______ cans.   b) $2\frac{1}{4}$ boxes hold ______ cans.   c) $3\frac{3}{4}$ boxes hold ______ cans.

9. If a bag holds 12 peas, then…

a) $1\frac{1}{12}$ bags hold ______ peas.   b) $2\frac{7}{12}$ bags hold ______ peas.   c) $3\frac{11}{12}$ bags hold ______ peas.

10. Write the mixed numbers as improper fractions.

a) $2\frac{1}{3} = \frac{}{3}$ b) $5\frac{1}{2} = \frac{}{2}$ c) $4\frac{2}{5} = \frac{}{5}$ d) $7\frac{1}{4} =$ e) $6\frac{3}{7} =$

11. Envelopes come in packs of 6. Alice used $2\frac{5}{6}$ packs. How many envelopes did she use? ______

12. Maia and her friends ate $4\frac{3}{4}$ pizzas. How many quarter-sized pieces did they eat? ______

13. **BONUS** ▶ How many quarters are there in $4\frac{1}{2}$ dollars? ______

14. **BONUS** ▶ Cindy needs $3\frac{2}{3}$ cups of flour.

a) How many scoops of cup A would she need? ______

b) How many scoops of cup B would she need? ______

A: $\frac{1}{3}$ cups

B: $\frac{1}{6}$ cups

How many whole pies are there in $\frac{13}{4}$ pies?

There are 13 pieces altogether, and each pie has 4 pieces.

So you can find the number of whole pies by dividing 13 by 4: **13 ÷ 4 = 3 remainder 1**

There are 3 whole pies and 1 quarter left over: 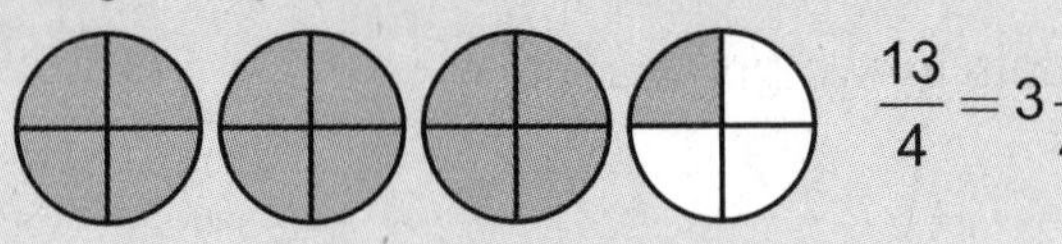 $\frac{13}{4} = 3\frac{1}{4}$

15. Find the number of whole pies in each amount by dividing.

a) $\frac{4}{2}$ pies = _____ whole pies b) $\frac{15}{3}$ pies = _____ whole pies c) $\frac{8}{4}$ pies = _____ whole pies

d) $\frac{21}{7}$ pies = _____ whole pies e) $\frac{20}{5}$ pies = _____ whole pies f) $\frac{24}{6}$ pies = _____ whole pies

16. Find the number of whole pies and the number of pieces remaining by dividing.

a) $\frac{5}{2}$ pies = ___*2*___ whole pies and ___*1*___ half pie = ___$2\frac{1}{2}$___ pies

b) $\frac{9}{2}$ pies = _______ whole pies and _______ half pie = _______ pies

c) $\frac{10}{3}$ pies = _______ whole pies and _______ third = _______ pies

d) $\frac{13}{4}$ pies = _______ whole pies and _______ fourth = _______ pies

17. Divide the numerator by the denominator to write each improper fraction as a mixed number.

a) $\frac{13}{3}$ 13 ÷ 3 = ___*4*___ R ___*1*___ So $\frac{13}{3} = 4\frac{1}{3}$

b) $\frac{13}{6}$ 13 ÷ 6 = ____ R ____ So $\frac{13}{6}$ = ________

c) $\frac{15}{4}$ 15 ÷ 4 = ____ R ____ So $\frac{15}{4}$ = ________

d) $\frac{3}{2}$ = ________ e) $\frac{8}{3}$ = ________ f) $\frac{22}{5}$ = ________

g) $\frac{29}{7}$ = ________ h) $\frac{57}{8}$ = ________ i) $\frac{68}{9}$ = ________

18. Write a mixed number and improper fraction for the total number of litres.

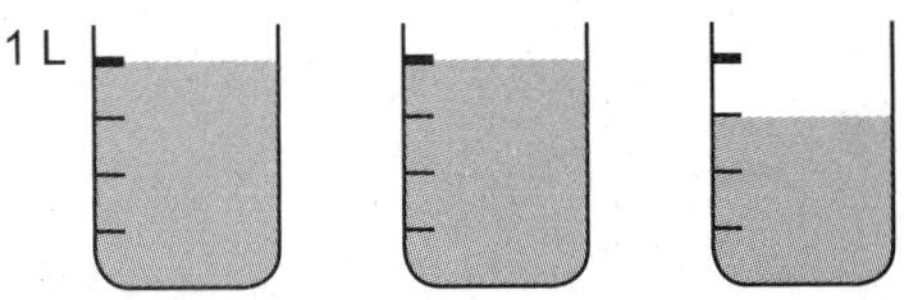

19. Write a mixed number and improper fraction for the length of the rope.

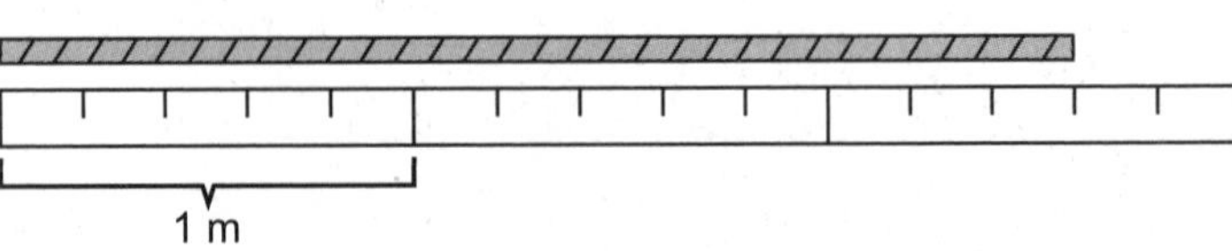

NS7-22 Fractions of Whole Numbers

There are 3 equal groups of dots, so each group is $\frac{1}{3}$ of 6.

There are 2 dots in each group, so $\frac{1}{3}$ of 6 is 2.

There are 4 dots in two groups, so $\frac{2}{3}$ of 6 is 4.

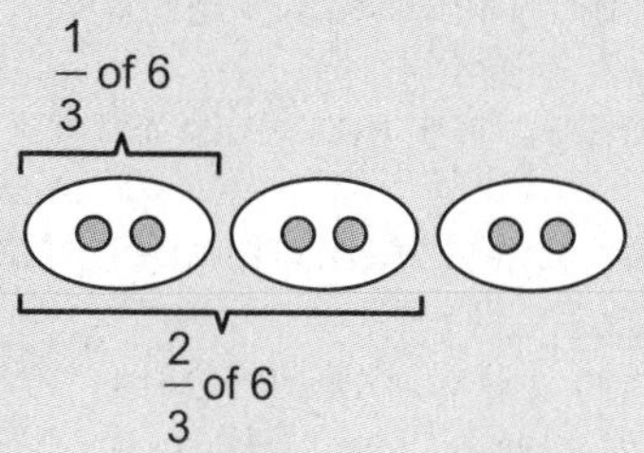

1. Write a fraction for the amount of dots shown.

a) 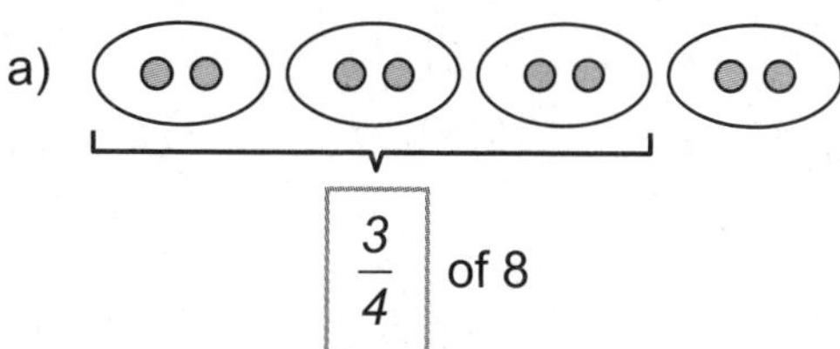

$\frac{3}{4}$ of 8

b) 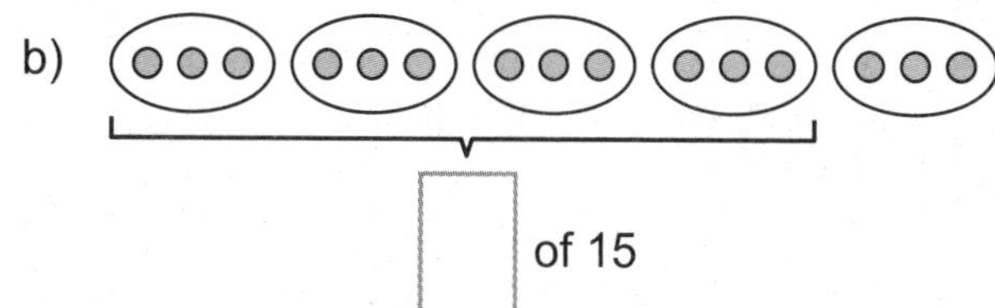

☐ of 15

2. Fill in the missing numbers.

a) $\frac{1}{3}$ of 6 =

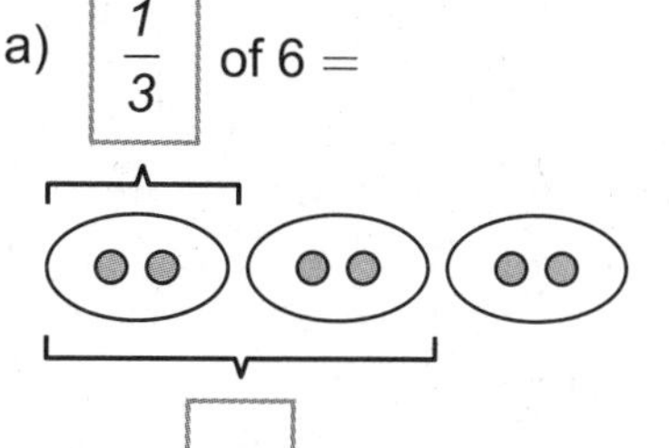

☐ of ____ = ____

b) ☐ of 8 = ______

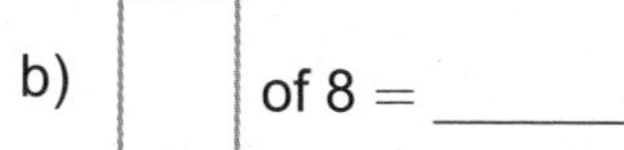

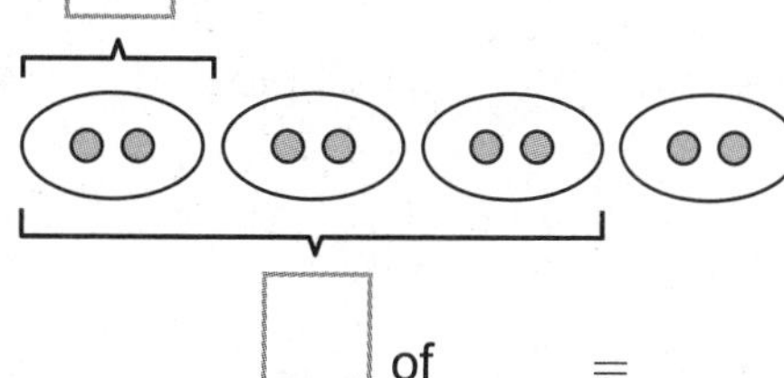

☐ of ____ = ____

c) ☐ of 9 = ______

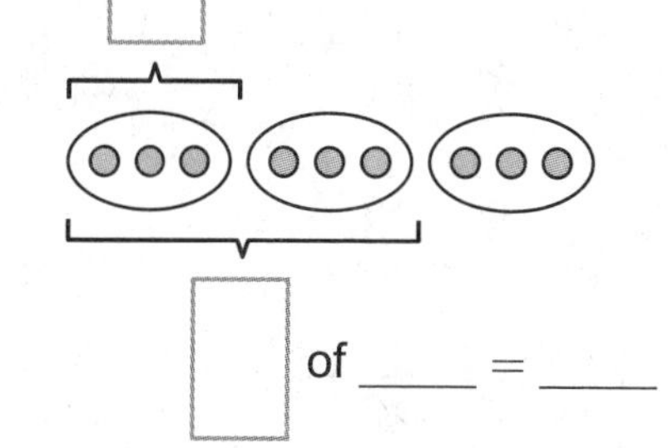

☐ of ____ = ____

d) 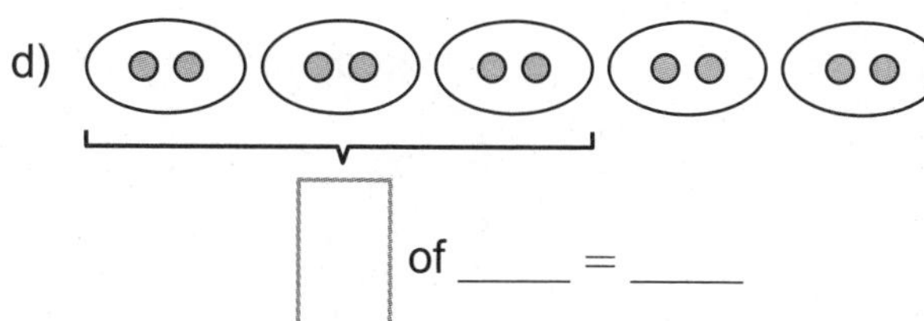

☐ of ____ = ____

e) 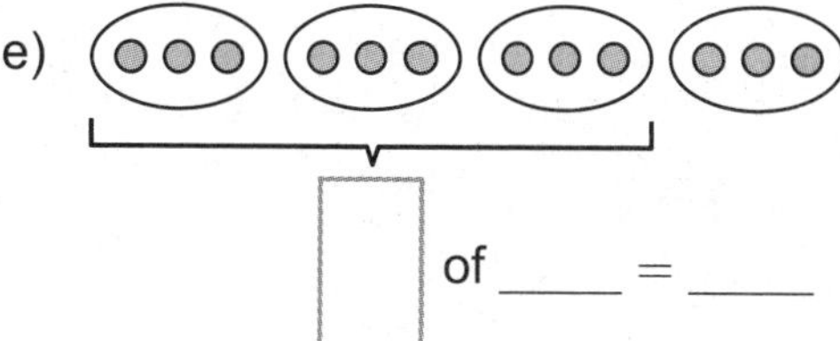

☐ of ____ = ____

3. Draw a circle to show the given amount.

a) $\frac{2}{3}$ of 6

b) $\frac{3}{4}$ of 8

4. Draw the correct number of dots in each circle, then draw a larger circle to show the given amount.

a) $\frac{2}{3}$ of 12

b) $\frac{1}{3}$ of 15

5. Find the fraction of the whole amount by drawing the correct number of circles and then filling in the correct number of dots in each circle.

a) $\frac{2}{3}$ of 9 is ______________. b) $\frac{3}{5}$ of 10 is ______________.

6. This is how Andy finds $\frac{2}{3}$ of 12.

Step 1: He finds $\frac{1}{3}$ of 12 by dividing 12 by 3. 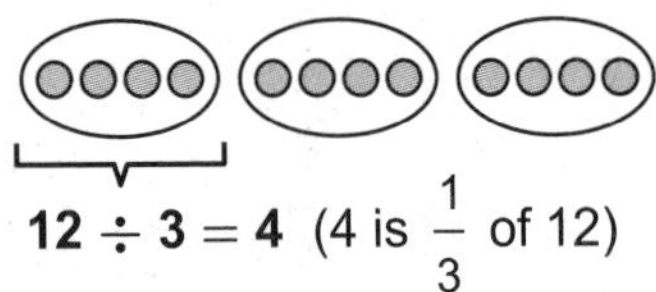 **12 ÷ 3 = 4** (4 is $\frac{1}{3}$ of 12)	**Step 3:** Then he multiplies the result by 2. 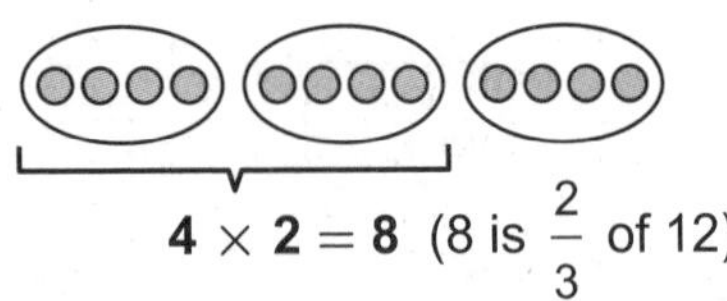 **4 × 2 = 8** (8 is $\frac{2}{3}$ of 12)

Find the following amounts using Andy's method.

a) $\frac{1}{3}$ of 9 = ____ So $\frac{2}{3}$ of 9 = ____

b) $\frac{1}{4}$ of 8 = ____ So $\frac{3}{4}$ of 8 = ____

c) $\frac{1}{3}$ of 15 = ____ So $\frac{2}{3}$ of 15 = ____

d) $\frac{1}{5}$ of 25 = ____ So $\frac{3}{5}$ of 25 = ____

e) $\frac{1}{3}$ of 27 = ____ So $\frac{2}{3}$ of 27 = ____

7. 20 students are on a bus. $\frac{3}{5}$ are boys. How many boys are on the bus? ______________

8. A store had 15 watermelons. They sold $\frac{2}{3}$ of the watermelons. How many watermelons were sold? ______________ How many were left? ______________

9. Shade $\frac{1}{4}$ of the squares. Draw stripes in $\frac{1}{6}$ of the squares. How many squares are blank? ______________

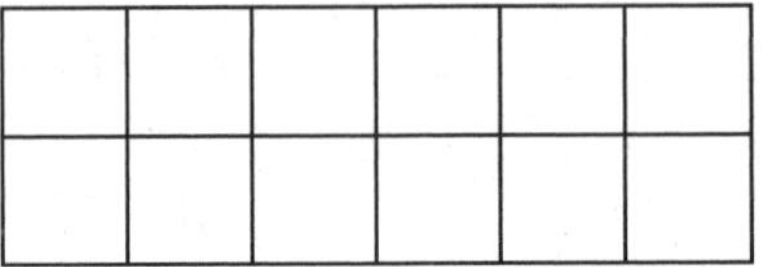

10. Ed has 20 sea shells. $\frac{2}{5}$ are turret shells. $\frac{1}{4}$ are scallops. The rest are conchs. How many shells are conchs?

11. Alan started studying at 8:15. He studied history for $\frac{1}{3}$ of an hour and math for $\frac{2}{5}$ of an hour. At what time did he stop studying?

12. Which is longer, 21 months or $1\frac{5}{6}$ of a year?

BONUS▶ There were 108 grapes. Sara ate $\frac{1}{2}$ of them, Jeff ate $\frac{1}{3}$ of them, and Ron ate $\frac{1}{6}$ of them. How many were left over?

NS7-23 Comparing Fractions — Introduction

1. Shade the given amount in each pie. Then circle the greater fraction in each pair.

a) $\frac{5}{8}$ $\frac{7}{8}$

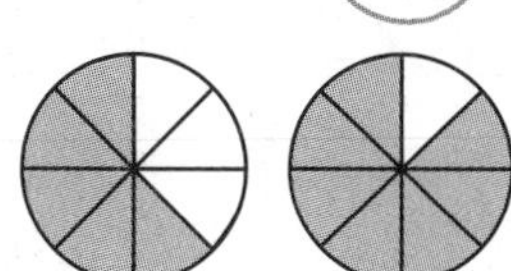

b) $\frac{6}{9}$ $\frac{4}{9}$

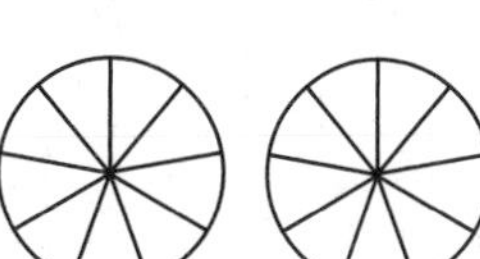

c) $\frac{8}{10}$ $\frac{7}{10}$

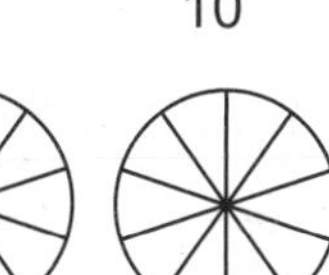

2. Two fractions have the same denominators (bottoms) but different numerators (tops). How can you tell which fraction is greater?

____

____

3. Shade the given amount in each pie. Then circle the greater fraction in each pair.

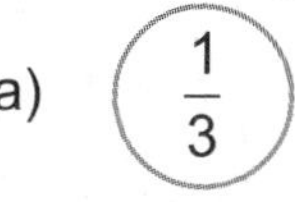

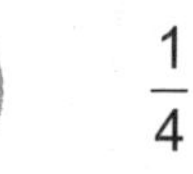

a) $\frac{1}{3}$ $\frac{1}{4}$

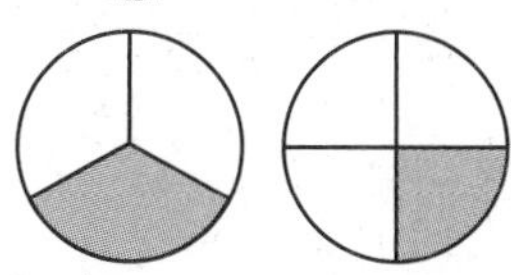

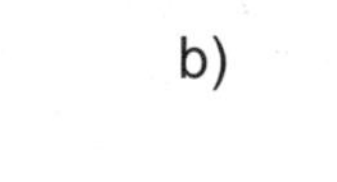

b) $\frac{1}{10}$ $\frac{1}{2}$

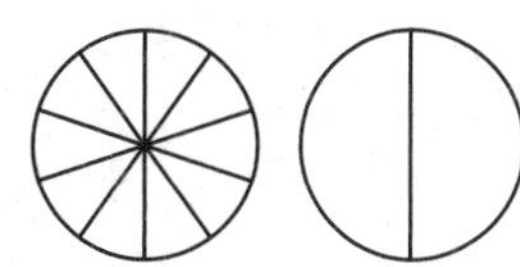

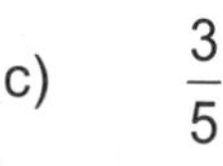

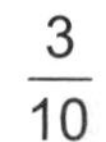

c) $\frac{3}{5}$ $\frac{3}{10}$

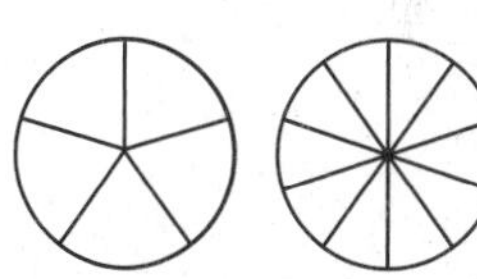

4. Two fractions have the same numerators (tops) but different denominators (bottoms). How can you tell which fraction is greater?

____

____

5. Write the fractions in order from least to greatest.

a) $\frac{1}{9}$ $\frac{1}{4}$ $\frac{1}{17}$ ____ ____ ____

b) $\frac{2}{11}$ $\frac{2}{5}$ $\frac{2}{7}$ $\frac{2}{16}$ ____ ____ ____ ____

c) $\frac{4}{5}$ $\frac{1}{5}$ $\frac{3}{5}$ ____ ____ ____

d) $\frac{9}{10}$ $\frac{2}{10}$ $\frac{1}{10}$ $\frac{5}{10}$ ____ ____ ____ ____

e) $\frac{5}{8}$ $\frac{7}{8}$ $\frac{5}{9}$ ____ ____ ____

f) $\frac{3}{7}$ $\frac{2}{7}$ $\frac{3}{5}$ ____ ____ ____

BONUS▸ $\frac{15}{19}$ $\frac{9}{23}$ $\frac{11}{21}$ $\frac{11}{19}$ $\frac{6}{23}$ $\frac{9}{22}$ $\frac{15}{17}$ $\frac{9}{21}$

6. Which fraction is greater? How do you know?

a) $\frac{7}{5}$ or $\frac{9}{5}$

b) $4\frac{1}{4}$ or $4\frac{3}{4}$

7. a) How much more do you need to shade to make a whole?

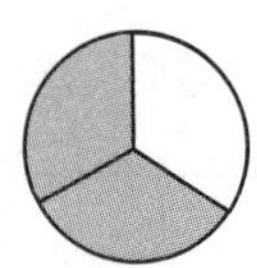 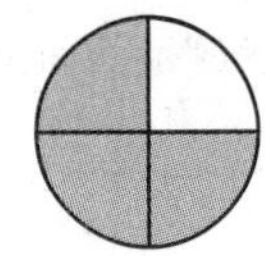 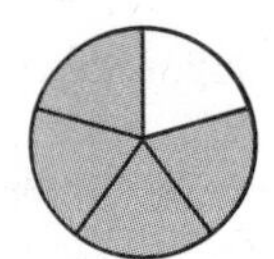 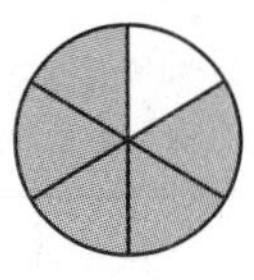

$\frac{2}{3} + \_\_\_\_\_ = 1$ $\frac{3}{4} + \_\_\_\_\_ = 1$ $\frac{4}{5} + \_\_\_\_\_ = 1$ $\frac{5}{6} + \_\_\_\_\_ = 1$

b) Which fraction is greater, $\frac{5}{6}$ or $\frac{6}{7}$? How do you know?

____

____

8. How much more do you need to make one whole?

$\frac{11}{13}$ [$\frac{2}{13}$] $\frac{14}{15}$ [ ] $\frac{7}{9}$ [ ] $\frac{19}{20}$ [ ] $\frac{5}{7}$ [ ] $\frac{12}{13}$ [ ]

9. a) Complete the chart.

Improper Fraction				$\frac{11}{5}$		$\frac{13}{3}$
Mixed Number	$6\frac{1}{2}$	$2\frac{3}{4}$	$3\frac{1}{4}$		$1\frac{5}{6}$	

b) Order the improper fractions from least to greatest. ____ ____ ____ ____ ____ ____

c) Order the mixed numbers from least to greatest. ____ ____ ____ ____ ____ ____

d) Explain why the lists in b) and c) should agree. If they do not, find your mistake.

10. Place these numbers on the number line. $\frac{1}{3}$ $\frac{4}{3}$ $2\frac{1}{3}$ $3\frac{1}{3}$ $\frac{13}{3}$

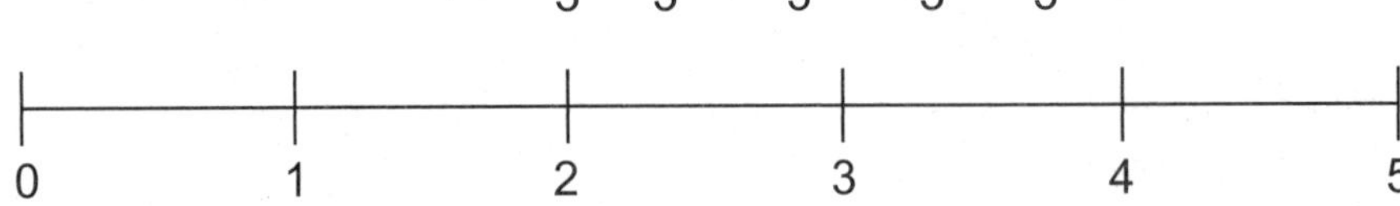

11. Is $2\frac{3}{4}$ closer to 2 or to 3? How do you know? ______________________

12. Place these numbers on the number line. $2\frac{3}{4}$ $\frac{11}{5}$ $\frac{6}{7}$ $\frac{9}{2}$ $\frac{11}{3}$ $\frac{9}{3}$

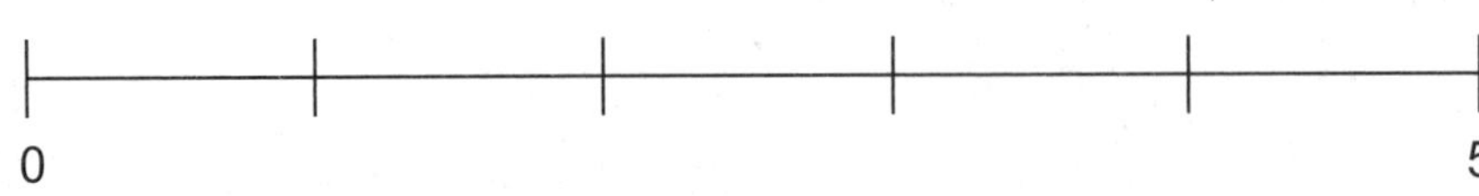

BONUS▶ Write the fractions from Question 8 from greatest to least. Explain how you compared the fractions.

NS7-24 Equivalent Fractions

1. Compare the fractions by shading to see which is more. Write > (more than), < (less than), or = (equal).

a) 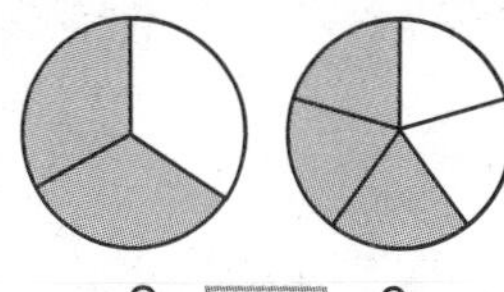 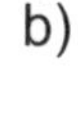

$\frac{2}{3}$ [>] $\frac{3}{5}$

b) 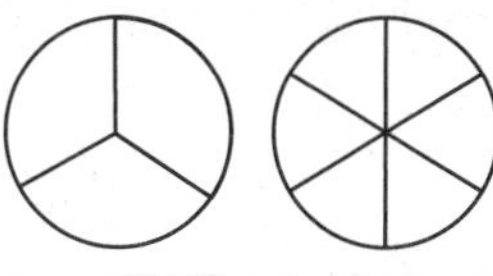 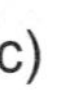

$\frac{2}{3}$ [ ] $\frac{4}{6}$

c) 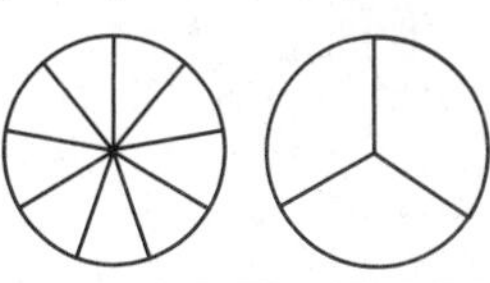

$\frac{5}{9}$ [ ] $\frac{2}{3}$

d) 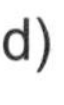 

$\frac{15}{20}$ [ ] $\frac{3}{4}$

e) 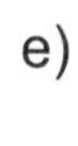 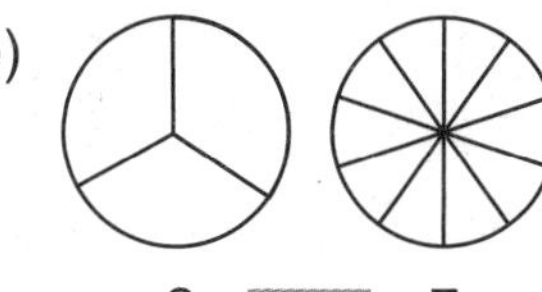

$\frac{2}{3}$ [ ] $\frac{7}{10}$

f)  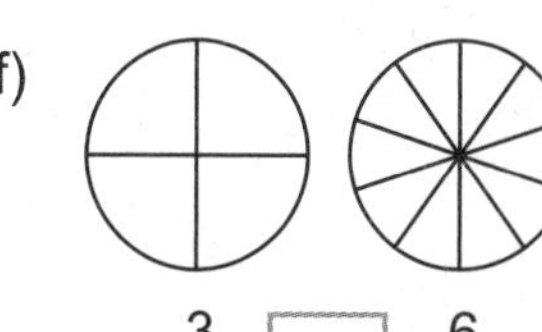

$\frac{3}{4}$ [ ] $\frac{6}{10}$

> Two fractions are said to be equivalent if they represent the same amount.

2. List two pairs of equivalent fractions from Question 1. _____ = _____ and _____ = _____

3. Group the squares into larger blocks to make an equivalent fraction.

a)  $\frac{6}{10} = \frac{3}{5}$

b) 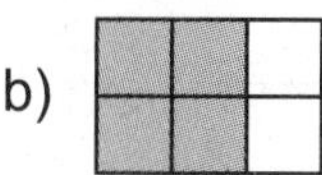 $\frac{4}{6} = \frac{\quad}{3}$

c)  $\frac{10}{12} = \frac{\quad}{6}$

4. Write three equivalent fractions for the amount shaded here.

________ ________ ________

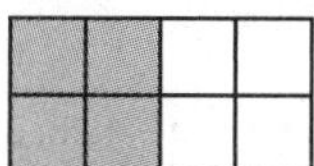

5. a) Draw lines to cut the pies into…

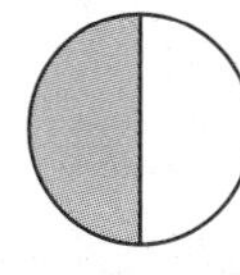
4 equal pieces

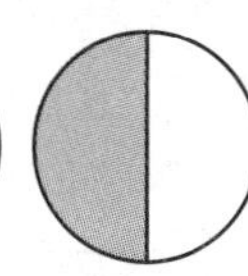
6 equal pieces

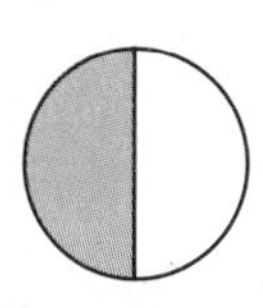
8 equal pieces

b) Fill in the numerators of the equivalent fractions.

$\frac{1}{2} = \frac{\quad}{4} = \frac{\quad}{6} = \frac{\quad}{8}$

6. Make an equivalent fraction by cutting each shaded piece into the same number of equal parts. Then cut the remaining pieces into that number of equal parts.

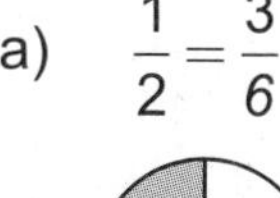

a) $\frac{1}{2} = \frac{3}{6}$

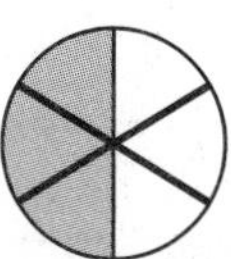

b) $\frac{2}{3} = \frac{4}{\quad}$

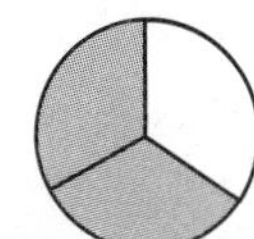

c) $\frac{2}{3} = \frac{6}{\quad}$

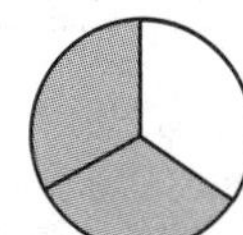

d) $\frac{2}{5} = \frac{8}{\quad}$

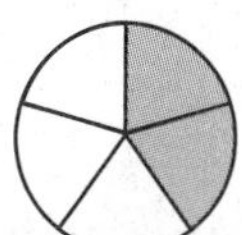

NS7-25 Comparing Fractions Using Equivalent Fractions

When you multiply the numerator and denominator of a fraction by the same number, you create an **equivalent fraction**.

$$\frac{1}{2} = \frac{1 \times 5}{2 \times 5} = \frac{5}{10}$$

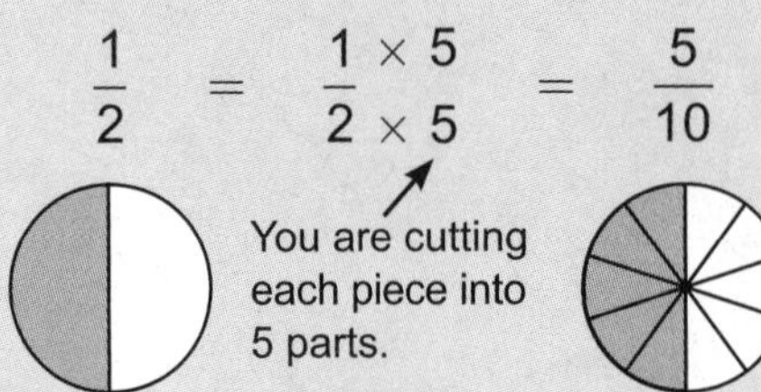
You are cutting each piece into 5 parts.

1. Make an equivalent fraction by multiplying the numerator and denominator by the same number.

a) $\frac{3}{5} = \frac{9}{}$ b) $\frac{2}{5} = \frac{}{20}$ c) $\frac{3}{10} = \frac{}{30}$ d) $\frac{5}{6} = \frac{20}{}$

e) $\frac{2}{3} = \frac{12}{}$ f) $\frac{2}{5} = \frac{20}{}$ g) $\frac{2}{3} = \frac{}{12}$ h) $\frac{3}{3} = \frac{12}{}$

2. Write six equivalent fractions for each by skip counting to find the numerators.

a) $\frac{2}{3} = \frac{}{6} = \frac{}{9} = \frac{}{12} = \frac{}{15} = \frac{}{18} = \frac{}{21}$

b) $\frac{3}{5} = \frac{}{10} = \frac{}{15} = \frac{}{20} = \frac{}{25} = \frac{}{30} = \frac{}{35}$

3. Which of the fractions in Question 2 is greater, $\frac{2}{3}$ or $\frac{3}{5}$? Find the answer two ways, as follows.

a) Select two fractions with the same denominators from the lists in Question 2. _______ and _______

Which of the two fractions is greater, $\frac{2}{3}$ or $\frac{3}{5}$? _______

How do you know? ____

b) Select two fractions with the same numerators from the lists in Question 2. _______ and _______

Which of the two fractions is greater, $\frac{2}{3}$ or $\frac{3}{5}$? _______

How do you know? ____

c) Did you get the same answer both ways? _______

4. a) Find four equivalent fractions for $\frac{4}{7}$. $\frac{4}{7} = \frac{}{14} = \frac{}{21} = \frac{}{28} = \frac{}{35}$

b) Write $\frac{2}{3}$, $\frac{3}{5}$, and $\frac{4}{7}$ in order from smallest to largest.

____ ____ ____

5. List equivalent fractions for each pair in order until you find two with the same denominator. Then compare the fractions.

a) $\frac{3}{4} = \frac{6}{8} = \frac{9}{12} = \frac{12}{16} = \frac{15}{20} = \frac{20}{24} = \frac{25}{28}$

$\frac{5}{7} = \frac{10}{14} = \frac{15}{21} = \frac{20}{28}$

$\frac{3}{4}$ [>] $\frac{5}{7}$

b) $\frac{2}{5}$

$\frac{1}{3}$

$\frac{2}{5}$ [ ] $\frac{1}{3}$

c) $\frac{5}{6}$

$\frac{7}{9}$

$\frac{5}{6}$ [ ] $\frac{7}{9}$

d) $\frac{5}{8}$ and $\frac{3}{4}$ e) $\frac{5}{8}$ and $\frac{7}{12}$ f) $\frac{3}{5}$ and $\frac{5}{9}$ g) $\frac{7}{12}$ and $\frac{8}{15}$

6. a) Write several fractions equivalent to $\frac{1}{2}$.

$\frac{1}{2} = \frac{\quad}{4} = \frac{\quad}{6} = \frac{\quad}{8} = \frac{\quad}{10} = \frac{\quad}{12} = \frac{\quad}{14} = \frac{\quad}{16} = \frac{\quad}{18} = \frac{\quad}{20}$

b) How much more than a half is each fraction below?

$\frac{3}{4}$ is _____ more than $\frac{1}{2}$. $\frac{4}{6}$ is _____ more than $\frac{1}{2}$. $\frac{5}{8}$ is _____ more than $\frac{1}{2}$.

c) Write the fractions from part b) in order from smallest to largest.

Does this agree with your answer from Question 5d) ? _______

BONUS▸ Which is bigger, $\frac{187}{372}$ or $\frac{214}{426}$? Explain your choice.

7. Create an equivalent fraction with denominator 24 by multiplying the numerator and denominator by the same number.

a) $\frac{1 \times 12}{2 \times 12} = \frac{12}{24}$ b) $\frac{3}{8} = \frac{\quad}{24}$ c) $\frac{5}{6} = \frac{\quad}{24}$ d) $\frac{3}{4} = \frac{\quad}{24}$

e) $\frac{2}{3} = \frac{\quad}{24}$ f) $\frac{7}{8} = \frac{\quad}{24}$ g) $\frac{1}{6} = \frac{\quad}{24}$ h) $\frac{5}{12} = \frac{\quad}{24}$

8. Write the fractions from Question 7 in order from smallest to largest.

NS7-26 Problems and Puzzles

1. The chart shows the number of walls in a house painted a particular colour.

   a) What fraction of the walls is painted green?

   b) What colour was used to paint one fifth of the walls?

   c) What colour was used to paint one half of the walls?

Colour	Number of Walls
White	10
Yellow	5
Blue	4
Green	1

2. Subdivide the line into ten equal parts using a ruler and then mark the fractions.

   $\frac{3}{10}$ $\frac{7}{10}$ $\frac{9}{10}$ $\frac{1}{2}$ $\frac{2}{5}$

3. $\frac{5}{6}$ of a pizza is covered in olives:

   $\frac{1}{3}$ of the pizza is covered in mushrooms:

   Each piece has at least one topping. Complete the picture.

   How many pieces are covered in olives **and** mushrooms? ________

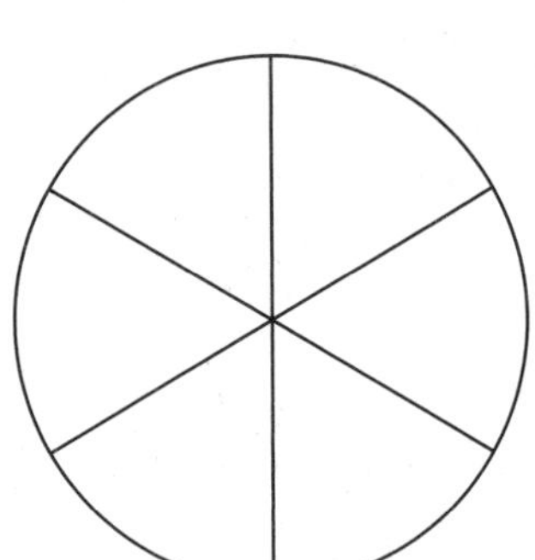
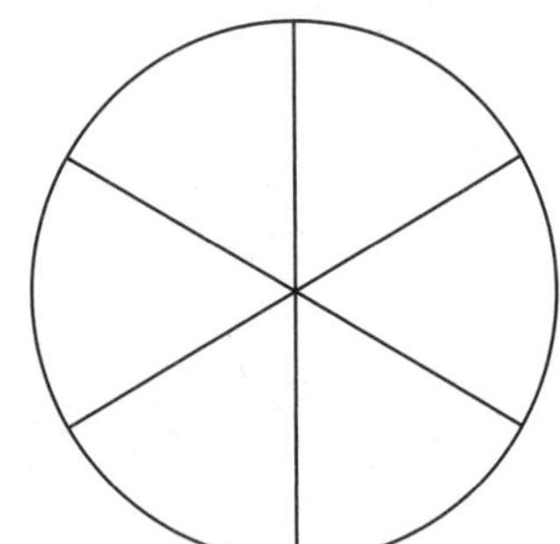

4. Equivalent fractions are said to be in the same **family**.
   Write two fractions in the same family as the fraction in each triangle.

a) 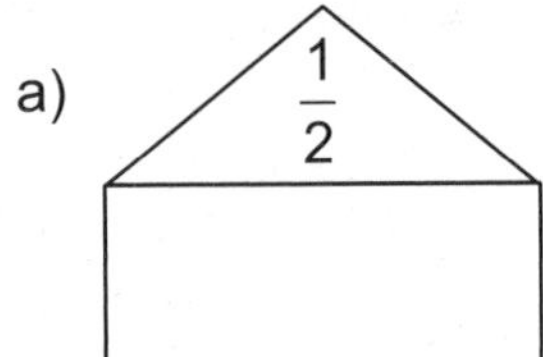

b) 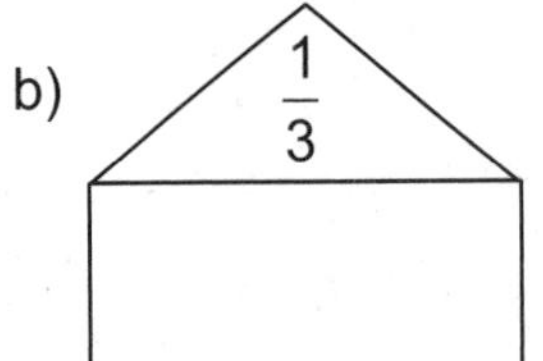

c) 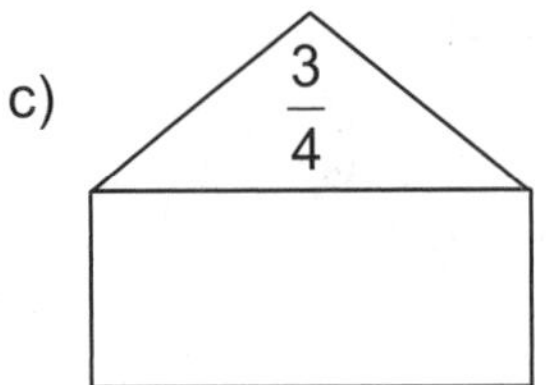

d) 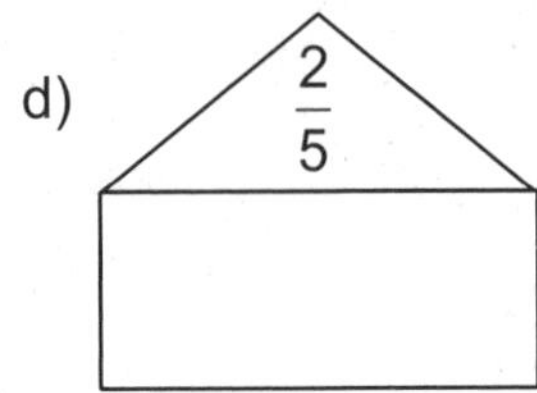

5. In each question, circle the **pair** of fractions that are in the same family.

   a) $\frac{1}{2}$ $\frac{4}{6}$ $\frac{5}{10}$ b) $\frac{3}{15}$ $\frac{16}{20}$ $\frac{4}{5}$ c) $\frac{2}{3}$ $\frac{4}{6}$ $\frac{1}{4}$

6. Find two fractions from the fraction family of $\frac{4}{12}$ with numerators smaller than 4. ________________

7. Find five fractions from the fraction family of $\frac{12}{24}$ with numerators smaller than 12. ________________

NS7-27 Adding and Subtracting Fractions

1. Imagine moving the shaded pieces from pies A and B into pie plate C.
Show how much of pie C would be filled, then write a fraction for pie C.

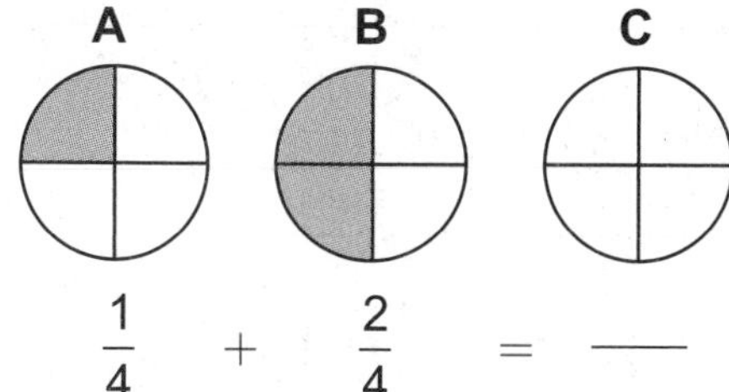

$\frac{1}{4} + \frac{2}{4} = \frac{}{}$

2. Imagine pouring the liquid from cups A and B into cup C.
Shade the amount of liquid that would be in C. Then complete the addition statements.

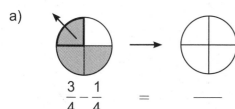

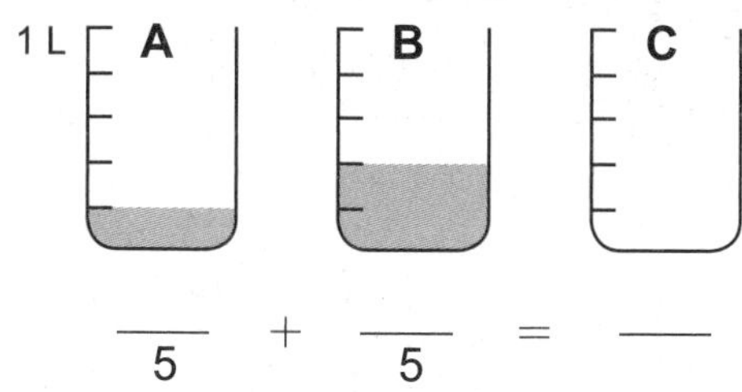

$\frac{}{5} + \frac{}{5} = \frac{}{}$

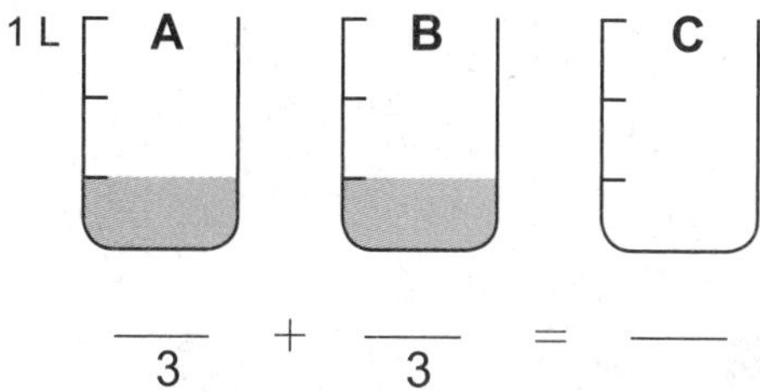

$\frac{}{3} + \frac{}{3} = \frac{}{}$

3. Add.

a) $\frac{3}{5} + \frac{1}{5} =$ b) $\frac{2}{4} + \frac{1}{4} =$ c) $\frac{3}{7} + \frac{2}{7} =$ d) $\frac{5}{8} + \frac{2}{8} =$

e) $\frac{3}{11} + \frac{7}{11} =$ f) $\frac{5}{17} + \frac{9}{17} =$ g) $\frac{11}{24} + \frac{10}{24} =$ h) $\frac{18}{57} + \frac{13}{57} =$

4. Show how much pie would be left if you took away the amount shown. Then complete the fraction statement.

a)

$\frac{3}{4} - \frac{1}{4} = \frac{}{}$

b)

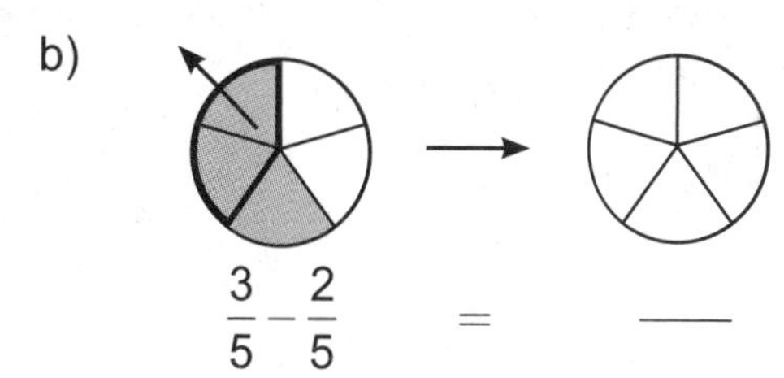

$\frac{3}{5} - \frac{2}{5} = \frac{}{}$

5. Subtract.

a) $\frac{2}{3} - \frac{1}{3} =$ b) $\frac{3}{5} - \frac{1}{5} =$ c) $\frac{6}{7} - \frac{3}{7} =$ d) $\frac{5}{8} - \frac{2}{8} =$

e) $\frac{9}{12} - \frac{2}{12} =$ f) $\frac{6}{19} - \frac{4}{19} =$ g) $\frac{9}{28} - \frac{3}{28} =$ h) $\frac{17}{57} - \frac{12}{57} =$

6. Calculate.

a) $\frac{2}{7} + \frac{1}{7} + \frac{3}{7} =$ b) $\frac{4}{11} + \frac{5}{11} - \frac{2}{11} =$ c) $\frac{10}{18} - \frac{7}{18} + \frac{5}{18} =$

To add fractions that have a common denominator, we can add the numerators.

Example: $\frac{3}{10} + \frac{4}{10} = \frac{7}{10}$

INVESTIGATION 1 ▶ To add fractions that have a common numerator, can we add the denominators?

Look at $\frac{5}{8} + \frac{5}{14}$. Could this equal $\frac{5}{8+14}$?

A. Which is larger, $\frac{5}{8} + \frac{5}{14}$ or $\frac{5}{8}$? How do you know? ______________________

____

B. Which is larger, $\frac{5}{8+14}$ or $\frac{5}{8}$? How do you know? ______________________

____

C. Does $\frac{5}{8} + \frac{5}{14} = \frac{5}{8+14}$? Explain. ______________________

____

INVESTIGATION 2 ▶ How can we add fractions with different denominators, such as $\frac{1}{3} + \frac{2}{5}$?

A. Make equivalent fractions until you find two with the same denominator, 15.

$\frac{1}{3} = \frac{}{6} = \frac{}{9} = \frac{}{12} = \frac{}{15}$

$\frac{2}{5} = \frac{}{10} = \frac{}{15}$

B. Add the two fractions that have the same denominator.

$\frac{}{15} + \frac{}{15} = \frac{}{15}$

C. What is $\frac{1}{3} + \frac{2}{5}$? How do you know? ______________________

Adding Fractions with Different Denominators

Step 1: Find the lowest common multiple (LCM) of the denominators. $\frac{1}{3} + \frac{2}{5}$

Multiples of 3: 0, 3, 6, 9, 12, **15**, 18

Multiples of 5: 0, 5, 10, **15**, 20, 25, 30 LCM (3, 5) = 15

Step 2: Create equivalent fractions with that denominator.

$$\frac{1}{3} + \frac{2}{5} = \frac{5 \times 1}{5 \times 3} + \frac{2 \times 3}{5 \times 3} = \frac{5}{15} + \frac{6}{15} = \frac{11}{15}$$

The LCM of the denominators is called the **lowest common denominator (LCD)** of the fractions.

7. Find the LCD of each pair of fractions. Then show what numbers you would multiply the numerator and denominator of each fraction by in order to add.

a) $\frac{3 \times 1}{3 \times 2} + \frac{2 \times 2}{3 \times 2}$ LCD = 6

b) $\frac{3}{4} + \frac{1}{8}$ LCD = ______

c) $\frac{1}{20} + \frac{1}{5}$ LCD = ______

d) $\frac{3}{4} + \frac{2}{3}$ LCD = ______

e) $\frac{3}{7} + \frac{1}{3}$ LCD = ______

f) $\frac{1}{4} + \frac{1}{6}$ LCD = ______

g) $\frac{2}{5} + \frac{1}{10}$ LCD = ______

h) $\frac{1}{8} + \frac{1}{7}$ LCD = ______

8. Add or subtract the fractions by changing them to equivalent fractions with denominator equal to the LCD of the fractions.

a) $\frac{2}{5} + \frac{1}{4}$

=

=

b) $\frac{4}{15} + \frac{2}{3}$

c) $\frac{2}{3} - \frac{1}{8}$

d) $\frac{2}{3} - \frac{1}{12}$

e) $\frac{3}{4} + \frac{1}{8}$

f) $\frac{1}{6} + \frac{11}{24}$

g) $\frac{5}{28} - \frac{1}{7}$

h) $\frac{2}{7} + \frac{1}{8}$

i) $\frac{4}{9} - \frac{1}{6}$

9. Add or subtract.

a) $\frac{1}{6} + \frac{5}{12}$

b) $\frac{17}{25} - \frac{3}{5}$

c) $\frac{6}{7} - \frac{1}{4}$

d) $\frac{4}{9} + \frac{2}{5}$

e) $\frac{5}{8} - \frac{7}{12}$

f) $\frac{2}{3} + \frac{1}{4} + \frac{1}{2}$

g) $\frac{3}{15} + \frac{2}{3} + \frac{1}{5}$

h) $\frac{7}{15} + \frac{1}{3} - \frac{3}{5}$

i) $\frac{1}{4} + \frac{17}{20} - \frac{3}{5}$

Lowest Terms

A fraction is reduced to **lowest terms** when the greatest common factor (GCF) of its numerator and denominator is the number 1.

$\frac{6}{8}$ is not in lowest terms because the GCF of 6 and 8 is 2.

Factors of 6: 1, **2**, 3, 6
Factors of 8: 1, **2**, 4, 8

$\frac{3}{4}$ is in lowest terms because the GCF of 3 and 4 is 1.

Factors of 3: **1**, 3
Factors of 4: **1**, 2, 4

1. Find the GCF of the numerator and denominator. Is the fraction in lowest terms? Write yes or no.

a) $\frac{3}{6}$ GCF = *3* *no*

b) $\frac{2}{5}$ GCF = ______ ______

c) $\frac{4}{5}$ GCF = ______ ______

d) $\frac{5}{10}$ GCF = ______ ______

e) $\frac{6}{10}$ GCF = ______ ______

f) $\frac{7}{10}$ g) $\frac{15}{16}$ h) $\frac{12}{10}$ i) $\frac{9}{5}$ j) $\frac{12}{8}$

Reducing a Fraction to Lowest Terms

Step 1: Find the GCF of the numerator and denominator.

Step 2: Divide both the numerator and denominator by the GCF.

2. Reduce the fractions below by dividing the numerator and the denominator by their GCF.

a) $\frac{2 \div 2}{10 \div 2} = \frac{1}{5}$ b) $\frac{2 \div}{6 \div}$ = ______ c) $\frac{2 \div}{8 \div}$ = ______ d) $\frac{2 \div}{12 \div}$ = ______

e) $\frac{6}{9}$ = ______ f) $\frac{3}{15}$ = ______ g) $\frac{4}{12}$ = ______ h) $\frac{20}{25}$ = ______

3. Add or subtract, then reduce your answer to lowest terms.

a) $\frac{5 \times 1}{5 \times 6} + \frac{1 \times 3}{10 \times 3}$

$= \frac{5}{30} + \frac{3}{30}$

$= \frac{8}{30} = \frac{4}{15}$

b) $\frac{13}{15} - \frac{1}{5}$ c) $\frac{5}{6} + \frac{3}{10}$ d) $\frac{25}{28} - \frac{1}{7}$

e) $\frac{1}{10} + \frac{1}{2} + \frac{1}{5}$ f) $\frac{3}{8} + \frac{1}{5} + \frac{1}{20}$ g) $\frac{4}{7} + \frac{2}{5} - \frac{4}{35}$ h) $\frac{5}{7} - \frac{8}{21} + \frac{2}{3}$

NS7-29 Adding and Subtracting Mixed Numbers

After a party, Chang's class has $2\frac{1}{2}$ pizzas left over.

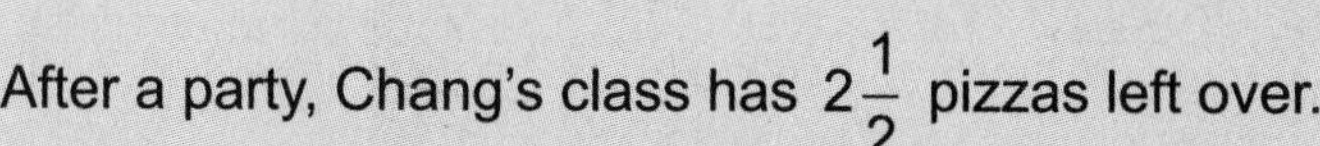

Alicia's class has $3\frac{1}{3}$ pizzas left over.

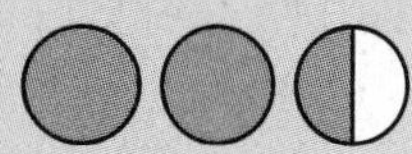

Chang's class

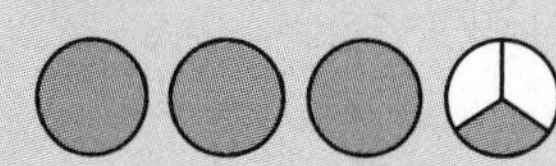

Alicia's class

To find out how much pizza is left over, Chang adds.

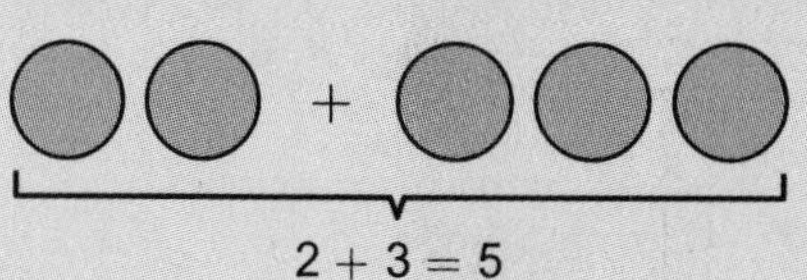

$2 + 3 = 5$

$\frac{1 \times 3}{2 \times 3} + \frac{1 \times 2}{3 \times 2} = \frac{3}{6} + \frac{2}{6} = \mathbf{\frac{5}{6}}$

There are $5\frac{5}{6}$ pizzas left over.

Here is how Chang shows his calculation: $2\frac{1}{2} + 3\frac{1}{3} = 2\frac{1 \times 3}{2 \times 3} + 3\frac{1 \times 2}{3 \times 2} = 2\frac{3}{6} + 3\frac{2}{6} = 5\frac{5}{6}$

1. Add or subtract.

a) $2\frac{1}{5} + 2\frac{2}{5} =$ b) $3\frac{3}{6} + 2\frac{1}{6} =$ c) $5\frac{7}{8} - 3\frac{2}{8} =$ d) $7\frac{9}{15} - 4\frac{4}{15} =$

2. Add or subtract by changing the fractions to equivalent fractions.

a) $2\frac{1 \times 3}{2 \times 3} + 1\frac{1 \times 2}{3 \times 2}$
$= 2\frac{3}{6} + 1\frac{2}{6}$
$= 3\frac{5}{6}$

b) $3\frac{3 \times 3}{4 \times 3} - 1\frac{1 \times 4}{3 \times 4}$
$= 3\frac{9}{12} - 1\frac{4}{12}$
$= 2\frac{5}{12}$

c) $5\frac{2}{3} - 2\frac{3}{5}$

d) $2\frac{2}{7} + 4\frac{1}{2}$

e) $4\frac{2}{5} - 1\frac{1}{6}$

f) $2\frac{3}{8} + 4\frac{1}{3}$

g) $1\frac{1}{4} + 2\frac{3}{7}$

h) $4\frac{1}{5} + 2\frac{4}{7}$

i) $8\frac{4}{5} - 5\frac{5}{9}$

j) $3\frac{2}{3} - 1\frac{1}{2}$

k) $5\frac{3}{4} - 3\frac{2}{3}$

l) $4\frac{4}{5} - 2\frac{3}{4}$

3. If you add $1\frac{1}{2} + 2\frac{2}{3}$ you will find that $1\frac{1}{2} + 2\frac{2}{3} = 3\frac{7}{6}$. How can you simplify this answer?

4. a) Change the improper fractions to mixed numbers.

i) $\frac{7}{6} = 1\frac{1}{6}$ ii) $\frac{11}{5} =$ iii) $\frac{13}{7} =$ iv) $\frac{7}{4} =$

v) $\frac{13}{8} =$ vi) $\frac{13}{10} =$ vii) $\frac{14}{9} =$ viii) $\frac{11}{6} =$

b) Rewrite each mixed number to make the improper fraction a proper fraction. Show the steps.

i) $3\frac{7}{6} = 3 + \frac{7}{6}$

$= 3 + 1\frac{1}{6}$

$= 4\frac{1}{6}$

ii) $2\frac{4}{3} =$ iii) $4\frac{8}{5} =$

iv) $2\frac{5}{4} =$ v) $3\frac{10}{9} =$ vi) $4\frac{12}{7} =$

c) Add by changing the fractions to equivalent fractions. Simplify your answer as in part b).

i) $2\frac{2}{5} + \frac{2}{3}$ ii) $3\frac{2}{3} + \frac{5}{6}$ iii) $4\frac{3}{4} + 2\frac{3}{5}$

iv) $5\frac{1}{6} + 5\frac{7}{8}$ v) $3\frac{5}{8} + 4\frac{1}{2}$ vi) $4\frac{5}{6} + 3\frac{4}{9}$

5. If you know that $\frac{4}{5}$ is greater than $\frac{1}{3}$, how can you subtract $4\frac{1}{3} - 2\frac{4}{5}$? Solve the problems below to find out.

a) Rewrite each mixed number below by regrouping 1 whole as a fraction. Example: $4\frac{1}{3} = 3 + \frac{3}{3} + \frac{1}{3} = 3\frac{4}{3}$

i) $8\frac{1}{4} = 7 + \frac{4}{4} + \frac{1}{4}$

$= 7\frac{5}{4}$

ii) $5\frac{1}{2} = 4 +$

iii) $1\frac{1}{6} =$ iv) $2\frac{3}{4} =$

b) Now try to regroup in your head. Follow the steps from part a).

i) $5\frac{2}{3} = 4\frac{5}{3}$ ii) $7\frac{3}{5} =$ iii) $4\frac{1}{6} =$ iv) $2\frac{7}{10} =$

c) Rewrite the mixed numbers as in part b), then subtract.

i) $3\frac{1}{5} - 1\frac{3}{4} = 3\frac{4}{20} - 1\frac{15}{20}$

$= 2\frac{24}{20} - 1\frac{15}{20}$

$= 1\frac{9}{20}$

ii) $4\frac{1}{3} - 2\frac{3}{5}$

iii) $2\frac{1}{4} - 1\frac{2}{3}$

iv) $7\frac{1}{2} - 3\frac{9}{10}$

6. Add or subtract by first changing the mixed fractions to improper fractions.

a) $3\frac{2}{3} + 1\frac{1}{2}$

$= \frac{2 \times 11}{2 \times 3} + \frac{3 \times 3}{2 \times 3}$

$= \frac{22}{6} + \frac{9}{6}$

$= \frac{31}{6}$

$= 5\frac{1}{6}$

b) $1\frac{1}{5} - \frac{2}{3}$

c) $3\frac{1}{4} - 2\frac{5}{6}$

d) $5\frac{1}{8} - 3\frac{1}{3}$

e) $1\frac{3}{5} + 2\frac{1}{6}$

f) $2\frac{4}{7} + 3\frac{1}{4}$

g) $4\frac{2}{3} + 2\frac{4}{5}$

h) $4\frac{1}{10} - 3\frac{4}{5}$

7. Alice walked $1\frac{3}{7}$ km in the first hour and $1\frac{1}{3}$ km in the second hour.
How many kilometres did she walk in two hours?

8. Steve bought $2\frac{3}{5}$ kg of apples, $1\frac{2}{3}$ kg of grapes, and $3\frac{4}{5}$ kg of oranges.
How many kilograms of fruit did he buy in total?

9. Tom and Andy worked together to paint a $12\frac{1}{6}$ metre fence.
On the first day, Tom painted $4\frac{2}{3}$ metres and Andy painted $5\frac{1}{2}$ metres.
How many metres of fence needed to be painted on the second day?

NS7-30 Mental Math

Sayaka subtracts $6 - 3\frac{2}{3}$ on a number line.

Step 1:

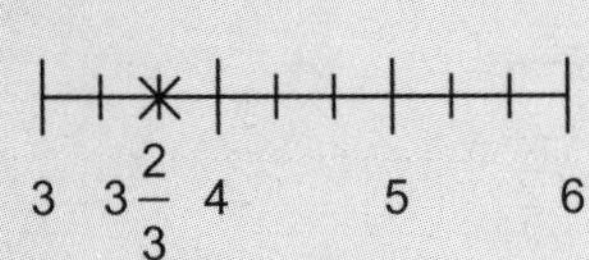

She marks the number she is subtracting ($3\frac{2}{3}$) on a number line.

Step 2:

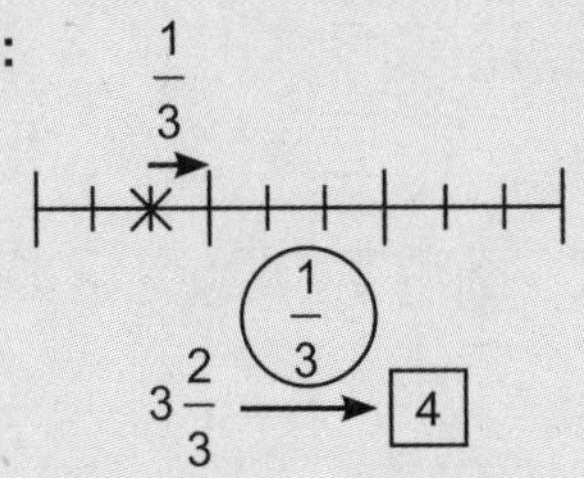

She draws an arrow to show the difference between $3\frac{2}{3}$ and the next whole number (4).

Step 3:

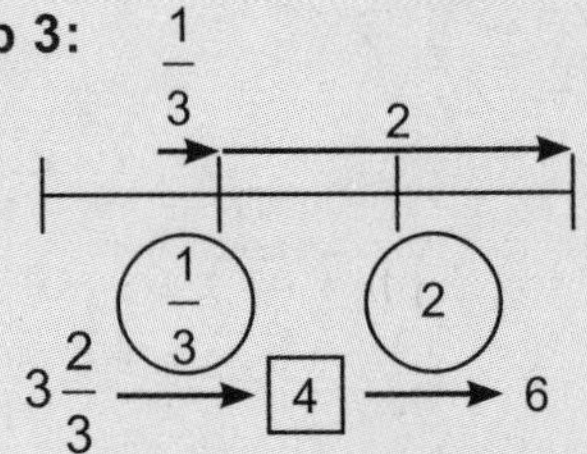

She draws an arrow to show the difference between 4 and 6.

She sees that $6 - 3\frac{2}{3} = 2 + \frac{1}{3} = 2\frac{1}{3}$.

1. Follow Sayaka's steps to find the differences.

a)

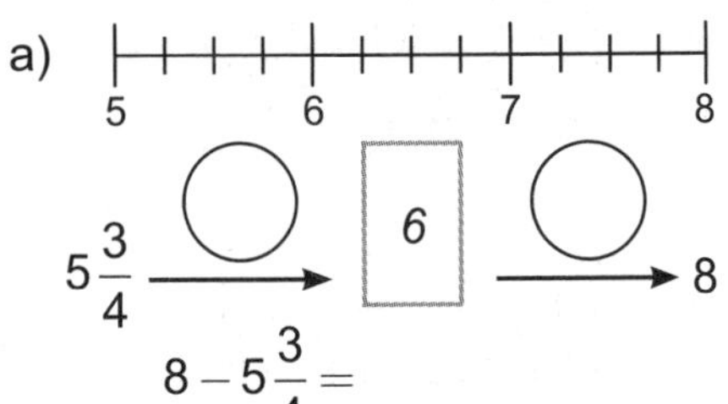

$8 - 5\frac{3}{4} =$

b) $7\frac{3}{5}$ → ◯ □ ◯ → 9

$9 - 7\frac{3}{5} =$

2. Find the differences.

a) $4\frac{3}{5}$ → ◯ □ ◯ → 6

$6 - 4\frac{3}{5} =$

b) $3\frac{1}{5}$ → ◯ □ ◯ → 8

$8 - 3\frac{1}{5} =$

c) $7\frac{5}{8}$ → ◯ □ ◯ → 10

$10 - 7\frac{5}{8} =$

3. Find the differences mentally.

a) $7 - 2\frac{1}{8} =$ b) $9 - 4\frac{7}{12} =$ c) $17 - 15\frac{3}{10} =$ d) $25 - 24\frac{1}{3} =$

4. Find the differences by following the steps.

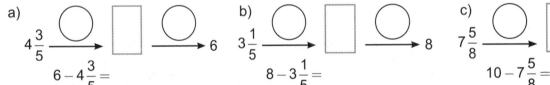

a) $5\frac{4}{5}$ → ($\frac{1}{5}$) next whole number ↓ [6] → (2) [8] → ($\frac{3}{5}$) → $8\frac{3}{5}$

$8\frac{3}{5} - 5\frac{4}{5} = \frac{1}{5} + 2 + \frac{3}{5} = 2\frac{4}{5}$

b) $3\frac{5}{8}$ → ◯ □ → ◯ □ → ◯ → $8\frac{1}{8}$

5. Find the differences mentally.

a) $4\frac{3}{7} - 3\frac{4}{7} =$ b) $7\frac{5}{9} - 3\frac{1}{9} =$ c) $10\frac{1}{5} - 5\frac{3}{5} =$ d) $12\frac{1}{6} - 5\frac{5}{6} =$

NS7-31 Problems and Puzzles

1. Write numbers in the boxes to make the equations true.

a) $\frac{3}{7} + \frac{\square}{7} = 1$ b) $\frac{6}{10} + \frac{4}{\square} = 1$ c) $1 - \frac{3}{5} = \frac{\square}{5}$

d) $1 - \frac{5}{11} = \frac{6}{\square}$ e) $\frac{1}{\square} + \frac{\square}{9} = \frac{7}{9}$ f) $\frac{\square}{12} - \frac{5}{\square} = \frac{3}{12}$

2. Sunitha ate $\frac{1}{5}$ of a pie. Kayla ate $\frac{1}{3}$. What fraction of the pie did they eat altogether?

3. Jennifer used $\frac{1}{2}$ a can of green olives and $\frac{2}{3}$ of a can of black olives to make pizza. How many cans of olives did she use altogether?

4. Rima needs $\frac{2}{3}$ of a cup of flour for a recipe. She only has $\frac{1}{5}$ of a cup. How much flour is she missing?

5. Karen wants to run $\frac{3}{4}$ of a kilometre today. She has already run $\frac{1}{2}$ a kilometre. How much farther must she run?

6. The chart shows how the students in a Grade 7 class get to school.

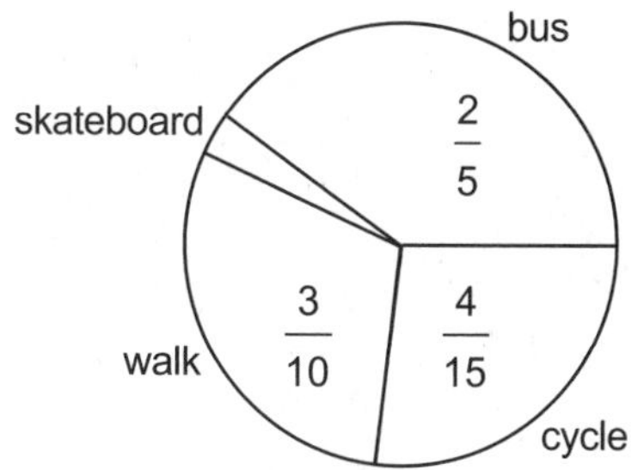

a) What fraction of the students skateboard to school?

b) There are 30 students in the class. How many take the bus to school?

7. The fractions in each row, column, and diagonal of the magic square add to 1.

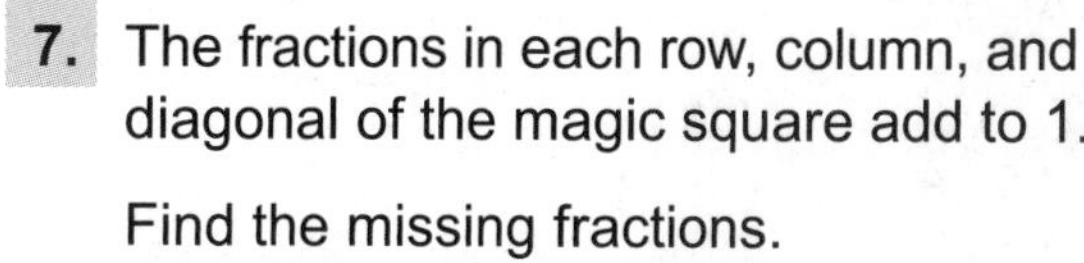

Find the missing fractions.

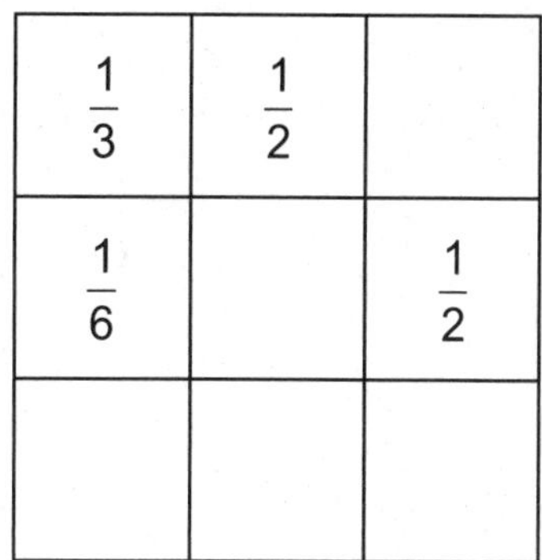

$\frac{1}{3}$	$\frac{1}{2}$	
$\frac{1}{6}$		$\frac{1}{2}$

8. Sudha had \$69. She spent $\frac{1}{3}$ of her money on books and half on a calculator. How much money did she have left?

9. Find two fractions with different denominators that add to $\frac{11}{12}$.

10. Write five fractions equivalent to 1.

11. Explain the mistake Fatima made in adding $\frac{1}{4} + \frac{1}{3} = \frac{2}{7}$.

12. Parts of the Arctic have 21 hours of daylight each summer day. What fraction of the day is dark? Write your answer in lowest terms.

13. Tina just turned 13 years old. How old was she $5\frac{1}{2}$ years ago?

14. Nevina got $\frac{1}{2}$ the questions right on a test, Sadia got $\frac{3}{4}$ of the questions right, and Tashi got $\frac{7}{10}$ of the questions right. Who got the most questions right?

15. Sadia picked $\frac{2}{5}$ of a basket of berries, Tashi picked $\frac{1}{3}$ of a basket, Shafma picked $\frac{4}{7}$ of a basket, and Marzuk picked $\frac{4}{5}$ of a basket. Did all their berries fit into 2 baskets?

16. Sally stretches for $\frac{1}{2}$ an hour, walks for $\frac{1}{3}$ of an hour, and jogs for $\frac{1}{4}$ of an hour. Calculate in two ways how many minutes she exercises for.

a) Add the fractions and then convert to minutes.

b) Convert the fractions to minutes and then add.

17. Write each fraction as a sum of exactly three fractions, each with numerator 1.

Example: $\frac{5}{6} = \frac{1}{2} + \frac{1}{6} + \frac{1}{6}$

Hint: How does finding the factors of the denominator help?

a) $\frac{7}{8}$ b) $\frac{17}{18}$ c) $\frac{13}{12}$ d) $\frac{13}{15}$ e) $\frac{11}{15}$

18. Decide whether each statement is true or false. Explain your answer.

a) If the numerator and denominator are both even, the fraction is never in lowest terms.

b) If the numerator and denominator are both odd, the fraction is always in lowest terms.

c) If the numerator is prime, the fraction is always in lowest terms.

19. Do you need to compare $\frac{1}{4}$ and $\frac{2}{9}$ in order to compare $6\frac{1}{4}$ and $5\frac{2}{9}$? Explain.

G7-1 Points and Lines

Object:	point	line	line segment	ray
		no endpoints	2 endpoints	1 endpoint
Diagram:	A	A B	A B	A B
Name:	*A*	*AB* (or *BA*)	*AB* (or *BA*)	*AB*

1. Draw a point on each line and choose a letter to name it.

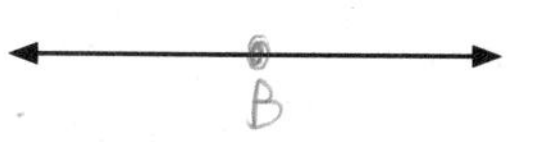

B D

2. Draw two points on each line. Name the lines.

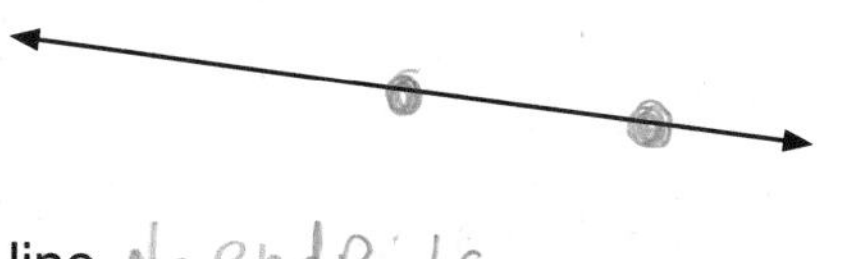

line No end Points   line No end Points

3. Draw and name any line.

1 end Point   2 end Points

4. Name each line in two ways.

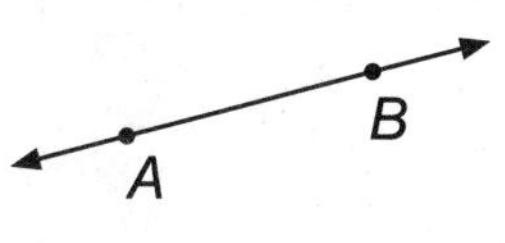

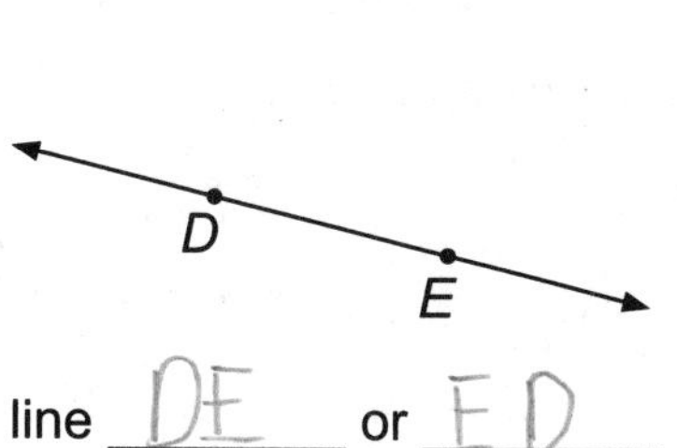

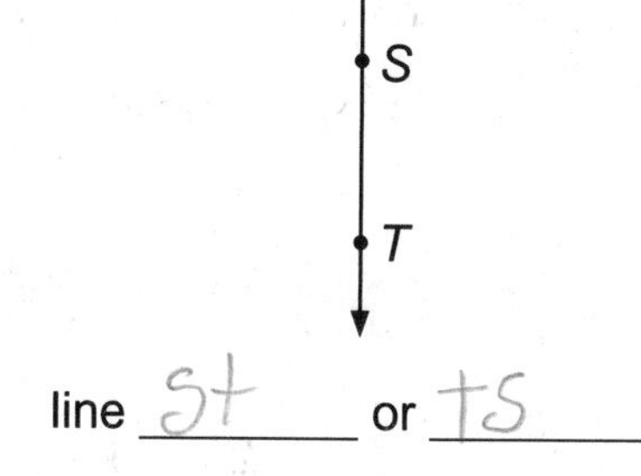

line ___AB___ or ___BA___   line ___DE___ or ___ED___   line ___St___ or ___tS___

5. a) Connect points *P* and *Q*.
   b) Is *PQ* a line, line segment, or ray? ___line Segment___

P Q

6. Measure line segment *EF*.

E F

length of *EF* = ___7cm___

7. Draw a line segment *PQ* of length 5 cm.

8. a) Circle the endpoint on each ray.

b) Name each ray.

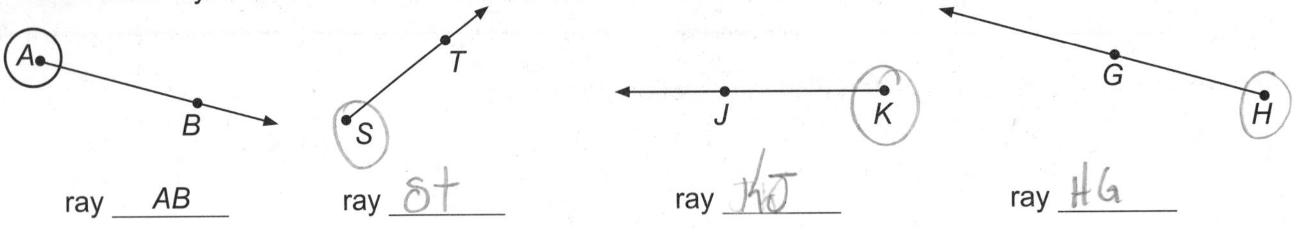

ray AB ray ST ray KJ ray HG

9. Name each ray.

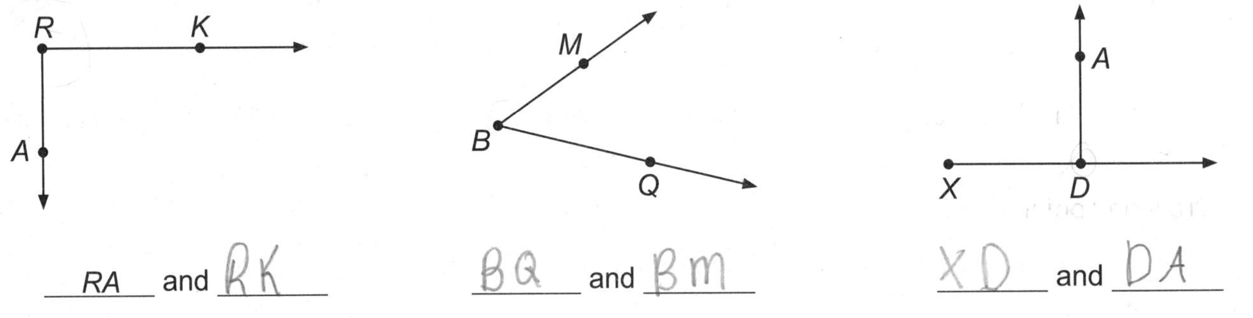

RA and RK BQ and BM XD and DA

10. Draw and name two rays.

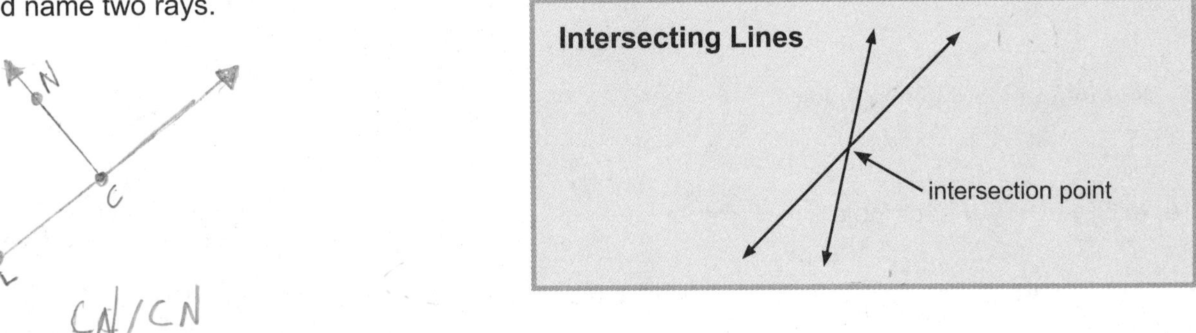

CN/CN

11. Give an example of intersecting lines in your classroom.

____

12. Name the intersecting lines, line segments, or rays and the intersection point.

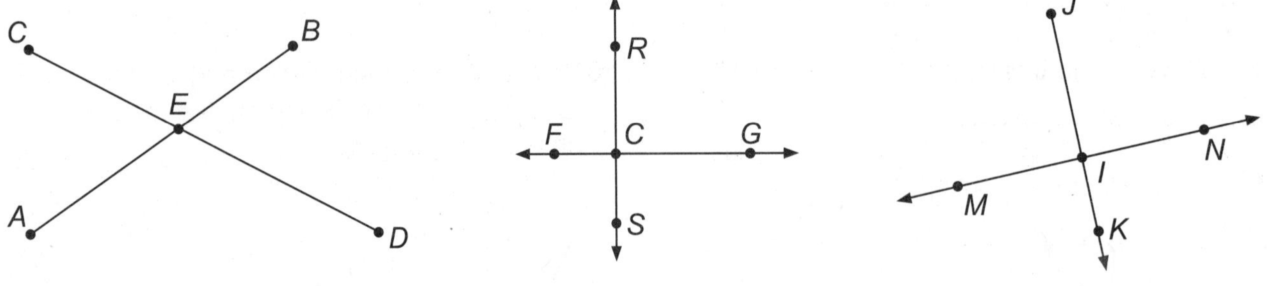

CD and AB intersect at E SR and FG intersect at C MN and JK intersect at I

You do not need to draw arrows and/or dots at the ends of lines, rays, or line segments, unless you especially want to show that what you are drawing is a line, ray, or line segment.

13. Name the intersecting lines and the intersection point.

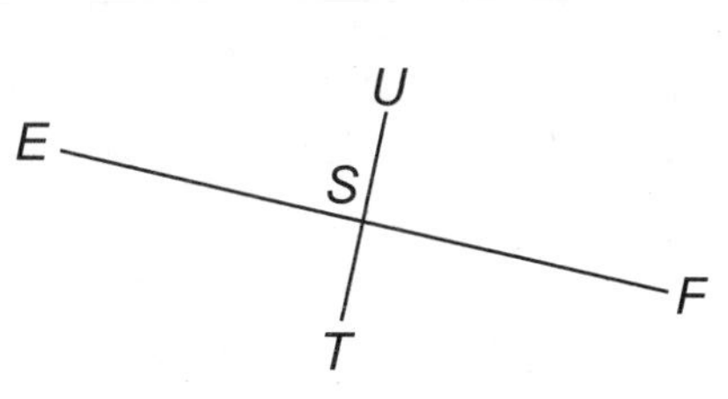

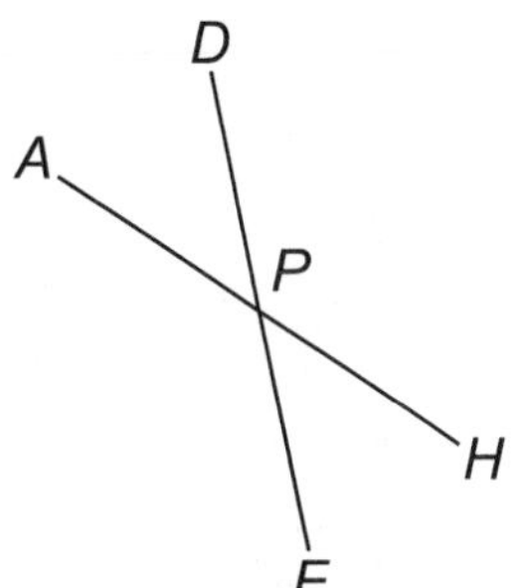

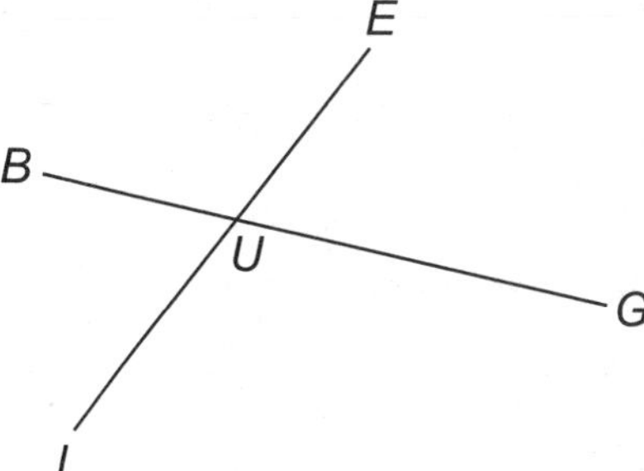

____ and ____ intersect at ____ ____ and ____ intersect at ____ ____ and ____ intersect at ____

14. a) Draw any point *P* on *AB*.

b) Draw a line segment *XY* that intersects *AB* at point *P*.

15. Circle the intersection point.

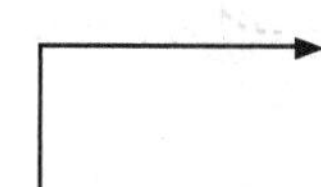

16. a) Find two of each object in this shape.

Points: __A__ and ____

Lines: ____ and ____

Line segments: ____ and ____

Rays: ____ and ____

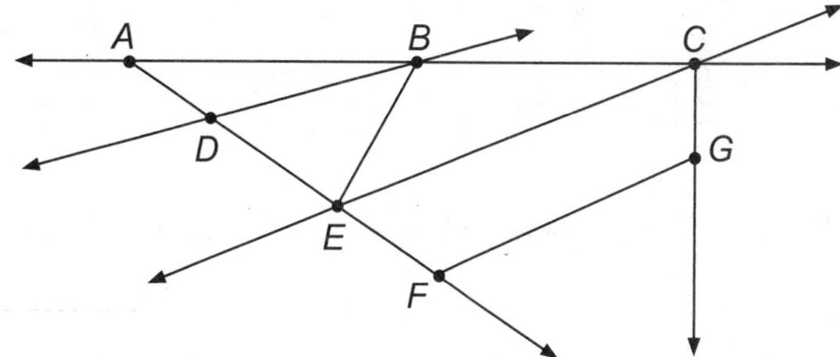

b) Find two pairs of intersecting lines and the intersection points.

____ and ____ intersect at ____ ____ and ____ intersect at ____

17. BONUS▶ Name this line in six ways.

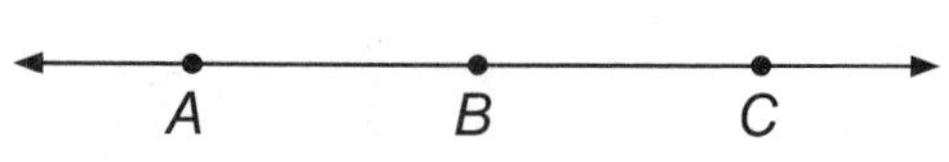

__AB__ , __AC__ , ____ , ____ , ____ , ____

18. BONUS▶ Two intersecting edges of the prism are marked. Trace another pair of intersecting edges.

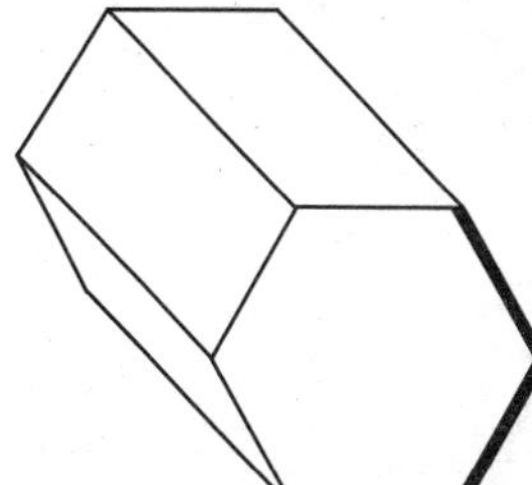

G7-2 Angles and Shapes

1. Circle the vertex on each angle.

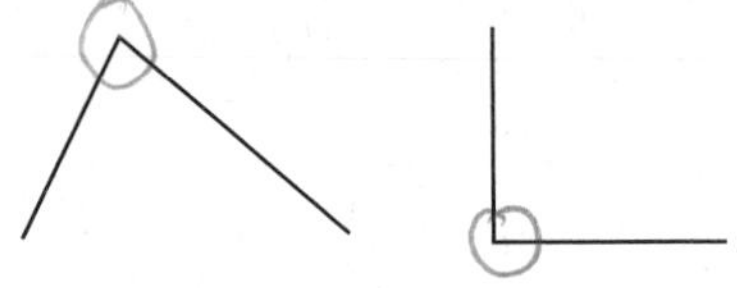

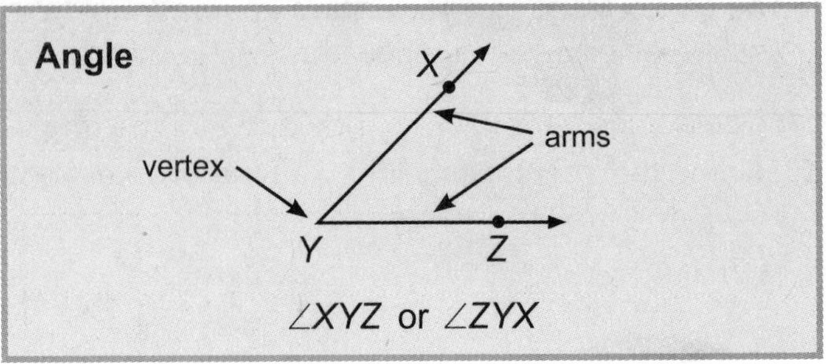

2. Fill in the blanks to name each angle in two ways.

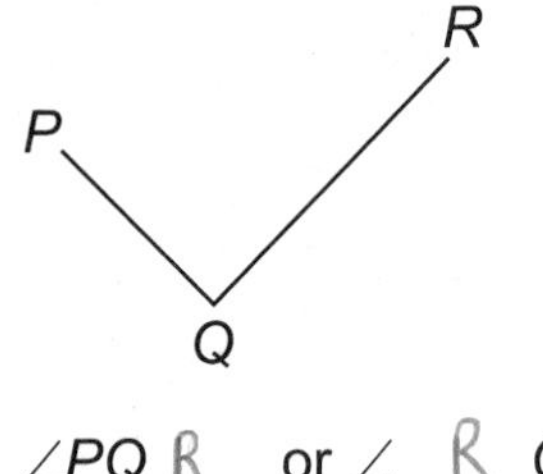

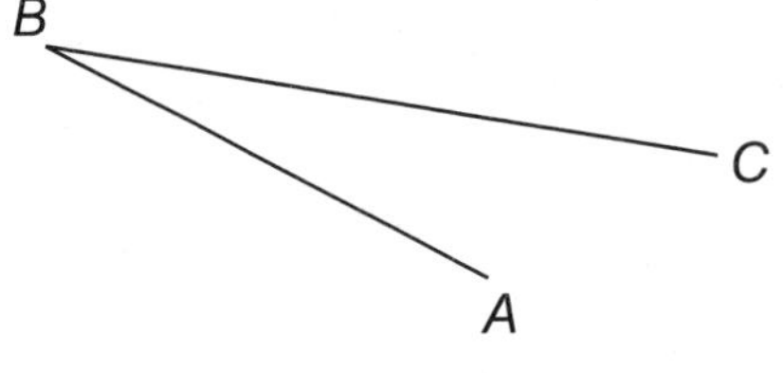

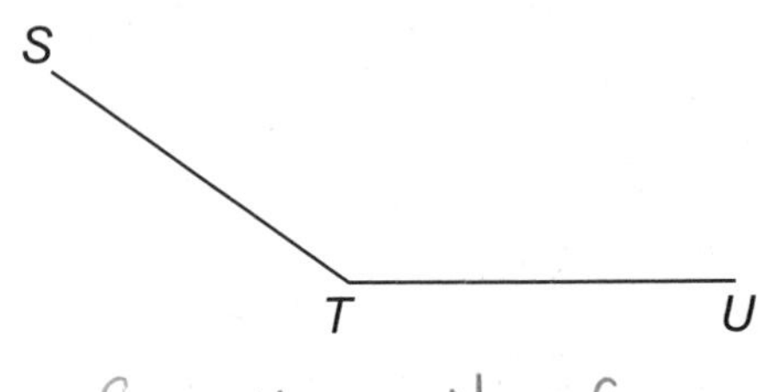

∠PQ R or ∠ R QP   ∠ A B C or ∠ C B A   ∠ S T U or ∠ U T S

3. Circle the vertex. Then name the angle.

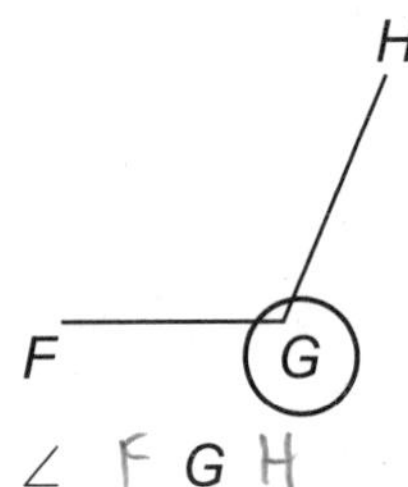

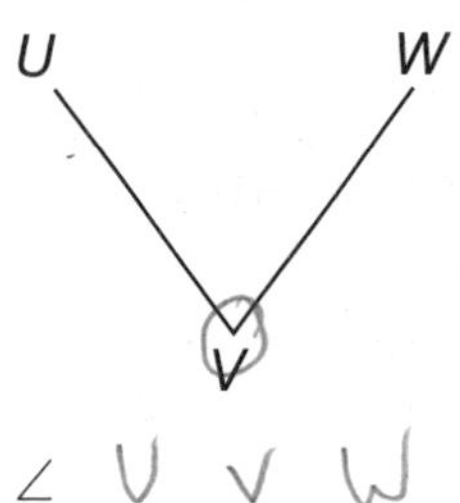

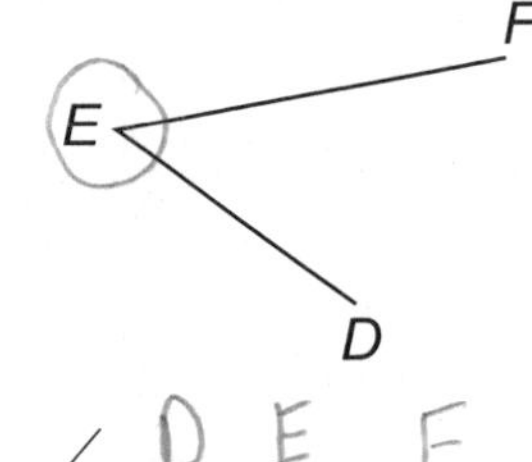

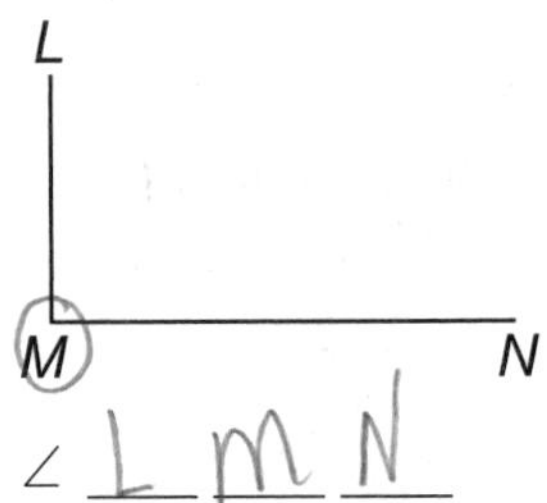

∠ F G H   ∠ U V W   ∠ D E F   ∠ L M N

4. Name each angle.

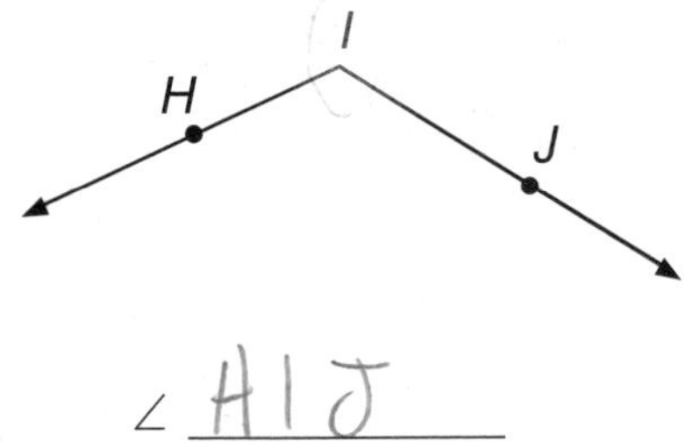

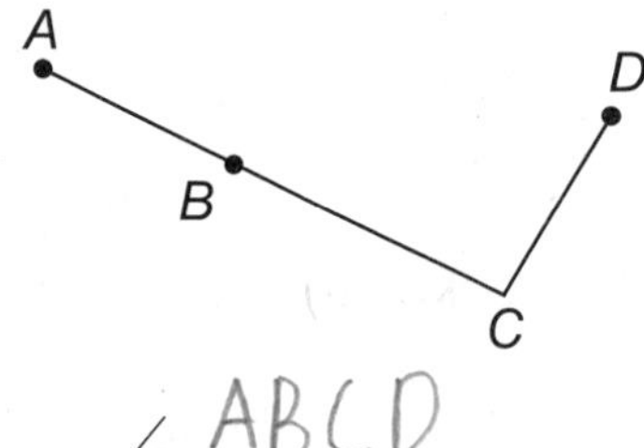

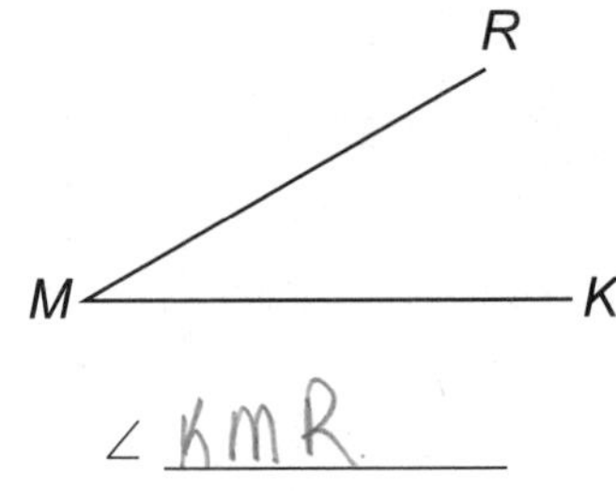

∠ HIJ   ∠ ABCD   ∠ KMR

BONUS▶ Name all the angles you can see.

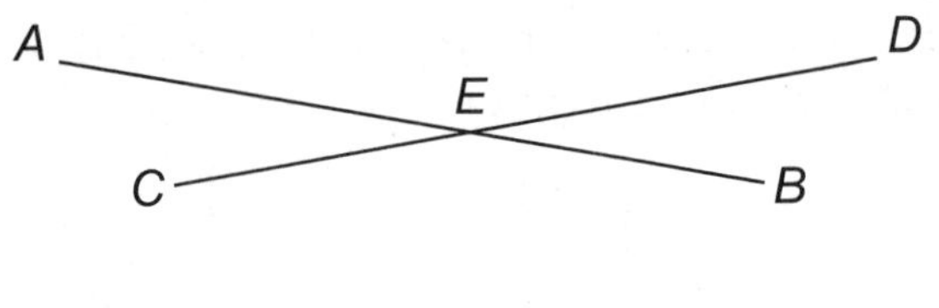

____

BONUS▶ Circle all the possible names for the angle.

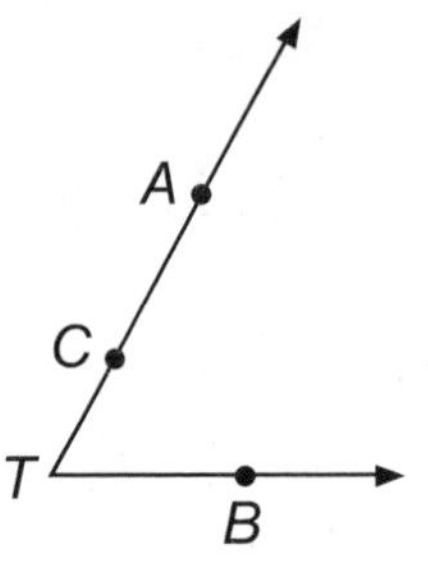

∠ACT or ∠TCA

∠ATB or ∠BTA

∠CBT or ∠TBC

∠CTB or ∠BTC

∠BCA or ∠ACB

The vertex letter can name an angle when there is no chance of confusion.

5. Circle each vertex. Write the names of the angles.

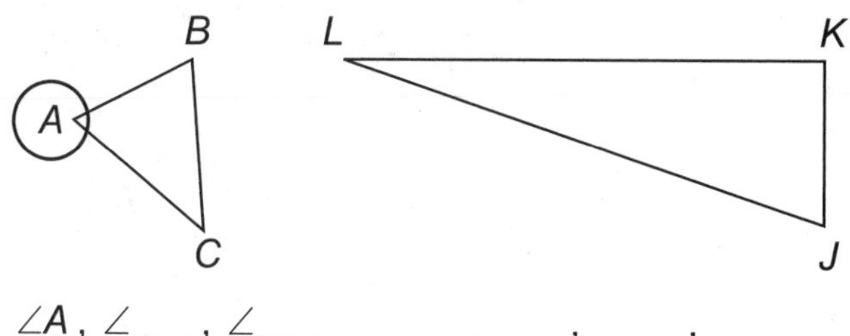

∠A , ∠___, ∠___ _____ , _____ , _____

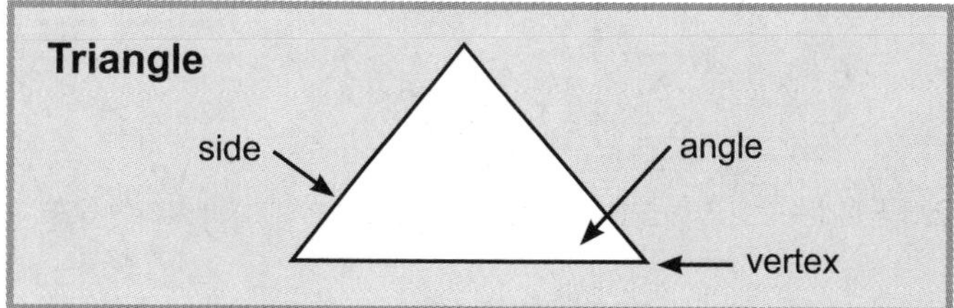

6. Name the sides of each triangle.

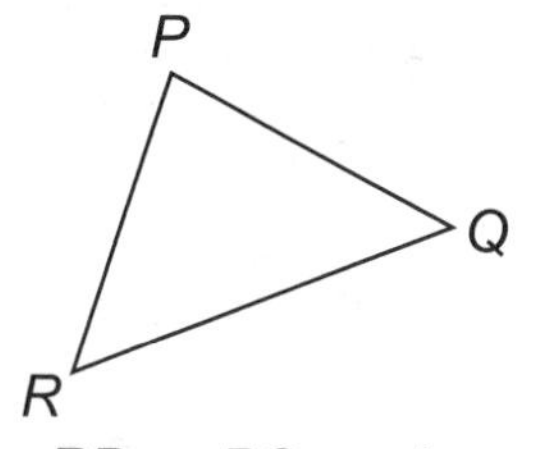

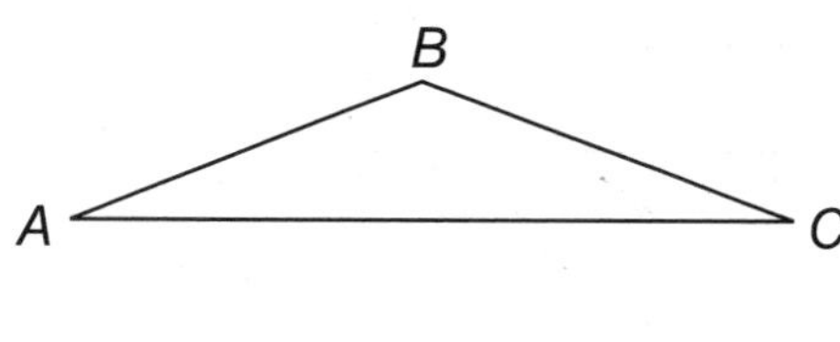

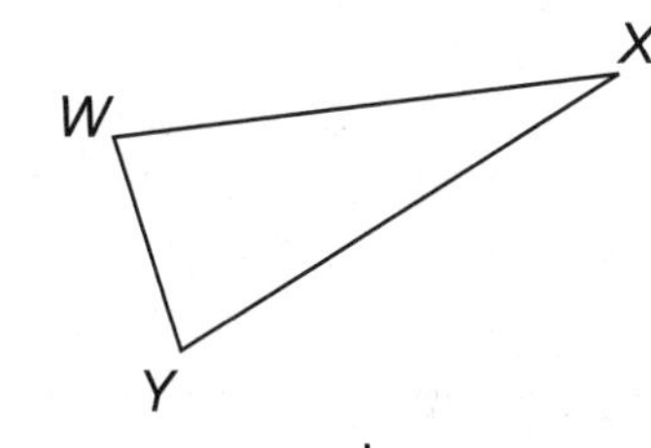

RP , PQ and ____ ____ , ____ and ____ ____ , ____ and ____

7. Name each triangle by writing the vertex letters in order (clockwise or counter-clockwise). You may start with any letter.

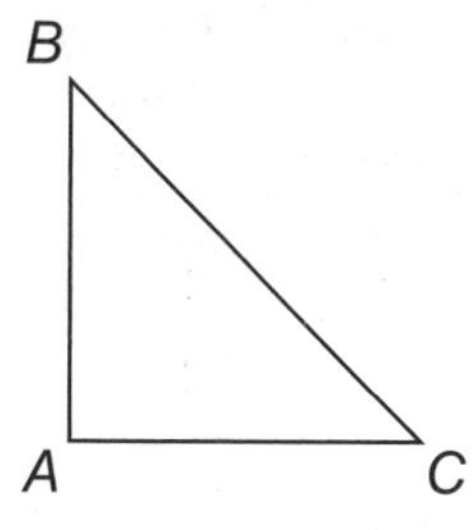

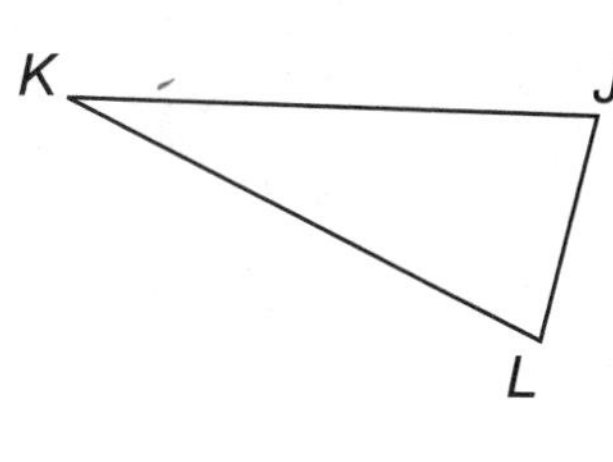

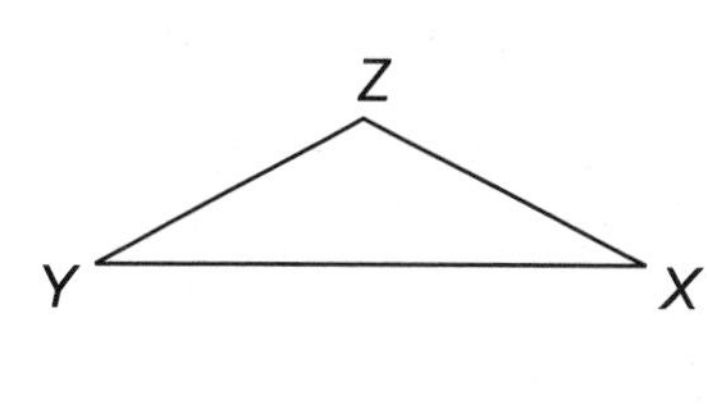

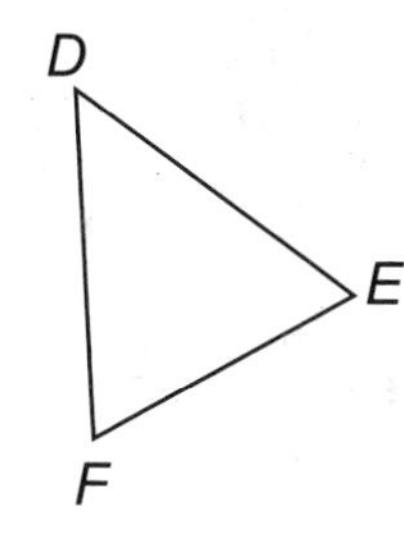

Δ ABC Δ ___ ___ ___ Δ ___ ___ ___ Δ ___ ___ ___

8. Label the vertices (clockwise or counter-clockwise) and name each polygon.

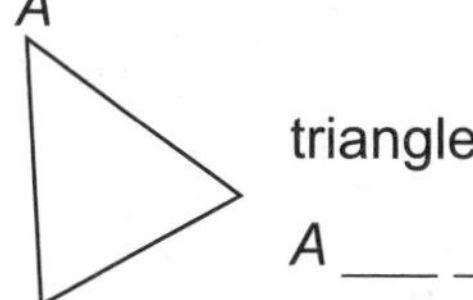

triangle

A ___ ___

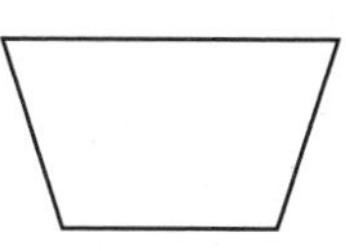

trapezoid

____

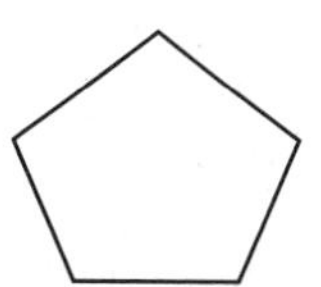

pentagon

____

BONUS▶ Label the vertices, then name the line segments that form each shape.

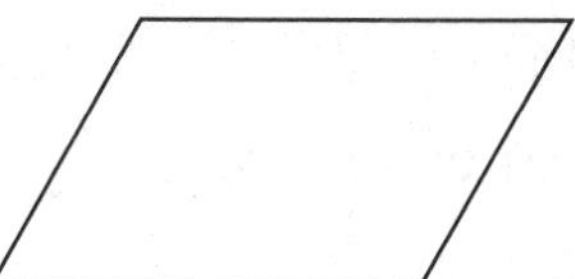

BONUS▶ Circle the angles you can name using only the vertex letter (if any).

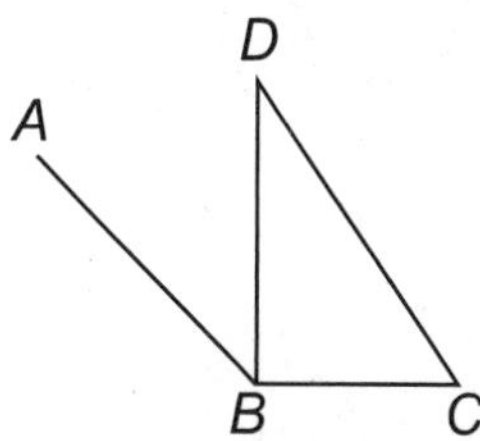

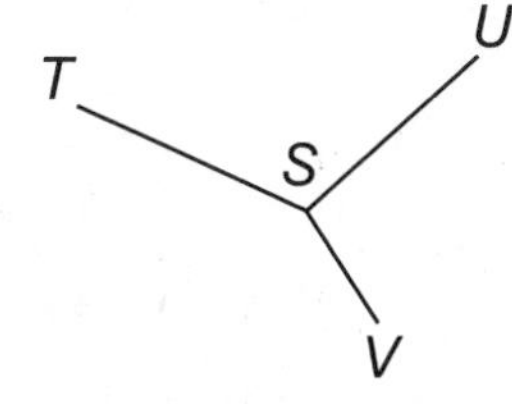

G7-3 Measuring and Drawing Angles and Triangles

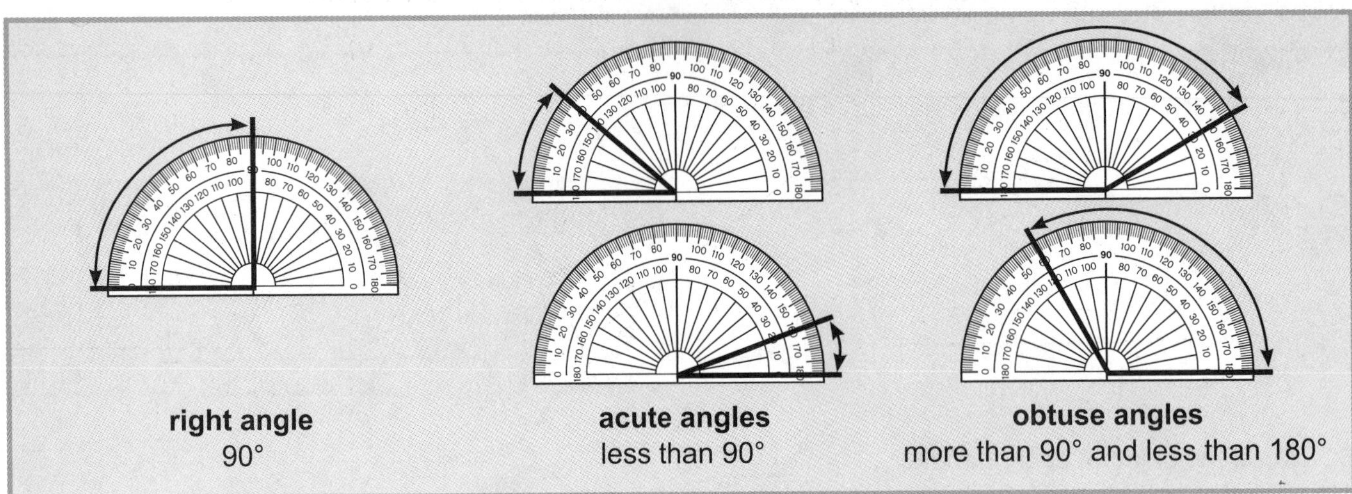

1. Without using a protractor, identify each angle as **acute** or **obtuse**.

a) b) c) d)

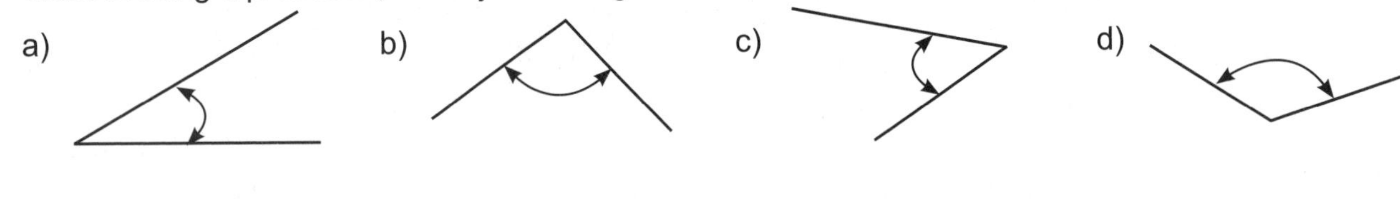

a) ____________ b) ____________ c) ____________ d) ____________

2. Practise choosing the correct scale to measure an angle.

Step 1: Is the angle acute or obtuse? Circle your answer.	**Step 2:** Circle the 2 numbers that the arm of the angle passes through.	**Step 3:** Choose the correct angle measure. Example: if the angle is acute, the measure is *less* than 90°.

a)

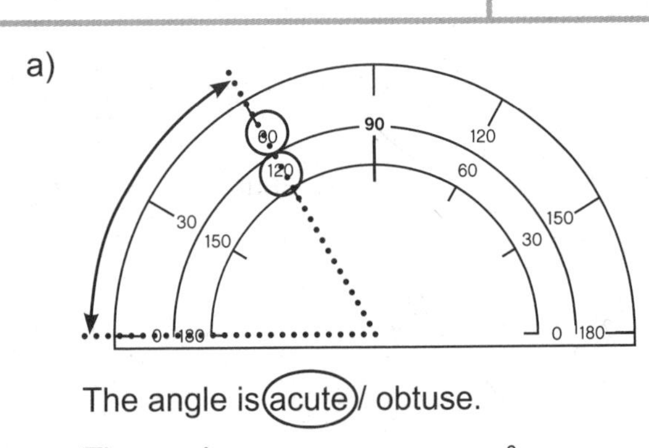

The angle is (acute) / obtuse.

The angle measures ________°.

b)

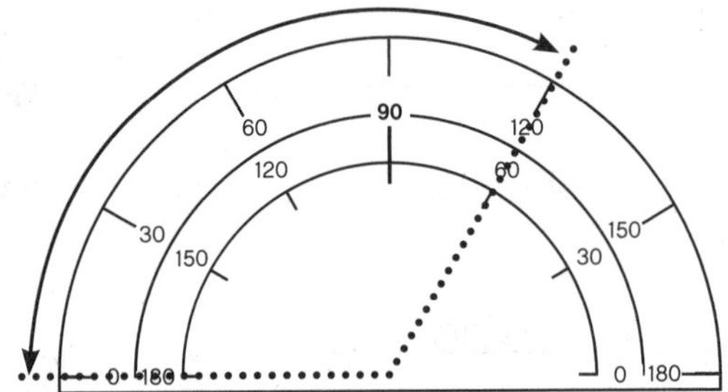

The angle is acute / obtuse.

The angle measures ________°.

c)

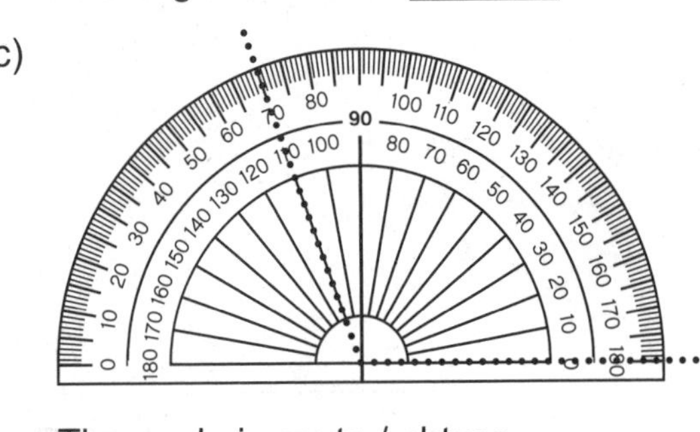

The angle is acute / obtuse.

The angle measures ________°.

d)

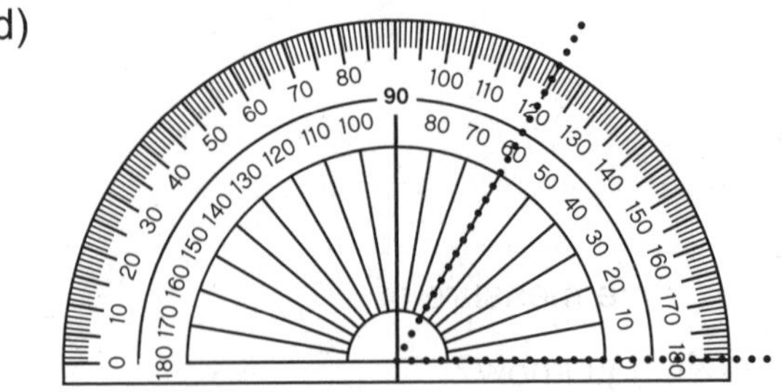

The angle is acute / obtuse.

The angle measures ________°.

3. Measure each angle. Hint: For parts d) and e), you will have to extend the arms.

a)

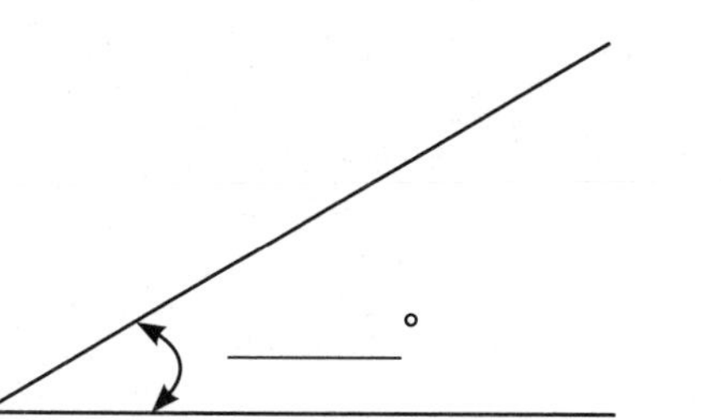

b)

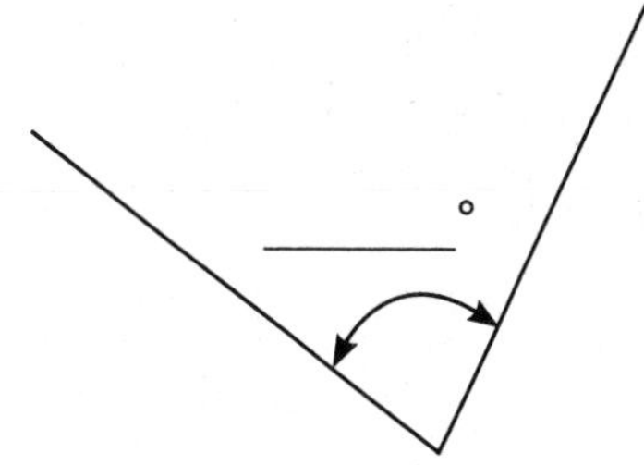

c)

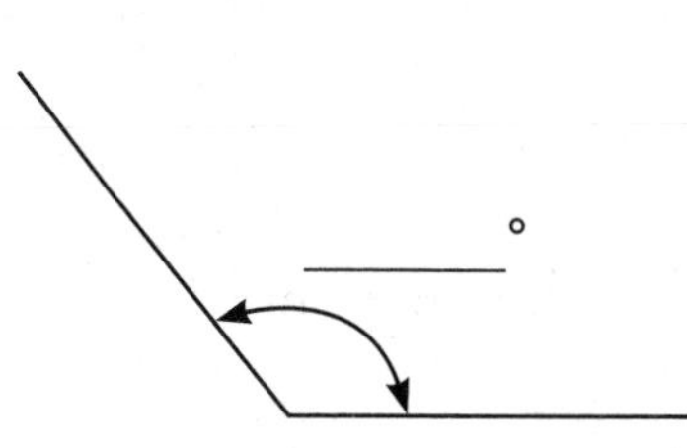

d)

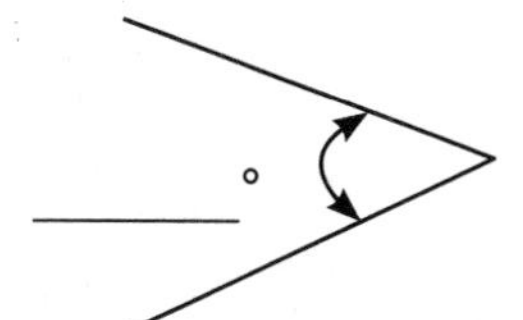

e)

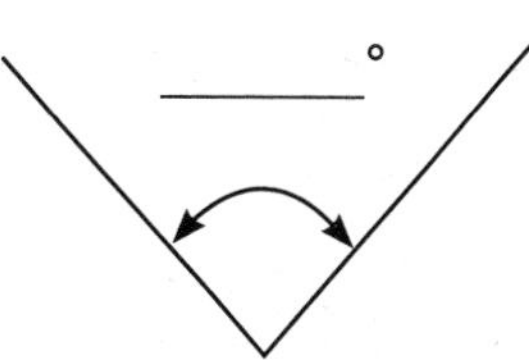

4. In each polygon, circle angle $\angle XYZ$. Then measure the angle.

a)

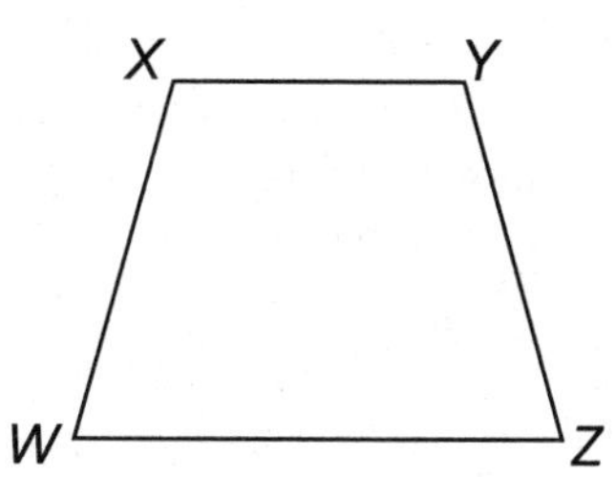

Measure of $\angle XYZ$: ________

b)

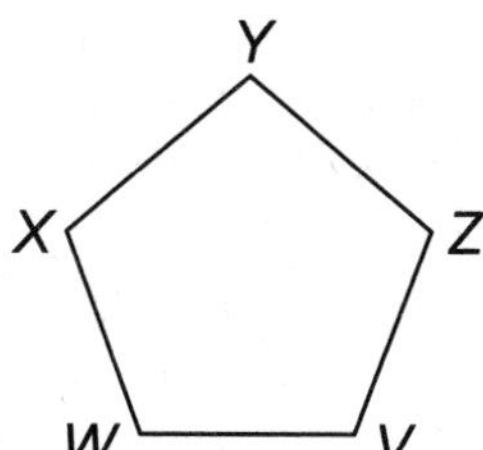

Measure of $\angle XYZ$: ________

c)

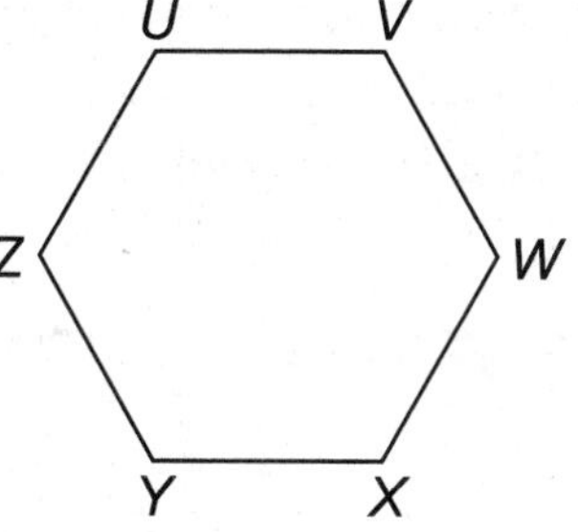

Measure of $\angle XYZ$: ______

5. $\angle ABC$ is 90°. $\angle ABD$ is 50°.

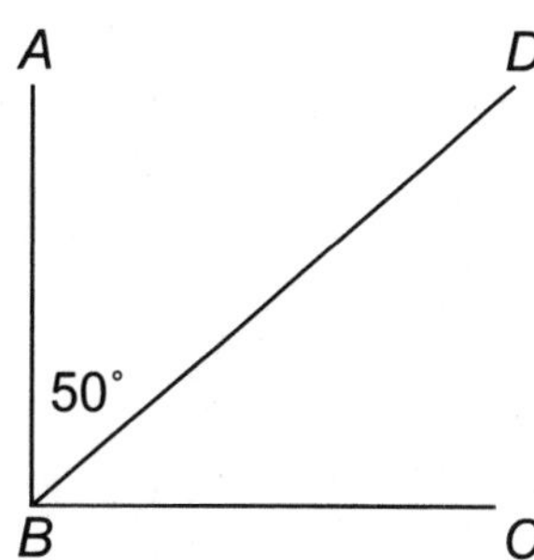

a) What is the measure of $\angle DBC$? __________

How do you know? ____

b) Measure $\angle DBC$ with a protractor to check your answer in a).

Drawing an Angle

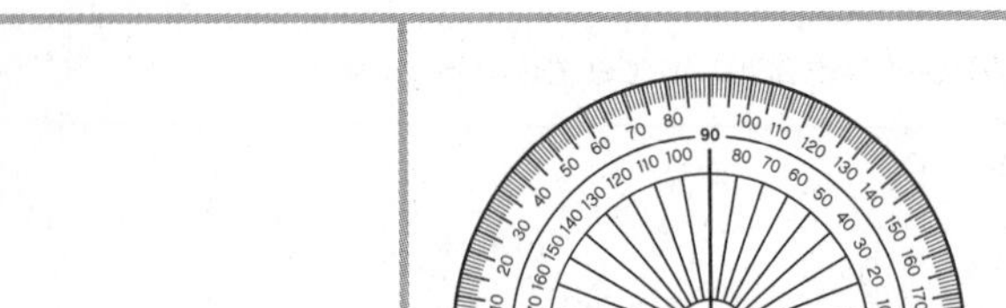

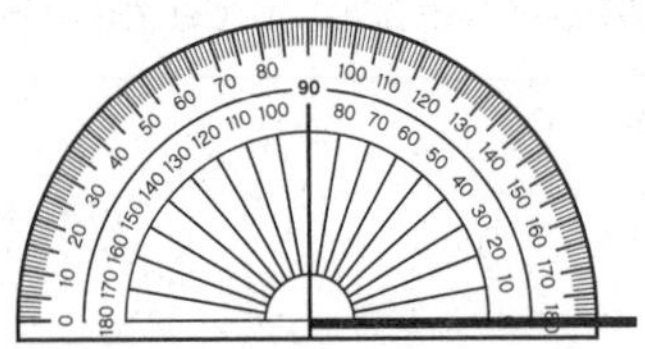

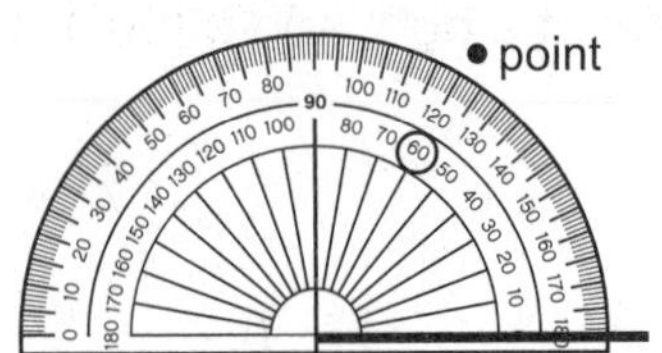

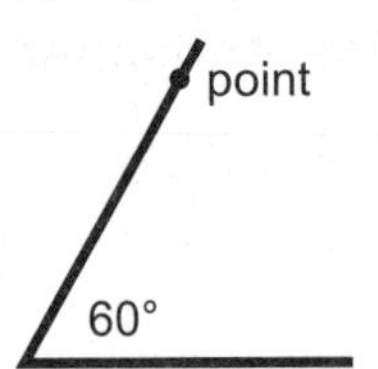

Step 1: Draw a line segment.	**Step 2:** Place the protractor with the origin on one endpoint. This point will be the vertex of the angle.	**Step 3:** Hold the protractor in place and mark a point at the angle measure you want.	**Step 4:** Draw a line from the vertex through the angle mark.

6. Draw the angles shown.

a) 30°

b) 120°

Drawing Lines That Intersect at an Angle

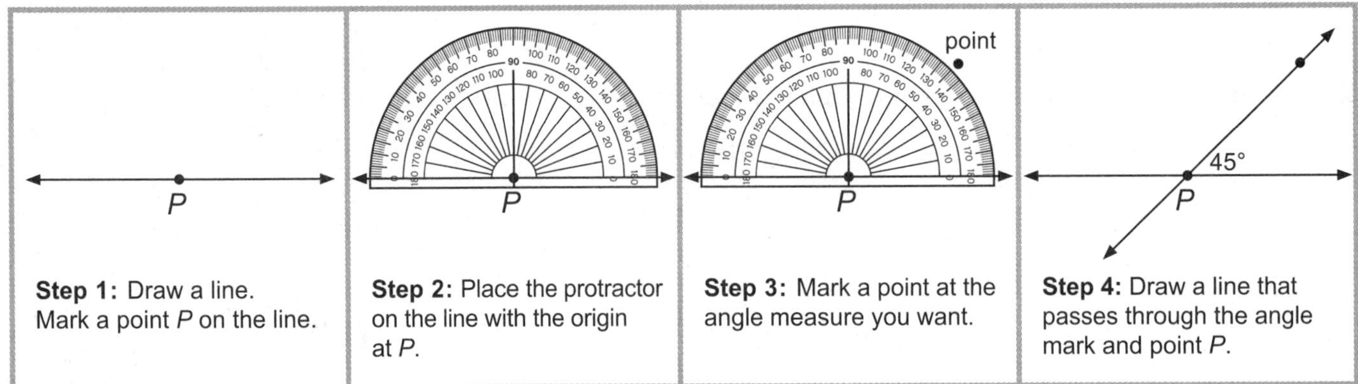

Step 1: Draw a line. Mark a point *P* on the line.	**Step 2:** Place the protractor on the line with the origin at *P*.	**Step 3:** Mark a point at the angle measure you want.	**Step 4:** Draw a line that passes through the angle mark and point *P*.

7. Draw each angle.

a) 30° b) 45° c) 60° d) 150° e) 10°

8. Construct two lines that intersect at…

a) 45° b) 30° c) 60° d) 90°

9. Draw the triangles with the side and two angles shown. (Lines are not drawn to scale.)

a) 40° 60°, 8 cm

b) 25° 110°, 6 cm

c) 90° 30°, 7 cm

d) 45° 45°, 9 cm

G7-4 Perpendicular Lines

Perpendicular lines meet at a right angle (90°). The ⊥ symbol means "is perpendicular to."

EG ⊥ *ZF*

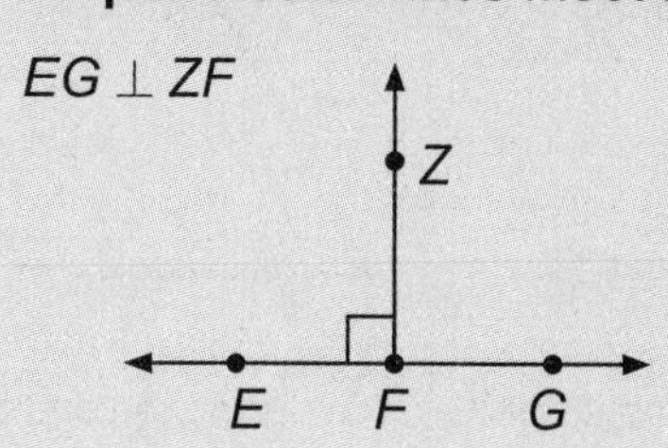

AB ⊥ *ST*

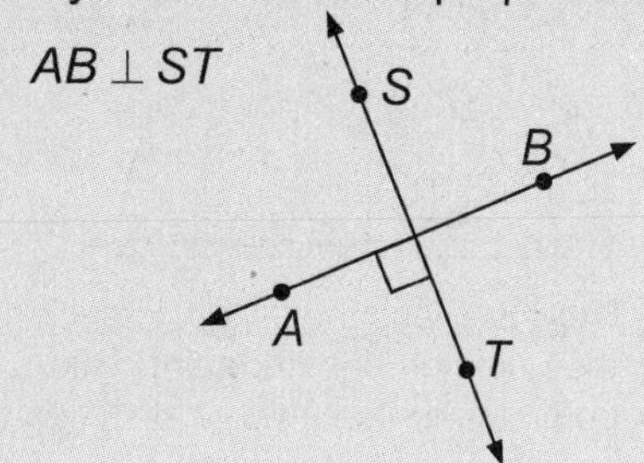

1. Name the perpendicular lines.

a)

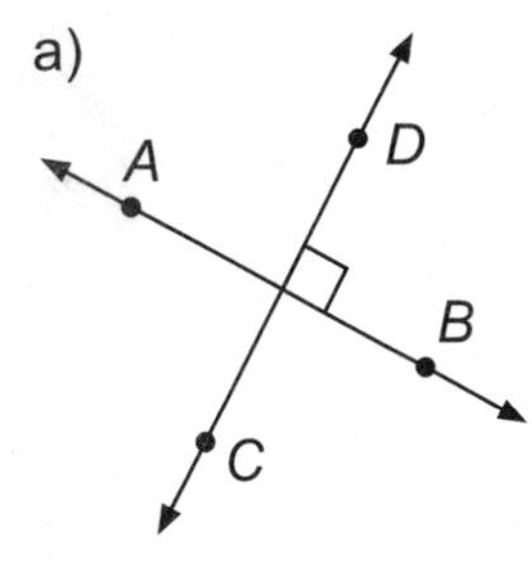

b)

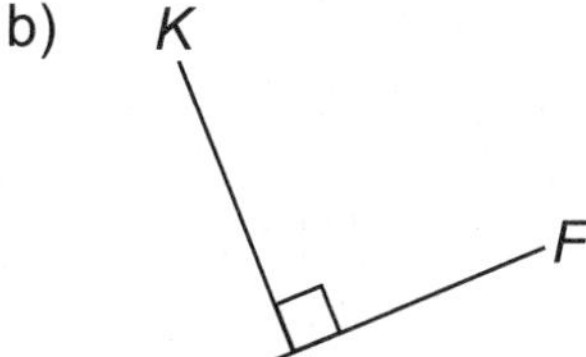

c)

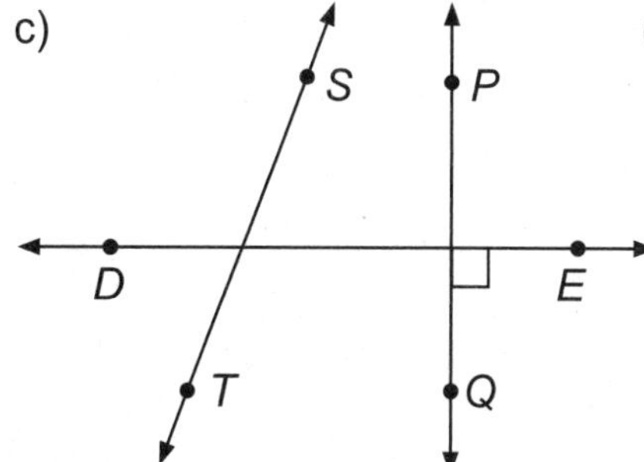

d)

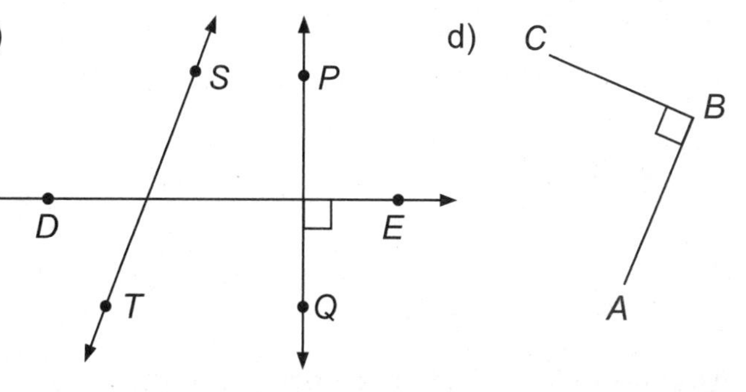

a) *AB* ⊥ ______ b) ______ ⊥ ______ c) ______ ⊥ ______ d) ______ ⊥ ______

2. Are the pairs of lines below perpendicular? Measure the angle where they meet to check.
Draw a square corner (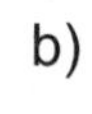) to show any perpendicular lines.

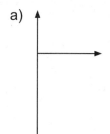

a) b) c) d)

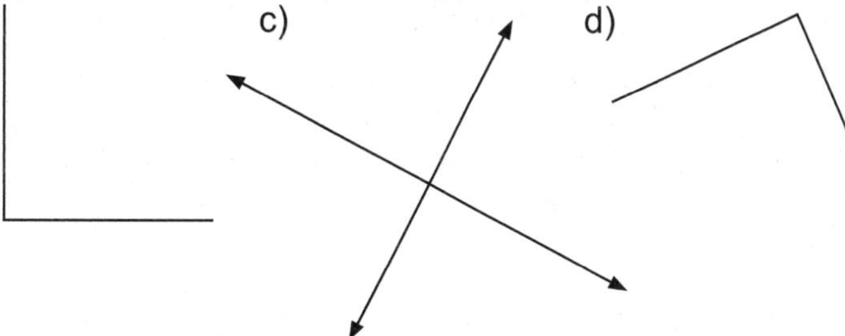

e)

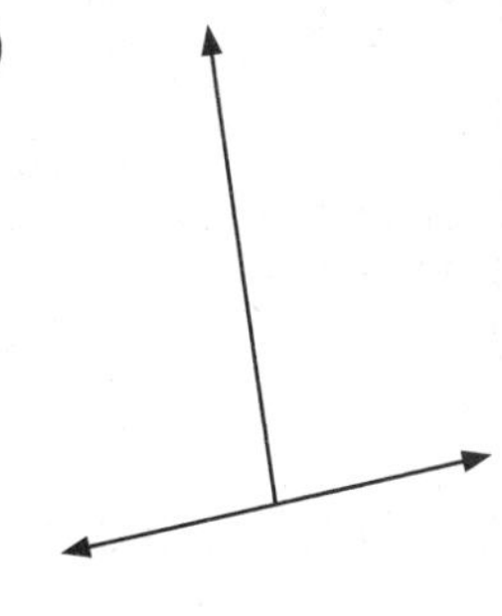

3. Match the diagrams to the descriptions.

A.

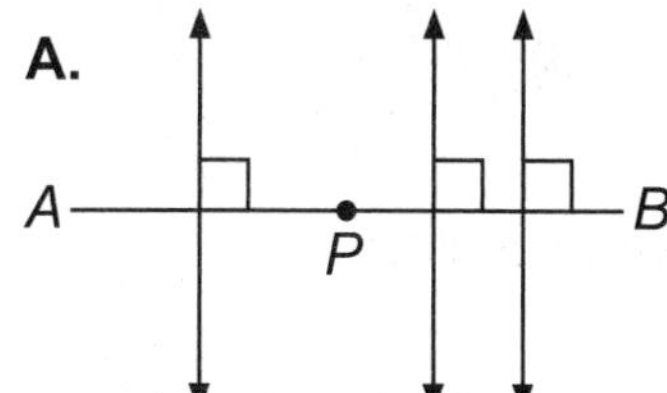

B.

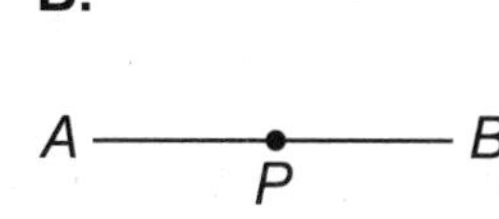

C.

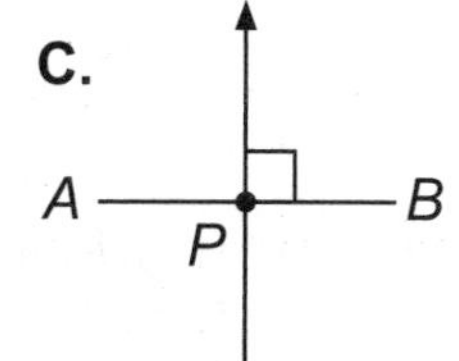

D.

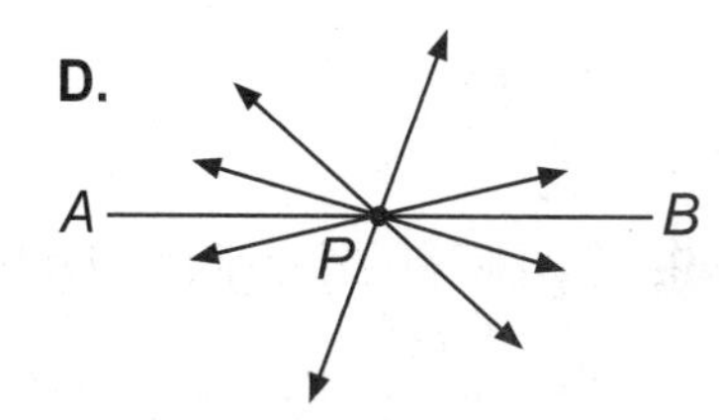

____ point *P* on line segment *AB*

____ lines perpendicular to *AB*

____ lines that pass through point *P* on *AB*

____ the line perpendicular to *AB* that passes through point *P*

Drawing a Line Segment Perpendicular to *AB* Through Point *P*

Using a Set Square

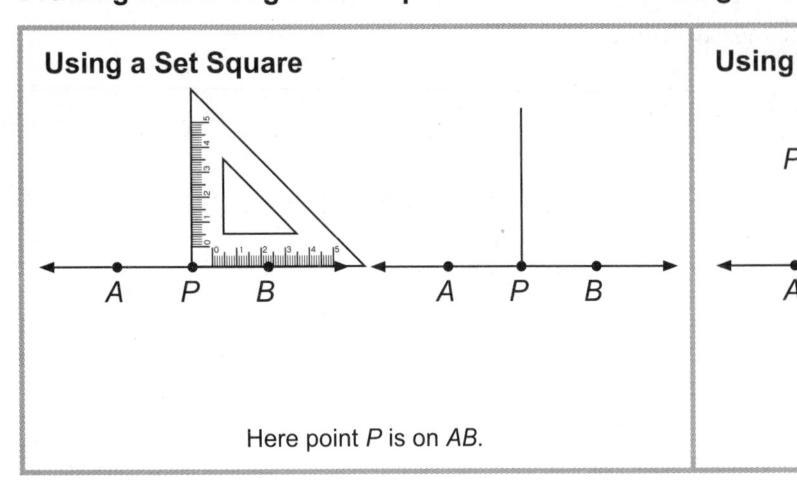

Here point *P* is on *AB*.

Using a Protractor

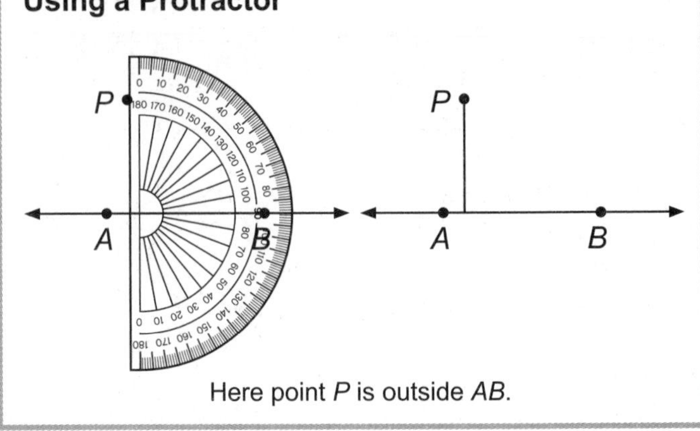

Here point *P* is outside *AB*.

4. Use a set square. Draw a line segment perpendicular to *AB* that passes through *P*.

a)

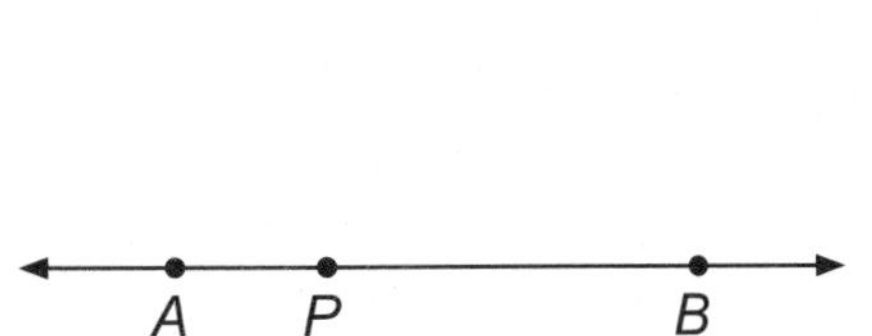

b)

P

A

B

5. Use a set square or a protractor.

a) Draw a line segment *AB*.
b) Draw a line segment *CD* perpendicular to *AB*.
c) Explain why the two lines are perpendicular.

6. Draw any line *CD*. Draw a point *P* not on *CD*. Draw any line *LM* that is perpendicular to *CD* and passes through *P*.

7. Use a protractor. Draw a line segment perpendicular to *AB* that passes through *P*.

a)

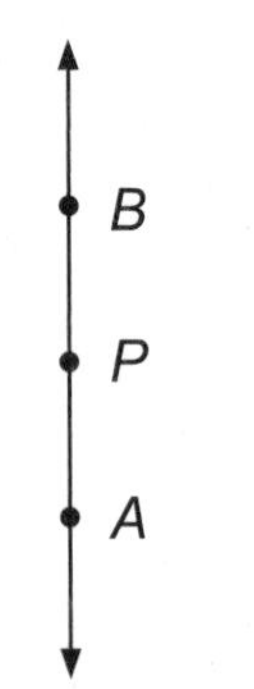

b)

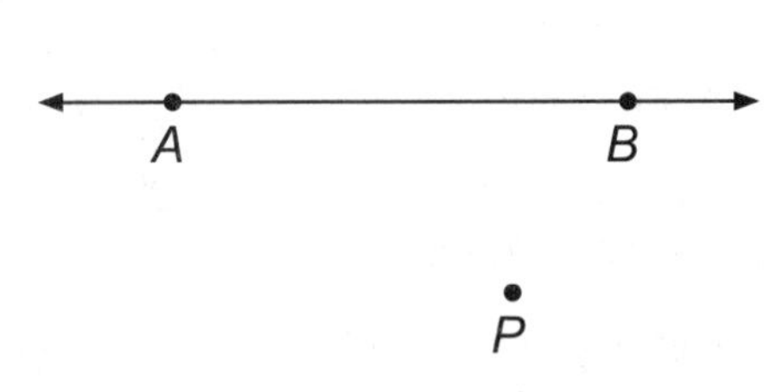

8. a) A rectangle has 4 right angles. Draw the missing sides to complete rectangle *ABCD*.

b) Name all the pairs of sides of *ABCD* that are perpendicular to one another.

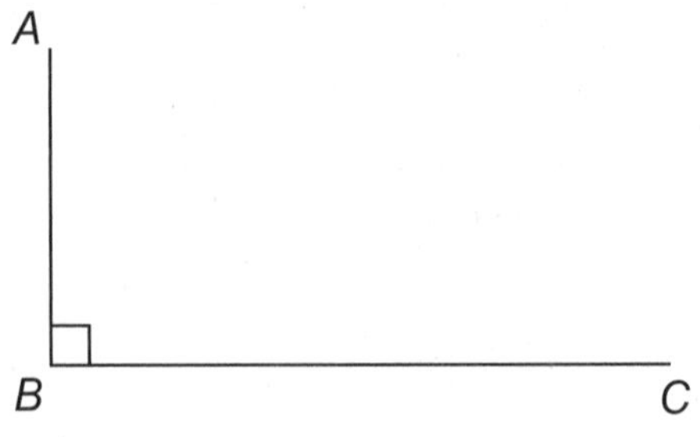

_______ ⊥ _______, _______ ⊥ _______, _______ ⊥ _______, _______ ⊥ _______

G7-5 Perpendicular Bisectors

1. Fill in the blanks to find the midpoint of this line segment.

A —/—•—/— B
M

M is the **midpoint** of *AB*.

Length of line segment = ____ cm

Length ÷ 2 = ____ cm

Mark the midpoint on the line.

2. Determine the midpoint of each line segment. Use a ruler.

a) Total length = _____cm

Length ÷ 2 = _____cm

Mark the midpoint on the line.
Label the midpoint *M*.

b) Total length = _____cm

Length ÷ 2 = _____cm

Mark the midpoint on the line.
Label the midpoint *M*.

3. Draw a line segment 8 cm in length. Mark the midpoint.

4. a) Name each midpoint shown in the figure and the line segment it is the midpoint of.

____ is the midpoint of ________

____ is the midpoint of ________

b) Can you tell from the diagram whether *E* is the midpoint of *FD*? Why or why not?

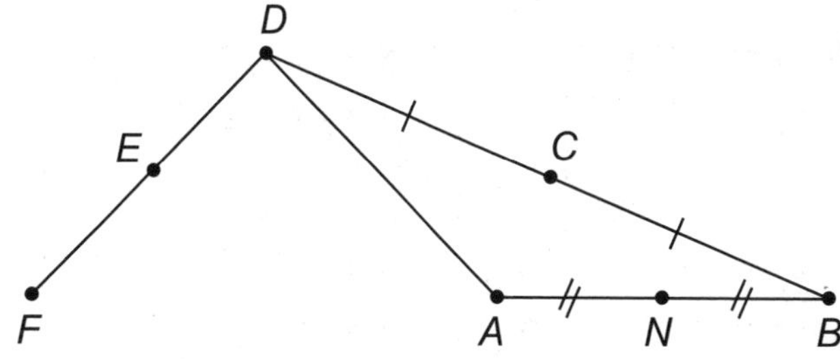

BONUS▶ Any line segment has a midpoint. But can a line have a midpoint? Explain.

5. a) Mark the midpoint of the line segment. Then draw 3 bisectors.

b) Draw another line segment with 3 bisectors.

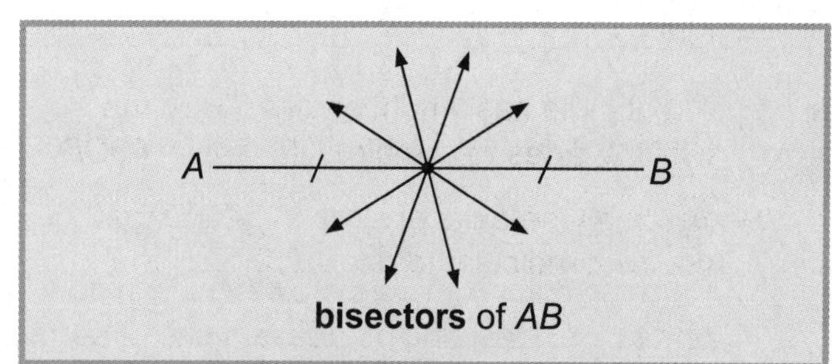

bisectors of *AB*

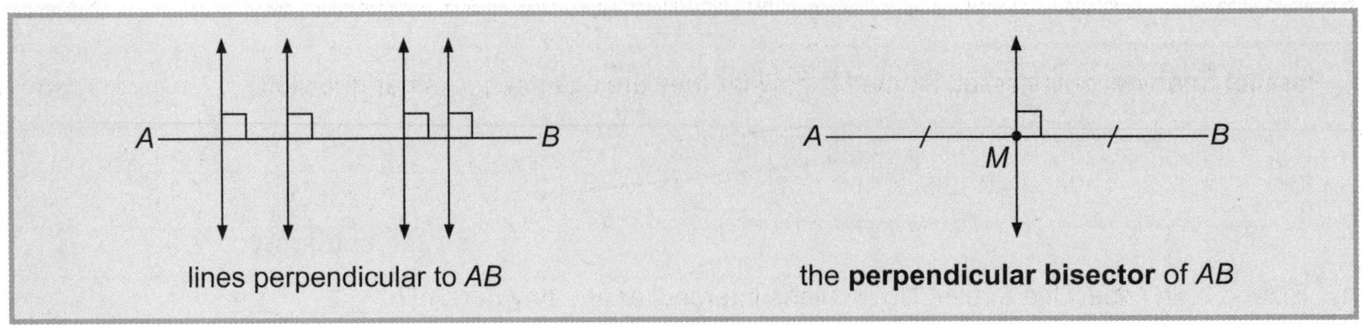

lines perpendicular to AB the **perpendicular bisector** of AB

6. Use a set square or a protractor to draw the perpendicular bisector of each line segment. The midpoint is marked.

a) b)

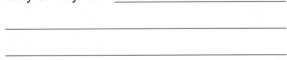

7. Draw the perpendicular bisector of each line segment.

a) b)

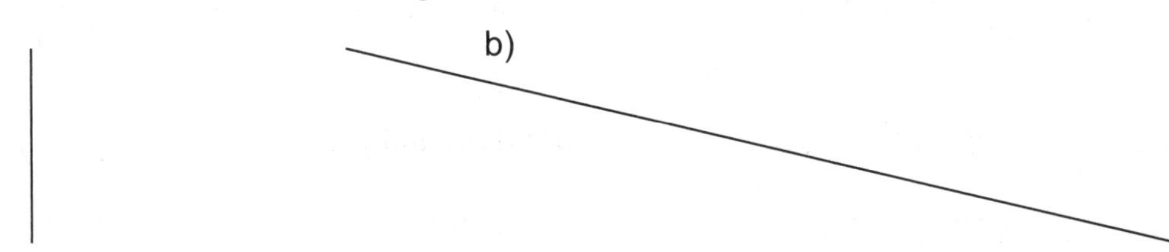

8. Use the diagram to fill in the blanks.

a) D is the midpoint of ____.

b) BH is perpendicular to ____.

c) The intersection point of CE and FG is ____.

d) FG is the perpendicular bisector of ____.

e) CE is a bisector of ____.

f) Can you tell for sure from the diagram whether $CB = BA$?

Why or why not? ________________________

____

____

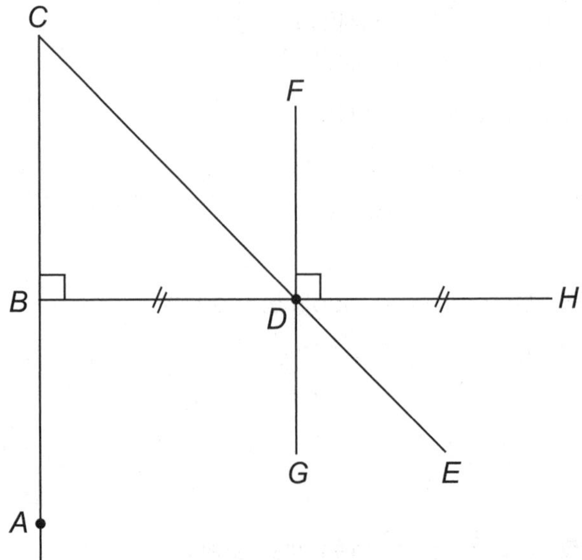

9. a) Circle the capital letters in the set below that contain perpendicular bisectors.

A E F H I K L M N T V W X Y Z

b) Perpendicular bisectors are seen in window frames, bookshelves, the letter E, and so on. Describe other examples of perpendicular bisectors seen in the world around you.

G7-6 Parallel Lines

Parallel lines never intersect, no matter how far they are extended in either direction.

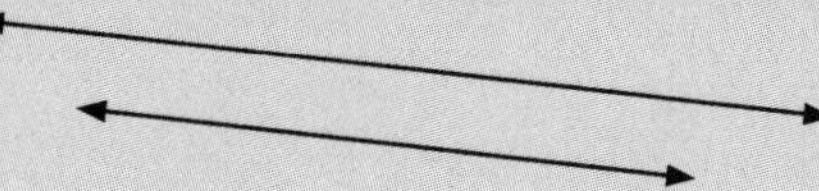

1. Extend both lines. Use a ruler. Do the lines intersect or are they parallel? ______________

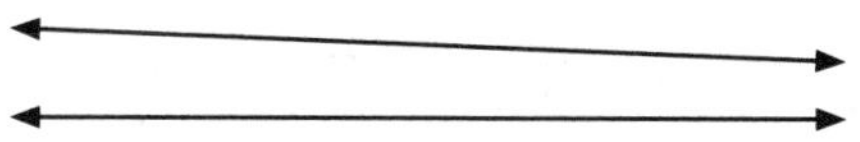

2. Match the descriptions to the lines.

   A. The lines intersect.
   B. If the lines were extended far enough, they would intersect.
   C. The lines are parallel.

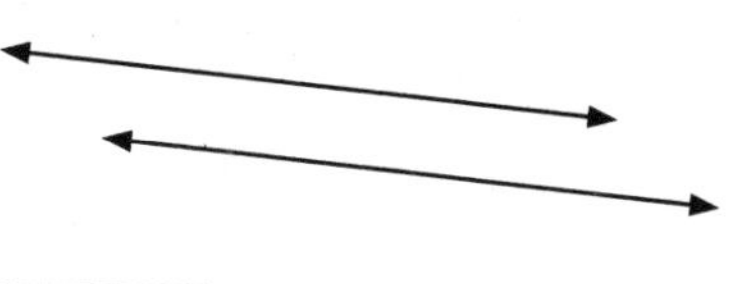

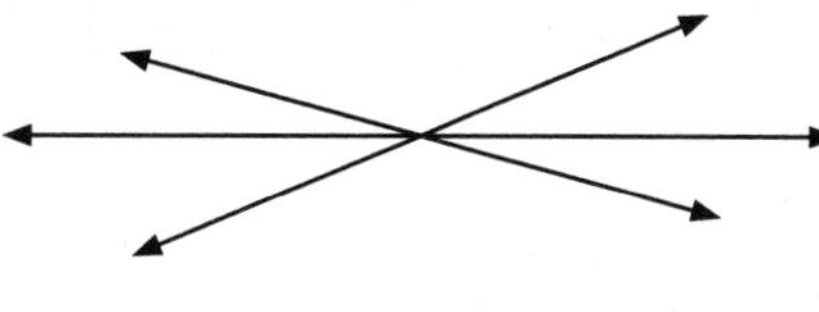

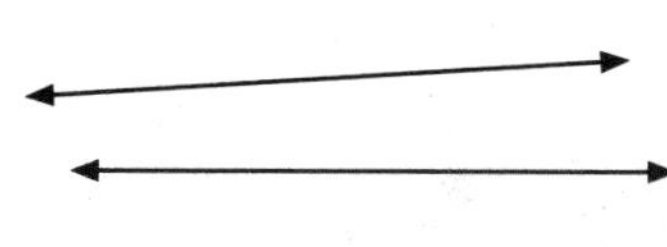

______ ______ ______

3. Give two examples of parallel lines in the world around you.

____

We mark parallel lines using an equal number of arrow symbols (>, >>, and so on). The || symbol means "is parallel to."

Example: AB || CD.

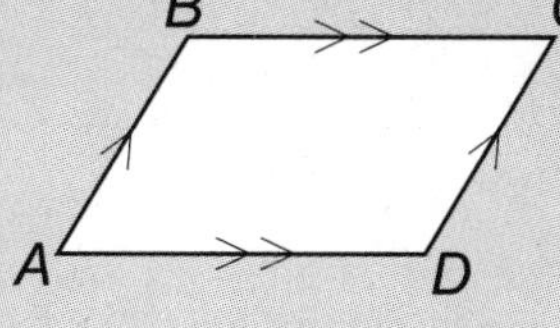

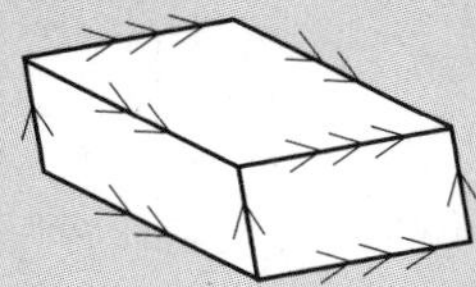

4. Use arrow symbols to mark the sides or edges of these shapes that look like they are parallel.

a) 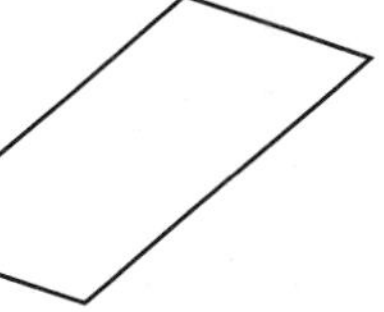

b) 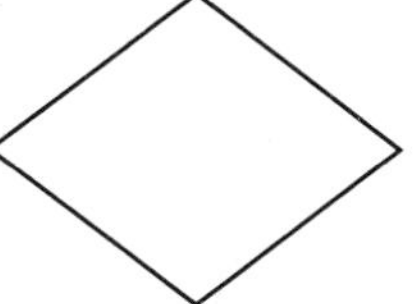

c) 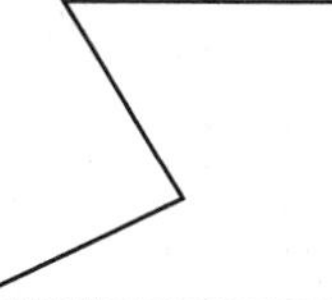

d) 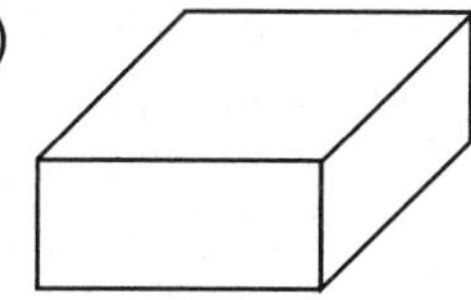

5. State which lines are parallel.

a) 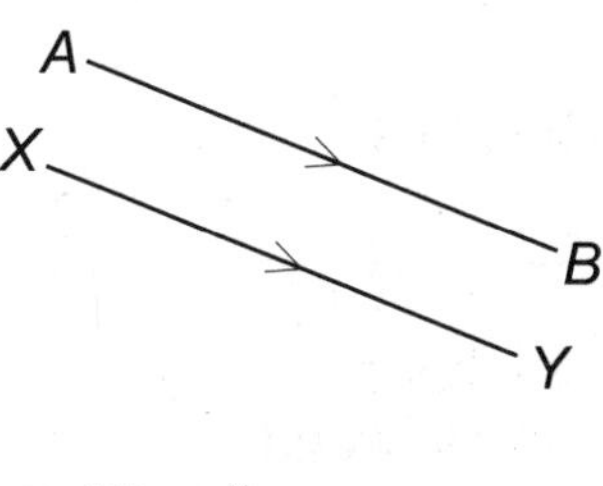

b) 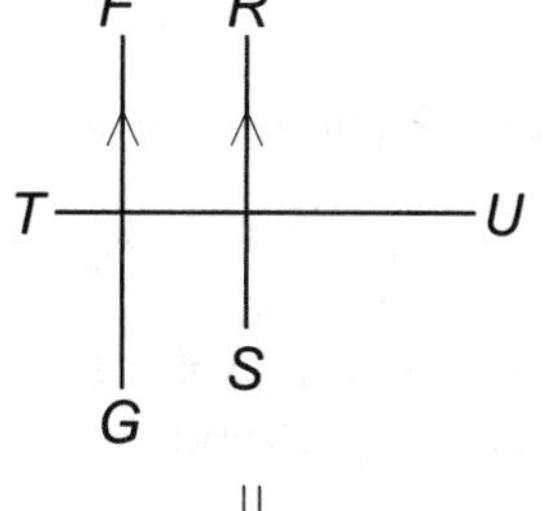

c) 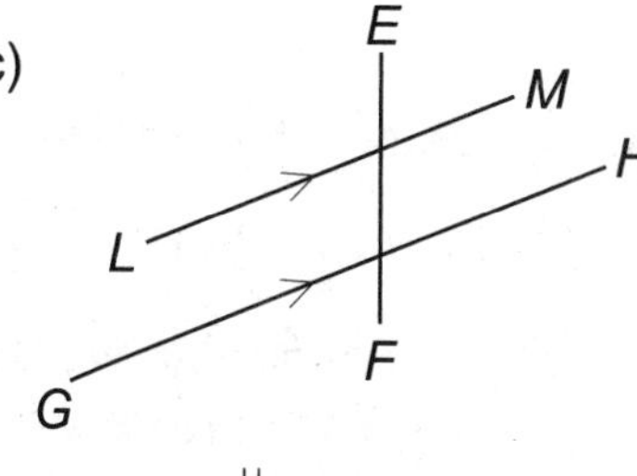

a) AB || ______ b) ______ || ______ c) ______ || ______

Determining If Two Lines Are Parallel

If two lines are perpendicular to another line, then they are parallel.

If two lines are parallel, any line perpendicular to one of the parallel lines will be perpendicular to the other.

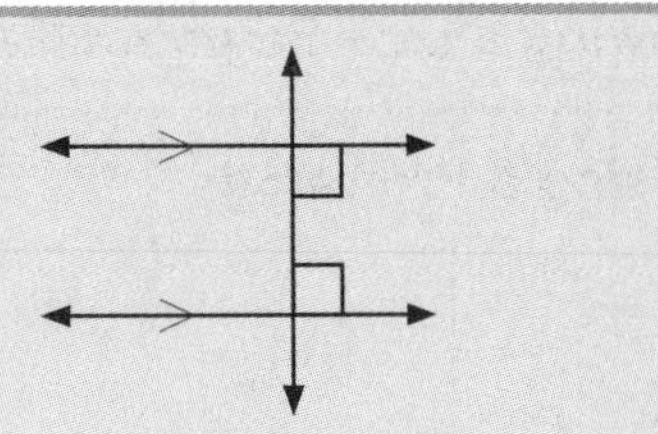

6. Mark any parallel lines. State which lines are parallel.

a) 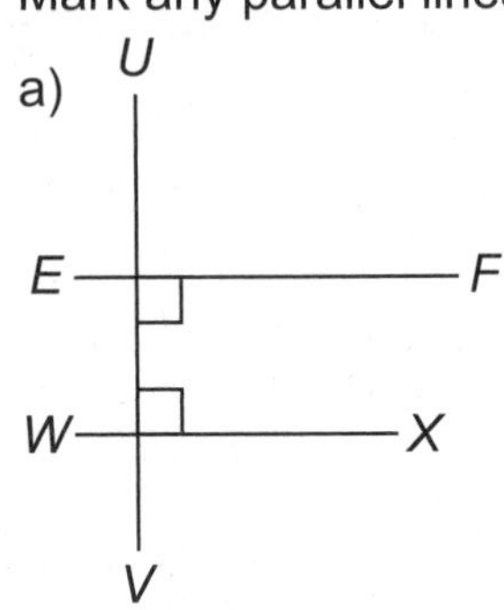

b) 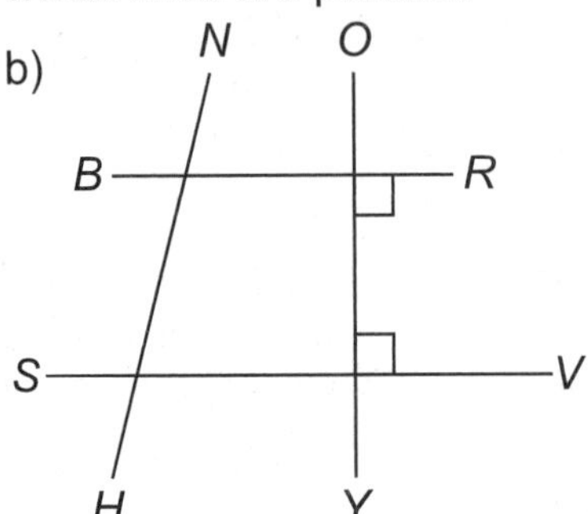

c) 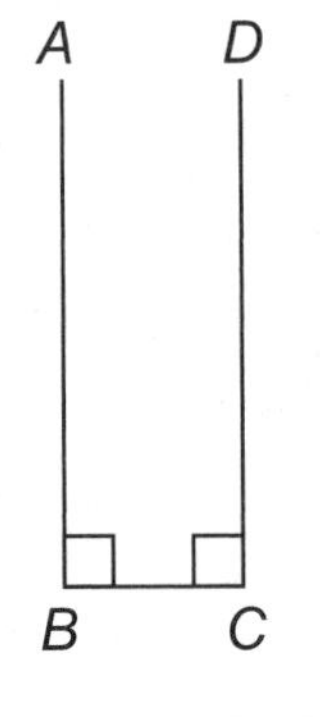

d) 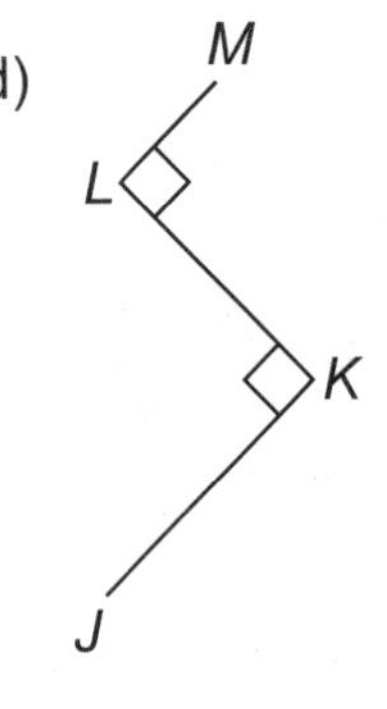

EF || ______   ______ || ______   ______ || ______   ______ || ______

7. Complete the statements.

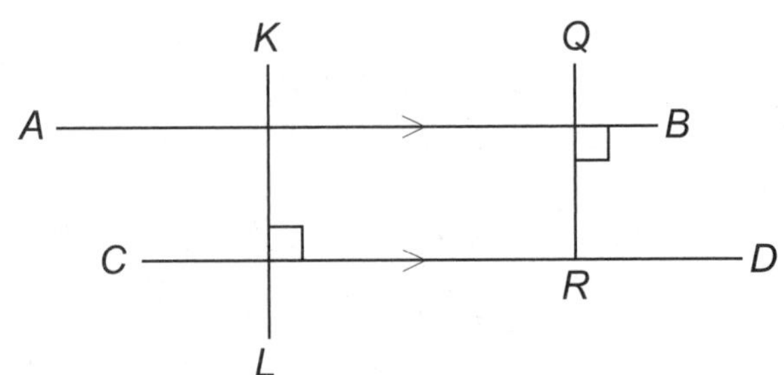

a) AB is parallel to ______ and

KL is perpendicular to CD, so

KL is also perpendicular to ______.

b) AB || ______ and $QR \perp$ ______, so, $QR \perp$ ______.

8. a) All the angles in a rectangle are right angles.

Mark the right angles on this rectangle.

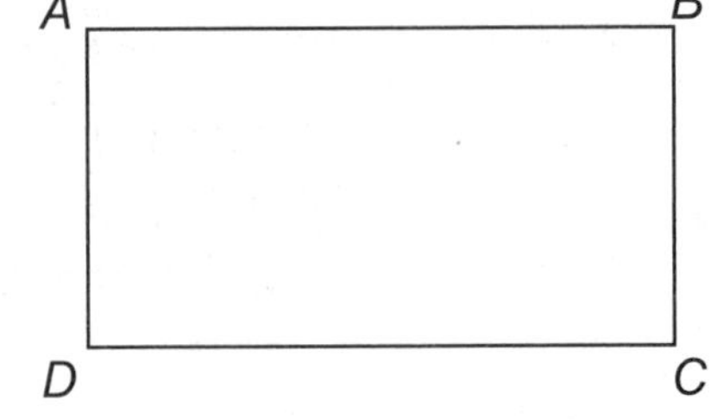

b) $AD \perp AB$ and $AD \perp$ ______, so AB || ______

$DC \perp AD$ and $DC \perp$ ______, so AD || ______

c) Explain how you know that these pairs of sides are parallel.

____

9. Circle the flags that contain parallel lines (not counting the edges of the flags).

Drawing a Line Segment Parallel to *AB* Through Point *P*

Using a Protractor

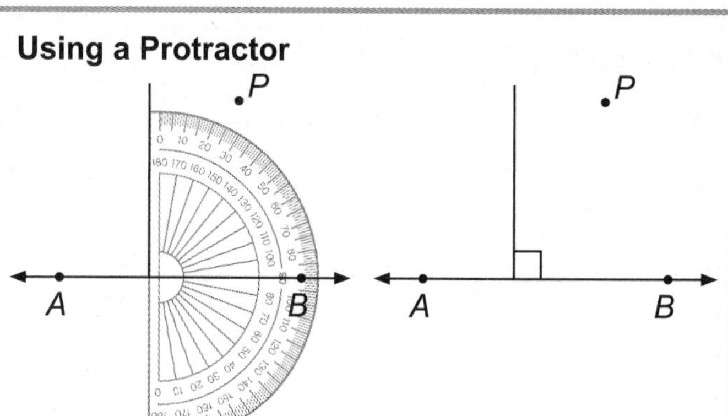

Step 1: Line up the 90° line on the protractor with *AB*. Use the base of the protractor to draw a line segment perpendicular to *AB*.

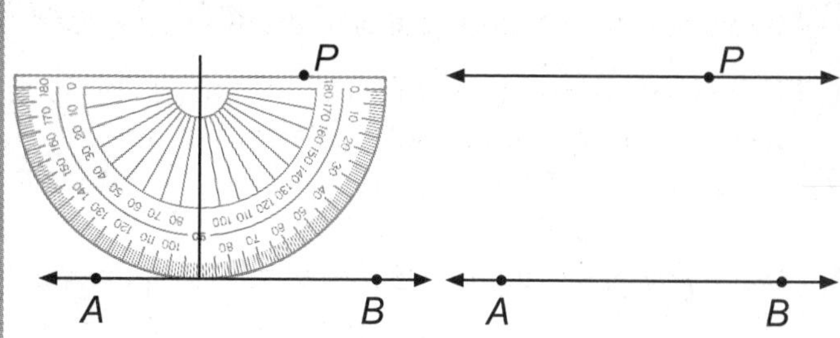

Step 2: Line up the 90° line on the protractor with the line segment drawn in step 1, and the base of the protractor with point *P*. Draw a line parallel to *AB*. Erase the first perpendicular you drew.

10. Draw a line through *P* parallel to *AB*.

a)

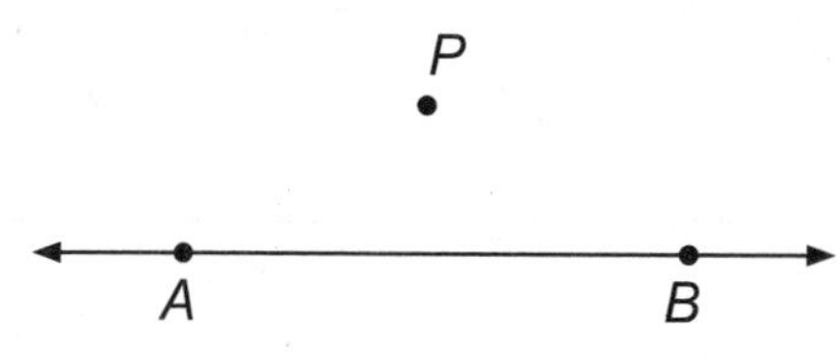

b)

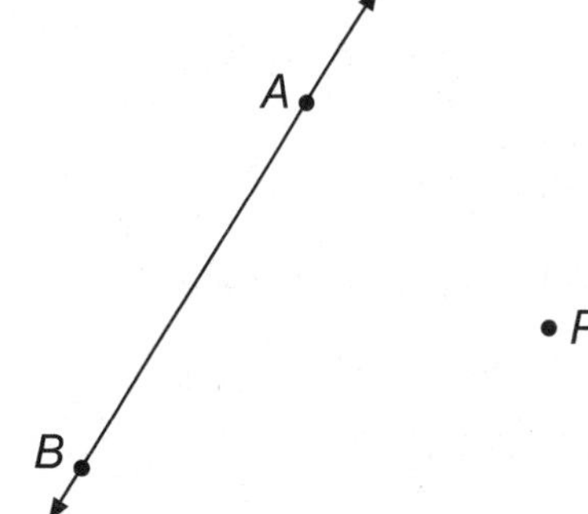

• *P*

11. A **regular** polygon has sides that are all the same length and angles that are all the same size.

a) Write the number of sides of each regular polygon below.

b) Mark all the pairs of parallel sides. Then write the number of pairs of parallel sides.

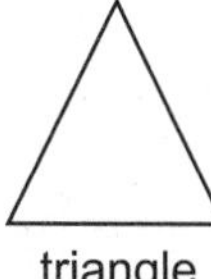
triangle

square

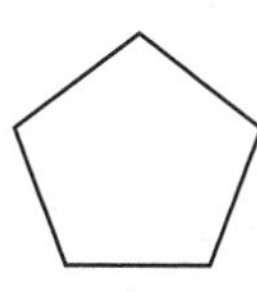
pentagon

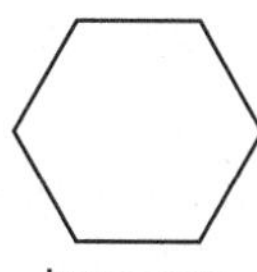
hexagon

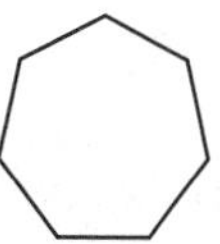
heptagon

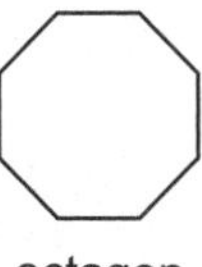
octagon

Number of sides	3	4	______	______	______	______
Pairs of parallel sides	0	2	______	______	______	______

c) Predict when a regular polygon will have parallel sides. How do you know?

BONUS▸ How many parallel sides could a non-regular quadrilateral (shape with 4 sides) have?

12. Use parallel and perpendicular lines to draw a rectangle.

G7-7 Angle Relationships

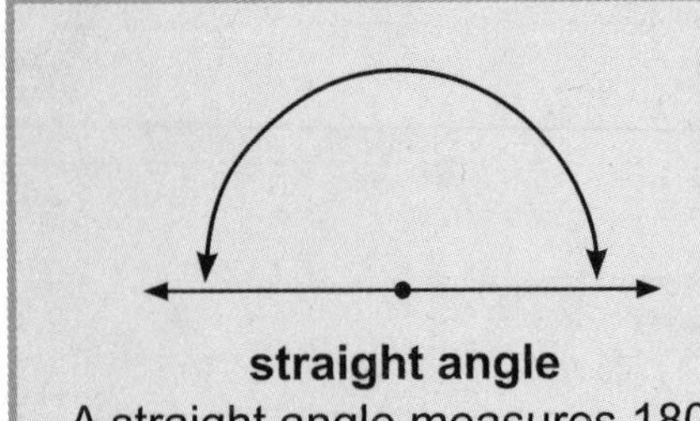

straight angle
A straight angle measures 180°.

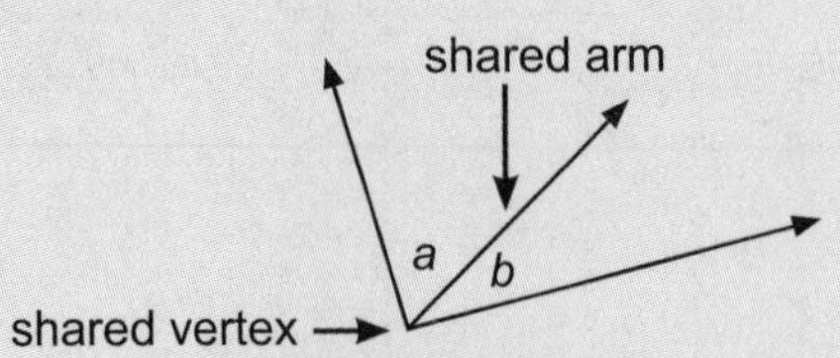

adjacent angles
Adjacent angles $\angle a$ and $\angle b$ have a shared vertex and arm.

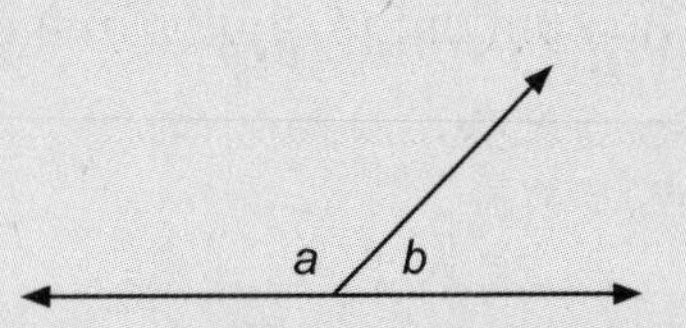

linear pair
The sum of the angles in a linear pair is 180°.

1. Match the diagrams to the names. Hint: The angles in a linear pair are also adjacent angles.

   straight angle: _____ adjacent angles: _____ linear pair: _____

   A. 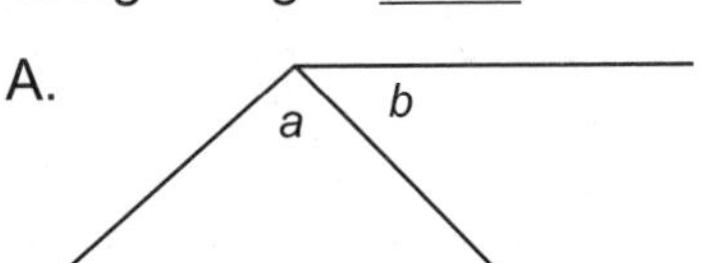

   B. 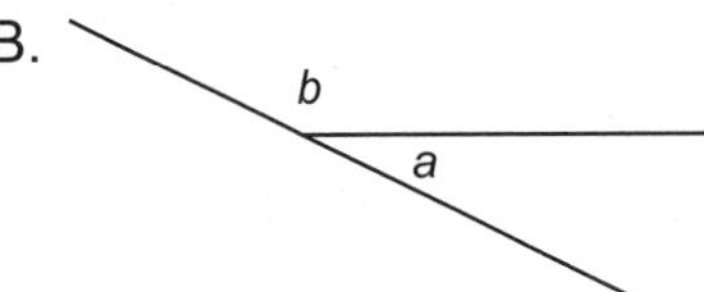

   C. 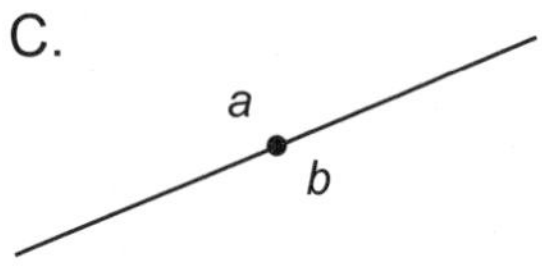

2. Calculate these angle sums.

   a) $10° + 25° =$ _____ b) $30° + 40° =$ _____ c) $12° + 28° =$ _____ d) $20° + 30° + 40° =$ _____

3. $\angle 1$ and $\angle 2$ are a linear pair. Identify the three other linear pairs in the diagram.

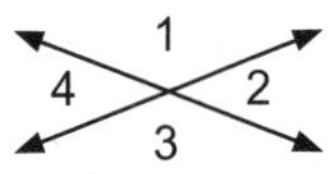

   $\angle$_____ and $\angle$_____ $\angle$_____ and $\angle$_____ $\angle$_____ and $\angle$_____

4. Determine the sum of the angles formed by **two lines that intersect at a right angle**.

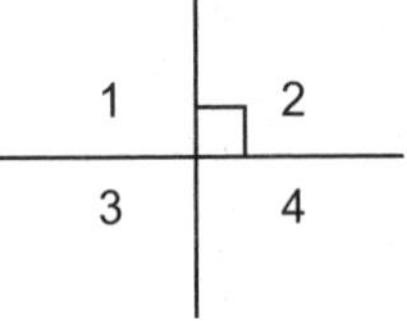

   $\angle 1 + \angle 2 = 90° + 90° =$ _____° $\angle 3 + \angle 4 = 90° + 90° =$ _____°

   So, $\angle 1 + \angle 2 + \angle 3 + \angle 4$ _____° + _____° = _____°

5. Determine the sum of the angles formed by **any two intersecting lines**.

   The sum of the angles in a linear pair is _____°.

   So, $\angle 1 + \angle 2 =$ _____° and $\angle 3 + \angle 4 =$ _____°

   So, $\angle 1 + \angle 2 + \angle 3 + \angle 4 =$ _____°

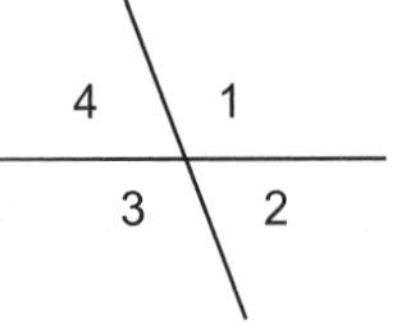

6. Predict the sum of the four angles around any point P. _____°

   Calculate these angle sums to check your prediction.

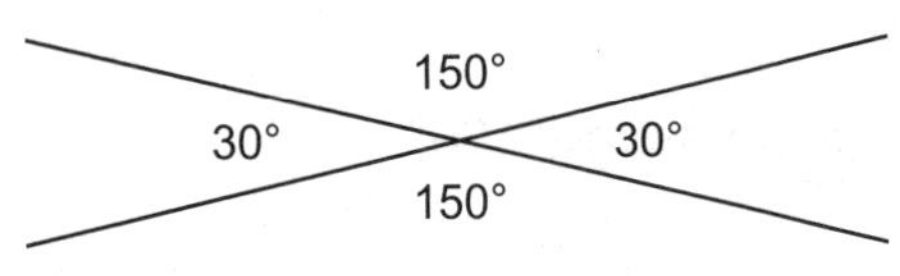

   $30° + 150° + 30° + 150° =$ _____

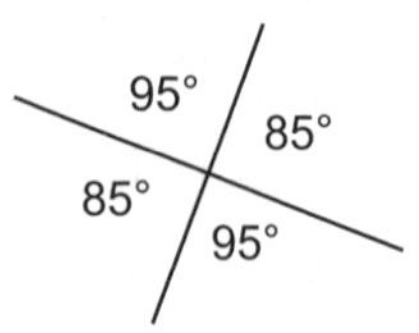

   $95° + 85° + 95° + 85° =$ _____

7. Determine the measure of $\angle XZY$.

The sum of the angles in a triangle is ____°.

So, $\angle XZY =$ ____° – (60° + 90°)

= ____° – ____°

= ____°

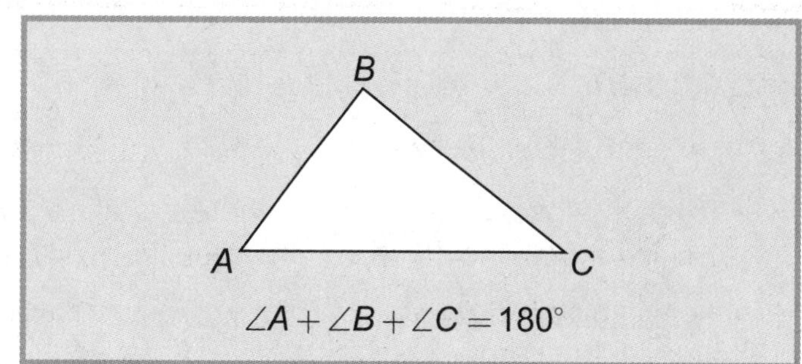

8. Determine the measure of $\angle A$ in each triangle.

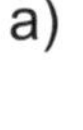
a)

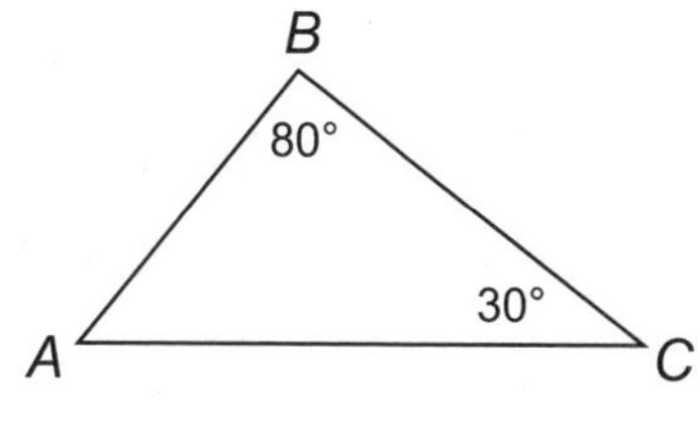

$\angle A = 180° - (80° + 30°)$

= ____°

b)

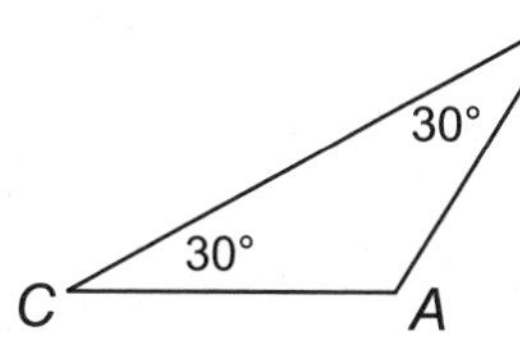

$\angle A = 180° -$ (____° + ____°)

= ____°

c)

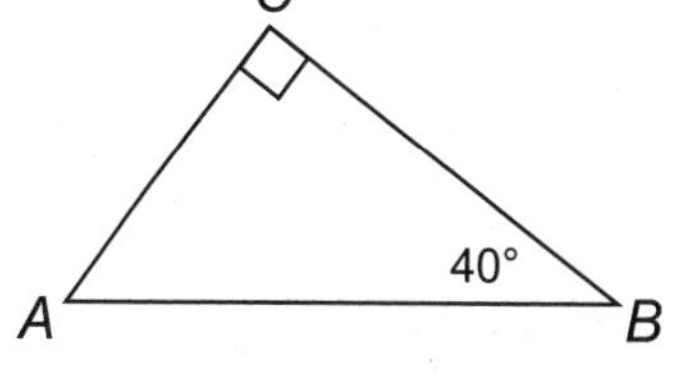

$\angle A =$ ____° – (____° + ____°)

= ____°

9. Determine the measure of $\angle F$ in ΔDEF without doing any calculations. _______

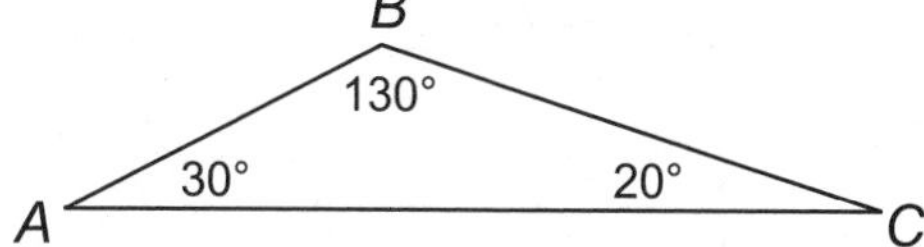

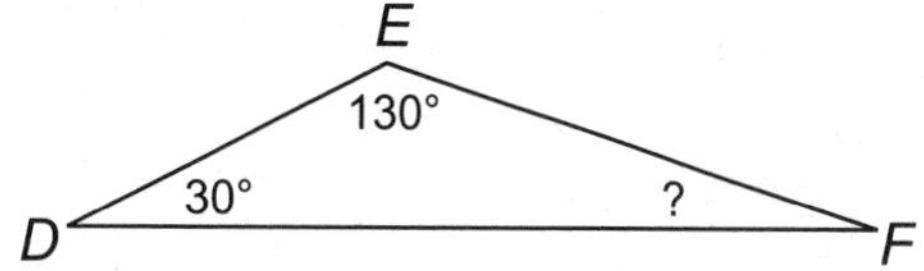

10. a) A triangle has a 30° angle and a 60° angle. What is the third angle in the triangle? ____

b) A triangle has two 45° angles. What is the third angle in the triangle? ____

c) A triangle has all angles equal. What is the measure of each angle? ____

11. a) Could a triangle ever have more than one obtuse angle? Use a sketch to help you explain.
b) Could a triangle ever have more than one right angle? Use a sketch to help you explain.

12. a) Measure and mark the angles on each set square.

b) Use set squares to draw two lines that intersect at a

i) 30° angle   ii) 45° angle   iii) 60° angle

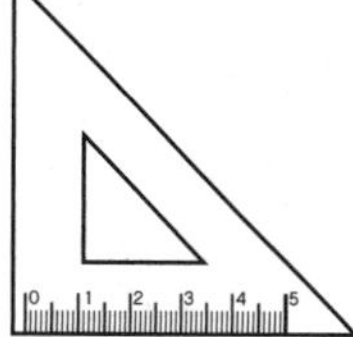

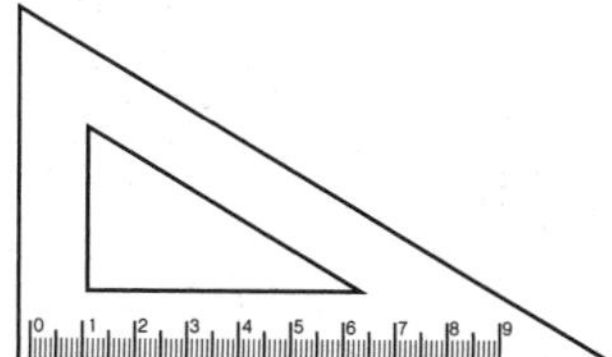

13. a) A triangle has two equal angles. One of the angles in this triangle measures 20°. What are the other angles? (Hint: There are two solutions. Try sketching the possibilities.)

b) A triangle has two equal angles. One of the angles in this triangle measures 100°. What are the other angles?

c) How are problems a) and b) different? Why do they have a different number of solutions?

G7-8 Triangle Properties

INVESTIGATION 1 ▶ Relating sides and angles

A. In each triangle below:

- Trace the longest side blue. (If there are 2 longest sides, trace both blue. If the 3 sides are all the same length, trace them all blue.)
- Trace the shortest side red. (If there are 2 shortest sides, trace them both red.)
- Circle the greatest angle in blue. (If there are 2 greatest angles, circle both in blue. If the 3 angles are all equal, circle them all in blue.)
- Circle the smallest angle in red. (If there are 2 smallest angles, circle both in red.)

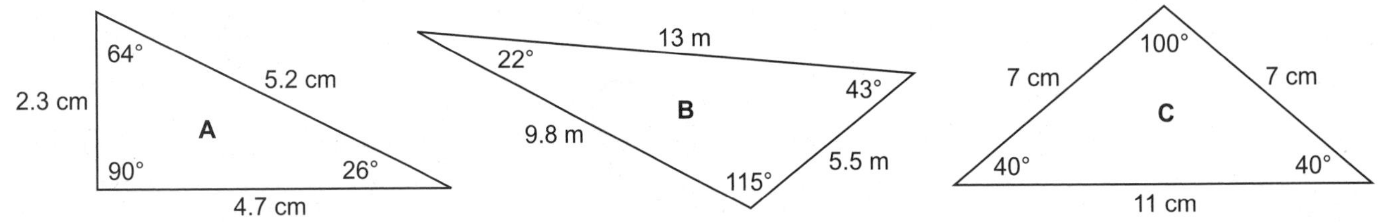

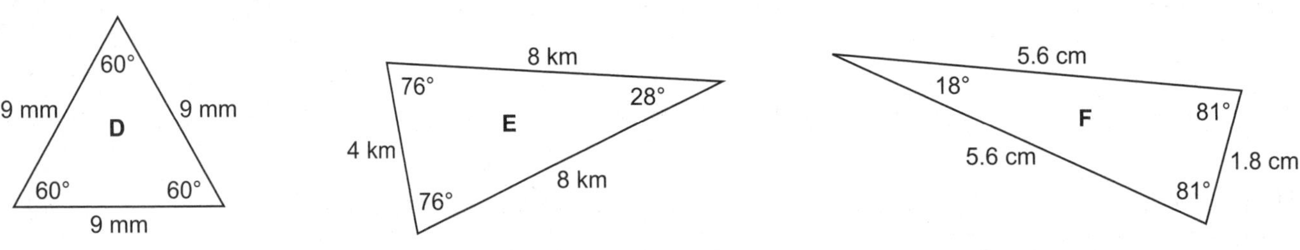

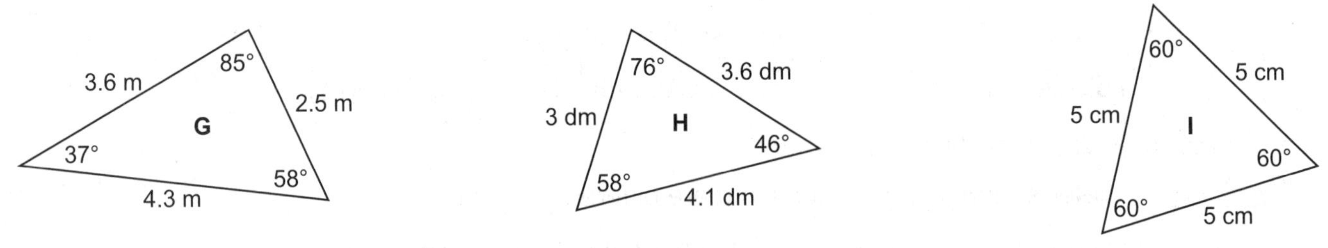

B. Mark each statement True or False. Use the triangles above to help you decide.

_______ The side opposite the greatest angle in a triangle is always the longest side.

_______ The side opposite the smallest angle in a triangle is always the shortest side.

_______ If one angle in a triangle is 90°, then two of the sides are equal.

_______ If two angles of a triangle are equal, then the sides opposite them are of equal length.

_______ If all three angles in a triangle are equal, then all three sides are also equal.

INVESTIGATION 2 ▶ Classifying triangles

In the triangles below:

- Obtuse angles are circled.
- Right angles have a square corner.
- All other angles are acute.

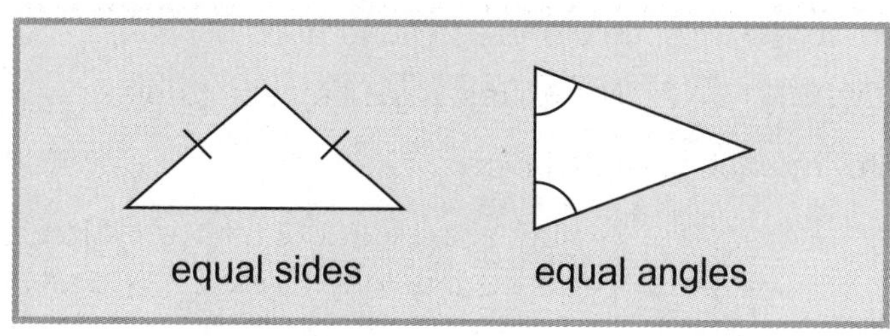

A. Which of the triangles match each description?

- All sides are equal. ____________
- 2 sides are equal. ____________
- No sides are equal. ____________
- 1 angle is a right angle. ____________
- All angles are acute. ____________
- 1 angle is obtuse. ____________

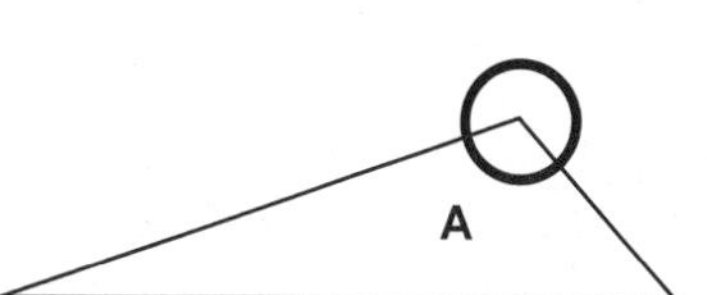

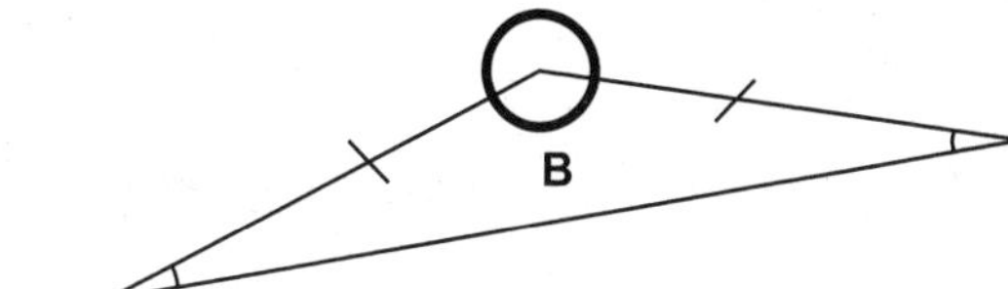

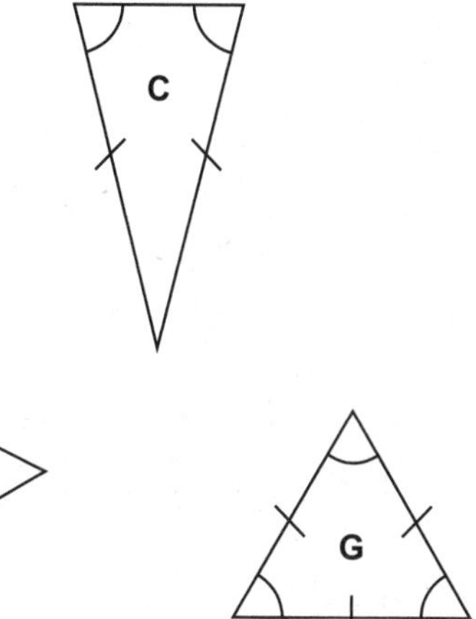

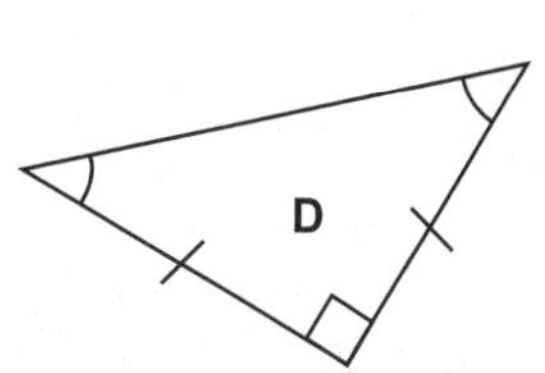

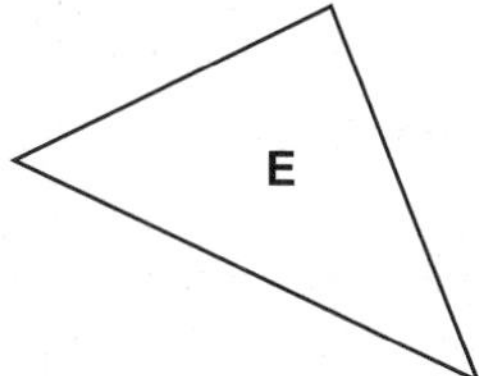

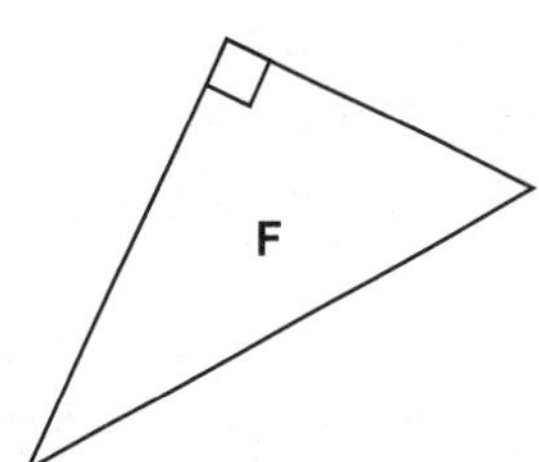

B. Match the triangles to the definitions. If more than one triangle matches the description, name both.

Classifying triangles by angle measures

_______ A **right** triangle has one right angle (90°).

_______ An **acute** triangle has all angles less than 90° (all acute angles).

_______ An **obtuse** triangle has one angle greater than 90° (1 obtuse angle).

Classifying triangles by side lengths

_______ A **scalene** triangle has 3 sides that are different lengths.

_______ An **isosceles** triangle has 2 sides that are the same length.

_______ An **equilateral** triangle has 3 sides that are the same length.

C. Look at the angle measures in the isosceles triangles. What do you notice?

____

Look at angle measures in the equilateral triangle. What do you notice?

____

1. Classify each triangle described below using angle measures. Determine the third angle before deciding.

   a) Two of the angles are 30°.
   The other angle is 180° − (30° + 30°) = ____°.
   This is an ______________ triangle.

   b) Two of the angles are 50° and 40°.
   The other angle is 180° − (50° + 40°) = ____°.
   This is a ______________ triangle.

   c) Two of the angles are 75° and 25°.
   The other angle is 180° − (75° + 25°) = ____°.
   This is an ______________ triangle.

2. Classify each triangle described below using side lengths.

   a) The sides are 5 cm, 6 cm, and 7 cm.
   There are ____ equal sides.
   This is a ______________ triangle.

   b) The sides are 8 cm, 7 cm, and 8 cm.
   There are ____ equal sides.
   This is an ______________ triangle.

   c) The sides are 5 m, 5 m, and 5 m.
   There are ____ equal sides.
   This is an ______________ triangle.

   BONUS ▶ Two of the sides are 10 cm.
   The triangle is __________ or __________ .

3. An isosceles triangle has sides 4 m and 6 m. What are the two possible lengths for the third side?

4. Draw an example of each of the six types of triangles. Use triangle grid or triangle dot paper. Mark equal sides and angles. Label each triangle. Your triangles can have any measurements so long as they match the definitions.

5. a) Check off the combinations that are possible triangles. (Example: a right scalene triangle is possible.)

   b) Two of the combinations are not possible. Which combinations are these? Explain why they are impossible.

	right	**acute**	**obtuse**
scalene	✓		
isosceles			
equilateral			

6. Name each triangle.

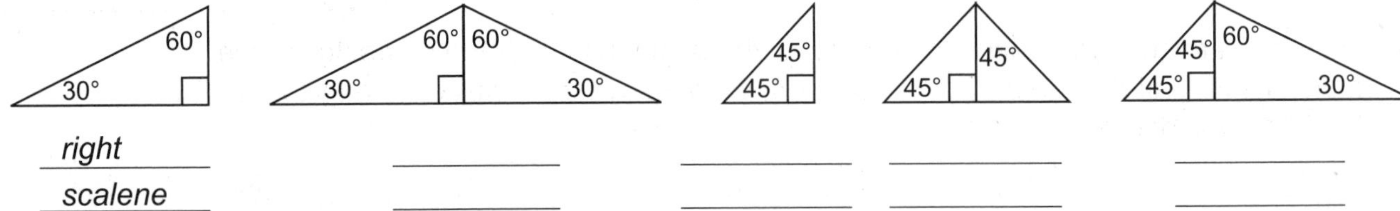

right ______ ______ ______ ______
scalene ______ ______ ______ ______

7. a) Draw and label these triangles. Mark any equal sides and angles.

   i) $\triangle JKL$, a right triangle with $\angle J = 60^\circ$
   ii) $\triangle ABC$, a right triangle with $\angle A = 90^\circ$ and $AC = 5$ cm
   iii) $\triangle MNO$, an equilateral triangle with $MN = 7$ cm and $\angle MNO = 60^\circ$

   b) For each triangle in part a), predict whether you can use the same instructions to draw a different triangle. Explain your prediction. Try to draw a different triangle to check your prediction.

G7-9 Angle Bisectors

1. Use small marks (like the ones you use to show equal sides of shapes) to show the equal angles formed by the angle bisectors.

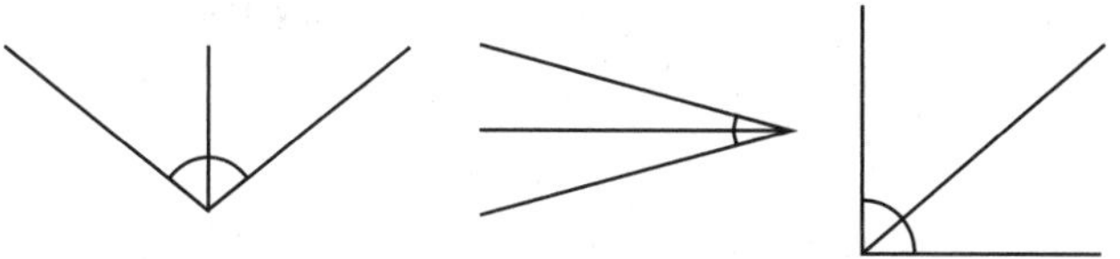

An **angle bisector** divides an angle in half.

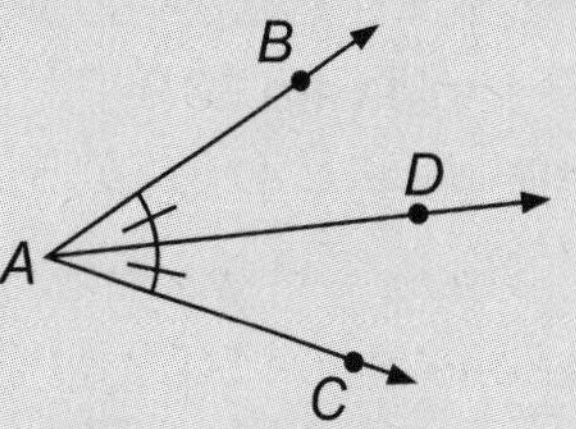

AD bisects $\angle BAC$, so $\angle BAD = \angle CAD$.

2. AD bisects $\angle CAB$. Determine the measure of $\angle BAD$ and $\angle BAC$.

a)

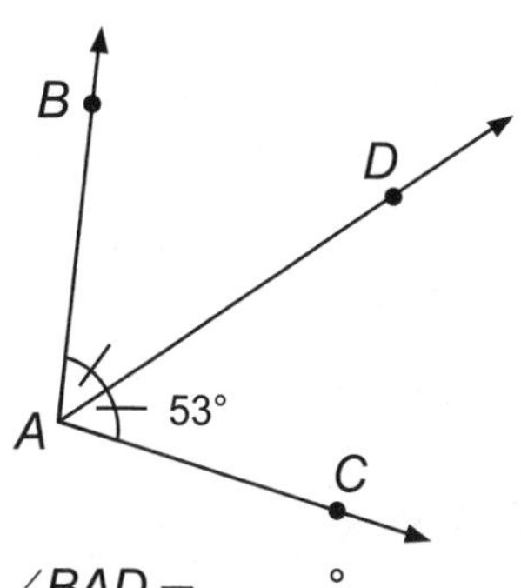

$\angle BAD =$ ____°

$\angle BAC =$ ____° + ____°

$=$ ____°

b)

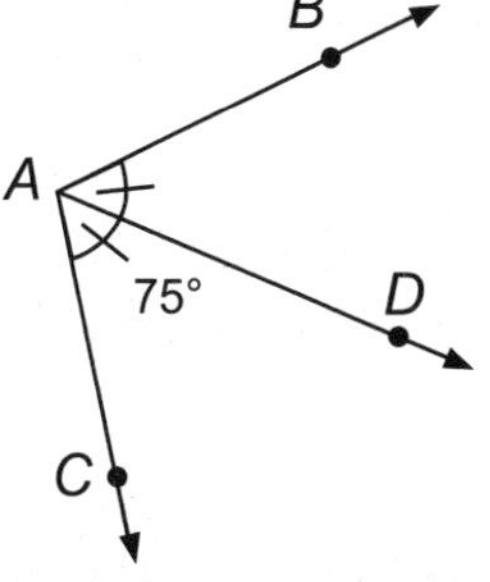

$\angle BAD =$ ____°

$\angle BAC =$ ____° + ____°

$=$ ____°

c)

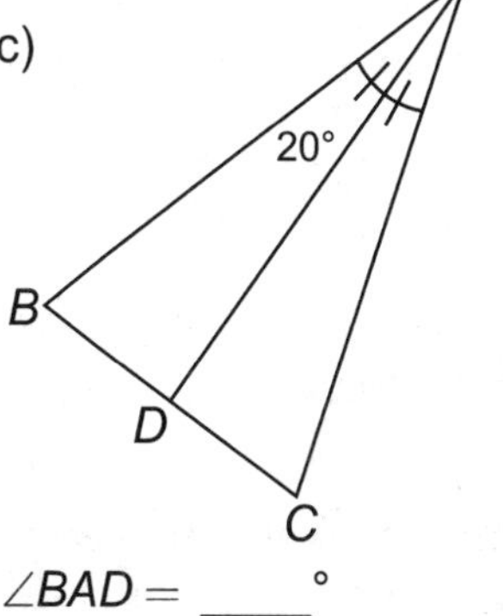

$\angle BAD =$ ____°

$\angle BAC =$ ____° + ____°

$=$ ____°

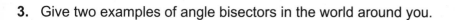

3. Give two examples of angle bisectors in the world around you.

____

4. A diagonal line connects two vertices of a rectangle. Is this line an angle bisector? Predict, then measure to check.

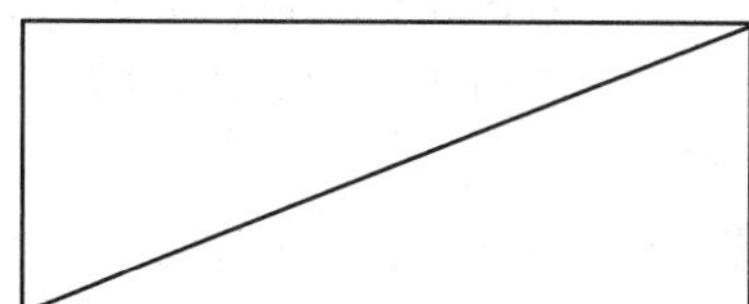

5. Draw each angle. Then draw the bisector of the angle. (Note: Some protractors have markings for half-degrees. If yours does not, estimate where to place the angle mark for a half of a degree.)

a) 38° b) 112° c) 98° d) 57° e) 69°

6. If an acute angle is bisected, the result is two smaller acute angles. If an obtuse angle is bisected, could the result be two obtuse angles? Explain.

Hint: An obtuse angle is between ____° and ____°,

so half of an obtuse angle is between ____° and ____°.

7. This angle bisector has divided the triangle into two identical triangles. Sketch a counter-example to show that this does not always happen.

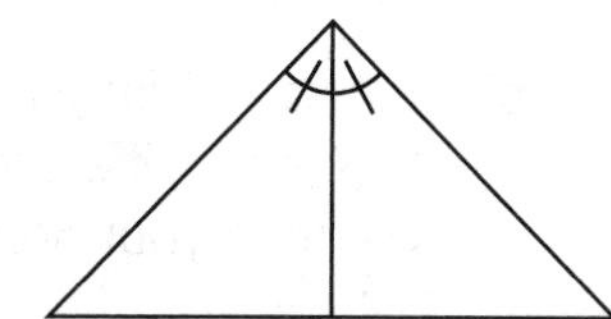

G7-10 Quadrilateral Properties

A **quadrilateral** is a polygon with 4 sides.

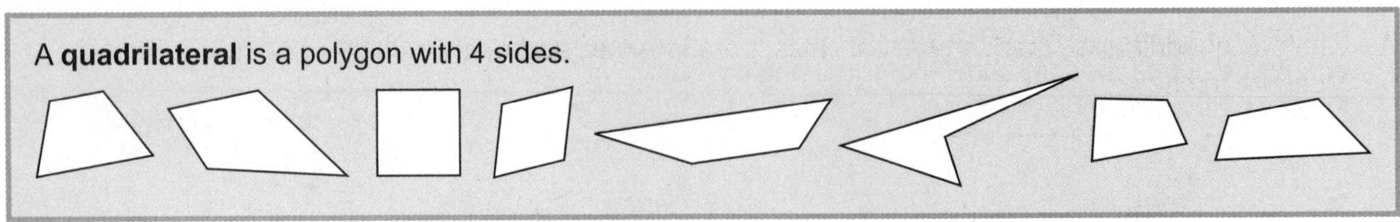

INVESTIGATION 1 ▶ Special quadrilaterals

A. Some quadrilaterals have **all sides equal**. Take 4 straws of equal length. Make at least three different quadrilaterals using these 4 straws. Sketch each quadrilateral you make.

B. Some quadrilaterals have **2 pairs of equal sides**. Take 2 straws of one length and 2 straws of another length. Make at least three different quadrilaterals using these 4 straws. Try placing the sides in different orders. Sketch each quadrilateral you make.

C. Some quadrilaterals have **2 pairs of parallel sides**. Look at the sketches you made. On your sketches, mark any pairs of sides you think are parallel.

pairs of equal sides

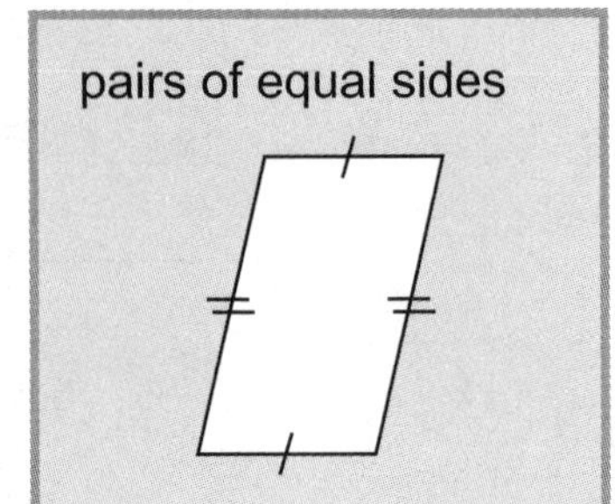

1. Check the properties these four quadrilaterals share.

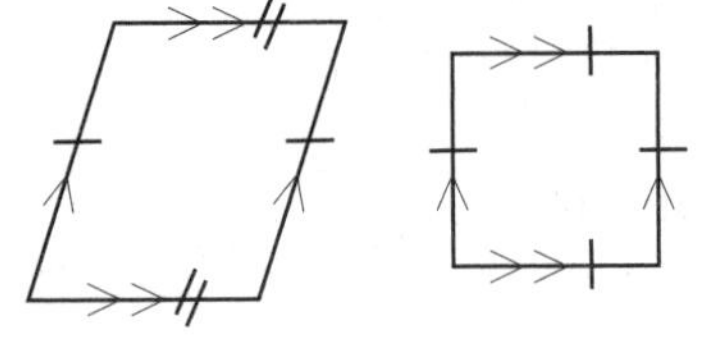
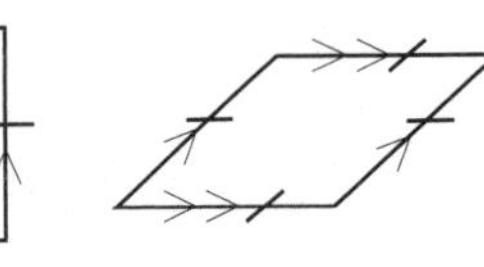
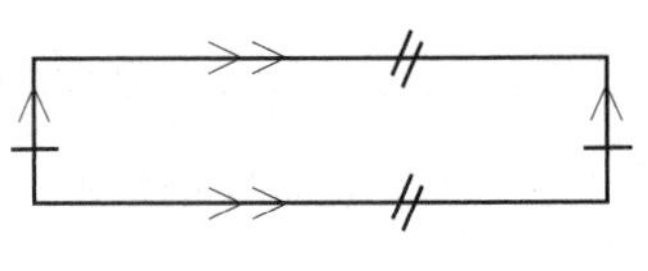

- ☐ all sides equal
- ☐ 2 pairs of equal sides
- ☐ 2 pairs of parallel sides

2. Check the properties these three quadrilaterals share.

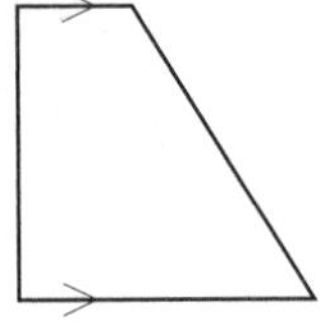
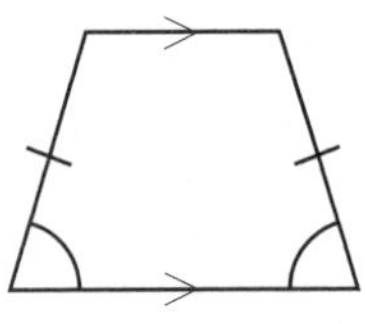
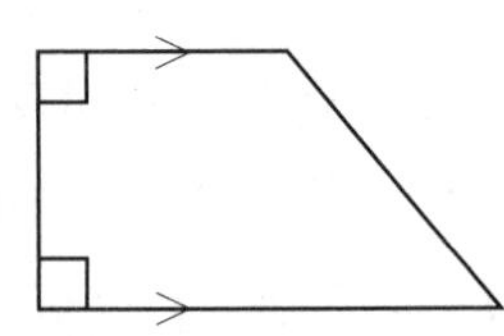

- ☐ all sides equal
- ☐ 1 pair of equal sides
- ☐ 1 pair of parallel sides

3. What is the same about these two quadrilaterals?

____

____

What is different? ____________________

____

____

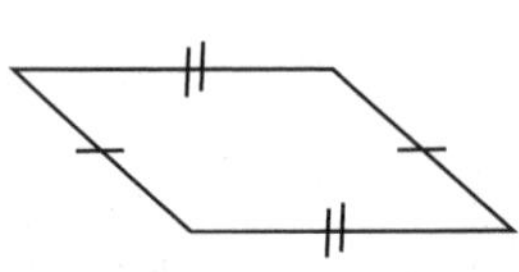
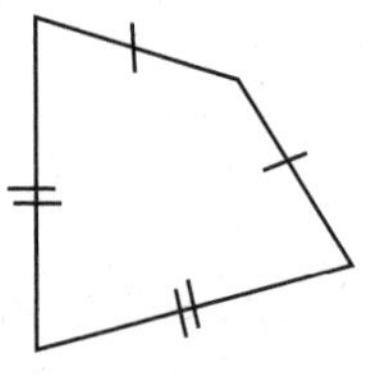

INVESTIGATION 2 ▶ Classifying quadrilaterals

A. On each quadrilateral, mark any equal sides, parallel sides, and right angles. Measure to check.

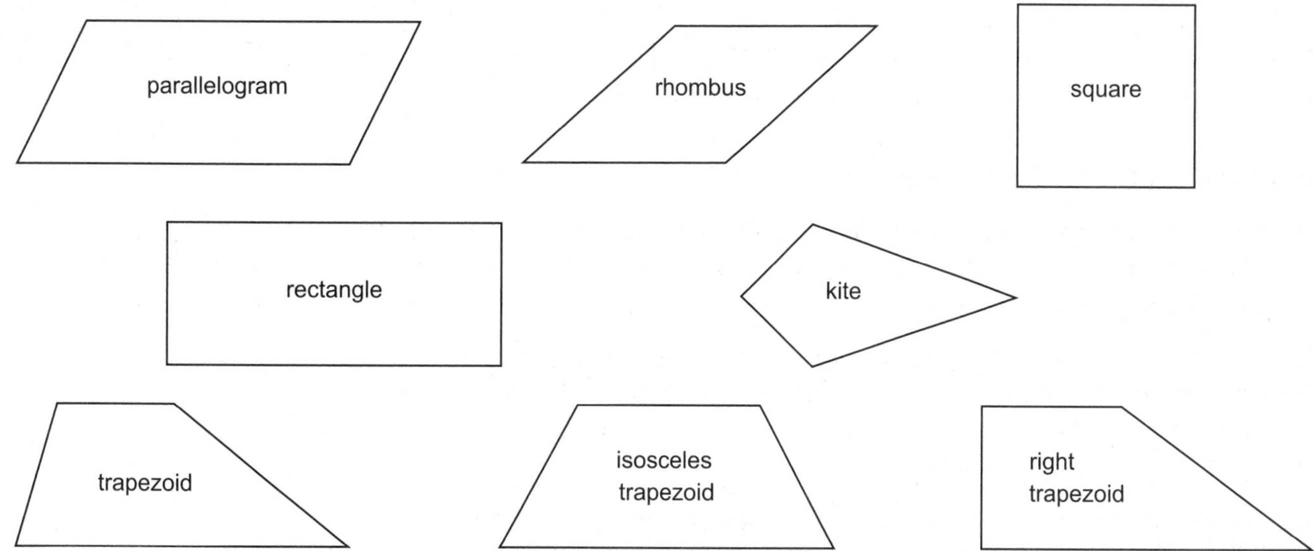

B. Read the definitions in part C. On the shapes in part A, mark any equal or parallel sides you missed.

C. List all the types of quadrilaterals that fit each definition.

i) A **parallelogram** has 2 pairs of parallel sides. _____ *parallelogram, rhombus,* _____

____

ii) A **rhombus** has all sides equal. _______________

iii) A **rectangle** has all right angles. _______________

iv) A **square** has all sides equal and all right angles. _______________

v) A **trapezoid** has exactly 1 pair of parallel sides.

An **isosceles trapezoid** also has 1 pair of equal sides.

A **right trapezoid** also has 2 right angles.

vi) A **kite** has 2 pairs of equal adjacent sides. ("Adjacent" means "right next to one another.")

____

D. Measure the angles in the quadrilaterals in part A. Mark any equal angles in each shape. Then list all the special quadrilaterals that have...

i) all angles equal. _______________

ii) opposite angles equal. _______________

iii) 2 pairs of equal angles. _______________

pairs of equal angles

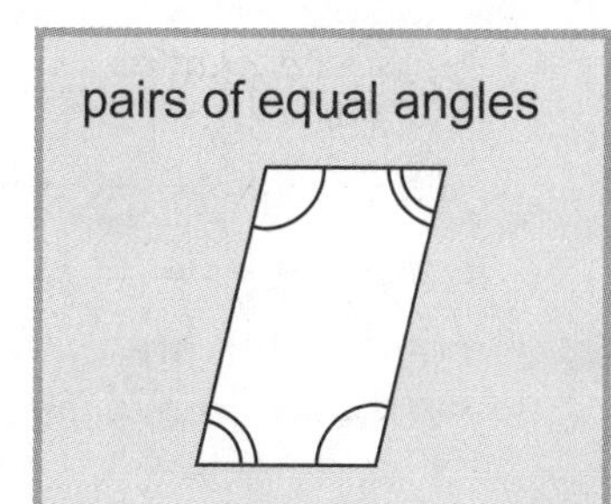

G7-11 Symmetry

A **line of symmetry** divides a figure into two parts that are exactly the same shape and size AND, if the figure is folded along the line of symmetry, the parts will fit on top of each other exactly.

This dotted line **is** a line of symmetry.

This dotted line **is not** a line of symmetry.

REMINDER▶ "Regular" means having all angles and sides equal.

INVESTIGATION 1▶

A. Draw all the lines of symmetry for each shape.

a)

equilateral triangle

b)

square

c)

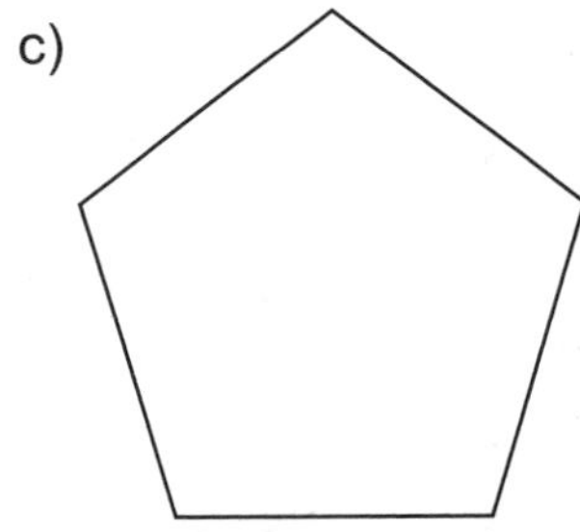

regular pentagon

d)

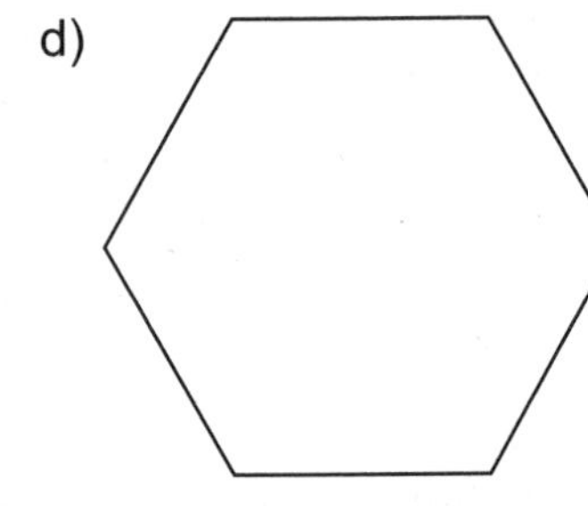

regular hexagon

B. Complete the chart.

Figure	Triangle	Square	Pentagon	Hexagon
Number of edges				
Number of lines of symmetry				

C. Describe any relation you see between the number of lines of symmetry in a regular polygon and the number of edges it has.

---

1. Brenda says the line shown here is a line of symmetry. Is she correct? ___________

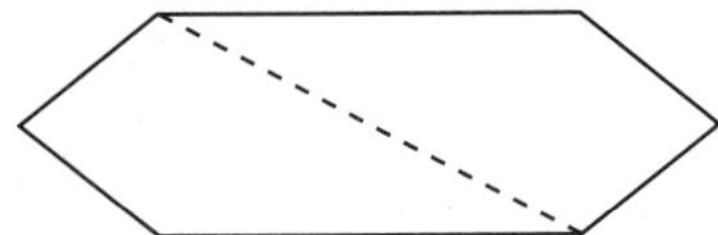

2. On grid paper, draw a figure with **exactly** two lines of symmetry. Explain how you know there are exactly two lines of symmetry.

Lines of symmetry in polygons are either angle bisectors or perpendicular bisectors of sides, or both.

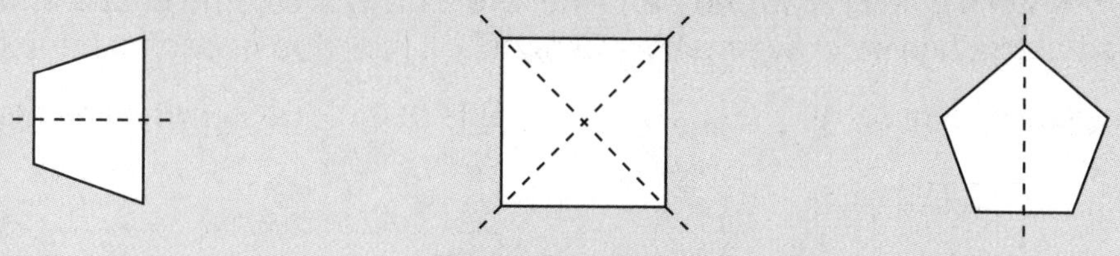

lines of symmetry

INVESTIGATION 2 ▶ Symmetry and bisectors

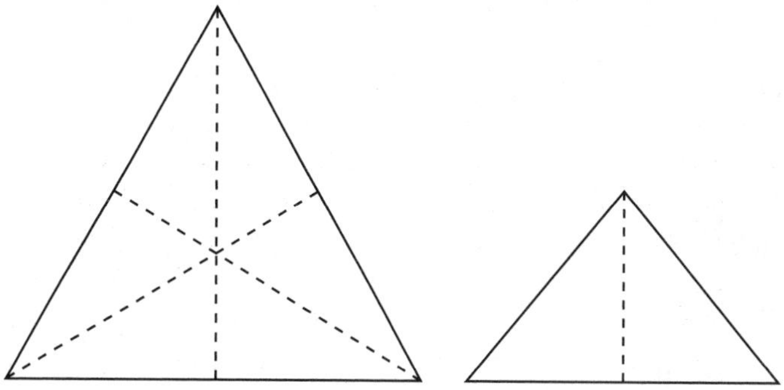

A. An equilateral triangle has 3 lines of symmetry.
An isosceles triangle has 1 line of symmetry.
Are these lines of symmetry angle bisectors?

______

Are these lines of symmetry perpendicular bisectors of sides? ______ Measure to check.

B.

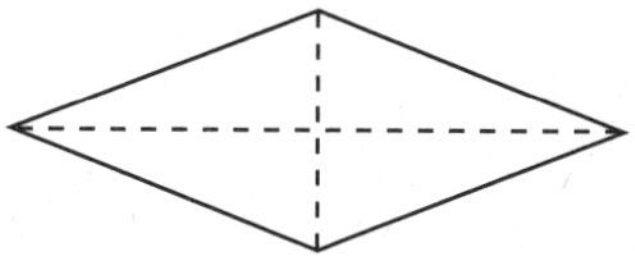

A rhombus has 2 lines of symmetry.

They are both ___*angle bisectors*___.

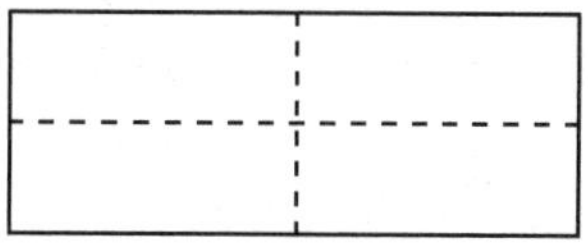

A rectangle has 2 lines of symmetry.

They are both ______________________.

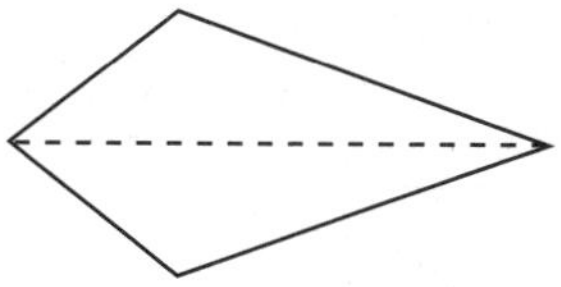

A kite has 1 line of symmetry.

It is an ______________________.

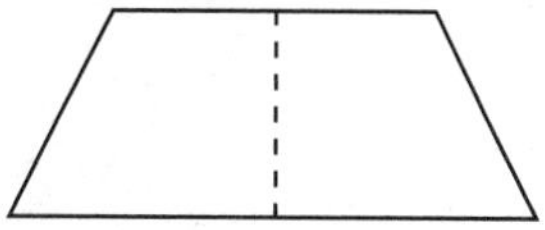

An isosceles trapezoid has 1 line of symmetry.

It is a ______________________.

C. On the square, draw the bisector of each angle and the perpendicular bisector of each side.

Describe what you notice. ______________________

____

____

____

G7-12 Making a Sketch

Work quickly—a sketch is not supposed to be perfect.

1. Sketch each figure.

   a) a rectangle divided into 2 triangles

   b) line segment *AB* intersecting line *CD*

   c) a parallelogram

Draw sides and angles roughly to scale.

2. Circle the sketch that is more to scale.

   a)

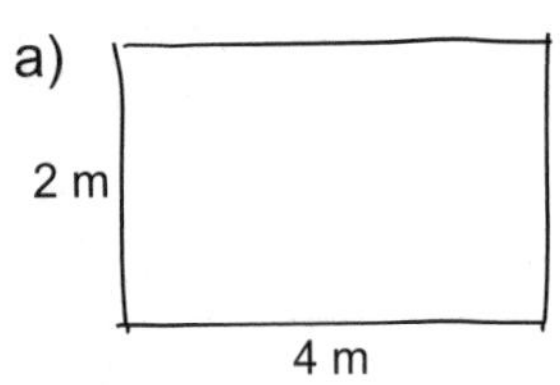

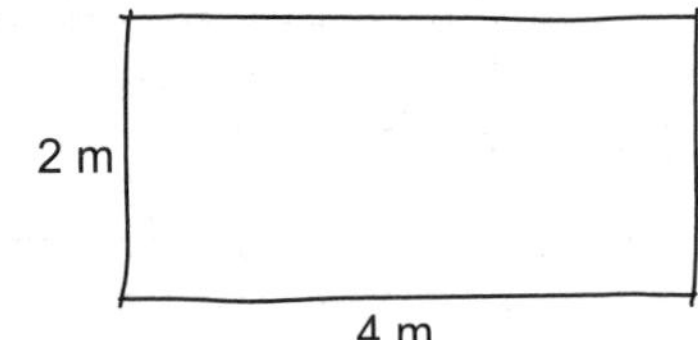

   b)

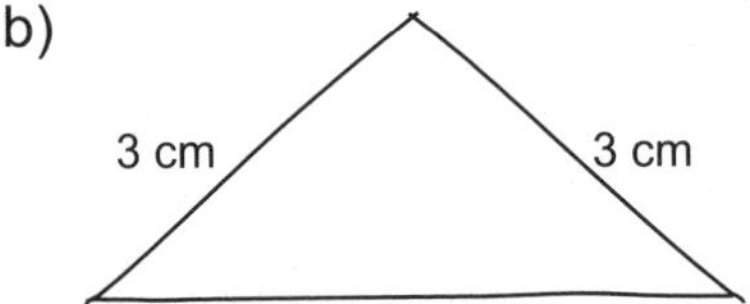

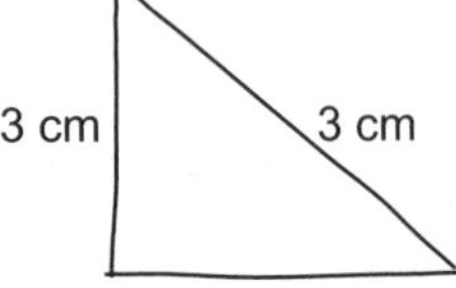

3. Circle the sketch that looks more like…

   a) a 90° angle.

   b) a 45° angle.

   c) a 135° angle.

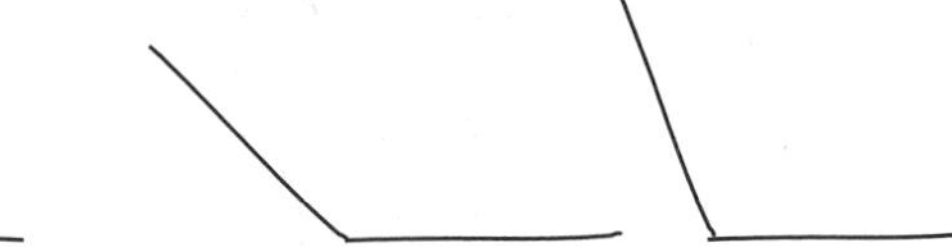

4. Circle the sketch that looks more like…

   a) an equilateral triangle.

   b) a right triangle.

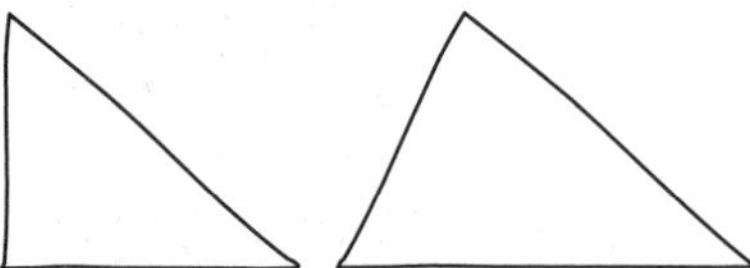

   c) an acute isosceles triangle.

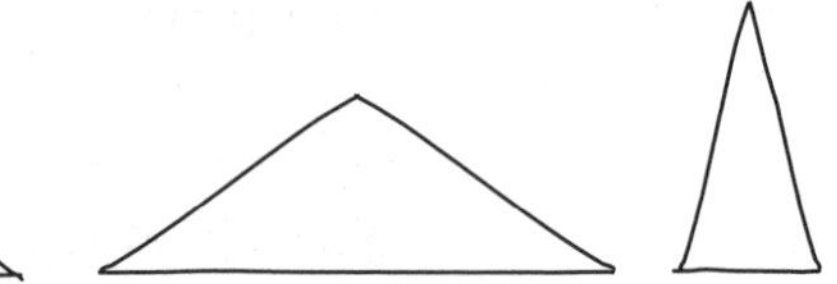

5. Make a better sketch.

   a)

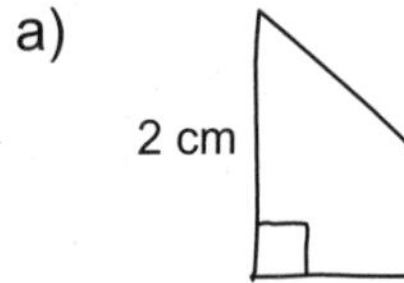
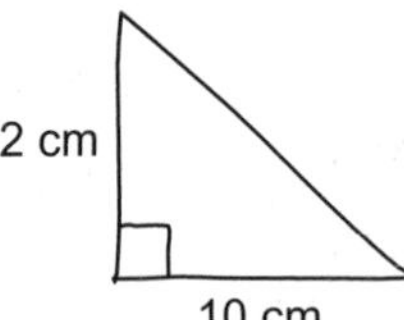

   b)

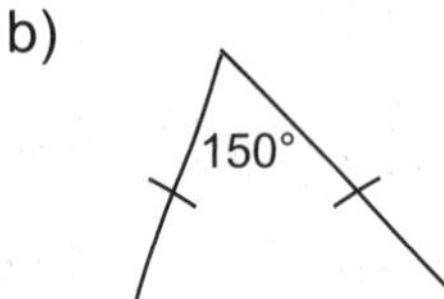

6. Sketch the figures. Add all necessary labels and side and angle markings.

   a) Line segment *AB* is twice as long as line segment *CD*.

   b) ΔABC has all sides equal. ΔTUV has all sides twice as long as ΔABC.

   c) ΔPQR is a right triangle with two 45° angles.

Include all the important information you have been given.

7. Circle the sketch that includes all the important information given.

a) Information: ΔABC has all sides equal.

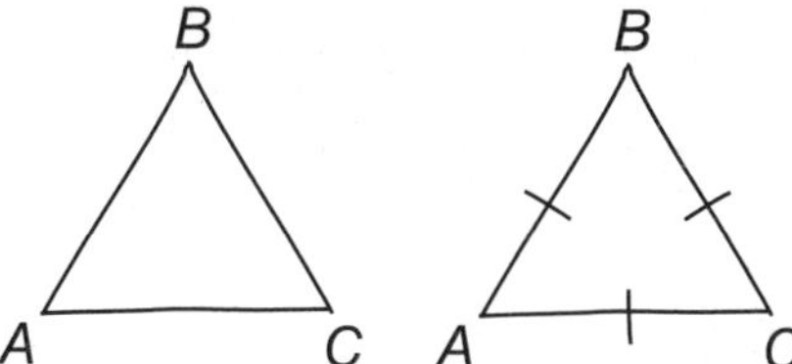

b) Information: ΔTUV is isosceles.

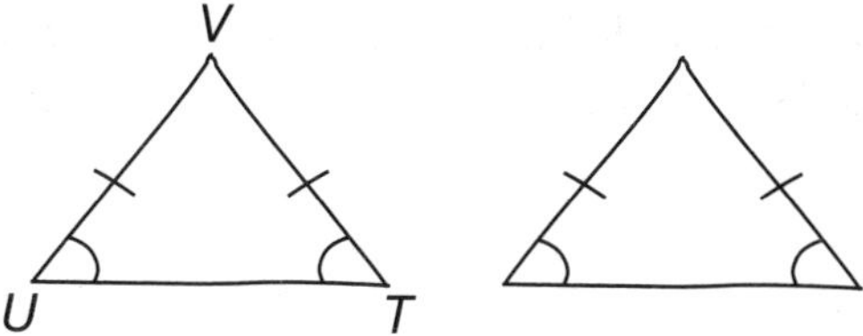

c) Information: GM is the perpendicular bisector of side FH in ΔFGH.

d) Information: Line DE is parallel to line segment XY.

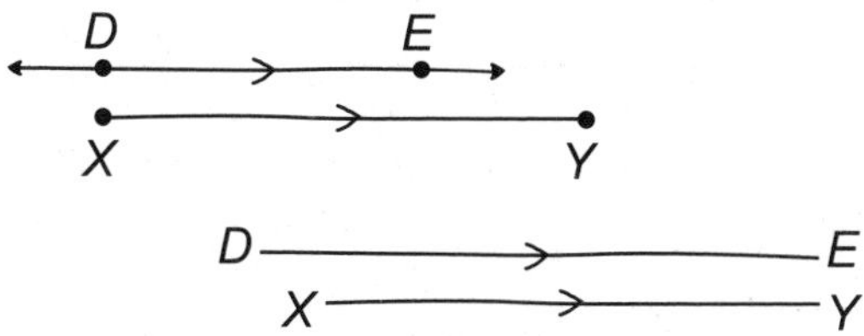

Leave out any information you are sure you do not need.

8. Cross out any information you do not need to solve the problem. Then sketch the problem.

	Problem	Sketch
a)	~~A strut on a bridge over a river is shaped like~~ a triangle with two equal sides. One angle of the triangle is 60°. What are the other two angles?	
b)	A caramel-filled chocolate bar has a gold-and-blue rectangular foil wrapper that is 15 cm long and 10 cm wide with a logo that is 3 cm wide. What is the area of the wrapper?	
c)	A rectangle with opposite sides parallel and all right angles is 7 m long and 3 m wide. What is its perimeter (distance around)?	

Be careful not to accidentally add in any information you do not know for sure.

9. Circle the sketch that has accidentally added information not known.

a) A trapezoid has an 8 cm base.

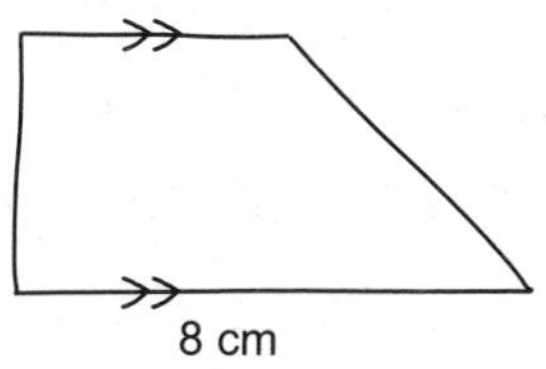

b) MF is perpendicular to GH.

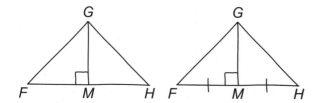

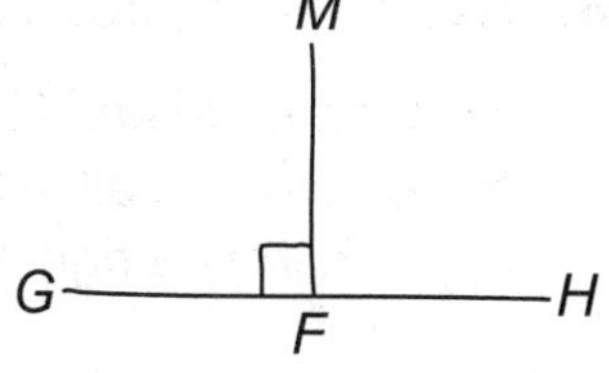

Sometimes you will want to make a few sketches to see the problem in different ways.

10. One angle of an isosceles triangle is 40°. What are the other angles?

Make two sketches to show that where you put the 40° angle on your sketch will make a difference to the answer.

Add other information you can deduce.

11. These sketches show the information given in a problem. What other information can you deduce? Mark this additional information on the sketch.

a) Hint: What is the sum of the 3 angles in a triangle?

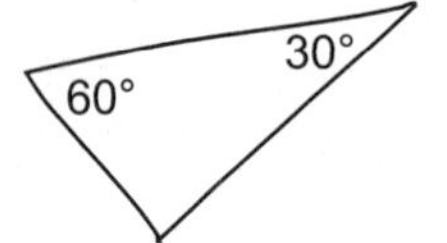

____

b) Hint: Which type of triangle is this? ______________

What do you know about the angles in this type of triangle?

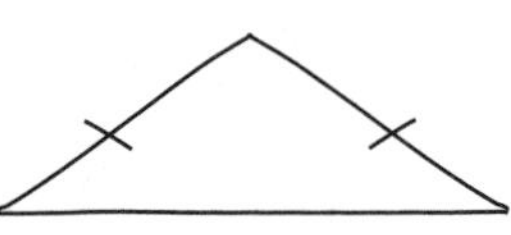

____

c) Hint: What do you know about the sum of the angles in a linear pair?

80°

____

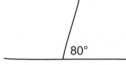

12. How many sides does each polygon have? How do you know? Identify the shape.

a) Polygon *DEFGH* has ________ sides. *A pentagon, because there are 5 vertex letters*.

b) Polygon *ABCD* has ________ sides. ______________________________.

c) Polygon *LMN* has ________ sides. ______________________________.

Use symbols instead of words to keep your sketch clear and uncluttered.

13. Circle the sketch that is better.

a)

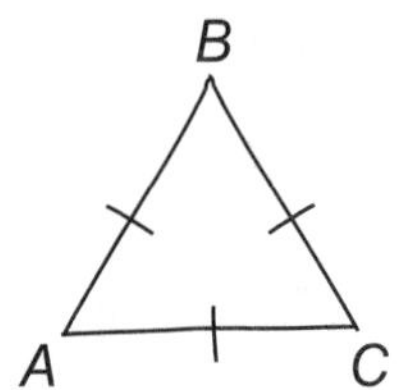

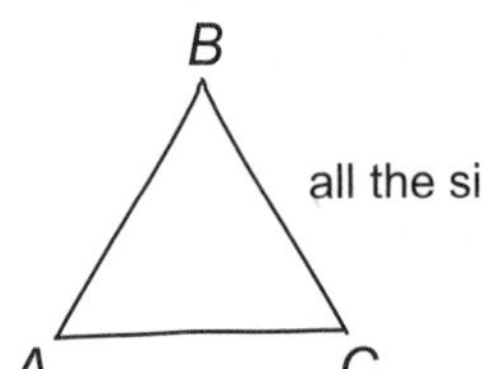

all the sides are equal

b)

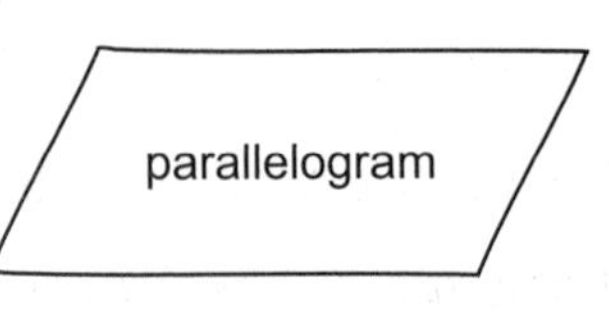

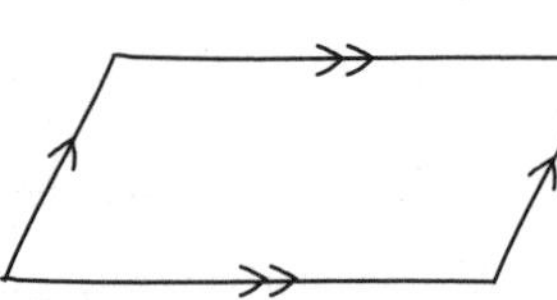

14. Sketch the triangle. Add all necessary labels and side and angle markings.

a) ΔABC is an obtuse triangle

b) ΔDEF is an isosceles triangle

c) ΔGHI is a right triangle

d) ΔJKL is a right isosceles triangle

e) a triangle with all equal sides

f) a 45°–45°–90° triangle

g) a 30°–60°–90° triangle

h) ΔXYZ is a scalene triangle

15. Sketch the polygon. Add all necessary labels and side and angle markings.

a) *ABCD* has all equal sides.
b) *PQRS* has 2 equal sides and 2 sides that are other lengths.
c) *JKLM* has two 90° angles.
d) *ABCDE* has no equal sides.

16. Problem: The foot of a ladder is 2 m from a vertical wall. The top of the ladder is 2 m up the wall. What angle does the ladder form with the ground, if the ground is horizontal?

A.

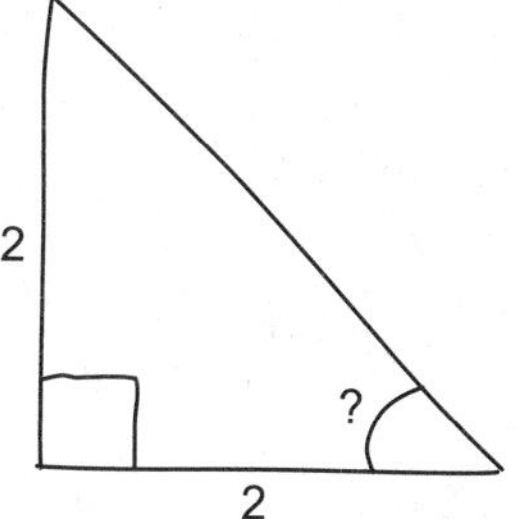

B.

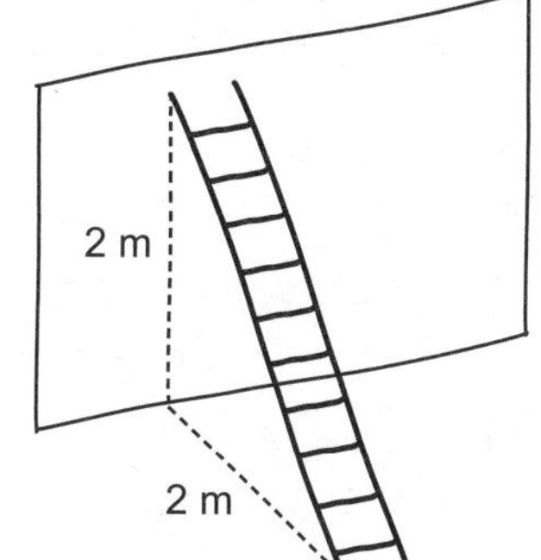

a) Do both of these sketches include all the important information given in the problem? Explain.

____

b) Does sketch B tell you anything more than sketch A does? ______________

c) Why does sketch A make it easier to see that the shape formed by the ladder against the wall is an isosceles triangle?

____

d) Sketch A shows that the angle between the two equal sides of the triangle is a right angle. How did the student who drew the sketch know that the angle is a right angle?

____

e) Which sketch tells what the problem is asking you to find? ______________

f) Which sketch will help the most to solve the problem? ______________

g) Solve the problem:

The triangle has a 90° angle, so the sum of the other 2 angles is _______°.

The triangle is isosceles, so the two other angles are ______________.

What angle does the ladder form with the ground? _______°

17. PROBLEM ▶ Use the clues to name the polygon.

- It is formed from two triangles that share a side.
- It has two pairs of opposite parallel sides.
- It has all right angles.
- Δ *ABC* shares side *BC* with Δ *DCB*.
- It has all sides equal.

SOLUTION ▶

a) You are told that the polygon is made from two triangles that share a side.

i) Sketch any triangle.
ii) Sketch another triangle that shares a side with the first triangle.
iii) Sketch a few other possible combinations.

How many sides do all polygons made from two triangles have? _______ or _______

Which of the clues implies the shape is not a triangle? ________________________________

This means that the shape is some kind of ________________________________.

b) You are told that one triangle is named Δ _______ and the other is named Δ ______.

You also know that the side the two triangles share is side _______.

i) On one of your sketches, label the vertices at the endpoints of that side.
ii) Then label the other two vertices of the shape.

The letter name of the polygon is *A* ___ ___ ___.

c) You are told that the shape has opposite sides parallel. That means that the shape is some kind of parallelogram.

i) Sketch two parallel line segments of equal length.

ii) Then sketch the other two sides of the parallelogram. Remember—you do not need to draw a perfect parallelogram; this is just a sketch.

d) You are told that the shape has all sides equal.

i) Sketch a parallelogram with all sides equal.
ii) Mark the equal sides.

e) You are told the shape has all right angles.

i) Sketch a shape with all right angles and all sides equal.

ii) Mark the equal sides and right angles. Which shape is the mystery polygon?

Polygon _______ is a ______________.

Some Sketching Tips

- Often, at the beginning of a problem, you only know part of what you need in order to solve the problem. You have to use what you are given to figure out more information. You do not know what you might find out, so do simple sketches that do not lock you in to one way of thinking about things.
- If you start a sketch and it does not seem to be helping, try doing a different sketch—or try another problem-solving strategy.

NS7-32 Decimal Fractions

1. Write the missing terms in each pattern.

   a) 1, 10, 100, ____, 10 000, …

   b) 1, ____, 100, 1 000, ________, …

   c) 10, 10×10, $10 \times 10 \times 10$, ______________, $10 \times 10 \times 10 \times 10 \times 10$, …

   d) $\frac{1}{10}$, $\frac{1}{100}$, $\frac{1}{\_\_\_\_}$, $\frac{1}{10000}$, …

   e) …, 1 000, 100, ____, 1, $\frac{1}{10}$, $\frac{1}{\_\_\_\_}$, $\frac{1}{1000}$, …

   f) …, 1 000, 100, 10, ____, $\frac{1}{10}$, $\frac{1}{100}$, $\frac{1}{\_\_\_\_}$, …

10, 100, 1 000, … are **powers of 10**. In a **decimal fraction**, the denominator is a power of ten.

2. Circle the decimal fractions (the denominator is a power of 10).

   $\frac{3}{10}$ $\frac{25}{100}$ $\frac{5}{6}$ $\frac{333}{1000}$ $\frac{7}{29}$ $\frac{1}{100}$ $\frac{100}{13}$ $\frac{4}{1000}$ $\frac{1}{55}$ $\frac{48}{10}$ $\frac{16}{101}$

There are 100 squares on a **hundredths grid**.

1 column $= \frac{10}{100} = \frac{1}{10} =$ 1 tenth

1 square $= \frac{1}{100} =$ 1 hundredth

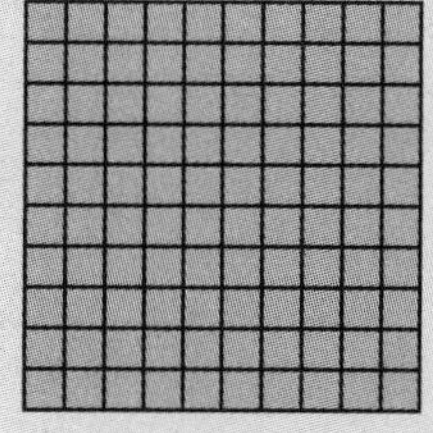
1 one

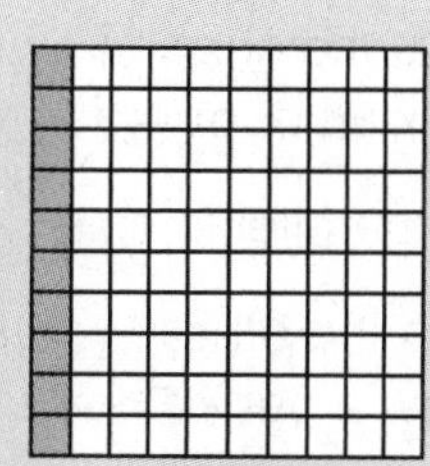
1 tenth

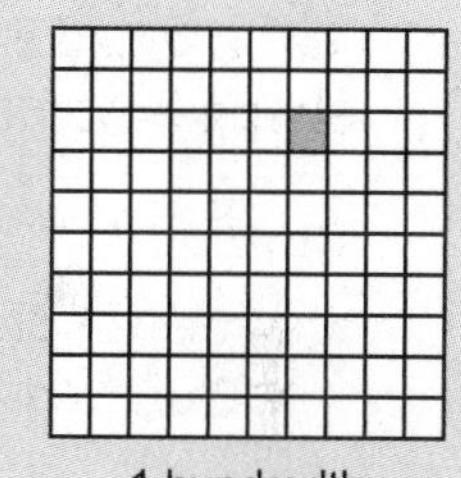
1 hundredth

3. Write two equivalent fractions for the shaded part of the grid. One column on the grid = 1 tenth.

   a) $\frac{2}{10} = \frac{\_\_}{100}$

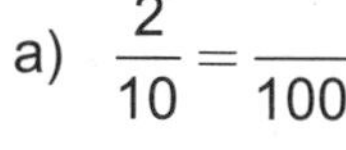

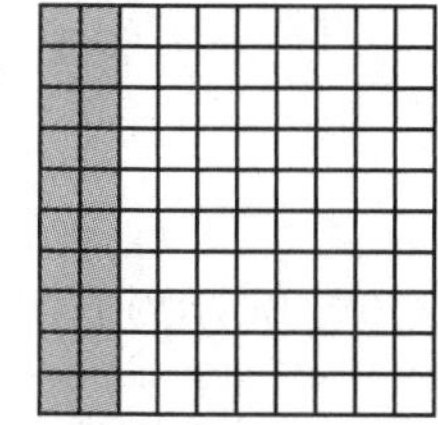

   b) $\frac{\_\_}{10} = \frac{\_\_}{100}$

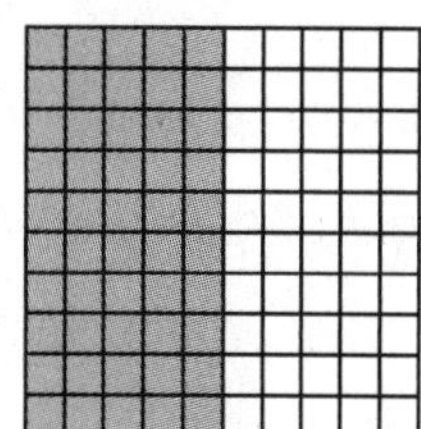

   c) $\frac{\_\_}{10} = \frac{\_\_}{100}$

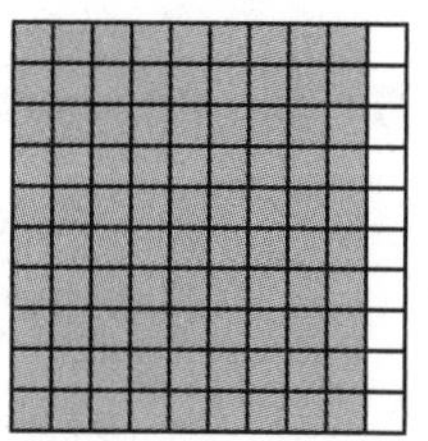

4. Write an equivalent fraction, then shade the grid to show the equivalent fractions.

   a) $\frac{6}{10} = \frac{\_\_}{100}$

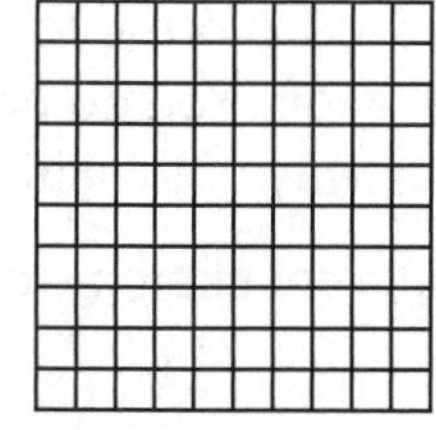

   b) $\frac{\_\_}{10} = \frac{70}{100}$

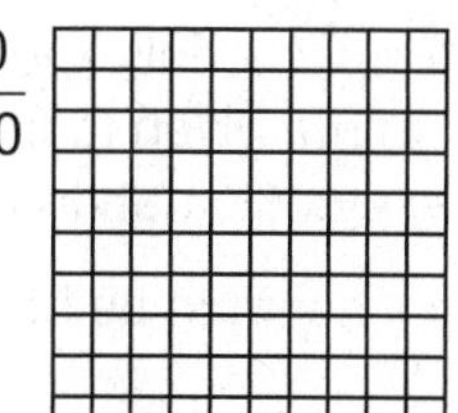

   c) $\frac{3}{10} = \frac{\_\_}{100}$

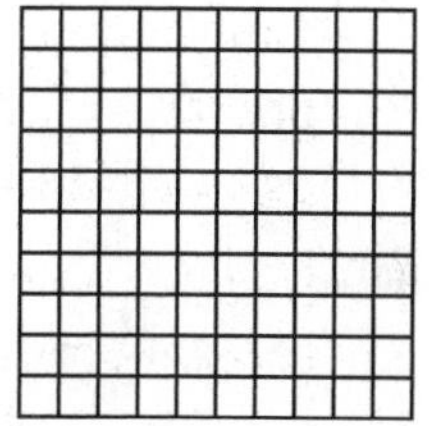

5. Write the fraction shown by the shaded part of the grid in two ways.

a) $\frac{23}{100} = \frac{2}{10} + \frac{\quad}{100}$

b) $\frac{\quad}{100} = \frac{\quad}{10} + \frac{\quad}{100}$

c) $\frac{\quad}{100} = \frac{\quad}{10} + \frac{\quad}{100}$

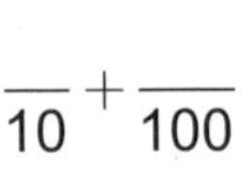

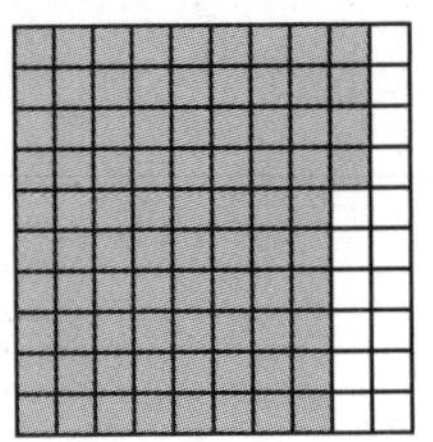

6. Shade the grid to show the fraction. Then write the fraction another way.

a) $\frac{47}{100} = \frac{\quad}{10} + \frac{\quad}{100}$

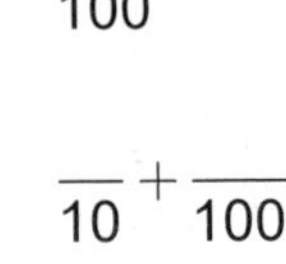

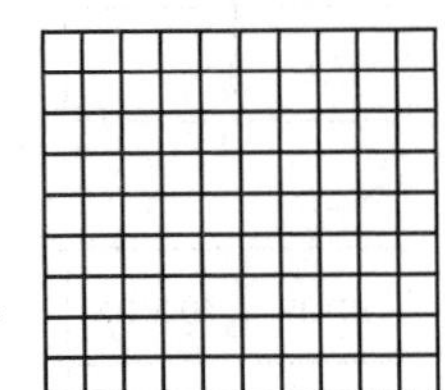

b) $\frac{91}{100} = \frac{\quad}{10} + \frac{\quad}{100}$

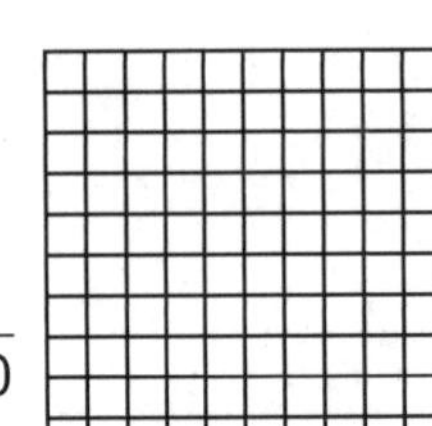

c) $\frac{36}{100} = \frac{\quad}{10} + \frac{\quad}{100}$

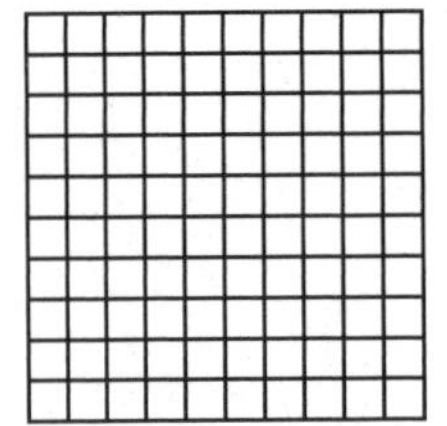

7. Multiply or divide the numerator and denominator by the same number to write an equivalent decimal fraction.

a) $\frac{2}{10} = \frac{\quad}{100}$ (× *10*, × *10*)

b) $\frac{6}{10} = \frac{\quad}{100}$ (× ____, × *10*)

c) $\frac{25}{100} = \frac{\quad}{1000}$ (× ____, × ____)

d) $\frac{81}{100} = \frac{\quad}{1000}$ (× ____, × ____)

e) $\frac{9}{10} = \frac{\quad}{1000}$ (× ____, × ____)

f) $\frac{80}{100} = \frac{\quad}{10}$ (÷ ____, ÷ ____)

g) $\frac{360}{1000} = \frac{\quad}{100}$ (÷ ____, ÷ ____)

h) $\frac{420}{1000} = \frac{\quad}{100}$ (÷ ____, ÷ ____)

i) $\frac{50}{1000} = \frac{\quad}{100}$ (÷ ____, ÷ ____)

j) $\frac{30}{100} = \frac{\quad}{10}$ (÷ ____, ÷ ____)

8. Determine the equivalent fraction.

a) $\frac{6}{10} = \frac{6 \times 10}{10 \times 10} = \frac{\quad}{100}$

b) $\frac{35}{100} = \frac{35 \times \_\_\_}{100 \times \_\_\_} = \frac{\quad}{1000}$

c) $\frac{2}{100} = \frac{2 \times \_\_\_}{100 \times \_\_\_} = \frac{\quad}{1000}$

d) $\frac{4}{10} = \frac{4 \times \_\_\_}{10 \times \_\_\_} = \frac{\quad}{1000}$

e) $\frac{30}{100} = \frac{30 \div \_\_\_}{100 \div \_\_\_} = \frac{\quad}{10}$

f) $\frac{710}{1000} = \frac{710 \div \_\_\_}{1000 \div \_\_\_} = \frac{\quad}{100}$

9. Write the equivalent fractions.

a) $\frac{5}{10} = \frac{\quad}{100} = \frac{\quad}{1000}$

b) $\frac{\quad}{10} = \frac{90}{100} = \frac{\quad}{1000}$

c) $\frac{\quad}{10} = \frac{\quad}{100} = \frac{300}{1000}$

d) $\frac{75}{100} = \frac{\quad}{1000}$

e) $\frac{70}{1000} = \frac{\quad}{100}$

f) $\frac{10}{10} = \frac{\quad}{100} = \frac{\quad}{1000}$

g) $\frac{78}{100} = \frac{\quad}{1000}$

h) $\frac{570}{1000} = \frac{\quad}{100}$

NS7-33 Place Value and Decimals

Decimals are a short way to write decimal fractions.

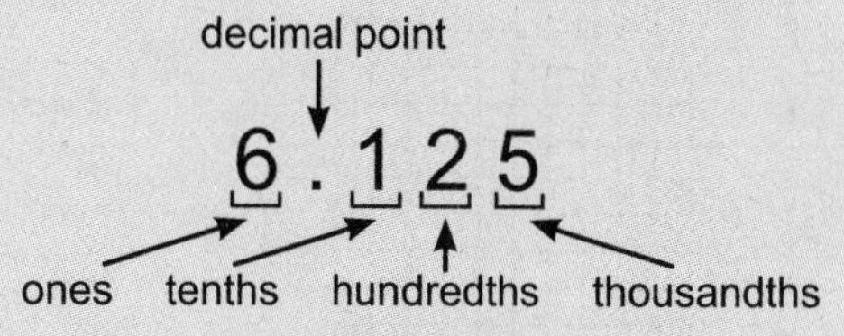

1. Write the decimal fraction in the place value chart. Then write the fraction as a decimal.

a) $\frac{3}{10}$

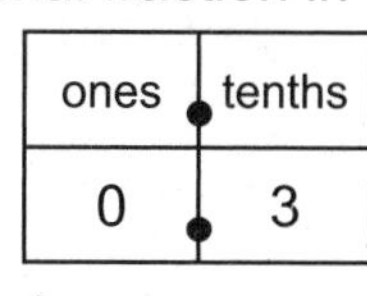

ones	tenths
0	3

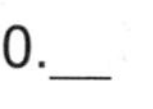

0.__

b) 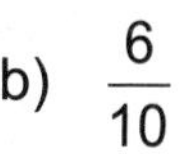 $\frac{6}{10}$

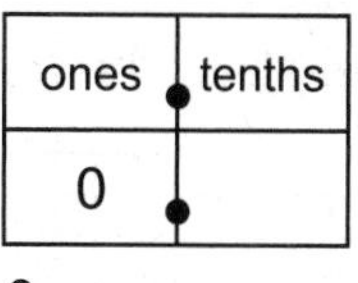

ones	tenths
0	

0.__

c) 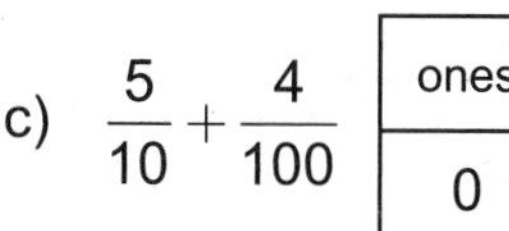 $\frac{5}{10} + \frac{4}{100}$

ones	tenths	hundredths
0	5	4

__.__ __

d) $\frac{1}{10} + \frac{8}{100}$

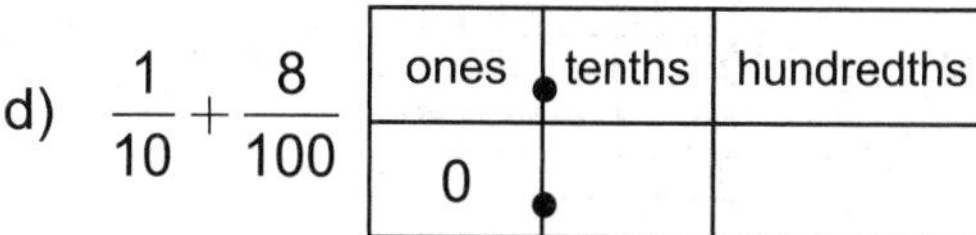

ones	tenths	hundredths
0		

__.__ __

e) $\frac{9}{10} + \frac{2}{100}$

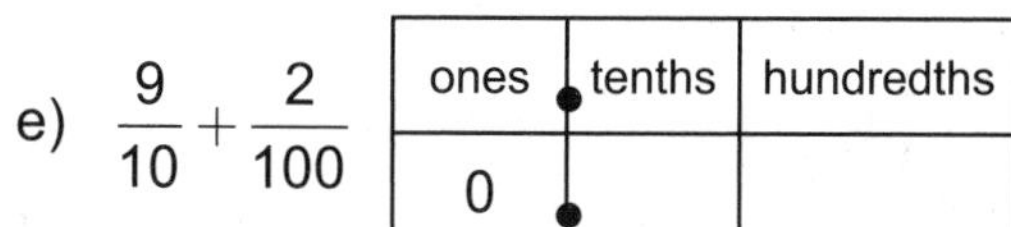

ones	tenths	hundredths
0		

__.__ __

f) $\frac{6}{10} + \frac{5}{100}$

ones	tenths	hundredths
0		

__.__ __

g) 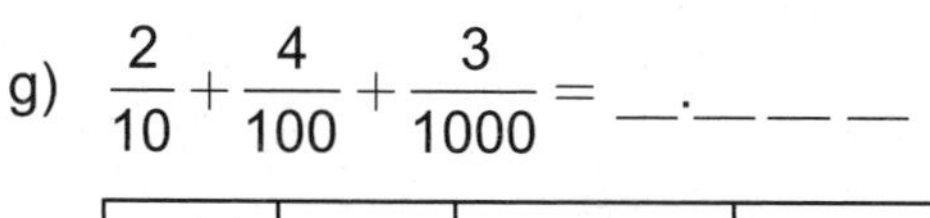 $\frac{2}{10} + \frac{4}{100} + \frac{3}{1000} =$ __.__ __ __

ones	tenths	hundredths	thousandths
0	2	4	3

h) $\frac{3}{10} + \frac{1}{100} + \frac{5}{1000} =$ __.__ __ __

ones	tenths	hundredths	thousandths
0			

2. Is the decimal point to the right or the left of the ones place? ☐ to the right ☐ to the left

3. Write the decimal in the place value chart.

	ones	tenths	hundredths	thousandths
a) 0.512	*0*	*5*	*1*	*2*
b) 0.3				
c) 0.763				

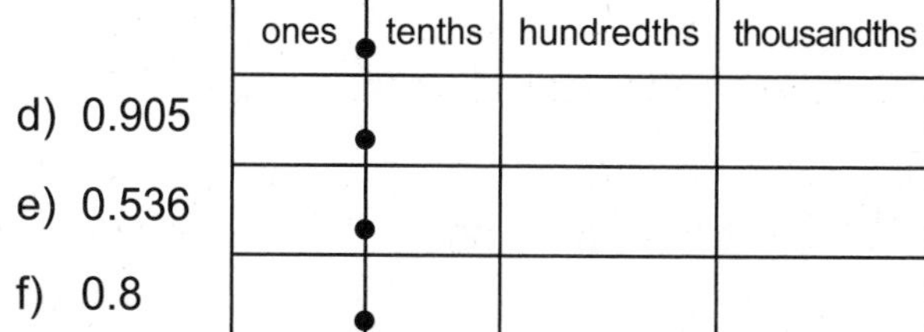

	ones	tenths	hundredths	thousandths
d) 0.905				
e) 0.536				
f) 0.8				

4. Write the value of the digit 9 in the decimal in words and as a fraction.

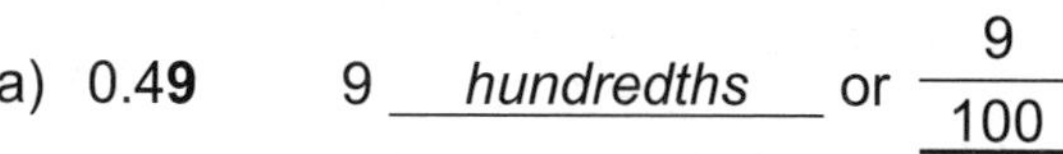

a) 0.4**9** 9 *hundredths* or  $\frac{9}{100}$

b) 0.34**9** 9 ______________ or $\frac{9}{\_\_\_}$

c) 0.**9**76 9 ______________ or $\frac{9}{\_\_\_}$

d) 0.3**9** 9 ______________ or $\frac{9}{\_\_\_}$

e) 0.**9**5 9 ______________ or $\frac{9}{\_\_\_}$

f) 0.32**9** 9 ______________ or $\frac{9}{\_\_\_}$

5. Write the number shown in the place value chart as a decimal, using 0 as a placeholder.

a)

ones •	tenths	hundredths
•		9

0 . *0* *9*

b)

ones •	tenths	hundredths	thousandths
•			5

___ . ___ ___ ___

c)

ones •	tenths	hundredths
•		3

___ . ___ ___

d)

ones •	tenths	hundredths	thousandths
•			1

___ . ___ ___ ___

6. Write the number as a decimal. Use zeros as placeholders.

a) 7 tenths = *0*.___ b) 3 tenths = ___.___ c) 9 tenths = ___.___

d) 7 hundredths = ___.___ ___ e) 5 hundredths = ___.___ ___ f) 4 hundredths = ___.___ ___

g) 7 thousandths = ___.___ ___ ___ h) 2 thousandths = ___.___ ___ ___ i) 6 thousandths = ___.___ ___ ___

7. Underline the smallest place value. Write the decimal in words.

a) 0.<u>6</u> = *six tenths* b) 0.07 = ______________

c) 0.005 = ______________ d) 0.02 = ______________

e) 0.3 = ______________ f) 0.005 = ______________

8. Which place is being held by the bolded zero in the decimal?

a) 0.**0**7 *tenths* place b) 0.1**0**5 ______________ place

c) 0.3**0**6 ______________ place d) 0.**0**44 ______________ place

9. Write the decimal in expanded form.

a) 0.407 = *4* tenths + *0* hundredths + *7* thousandths

b) 0.163 = ___ tenths + ___ hundredths + ___ thousandths

c) 0.08 = ___ tenths + ___ hundredths

d) 0.76 = ___ tenths + ___ hundredths

e) 0.201 = ___ tenths + ___ hundredths + ___ thousandths

10. Write the number in expanded form as a decimal.

a) 3 tenths + 5 hundredths + 2 thousandths = *0* . ___ ___ ___

b) 4 tenths + 1 hundredth + 6 thousandths = ___ . ___ ___ ___

c) 5 tenths = ___ . ___

d) 8 tenths + 2 hundredths = ___ . ___ ___

e) 3 hundredths + 5 thousandths = ___ . ___ ___ ___

f) 5 tenths + 3 thousandths = ___ . ___ ___ ___

11. Put a decimal point in the number so the digit 3 has the value $\frac{3}{100}$. Add zeros if you need to.

a) 3 2 b) 1 3 5 c) 9 8 7 3 d) 3

NS7-34 Fractions and Decimals

1. Complete the chart below.

Drawing	Fraction	Decimal	Equivalent Decimal	Equivalent Fraction	Drawing
	$\frac{5}{10}$	0.5	0.50	$\frac{50}{100}$	
	$\frac{\_\_}{10}$	__ . __	__ . __ __	$\frac{\_\_}{100}$	

2. Fill in the missing numbers. Remember: $\frac{1}{10} = \frac{10}{100}$

a) $0.8 = \frac{8}{10} = \frac{\_\_}{100} = 0.80$ b) $0.\_\_ = \frac{\_\_}{10} = \frac{40}{100} = 0.\_\_\ \_\_$ c) $0.\_\_ = \frac{\_\_}{10} = \frac{\_\_}{100} = 0.30$

3. Fill in the missing numbers. Remember: $\frac{1}{100} = \frac{10}{1000}$

a) $0.03 = \frac{3}{100} = \frac{\_\_}{1000} = 0.030$ b) $0.\_\_\ \_\_ = \frac{2}{100} = \frac{\_\_}{1000} = 0.020$

c) $0.\_\_\ \_\_ = \frac{\_\_}{100} = \frac{70}{1000} = 0.\_\_\ \_\_\ \_\_$ d) $0.\_\_\ \_\_ = \frac{\_\_}{100} = \frac{\_\_}{1000} = 0.090$

4. How many tenths and hundredths are shaded? Write a fraction and a decimal to represent them.

a) _47_ hundredths = _4_ tenths _7_ hundredths $\frac{47}{100} = 0.\_\_\ \_\_$

b) __ hundredths = __ tenths __ hundredths $\frac{\_\_}{100} = 0.\_\_\ \_\_$

c) __ hundredths = __ tenths __ hundredths $\frac{\_\_}{100} = 0.\_\_\ \_\_$

d) __ hundredths = __ tenths __ hundredths $\frac{\_\_}{100} = 0.\_\_\ \_\_$

5. Write a decimal for the fraction.

a) $\frac{35}{100} = 0.\_\_\ \_\_$ b) $\frac{61}{100} = 0.\_\_\ \_\_$ c) $\frac{18}{100} = 0.\_\_\ \_\_$ d) $\frac{3}{100} = 0.\_\_\ \_\_$

6. Describe the decimal in two ways.

a) 0.52 = ____ tenths ____ hundredths = ____ hundredths

b) 0.40 = ____ tenths ____ hundredths = ____ hundredths

c) 0.93 = ____ tenths ____ hundredths = ____ hundredths

7. Write the number as a decimal.

a) 23 hundredths = 0.___ ___   b) 61 hundredths = 0.___ ___   c) 12 hundredths = 0.___ ___

8. Fill in the blanks.

a) 715 thousandths = ____ tenths ____ hundredths ____ thousandths $\frac{715}{1000}$ = 0. ___ ___ ___

b) 164 thousandths = ____ tenths ____ hundredths ____ thousandths $\frac{\_\_\_}{1000}$ = 0. ___ ___ ___

c) 42 thousandths = ____ hundredths ____ thousandths $\frac{\_\_\_}{1000}$ = 0. ___ ___ ___

9. Write a decimal for the fraction.

a) $\frac{275}{1000}$ = 0. ___ ___ ___   b) $\frac{602}{1000}$ = 0. ___ ___ ___

c) $\frac{199}{1000}$ = 0. ___ ___ ___   d) $\frac{56}{1000}$ = 0. ___ ___ ___

10. Describe the decimal in two ways.

a) 0.345 = ____ tenths ____ hundredths ____ thousandths = ____ thousandths

b) 0.629 = ____ tenths ____ hundredths ____ thousandths = ____ thousandths

c) 0.118 = ____ tenths ____ hundredths ____ thousandths = ____ thousandths

11. Write the number as a decimal.

a) 765 thousandths = *0.765*   b) 123 thousandths = ______   c) 204 thousandths = ______

d) 42 thousandths = *0.042*   e) 18 thousandths = ______   f) 79 thousandths = ______

12. Say the name of the fraction and decimal to yourself. Circle the equalities that are incorrect.

a) $0.36 = \frac{36}{100}$ b) $0.9 = \frac{9}{100}$ c) $0.6 = \frac{6}{10}$ d) $\frac{27}{100} = 0.27$ e) $\frac{125}{1000} = 0.125$

f) $0.75 = \frac{74}{100}$ g) $0.03 = \frac{3}{10}$ h) $\frac{200}{1000} = 0.020$ i) $0.08 = \frac{8}{100}$ j) $0.40 = \frac{40}{10}$

13. Write the decimal as a fraction.

a) 0.3   b) 0.57   c) 0.654   d) 0.45   e) 0.03

f) 0.056   g) 0.002   h) 0.1   i) 0.704   j) 0.069

NS7-35 Decimals, Money, and Measurements

A **dime** is **one tenth** of a dollar. A **penny** is one **hundredth** of a dollar.

1. Express the value of each decimal in four different ways.

a) 0.64

6 dimes and 4 pennies

6 tenths and 4 hundredths

64 pennies

64 hundredths

b) 0.31

______
______
______
______

c) 0.73

______
______
______
______

d) 0.31

______
______
______
______

A **decimetre** is **a tenth** of a metre. A **centimetre** is **a hundredth** of a metre.

2. Express the value of each measurement in four different ways.

a) 0.28 m

2 decimetres 8 centimetres

______
______
______

b) 0.16 m

______
______
______
______

3. Express the value of each decimal in four different ways.

Hint: Add a zero in the hundredths place if there are no hundredths.

a) 0.32 ____ dimes ____ pennies
____ tenths ____ hundredths
____ pennies
____ hundredths

0.3 ____ dimes ____ pennies
____ tenths ____ hundredths
____ pennies
____ hundredths

b) 0.36 ____ dimes ____ pennies
____ tenths ____ hundredths
____ pennies
____ hundredths

0.4 ____ dimes ____ pennies
____ tenths ____ hundredths
____ pennies
____ hundredths

4. Kieko says 0.73 is greater than 0.9 because 73 is greater than 9. Can you explain her mistake?

5. What unit of measurement does the 5 in 0.725 m represent?

NS7-36 Decimals and Fractions Greater Than 1

The whole-number part of a decimal is the digits to the left of the decimal point.

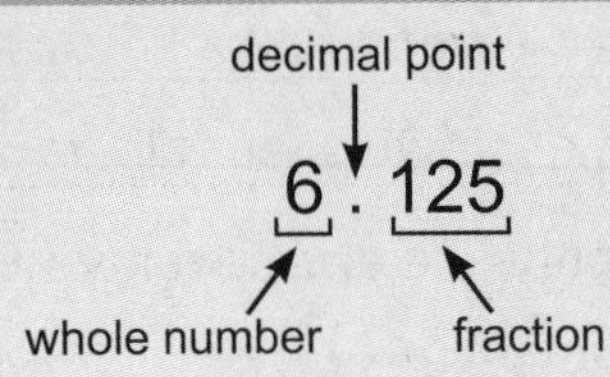

1. Underline the whole-number part of the decimal.

a) 36.497 b) 196.4 c) 25.76

d) 8.036 e) 0.38 f) 10.004

2. Write the decimal in expanded form.

a) 7.5 = ___ ones + ___ tenths

b) 4.32 = ___ ones + ___ tenths + ___ hundredths

c) 36.726 = _3_ tens + _6_ ones + _7_ tenths + ___ hundredths + ___ thousandths

d) 25.04 = ___ tens + ___ ones + ___ tenths + ___ hundredths

e) 7.015 = ___ ones + ___ tenths + ___ hundredths + ___ thousandths

3. Write the number as a decimal.

a) 2 tens + 4 ones + 3 tenths + 5 hundredths + 2 thousandths = ___ ___ . ___ ___ ___

b) 9 ones + 4 tenths + 1 hundredth + 6 thousandths = ____________

c) 4 tens + 8 ones + 7 tenths + 2 hundredths = ____________

d) 3 hundreds + 3 tens + 3 ones + 3 tenths + 3 hundredths = ____________

4. Write the decimal in the place value chart.

	thousands	hundreds	tens	ones	tenths	hundredths	thousandths
a) 17.34			1	7	3	4	
b) 8.675							
c) 250.93							
d) 6700.5							
e) 49.007							

5. Write the whole number and how many hundredths or thousandths.

a) 6.45 _six_ and _forty-five_ hundredths

b) 1.32 ________ and ________ hundredths

c) 36.007 ________ and ________ thousandths

d) 7.052 ________ and ________ thousandths

e) 20.104 ________ and ________ thousandths

6. Fill in the blanks to show how to read the decimal.

a) 6.8 is read as " *six and eight tenths* "

b) 3.02 is read as " ______ and two ______ "

c) 25.79 is read as " twenty-five and seventy-nine ______ "

d) 15.285 is read as " ______ and two hundred eighty-five ______ "

A decimal can be written as a mixed number. Example: $3.75 = 3\frac{75}{100}$

7. Write the number represented on the grids in three ways.

a) 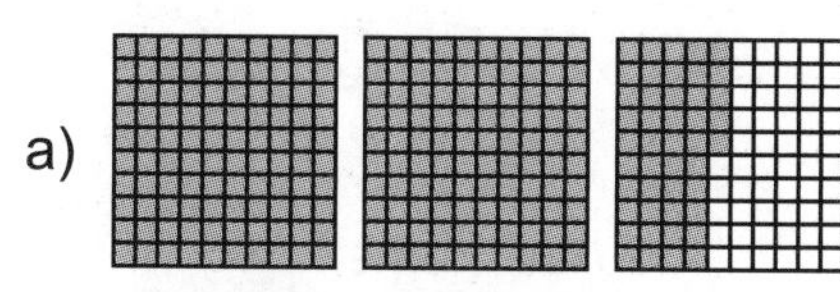 *2* ones *45* hundredths  $2\frac{\_\_}{100}$

b) 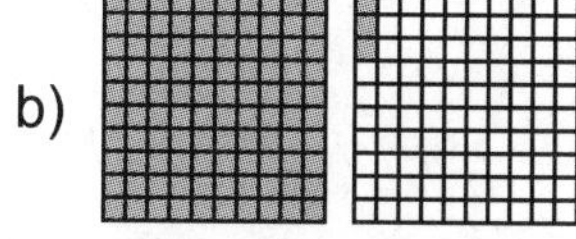 ___ ones ___ hundredths ___ . ___ ___ $\_\frac{\_\_}{100}$

c) 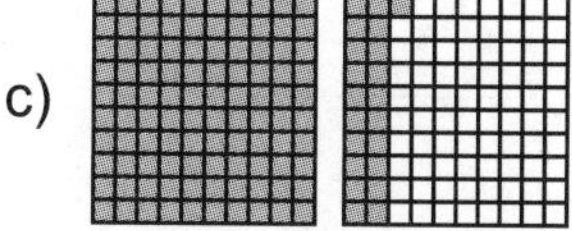 ___ ones ___ hundredths ___ . ___ ___ $\_\frac{\_\_}{100}$

d) 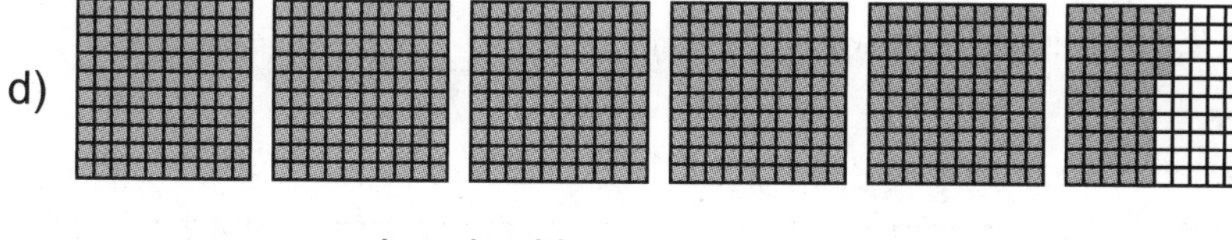

___ ones ___ hundredths ___ . ___ ___ $\_\frac{\_\_}{100}$

8. Write a mixed number for the decimal.

a) 3.21 b) 1.62 c) 8.6 d) 9.137

e) 31.76 f) 23.665 g) 1.7 h) 82.505

9. Write a decimal for the mixed number.

a) $2\frac{17}{100}$ b) $1\frac{67}{100}$ c) $76\frac{7}{10}$ d) $5\frac{375}{1000}$ e) $3\frac{9}{100}$ f) $29\frac{5}{1000}$

10. Which is larger, 12.057 or $12\frac{52}{100}$? Explain.

NS7-37 Comparing and Ordering Tenths and Hundredths

This number line is divided into tenths. The number represented by point **A** is $2\frac{3}{10}$ or 2.3.

1. Write a fraction or a mixed number for each point.

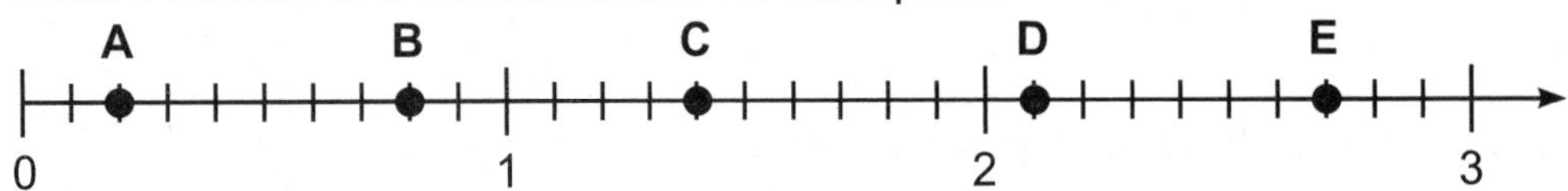

A ______ **B** ______ **C** ______ **D** ______ **E** ______

2. a) Write a decimal for each mark on the number line.

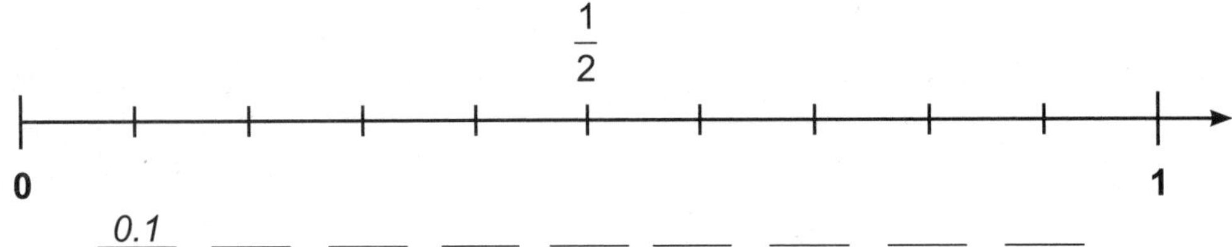

0.1 ____ ____ ____ ____ ____ ____ ____ ____

b) Which decimal is equal to one half? $\frac{1}{2}$ = ______

3. Use the number line in Question 2 to say whether the decimal is closer to 0, $\frac{1}{2}$, or 1.

a) 0.2 is closer to ______ b) 0.8 is closer to ______ c) 0.7 is closer to ______

d) 0.9 is closer to ______ e) 0.3 is closer to ______ f) 0.1 is closer to ______

4. a) Mark each point with a dot and label the point with the correct letter.

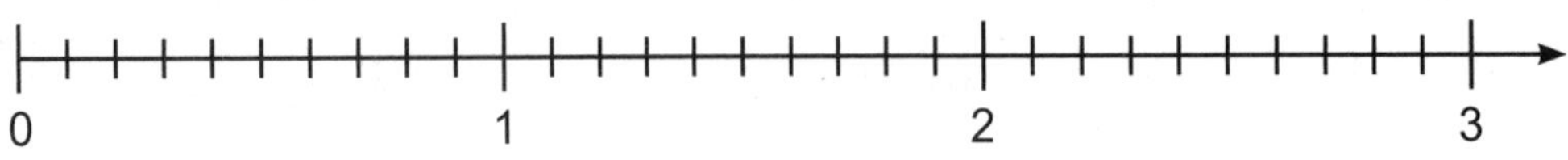

A 1.3 **B** 2.7 **C** 0.7 **D** $2\frac{1}{10}$ **E** $\frac{3}{4}$

F nine tenths **G** one and five tenths

b) Use the number line to order the points from least to greatest. *C*, ___, ___, ___, ___, ___, ___

5. a) This number line is divided into hundredths. Mark 0.50 on the number line. In your notebook, explain how you decided where to mark this point.

b) Mark and label these points on the number line above. In your notebook, explain the strategy you used to place each number on the line.

A 0.72 **B** $\frac{34}{100}$ **C** 0.05 **D** $\frac{51}{100}$

c) Use the number line to order the points from least to greatest. ___, ___, ___, ___

6.

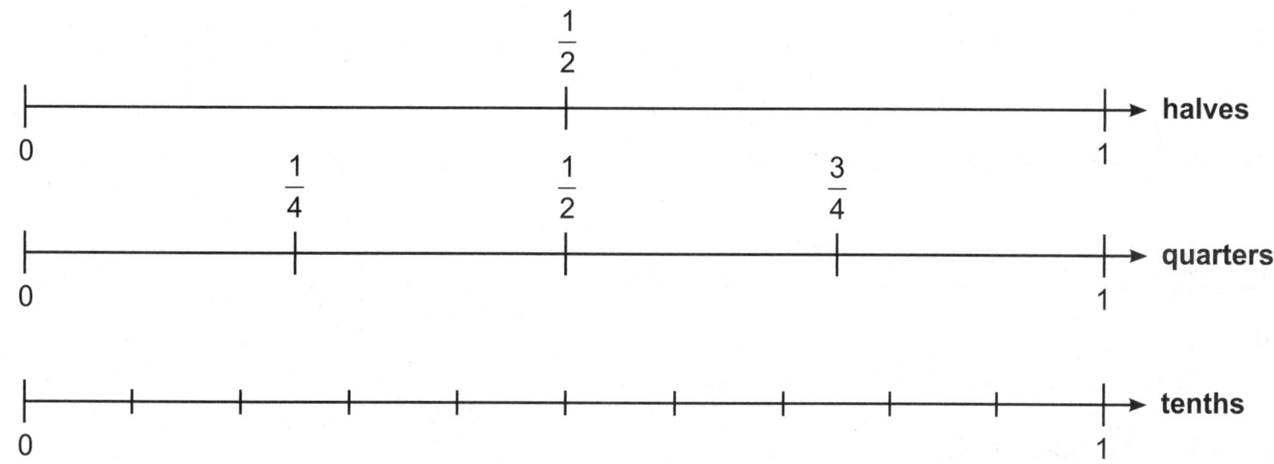

Use the number lines above to compare the pairs of numbers below. Write < (less than) or > (greater than) between each pair of numbers.

a) 0.7 ☐ $\frac{3}{4}$ b) 0.4 ☐ $\frac{7}{10}$ c) 0.8 ☐ $\frac{1}{2}$ d) 0.2 ☐ $\frac{1}{4}$

e) 0.4 ☐ $\frac{1}{2}$ f) 0.35 ☐ $\frac{1}{4}$ g) 0.07 ☐ $\frac{1}{2}$ h) $\frac{3}{4}$ ☐ 0.65

7. a) Circle the numbers that are placed on the line incorrectly. Draw the correct point(s).

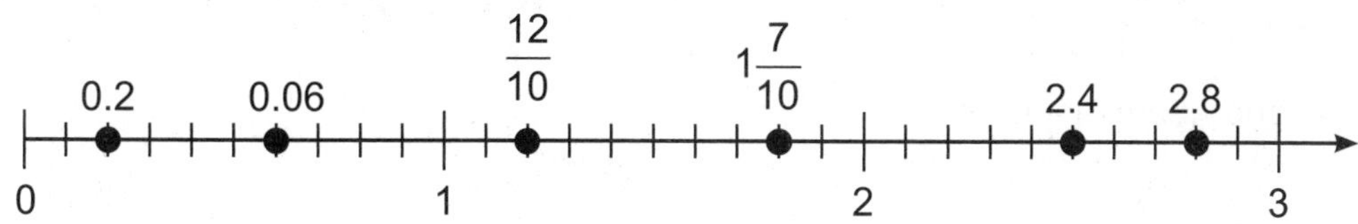

b) Write a number between each pair of numbers.

i) 0.2, ______, $\frac{12}{10}$ ii) $\frac{12}{10}$, ______, $1\frac{7}{10}$ iii) $1\frac{7}{10}$, ______, 2.4 iv) 2.4, ______, 2.8

NS7-38 Ordering Decimals and Fractions to Thousandths

1. Write the fractions with a common denominator. Then order the fractions from least to greatest.

a) $\frac{50}{100}$ $\frac{4}{10} = \frac{}{100}$ $\frac{6}{10} = \frac{}{100}$ ______, ______, ______

b) $\frac{30}{100}$ $\frac{2}{10} =$ $\frac{9}{10} =$ ______, ______, ______

2. Write the decimal as a fraction with denominator 100 by first adding a zero to the decimal.

a) $0.7 = \underline{\ 0.70\ } = \frac{70}{100}$ b) $0.9 =$ ______ $= \frac{}{100}$ c) $0.1 =$ ______ $= \frac{}{100}$

3. Add a zero to change the decimal tenths to hundredths. Then circle the greatest decimal hundredth.

a) 0.4*0* 0.32 (0.41) b) 0.72 0.8 0.7 c) 3.5 3.45 3.6

4. Write the fractions with a common denominator. Then order the fractions from least to greatest.

a) $\frac{72}{1000}$ $\frac{64}{100} = \frac{}{1000}$ $\frac{68}{100} = \frac{}{1000}$ ______, ______, ______

b) $\frac{54}{100} = \frac{}{1000}$ $\frac{504}{1000}$ $\frac{5}{10} = \frac{}{100} = \frac{}{1000}$ ______, ______, ______

5. Write the decimal as a fraction with denominator 1 000 by first adding one or two zeros to the decimal.

a) $0.75 =$ ______ $= \frac{}{1000}$ b) $0.93 =$ ______ $= \frac{}{1000}$ c) $0.2 =$ ______ $= \frac{}{1000}$

6. Add zero(s) where necessary to change the decimals to thousandths. Then circle the greatest decimal thousandth.

a) 0.12 0.046 0.4 b) 0.2 0.68 0.092 c) 7.5 7.45 7.6

7. Write each decimal as an improper fraction with the denominator shown. Then order the decimals from greatest to least.

a) $4.6 = \frac{46}{10}$ $3.7 = \frac{}{10}$ $4.4 = \frac{}{10}$ *4.6*, ______, ______

b) $2.97 = \frac{297}{100}$ $3.05 = \frac{}{100}$ $2.76 = \frac{}{100}$ ______, ______, ______

c) $1.3 = \frac{1300}{1000}$ $1.7 = \frac{}{1000}$ $1.4 = \frac{}{1000}$ *1.7*, ______, ______

d) $7.2 = \frac{7200}{1000}$ $7.587 = \frac{}{1000}$ $7.98 = \frac{}{1000}$ ______, ______, ______

8. Write a decimal that matches each description.

a) between 0.83 and 0.89 0. ____________ b) between 0.6 and 0.70 0. ____________

c) between 0.385 and 0.39 0. ____________ d) between 0.457 and 0.5 0. ____________

9. Write the numbers in the place value chart. Order the numbers from greatest to least.

a) 0.242, 1.368, 1.70, 2.05

tens	ones	tenths	hundredths	thousandths
	0	2	4	2

________, ________, ________, ________

b) 37.03, 7.306, 3.706, 6.73

tens	ones	tenths	hundredths	thousandths

________, ________, ________, ________

c) 45.25, 45.29, 45.193, 45.210

tens	ones	tenths	hundredths	thousandths

________, ________, ________, ________

d) 0.654, 0.555, 0.655, 0.554

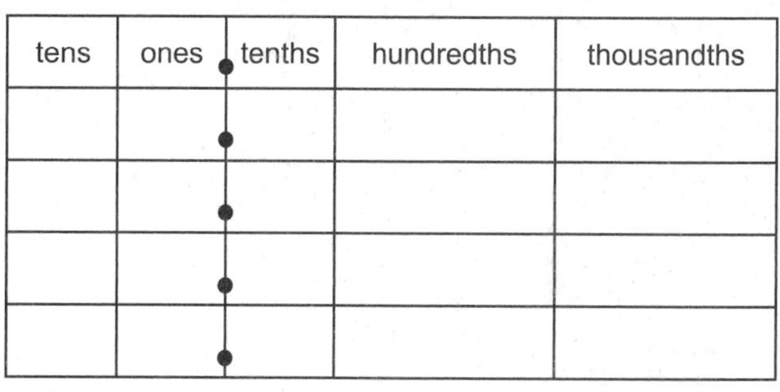

tens	ones	tenths	hundredths	thousandths

________, ________, ________, ________

10. Complete the number pattern.

a) 7.5, 7.6, 7.___, 7.8, 7.9, 8.___, 8.___

b) 10.5, 11.5, 12.5, ______, ______

c) ______, 9.40, 9.35, ______, 9.25, 9.20

d) 0.005, 0.010, 0.015, ______, 0.025, 0.030

e) 25.6, ______, ______, 28.6, 29.6

f) 50.63, 50.53, ______, 50.33, ______

11. Arrange the numbers in increasing order.

a) 22.546, 22.456, 22.466

________, ________, ________

b) 60.765, 60.756, 60.657

________, ________, ________

c) 3.67, 3.076, 367

________, ________, ________

d) 53.760, 53.670, 53.607

________, ________, ________

12. Arrange the numbers in decreasing order.

a) 75.240, 75.704, 77.740

________, ________, ________

b) 0.004, 0.040, 0.041, 4.001

________, ________, ________, ________

13. Write five decimals greater than 1.32 and less than 1.33.

14. 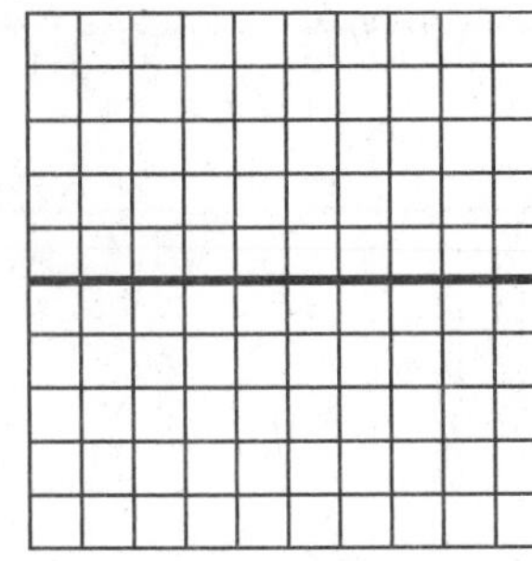

Shade $\frac{1}{2}$ of the squares. Write 2 fractions and 2 decimals for $\frac{1}{2}$.

Fractions: $\frac{1}{2} = \frac{\_\_}{10} = \frac{\_\_}{100}$

Decimals: $\frac{1}{2}$ = __.____ = __.____

15. 

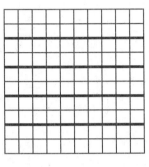

Shade $\frac{1}{5}$ of the boxes. Write 2 fractions and 2 decimals for $\frac{1}{5}$.

Fractions: $\frac{1}{5} = \frac{\_\_}{10} = \frac{\_\_}{100}$

Decimals: $\frac{1}{5}$ = __.____ = __.____

16. Write equivalent fractions.

a) $\frac{2}{5} = \frac{\_\_}{10} = \frac{\_\_}{100}$ b) $\frac{3}{5} = \frac{\_\_}{10} = \frac{\_\_}{100}$ c) $\frac{4}{5} = \frac{\_\_}{10} = \frac{\_\_}{100}$

17. 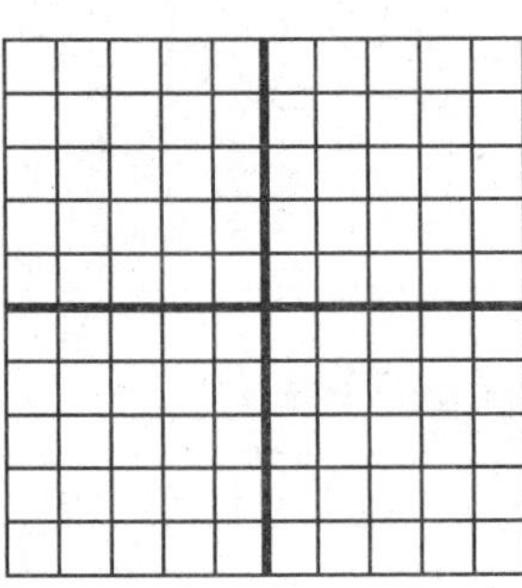

Shade $\frac{1}{4}$ of the squares. Write a fraction and a decimal for $\frac{1}{4}$ and $\frac{3}{4}$.

Fraction: $\frac{1}{4} = \frac{\_\_}{100}$ *Fraction:* $\frac{3}{4} = \frac{\_\_}{100}$

Decimal: $\frac{1}{4}$ = __.____ *Decimal:* $\frac{3}{4}$ = __.____

18. Circle the greater number. Hint: First change all fractions and decimals to fractions with denominator 100 or 1 000. (Note: $4 \times 250 = 1\,000$)

a) $\frac{1}{2}$ 0.51 b) $\frac{4}{5}$ 0.85 c) $\frac{3}{4}$ 0.734

19. Write the numbers in order from least to greatest. Explain how you found your answer.

a) 0.7 0.34 $\frac{3}{5}$ b) 0.817 $\frac{77}{100}$ $\frac{4}{5}$ c) $\frac{3}{5}$ 0.425 $\frac{1}{2}$

20. How does knowing that $\frac{1}{4} = 0.25$ help you find the decimal form of $\frac{3}{4}$?

21. Explain how you know 0.635 is greater than $\frac{1}{2}$.

Regrouping Decimals

A Base Ten Model for Decimal Tenths and Hundredths

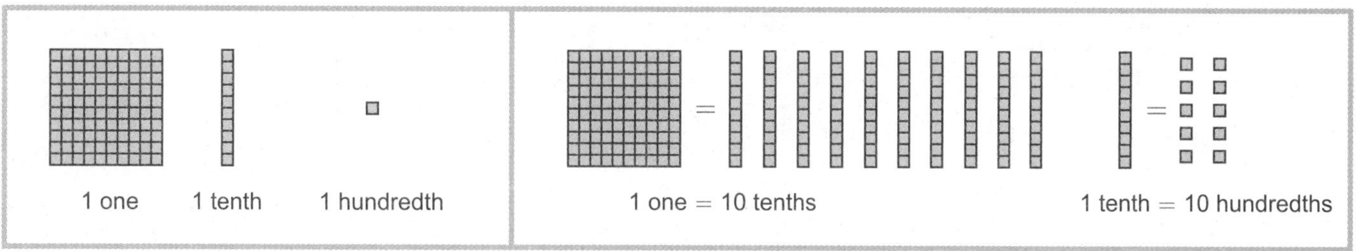

1. a) This model represents the decimal _2_.___ ___.

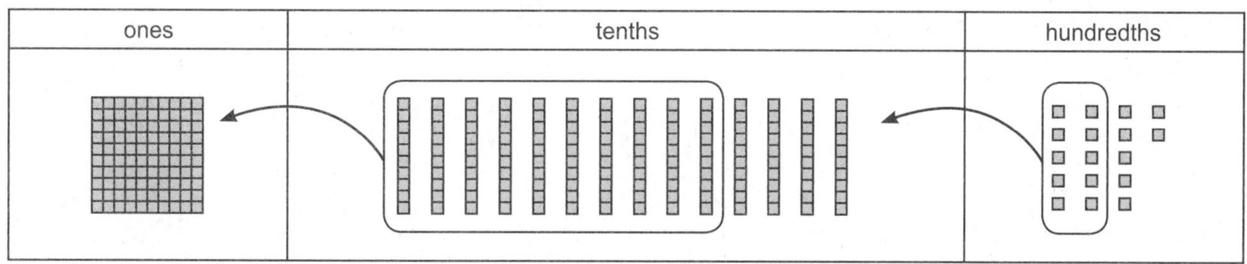

b) Regroup as many of the blocks into bigger blocks as you can. This model represents ___.___ ___.

ones	tenths	hundredths

c) Regroup as many of the blocks into bigger blocks as you can. This model represents ___.___ ___.

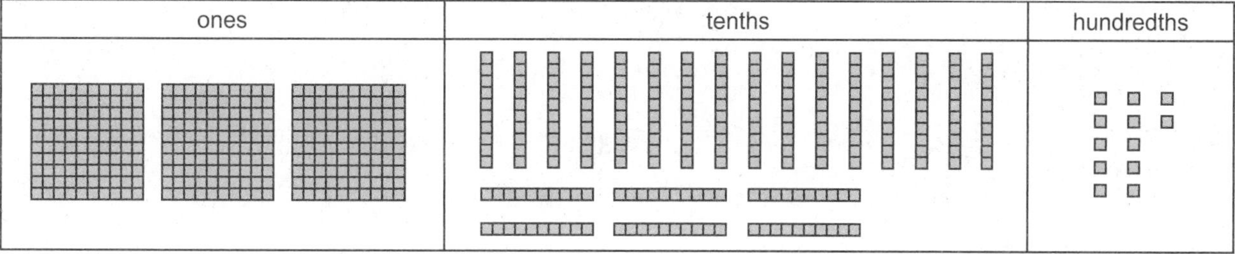

2. Regroup.

a) 27 tenths = _2_ ones + ___ tenths

b) 36 tenths = ___ ones + ___ tenths

c) 74 hundredths = ___ tenths + ___ hundredths

d) 19 hundredths = ___ tenths + ___ hundredths

3. Regroup so that each place value has a single digit.

a) 2 ones + 14 tenths = _3_ ones + _4_ tenths

b) 6 tenths + 17 hundredths = ___ tenths + ___ hundredths

c) 5 hundredths + 11 thousandths = ___ hundredths + ___ thousandth

4. Exchange 1 tenth for 10 hundredths or 1 hundredth for 10 thousandths.

a) 6 tenths + 0 hundredths = ___5___ tenths + ___10___ hundredths

b) 9 tenths + 0 hundredths = _______ tenths + _______ hundredths

c) 7 hundredths + 0 thousandths = _______ hundredths + _______ thousandths

d) 4 tenths + 0 hundredths = _______ tenths + _______ hundredths

5. Exchange one of the larger unit for 10 of the smaller unit.

a) 3 hundredths + 4 thousandths = ___2___ hundredths + ___14___ thousandths

b) 6 tenths + 7 hundredths = _______ tenths + _______ hundredths

c) 4 ones + 5 tenths = _______ ones + _______ tenths

d) 9 hundredths + 1 thousandth = _______ hundredths + _______ thousandths

6. Underline the smallest place value in the decimal. Then write the decimal as an improper fraction.

a) $2.3 = \frac{23}{10}$ b) $4.5 =$ c) $7.6 =$ d) $3.55 = \frac{\quad}{100}$ e) $6.18 =$

f) $9.76 =$ g) $1.23 =$ h) $1.254 = \frac{\quad}{1000}$ i) $5.355 =$ j) $3.112 =$

7. Add zeros to rewrite the whole number as decimal tenths, hundredths, and thousandths.
Example: 2 = 2.0 = 2.00 = 2.000

a) 7 = __________
= __________
= __________

b) 15 = __________
= __________
= __________

c) 230 = __________
= __________
= __________

8. Regroup the whole number as ones, tenths, hundredths, and thousandths.

a) 8 = _______ ones = _______ tenths = _______ hundredths = _______ thousandths

b) 16 = _______ ones = _______ tenths = _______ hundredths = _______ thousandths

9. Complete the statements.

a) 1.7 = _______ tenths

b) 5.2 = _______ tenths

c) 13.4 = _______ tenths

d) 75.3 = _______ tenths

e) 13.4 = _______ hundredths

f) 75.3 = _______ hundredths

g) 10.36 = _______ hundredths

h) 1.25 = _______ hundredths

i) 10.36 = _______ thousandths

j) 1.25 = _______ thousandths

NS7-40 Addition Strategies for Decimals

1. Write an addition statement that corresponds to the grids.

a) 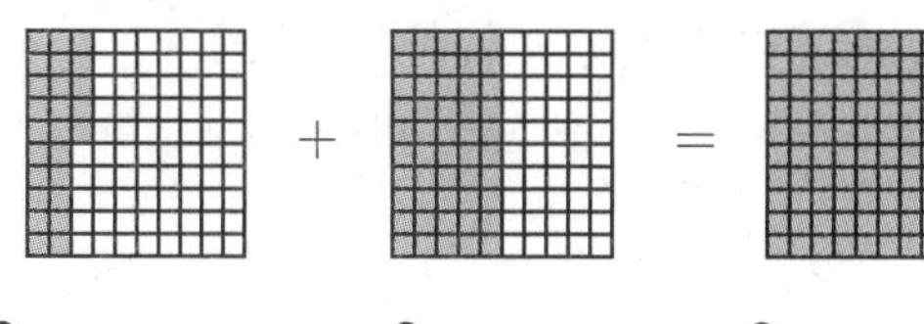

0.______ + 0.______ = 0.______

b) 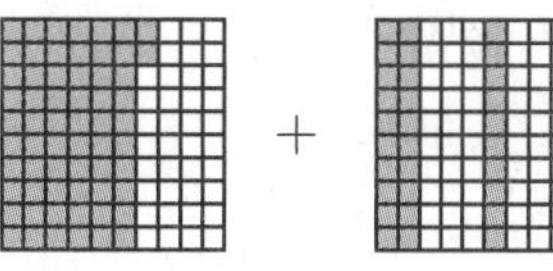 = 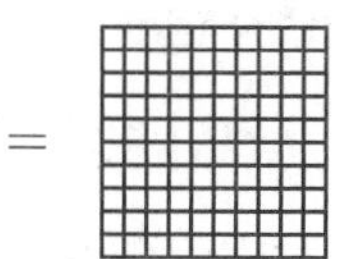

0.______ + 0.______ = 0.______

2. Add by sketching a base ten model. Note: Use a hundreds block for a one and a tens block for a tenth.

a) 1.23 + 1.12

= 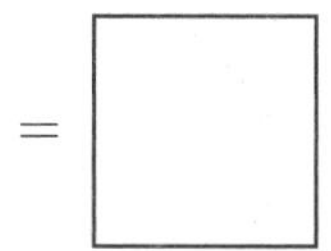 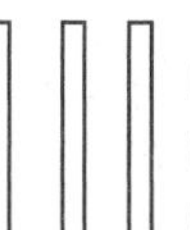 + 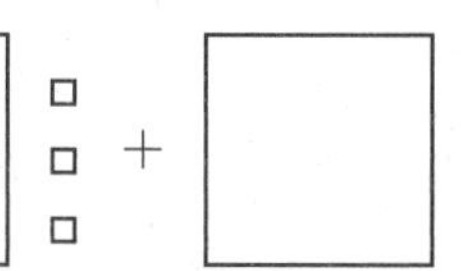

= 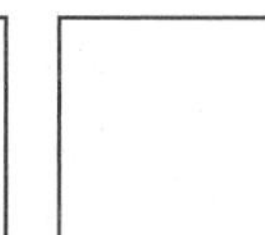  = ______

b) 1.46 + 1.33

3. Use equivalent fractions to calculate the decimal sums.

a) $0.3 + 0.4 = \frac{3}{10} + \frac{}{10} = \frac{}{10} = 0.$______

b) $0.65 + 0.22 = \frac{}{100} + \frac{}{100} = \frac{}{100} = 0.$______

c) $0.56 + 0.05 = \frac{}{100} + \frac{}{100} = \frac{}{100} = 0.$______

d) $0.123 + 0.44 = \frac{}{1000} + \frac{}{1000} = \frac{}{1000} = 0.$______

4. Write the decimals as fractions with a common denominator to calculate the sums.

a) $0.27 + 0.6 = \frac{27}{100} + \frac{6}{10} = \frac{27}{100} + \frac{}{100} = \frac{}{100} =$ ___.___ ___

b) $0.57 + 0.765 = \frac{57}{100} + \frac{765}{1000} = \frac{}{1000} + \frac{765}{1000} = \frac{}{1000} =$ ___.___ ___ ___

c) $2.025 + 0.99 = \frac{}{1000} + \frac{}{100} = \frac{}{1000} + \frac{}{1000} = \frac{}{1000} =$ ___.___ ___ ___

5. Write both decimals using the smallest place value to calculate the sums.

a) 2.15 + 6.3

= *215* hundredths + *63* tenths

= *215* hundredths + *630* hundredths

= *845* hundredths

= *8* . *4* *5*

b) 4.054 + 2.93

= _____ thousandths + _____ hundredths

= _____ thousandths + _____ thousandths

= _____ thousandths

= ___.___ ___ ___

6. Add by adding each place value.

a) 3.3 + 2.4

= (3 ones + 3 tenths) + (2 ones + 4 tenths)

= (3 ones + 2 ones) + (3 tenths + 4 tenths)

= ___ ones + ___ tenths

= ___.___

b) 7.6 + 1.3

= (___ ones + ___ tenths) + (___ ones + ___ tenths)

= (___ ones + ___ ones) + (___ tenths + ___ tenths)

= ___ ones + ___ tenths

= ___.___

7. Add by adding each place value.

a)

	tens	ones	tenths	hundredths
	3	2	1	
+		6	7	8
	3	8	8	8

b)

	tens	ones	tenths	hundredths
	4	0	5	3
+	2	7	2	

8. Add by adding each place value. Then regroup wherever necessary.

Example:

	ones	tenths
	1	7
+	4	7
	5	14

14 tenths =

1 one + 4 tenths,

so the sum is

6	4

a)

	ones	tenths	hundredths
		6	4
+	8	2	9

___ hundredths =

___ tenths + ___ hundredths,

so the sum is

b)

	ones	tenths	hundredths	thousandths
	2	5	0	7
+		3	6	8

___ thousandths =

___ hundredths + ___ thousandths

so the sum is

9. Use the place value chart to add the decimals. Then regroup.

a) 0.723 + 3.146 + 0.5

	tens	ones	tenths	hundredths	thousandths
+					

Regroup:

b) 0.23 + 45.652 + 2.4

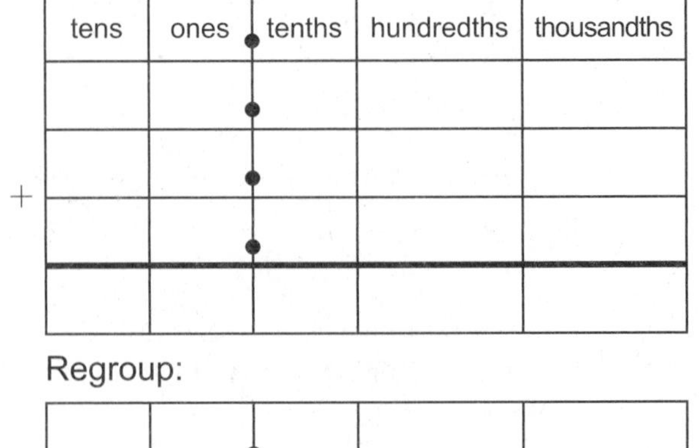

	tens	ones	tenths	hundredths	thousandths
+					

Regroup:

BONUS ▶ Regroup twice to add: 0.025 + 0.348 + 0.534

NS7-41 Adding and Subtracting Decimals

Adding Decimals

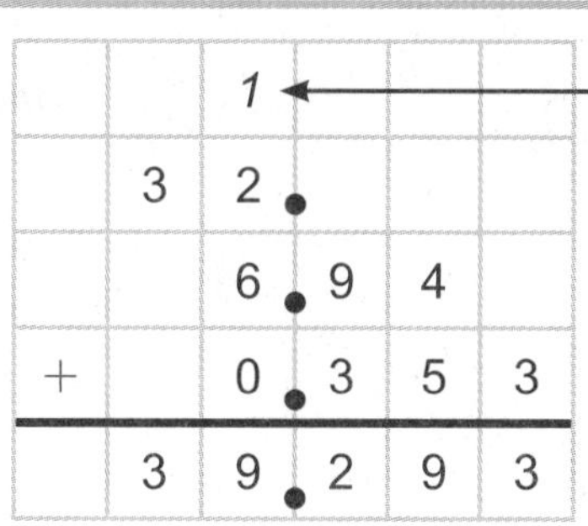

12 tenths were regrouped as 1 one and 2 tenths.

		1			
	3	2.			
		6.	9	4	
+		0.	3	5	3
	3	9.	2	9	3

1. Add the decimals.

a) 0.32 + 0.54
b) 5.71 + 3.26
c) 0.416 + 0.573
d) 9.117 + 0.162

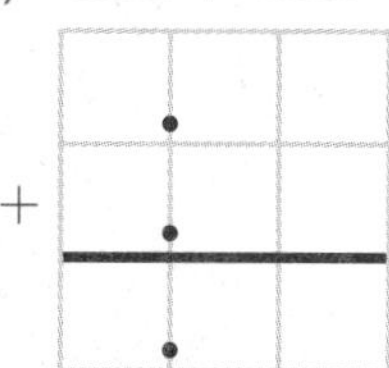

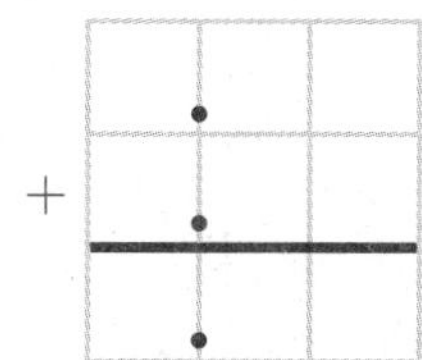

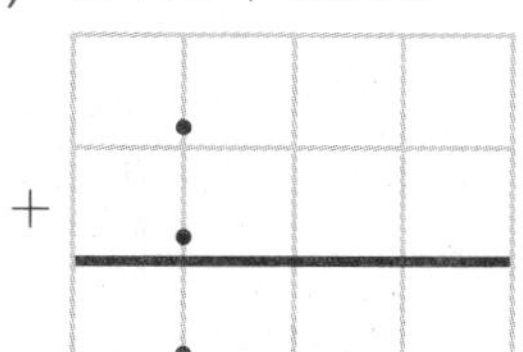

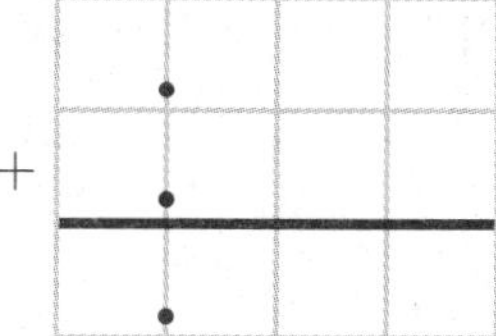

2. Add the decimals by lining up the decimal points.

a) 0.81 + 0.58
b) 2.56 + 7.27
c) 0.583 + 1.251
d) 5.555 + 4.078

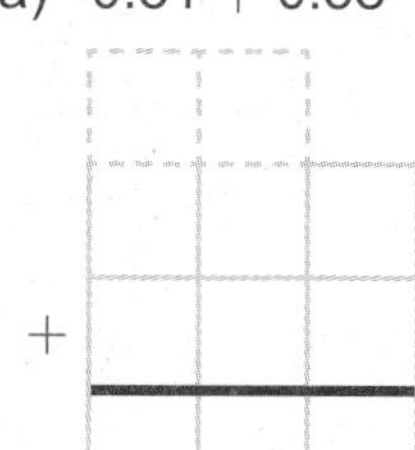

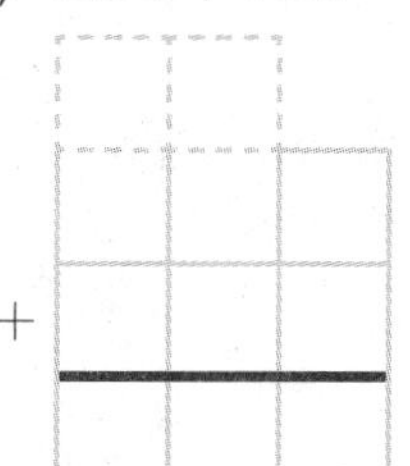

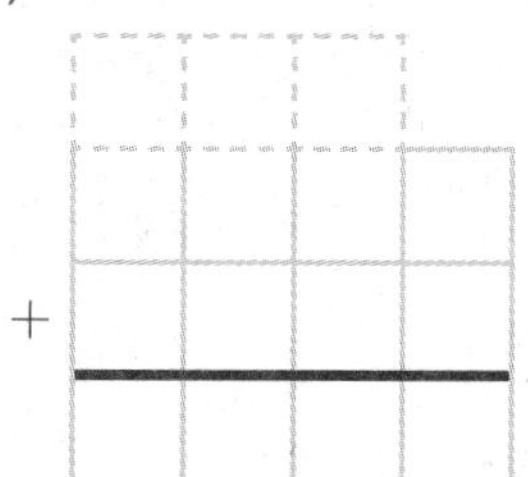

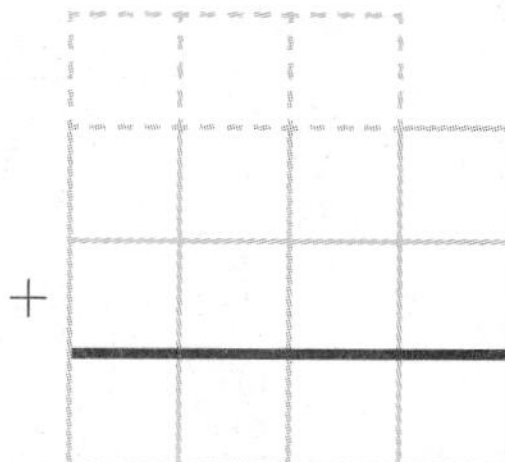

e) 0.45 + 0.08 + 0.32
f) 5.6 + 1.42 + 0.8
g) 1.275 + 0.56 + 6.304
h) 0.9 + 0.99 + 0.999

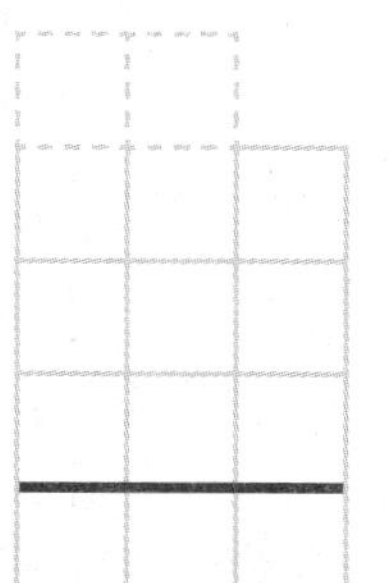

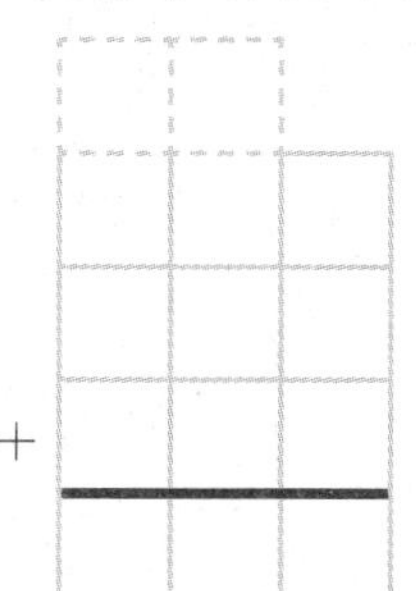

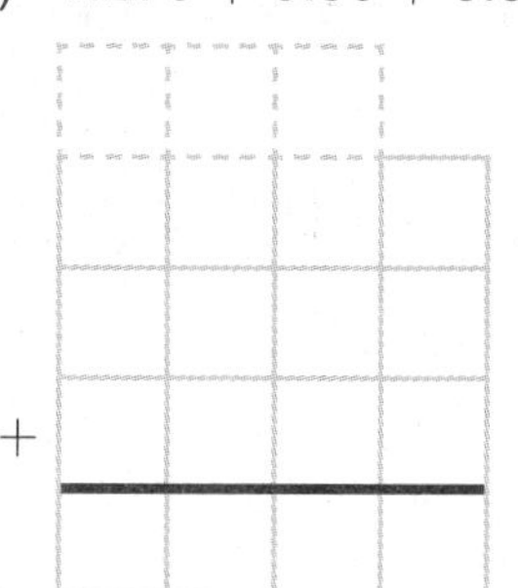

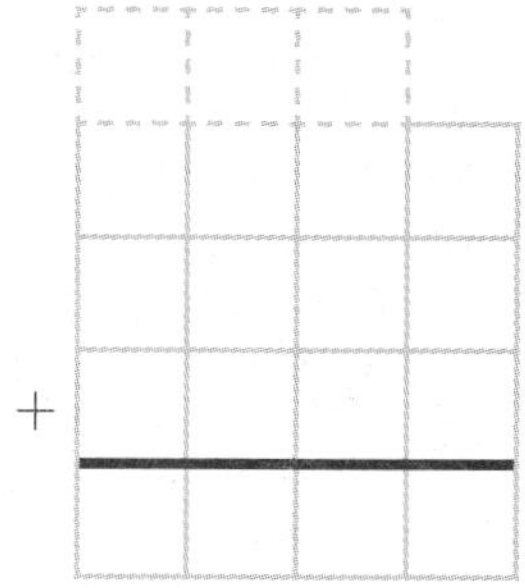

3. Add the decimals on grid paper.

a) 4.32 + 2.77
b) 3.64 + 5.83
c) 9.465 + 3.12
d) 0.87 + 0.026
e) 7.098 + 2.169 + 5.43
f) 0.076 + 2.84 + 0.639
g) 47.5 + 3.003 + 16.87

4. a) The mass of a nickel is 3.95 g and the mass of a penny is 2.35 g. What is the total mass of 1 nickel and 2 pennies?

b) The mass of a dime is 1.75 g, and the mass of a quarter is 4.4 g. What is heavier, five dimes or two quarters?

5. Bill adds 43.4 + 5.65 on grid paper. He gets 99.9. What mistake did he make? Explain.

Subtracting Decimals

Add zeros to make each decimal end at the same place value.

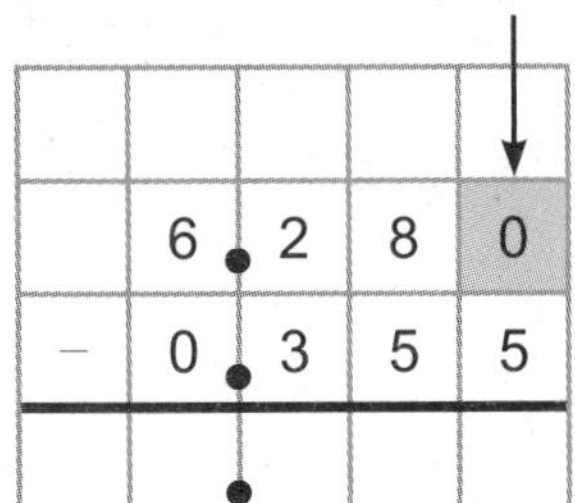

If the top digit in a column is **less than the digit below it**, take 1 from the column to the left and add 10 to the top digit.

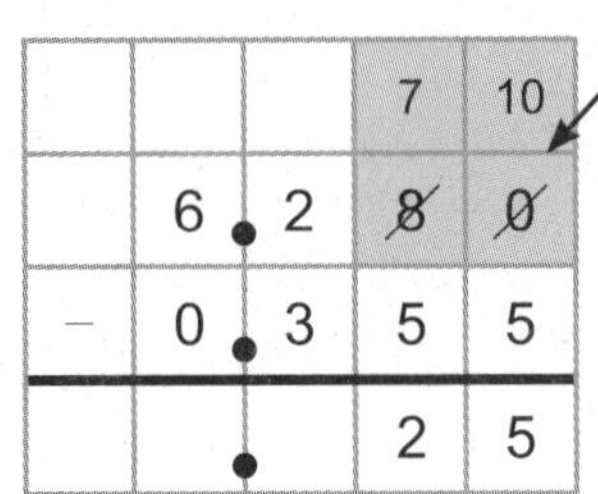

	5	12	7	10
	~~6~~	. ~~2~~	~~8~~	~~0~~
−	0	. 3	5	5
	5	. 9	2	5

6. Subtract the decimals.

a) 0.53 – 0.21

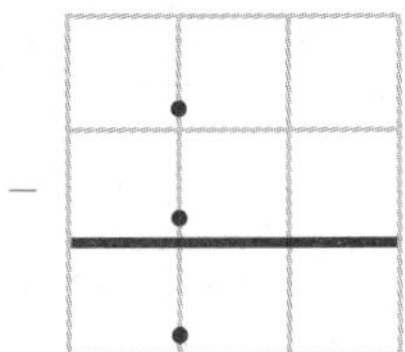

b) 0.76 – 0.24

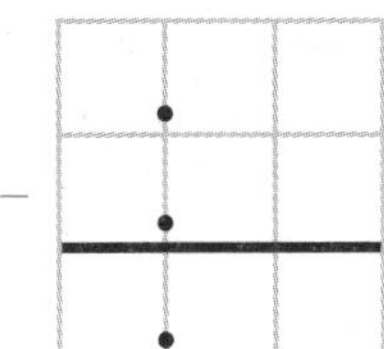

c) 3.47 – 2.2

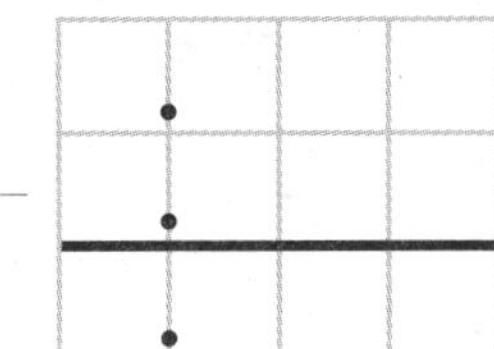

d) 6.49 – 0.35

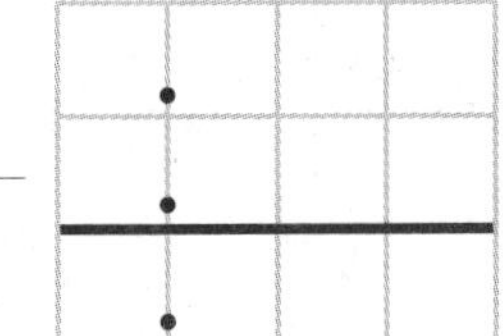

7. Subtract the decimals by lining up the decimal points.

a) 0.81 – 0.58

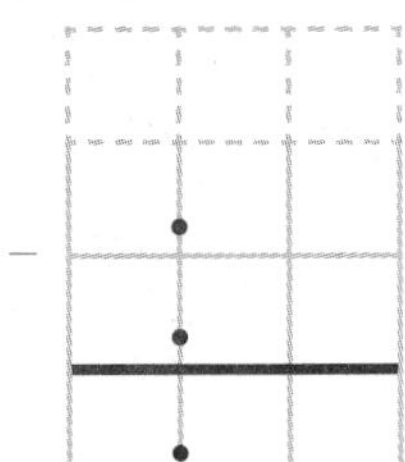

b) 5.72 – 3.56

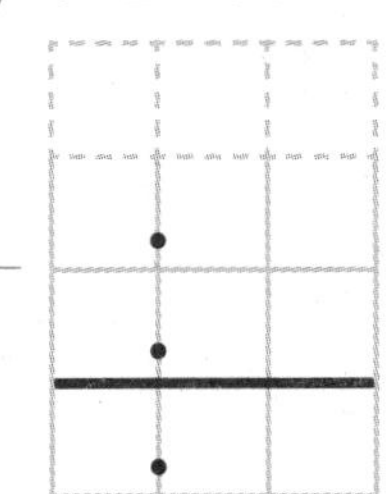

c) 6.156 – 4.25

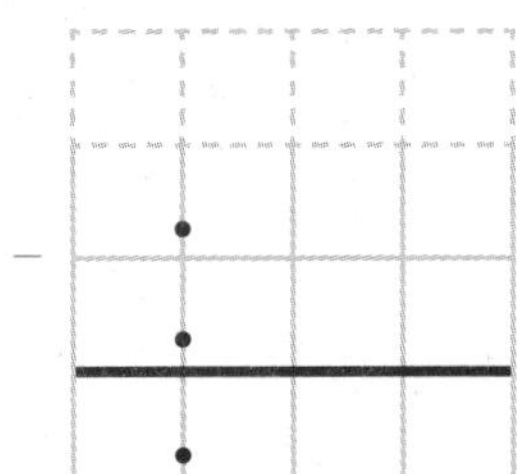

d) 2.463 – 0.271

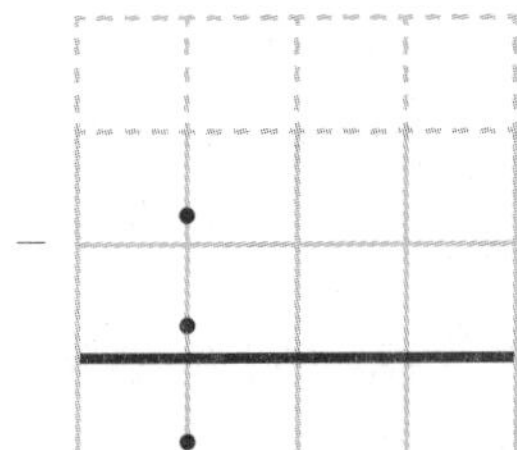

e) 4.5 – 2.65

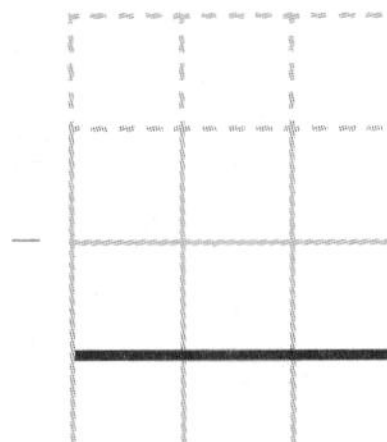

f) 31.1 – 22.2

g) 7.455 – 6.68

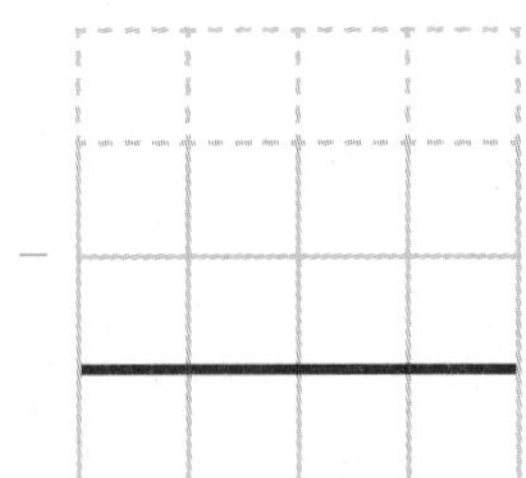

h) 5.207 – 1.238

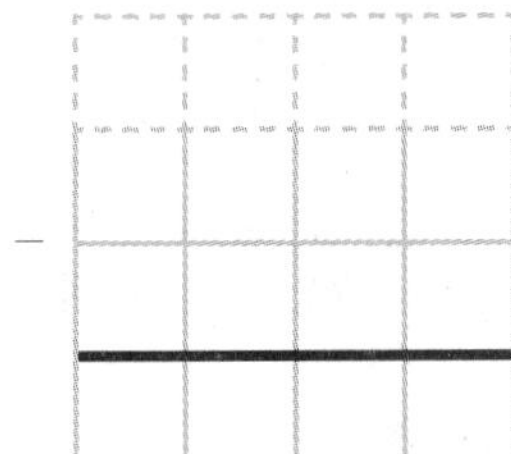

8. Subtract the decimals on grid paper.

a) 0.87 – 0.026 b) 9.465 – 3.12 c) 5.83 – 3.69 d) 4.35 – 2.72

9. What is the difference in thickness of these coins?

a) a penny (1.45 mm) and a dime (1.22 mm)

b) a dollar (1.95 mm) and a quarter (1.58 mm)

NS7-42 Rounding Review

1. Underline the digit you wish to round to. Then say whether you would round up or down.

a) thousands

b) ten thousands

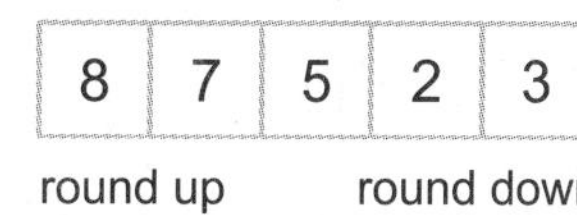

c) hundreds

d) tens

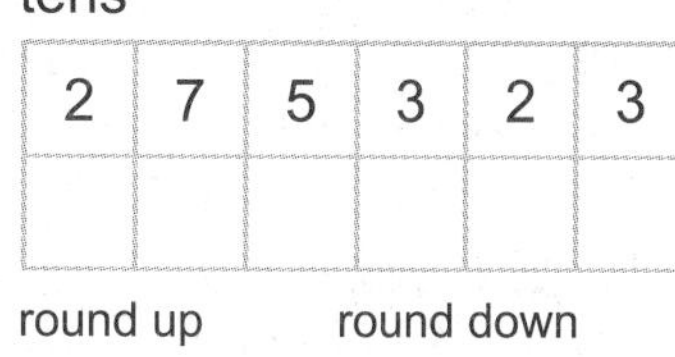

e) thousands

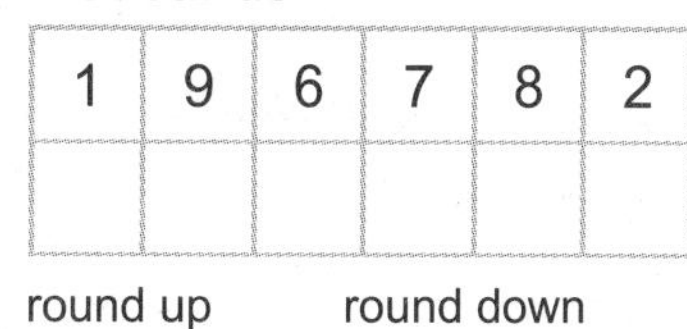

f) thousands

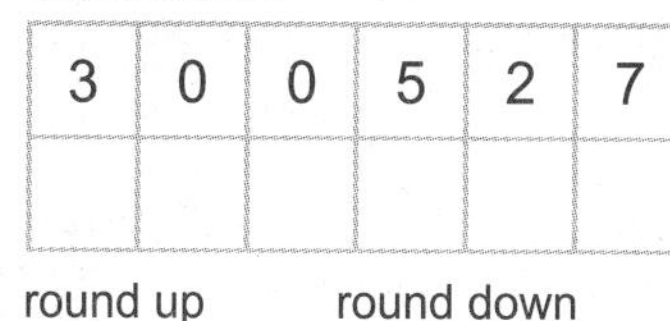

2. Complete the two steps from Question 1. Then follow the two steps below.

Step 1: Round the digit underlined up or down.

- To round up, add 1 to the digit.
- To round down, keep the digit the same.

4	5	7	3	4	5	ru
			3			(rd)

Step 2: The digits to the right of the rounded digit become zeros.

The digits to the left remain the same.

4	5	7	3	4	5	ru
		7	3	0	0	(rd)

a) thousands

b) ten thousands

c) ten thousands

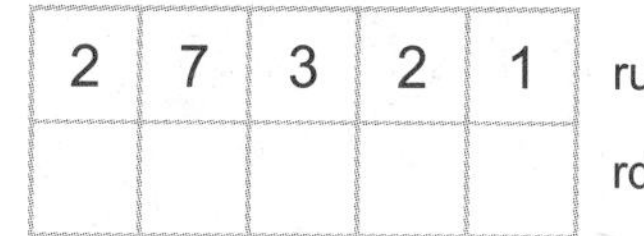

d) hundred thousands

e) ten thousands

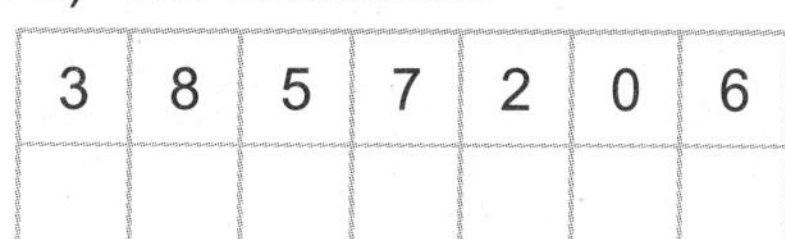

f) hundred thousands

g) hundreds

2	3	0	1	3	2	5	ru
							rd

h) tens

3	2	9	7	8	7	6	ru
							rd

i) thousands

3. Sometimes in rounding, you have to regroup.

Example: Round 37 952 to the nearest hundred.

3	7	9	5	2

Step 1: 900 rounds to 1 000.

3	7	9	5	2
	8	0		

Step 2: Regroup the 10 hundreds as 1 (thousand) and add it to the 7 (thousand).

3	7	9	5	2
3	8	0	0	0

Step 3: Complete the rounding.

Round each number to the digit given (regrouping if necessary).

a) 385 721 ten thousands b) 987 832 thousands c) 39 823 ten thousands d) 427 296 tens

e) 20 175 hundreds f) 8 729 738 hundred thousands g) 97 231 ten thousands h) 3 952 793 hundred thousands

NS7-43 Rounding Decimals

1. What is the length, to the nearest centimetre?

a) ______ cm, to the nearest centimetre

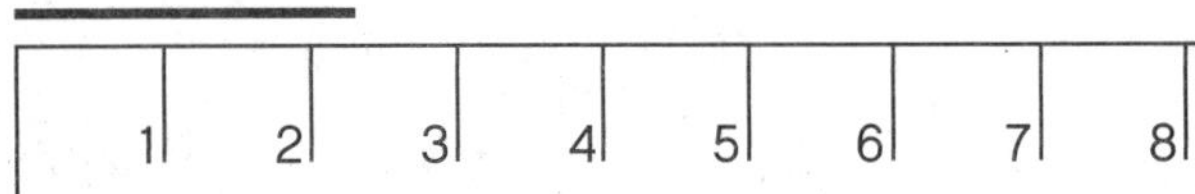

b) ______ cm, to the nearest centimetre

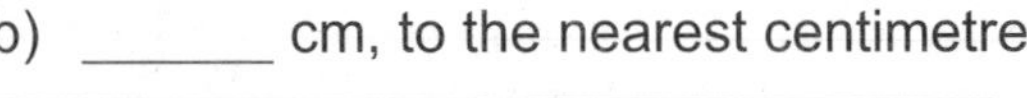

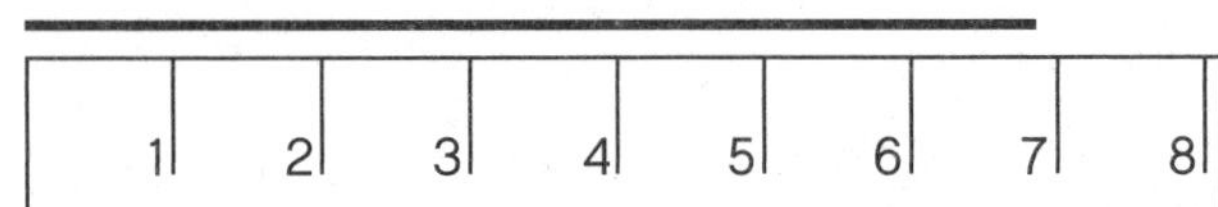

2. What is the length, to the nearest centimetre?

a) 5.4 cm is approximately ______ cm.

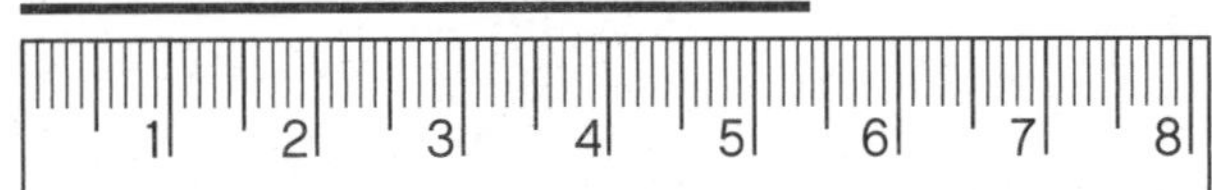

b) 7.7 cm is approximately ______ cm.

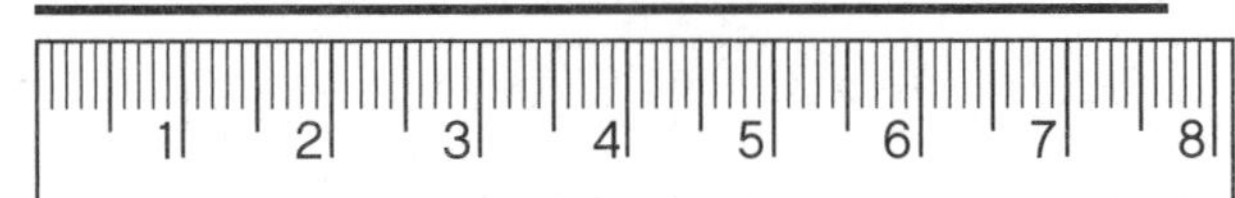

3. a) Is 3.76 closer to 3.7 or 3.8? Closer to ______

So, 3.76 is approximately equal to ______.

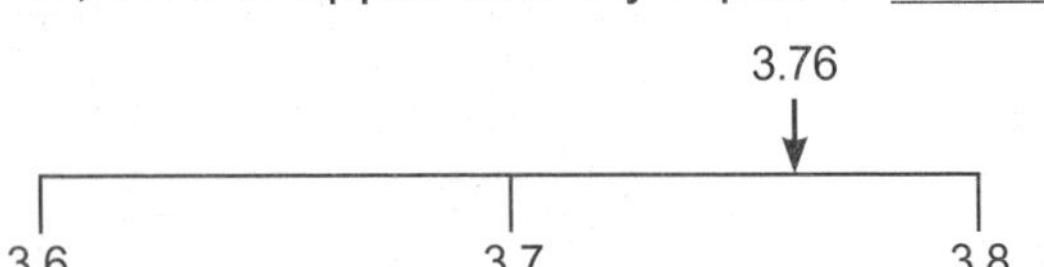

b) Is 4.254 closer to 4.25 or 4.26? Closer to ______

So, 4.254 is approximately equal to ______.

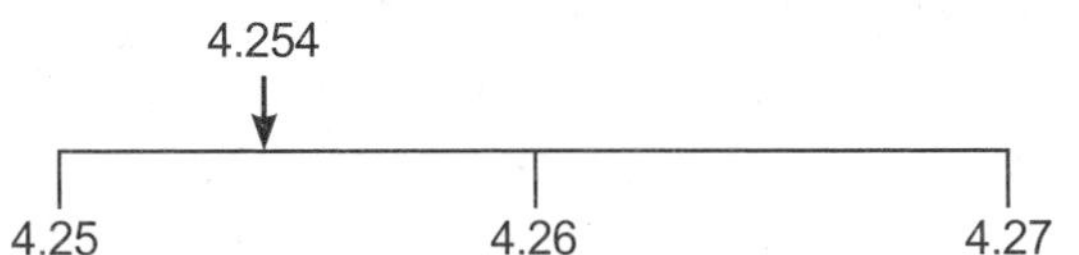

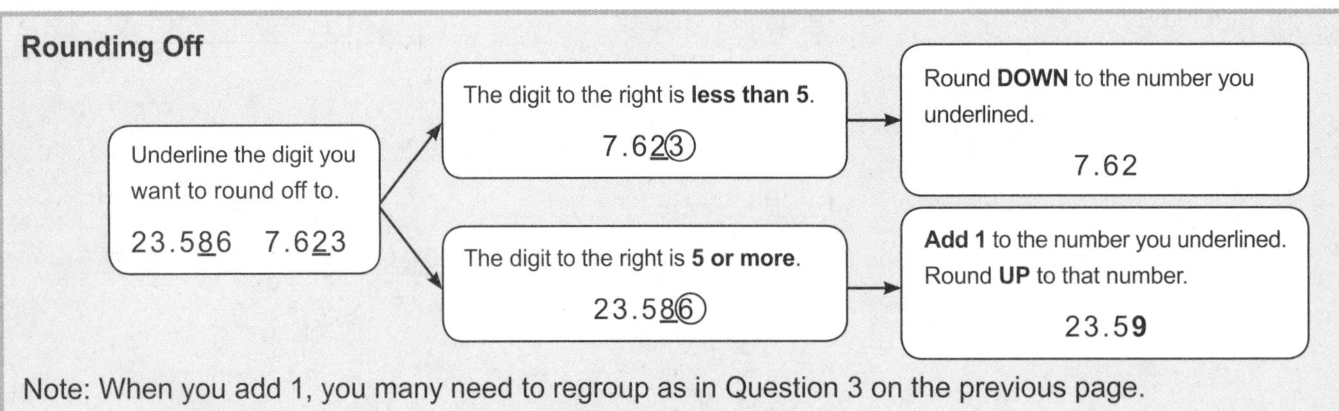

Rounding Off
Underline the digit you want to round off to.
23.586 7.623
The digit to the right is less than 5.
7.623
Round DOWN to the number you underlined.
7.62
The digit to the right is 5 or more.
23.586
Add 1 to the number you underlined. Round UP to that number.
23.59
Note: When you add 1, you many need to regroup as in Question 3 on the previous page.

4. Follow the steps above to round the decimals.
Hint: Do not forget to write the decimal point in your answer.

a) tenths

2 . 3 7 5

b) hundredths

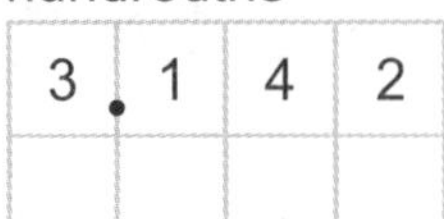

c) tenths

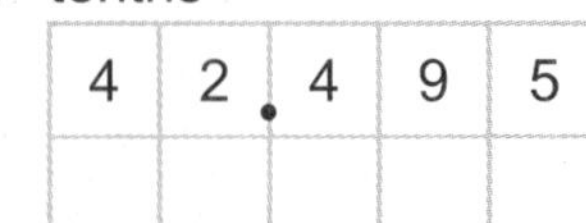

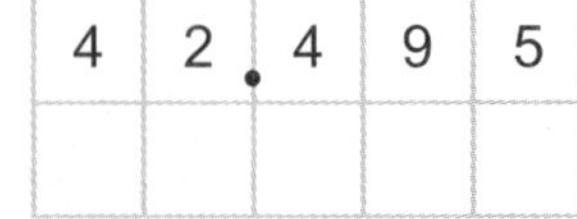

d) ones

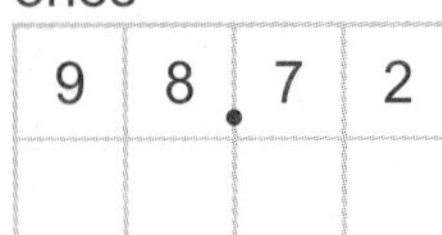

e) tens

f) ones

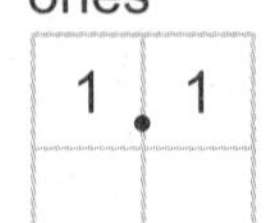

g) tenths

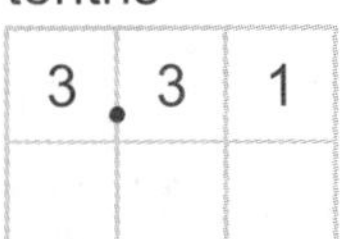

h) hundredths

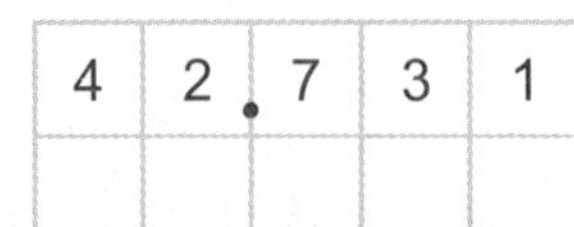

i) thousandths

3 . 2 7 0 6

j) tenths

9	2.	1	5	7

k) hundredths

3	6.	2	8	3

l) ones

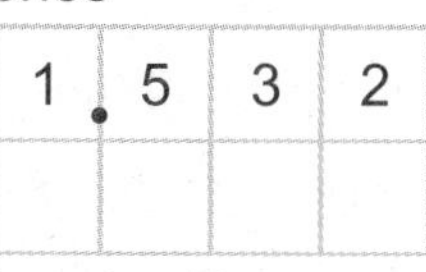

1.	5	3	2

m) ones

7.	6	2

n) tens

4	8.	0	5

o) hundredths

5.	2	9	9

5. Round off the decimal to the nearest thousandth, hundredth, and tenth.

REMINDER▶ The symbol ≈ means "is approximately equal to".

a) 0.1234 ≈ 0.__ __ __ ≈ 0.__ __ ≈ 0.__ b) 4.6789 ≈ 4.__ __ __ ≈ 4.__ __ ≈ 4.__

c) 0.6327 ≈ 0.__ __ __ ≈ 0.__ __ ≈ 0.__ d) 5.1774 ≈ 5.__ __ __ ≈ 5.__ __ ≈ 5.__

6. Round off the measurement to the nearest tenth.

a) 35.234 kg ≈ ____ kg b) 0.593 km ≈ ____ km c) 349.67 L ≈ ____ L d) 100.06 m ≈ ____ m

e) 0.067 cm ≈ ____ cm f) 921.58 g ≈ ____ g g) 7.008 mm ≈ ____ mm h) 4.96 mg ≈ ____ mg

7. Round the decimal to either 0 or 1, whichever is closer. Examples: 0.9 ≈ 1 and 0.3 ≈ 0.

a) 0.8 ≈ ____ b) 0.2 ≈ ____ c) 0.5 ≈ ____ d) 0.97 ≈ ____ e) 0.43 ≈ ____ f) 0.55 ≈ ____

8. Calculate using a calculator. Then round off to the nearest hundredth.

a) 1 ÷ 3 ≈ 0.__ __ b) 2 ÷ 3 ≈ 0.__ __ c) 22 ÷ 7 ≈ 3.__ __ d) 45 ÷ 13 ≈ 3.__ __

9. Estimate the value by rounding off to the nearest whole number.

a) 32.7 + 4.16 ≈ ____ + ____ = ____

b) 25.3 − 10.657 ≈ ____ − ____ = ____

c) 2.7 × 5.3 ≈ ____ × ____ = ____

d) 34.826 + 7.25 ≈ ____ + ____ = ____

e) 0.65 + 0.213 ≈ ____ + ____ = ____

f) 4.37 × 2.567 ≈ ____ × ____ = ____

g) 23.82 ÷ 2.57 ≈ ____ ÷ ____ = ____

h) 73.54 − 20.66 ≈ ____ − ____ = ____

i) 39.86 ÷ 4.874 ≈ ____ ÷ ____ = ____

10. a) Estimate by rounding both numbers to the nearest whole number. Use your estimate to predict whether the answer given is reasonable.

i) 32.7 + 4.16 = 73.8 ii) 0.7 × 8.3 = 5.81 iii) 9.2 × 10.3 = 947.6

iv) 97.2 ÷ 0.9 = 0.8 v) 88.2 ÷ 9.8 = 9 vi) 54.3 ÷ 5.6 = 35.7

b) Use a calculator to calculate the answers in a). Were your predictions correct?

11. The decimal hundredths that could be rounded off to 5.3 are from 5.25 to 5.34. Which decimal hundredths could be rounded off to 7.2? Explain.

NS7-44 Estimating Decimal Sums and Differences

1. a) Estimate the sum or difference using the whole number parts of the decimals.

Example: For 32.456 + 6.71 + 0.253, estimate 32 + 6 + 0 = 39.
So the sum is close to 39.

i) 2.785 + 3.76 + 20.4 ≈ ____ + ____ + ____ = ____

ii) 12.348 – 4.97 ≈ ____ – ____ = ____

iii) 12.75 + 10.603 + 0.24 ≈ ____ + ____ + ____ = ____

iv) 562.403 – 140.624 ≈ ____ – ____ = ____

b) Now calculate the sums and differences. Use your estimates to check your calculations.

Example: On a calculator, 32.456 + 6.71 + 0.253 = 39.419.
This is close to 39, as expected.

i) 2.785 + 3.76 + 20.4 = ________. Is this close to your estimate from part a)? ________

ii) 12.348 – 4.97 = ________. Is this close to your estimate from part a)? ________

iii) 12.75 + 10.603 + 0.24 = ________. Is this close to your estimate from part a)? ________

iv) 562.403 – 140.624 = ________. Is this close to your estimate from part a)? ________

2. a) Estimate by rounding to the nearest tenth.

Example: For 2.877 + 3.62, you could estimate 2.9 + 3.6.
So the sum is approximately 6.5.

i) 0.769 – 0.35 ≈ ____ – ____ = ____

ii) 25.08 + 0.004 + 4.53 ≈ ____ + ____ + ____ = ____

iii) 3.25 + 2.67 + 0.48 ≈ ____ + ____ + ____ = ____

iv) 5.467 – 2.78 ≈ ____ – ____ = ____

b) Calculate the sums and differences in part a) using a calculator.
Use your estimates to check your calculations.

3. a) Estimate by using the digits of the two highest place values.

Examples: **3.2**85 – **0.7**6 ≈ 3.2 – 0.7 = 2.5
0.**54**6 + 0.**06**7 ≈ 0.54 + 0.06 = 0.60

Put zeros in the other places if you need to.
4356.75 + **67**40.39 ≈ 4 300 + 6 700 = 11 000

i) 9.182 + 1.868 ≈ ____ + ____ = ____

ii) 3.29 + 2.547 + 4.166 ≈ ____ + ____ + ____ = ____

iii) 0.239 – 0.147 ≈ ____ – ____ = ____

iv) 685.6 – 479.2 ≈ ____ – ____ = ____

b) Calculate the sums and differences in part a) using a calculator.
Use your estimates to check your calculations.

For greater numbers, you can estimate by rounding to the nearest 10, 100, or 1 000.

Examples: $453.56 + 38.027 \approx 450 + 40 = 490$
$8\,739.57 - 2\,476.82 \approx 8\,700 - 2\,500 = 6\,200$

4. a) Estimate by rounding to the nearest 10, 100, or 1 000.

i) $7\,652.73 + 6\,281.56 \approx$ _____ + _____ = _____

ii) $341.8 + 756.4 + 523.9 \approx$ _____ + _____ + _____ = _____

iii) $753.8 - 684.2 \approx$ _____ − _____ = _____

iv) $5\,416.347 - 4\,675.096 \approx$ _____ − _____ = _____

b) Calculate the sums and differences in part a) using a calculator.
Use your estimates to check your calculations.

5. a) Use the three methods in Questions 1 to 3 to estimate $4.768 + 5.385$.

b) Calculate $4.768 + 5.385$.

c) Which methods give the closest estimate? _______________

For the problems below, estimate the solution before calculating.

6. Anika wants to buy three items that cost \$15.79, \$12.25, and \$37.50.
If she has \$65 with her, does she have enough money to buy all three items?

7. Mercury is 57.6 million km from the Sun. Earth is 148.64 million km from the Sun.
How much farther from the Sun is Earth than Mercury?

8. The average temperature in Jakarta is 30.33°C and, in Toronto, it is 11.9°C.
How many degrees warmer is Jakarta than Toronto, on average?

9. Each wing of a butterfly is 3.72 cm wide. Its body is 0.46 cm wide. How wide is the butterfly?

10. John cut 2.73 m off a 10-m rope. Thomson cut another 4.46 m off. How much rope was left?

11. a) A slice of cheese pizza has 4.838 g of saturated fat, 2.802 g of monounsaturated fat, and 1.765 g of polyunsaturated fat. What is the total amount of fat?

b) A slice of pepperoni pizza has 4.995 g of saturated fat, 3.857 g of monounsaturated fat, and 1.953 g of polyunsaturated fat. What is the total amount of fat?

c) How much less fat does the cheese slice have than the pepperoni slice?

12. Suppose you had \$755.50 and spent \$326.87. If you were shopping, which of the methods from Questions 1-3 would you use to estimate how much money you have left? Explain your choice.

NS7-45 Multiplying Decimals by 10

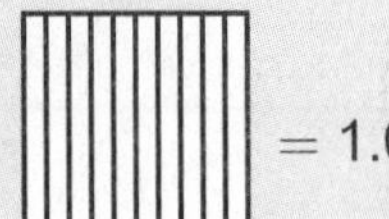 = 1.0 | = 0.1 ⟶ 10 × | =

If a hundreds block represents 1 whole (1.0), then a tens block represents 1 tenth (0.1).

10 × 0.1 = 1.0
10 tenths make 1 whole

1. Multiply the number of tens blocks by 10. Draw the number of hundreds blocks you would have, then complete the multiplication sentence.

a) 10 × 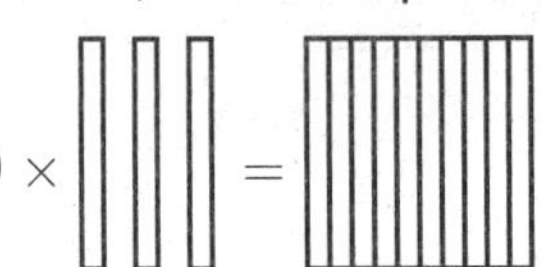 = 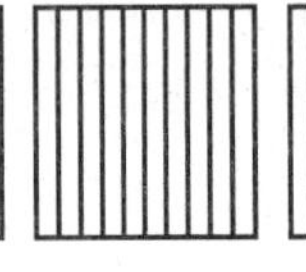

10 × 0.3 = *3*

b) 10 × =

10 × 0.2 = _____

c) 10 × =

10 × 0.5 = _____

2. To multiply by 10, shift the decimal one place to the right.

a) 10 × 0.5 = *5* b) 10 × 0.6 = _____ c) 10 × 1.4 = _____ d) 10 × 0.8 = _____

e) 10 × 2.4 = _____ f) 3.5 × 10 = _____ g) 14.5 × 10 = _____ h) 11.2 × 10 = _____

i) 10 × 2.06 = *20.6* j) 10 × 2.75 = _____ k) 10 × 97.6 = _____ l) 52.36 × 10 = _____

To change metres to decimetres, multiply by 10.

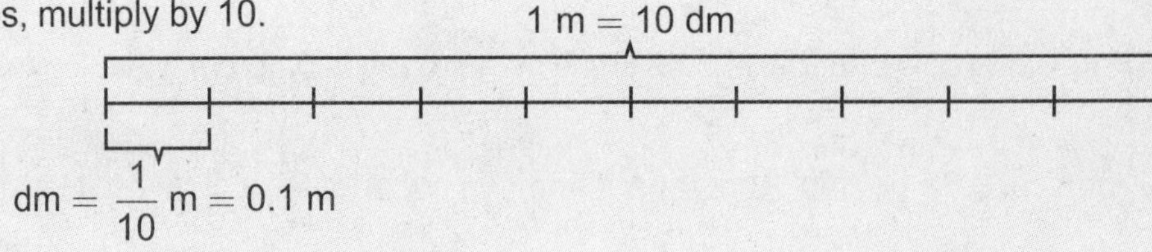

3. Find the answers.

a) 0.4 m = _____ dm b) 0.8 m = _____ dm c) 7.5 m = _____ dm

4. 10 × 4 can be written as a sum: 4 + 4 + 4 + 4 + 4 + 4 + 4 + 4 + 4 + 4.

Write 10 × 0.4 as a sum and skip count by 0.4 to find the answer.

5. A dime is a tenth of a dollar (10¢ = $0.10). Draw a picture or use play money to show that 10 × $0.30 = $3.00.

NS7-46 Multiplying Decimals by 100 and 1 000

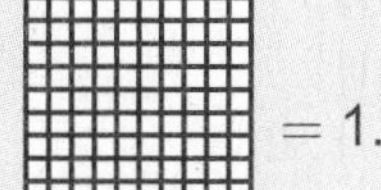

= 1.0   □ = 0.01 ⟶ 100 × □ = [hundreds block]

If a hundreds block represents 1 whole (1.0), then a ones block represents 1 hundredth (0.01).

100 × 0.01 = 1.0
100 hundredths makes 1 whole

1. Write a multiplication sentence for each picture.

   a) 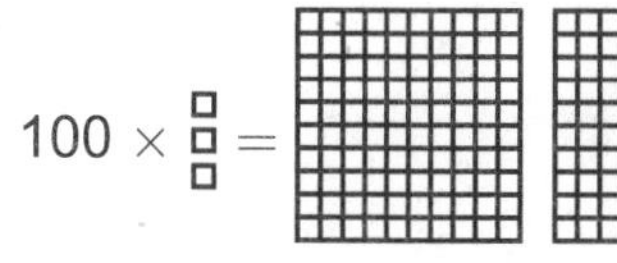 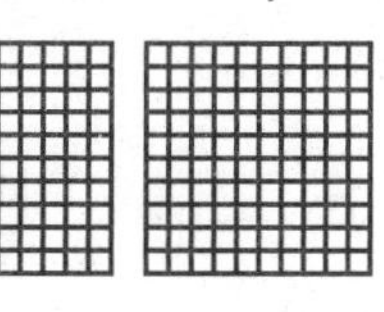

   100 × [3 ones blocks] = [3 hundreds blocks]

   100 × 0.03 = ______

   b) 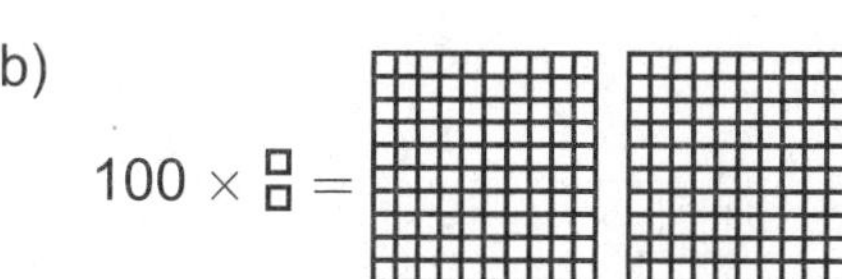

   100 × [2 ones blocks] = [2 hundreds blocks]

   ______ = ______

The picture shows why the decimal shifts two places to the right when you multiply by 100.

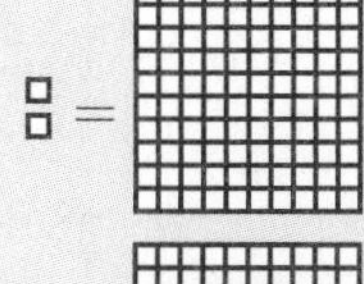

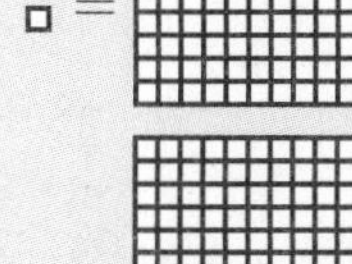

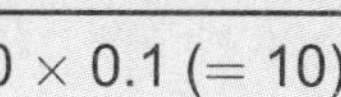

100 × 0.12 = 100 × 0.1 (= 10) + 100 × 0.02 (= 2) = 12

2. To multiply by 100, shift the decimal two places to the right.

   a) 100 × 0.8 = *80*   b) 100 × 3.5 = ______   c) 7.2 × 100 = ______

   d) 6.3 × 100 = ______   e) 100 × 2.1 = ______   f) 6.0 × 100 = ______

   g) 100 × 0.34 = ______   h) 0.76 × 100 = ______   i) 100 × 0.07 = ______

3. Multiply.

   a) 100 × 0.05 = *5*   b) 100 × 0.02 = ______   c) 0.63 × 100 = ______   d) 0.45 × 100 = ______

   e) 2.72 × 100 = ______   f) 100 × 3.09 = ______   g) 100 × 0.23 = ______   h) 100 × 0.7 = ______

   i) 1.4 × 100 = ______   j) 100 × 0.06 = ______   k) 11.3 × 100 = ______   l) 2.4 × 100 = ______

4. a) What do 1 000 thousandths add up to? ______   b) What is 1 000 × 0.001? ______

5. Look at your answer to Question 4 b).

   How many places right does the decimal shift when you multiply by 1 000? ______

6. Multiply the numbers by shifting the decimal.

   a) 1 000 × 0.93 = ______   b) 1 000 × 0.726 = ______   c) 6.325 × 1 000 = ______

   d) 1 000 × 0.27 = ______   e) 1 000 × 3.21 = ______   f) 2.8 × 1 000 = ______

NS7-47 Dividing Decimals by 10 and 100

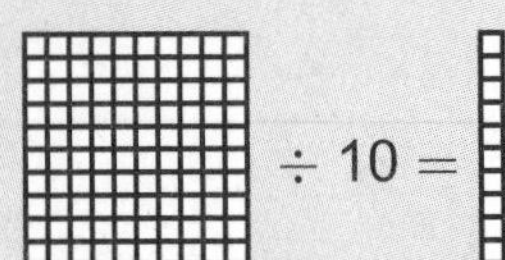

Divide 1 whole into 10 equal parts; each part is 1 tenth.

1.0 ÷ 10 = 0.1

÷ 10 = ▫

Divide 1 tenth into 10 equal parts; each part is 1 hundredth.

0.1 ÷ 10 = 0.01

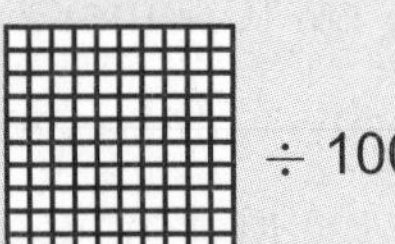

Divide 1 whole into 100 equal parts; each part is 1 hundredth.

1.0 ÷ 100 = 0.01

1. Complete the picture and write a division sentence for each picture.

a) 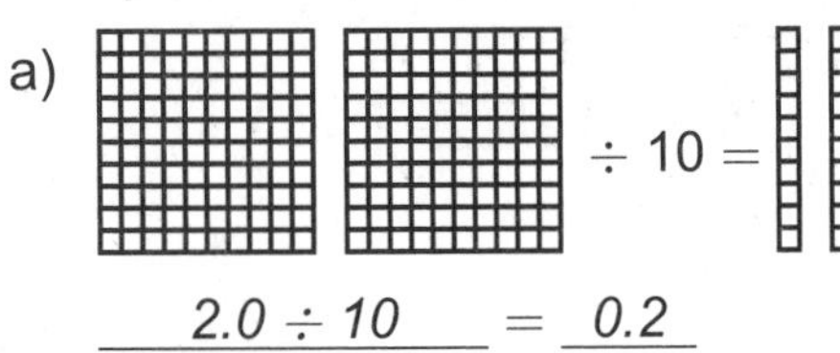

2.0 ÷ 10 = *0.2*

b) 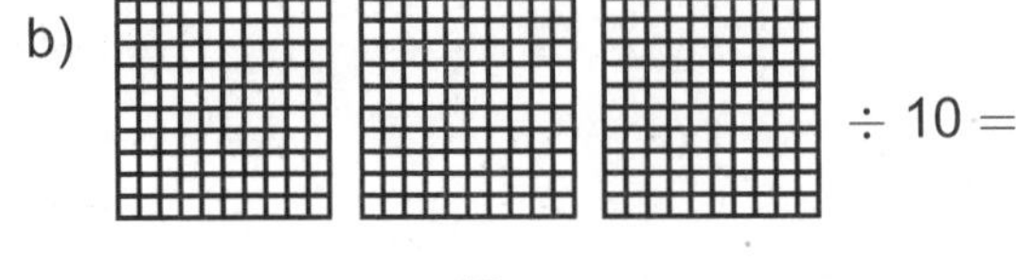

________ = _____

c) 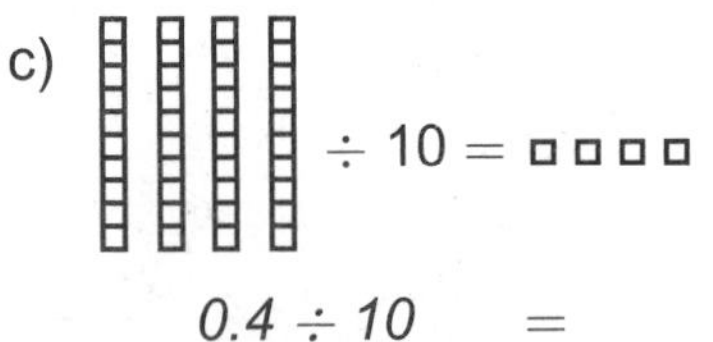

0.4 ÷ 10 = _____

d) 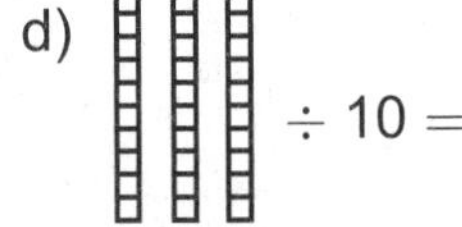

________ = _____

e) 

________ = _____

f) 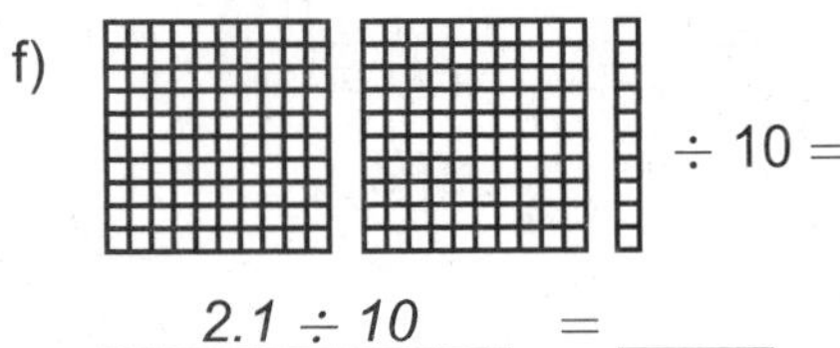

2.1 ÷ 10 = _____

g) 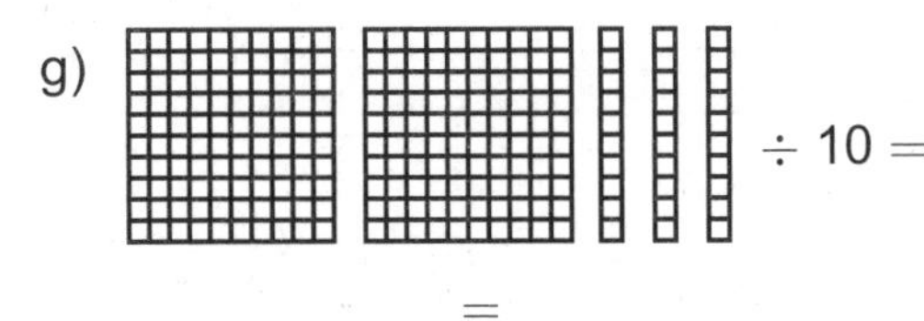

________ = _____

2. Division undoes multiplication. How do you undo multiplying by 10 or 100?

a) To multiply by 10, I move the decimal point _____ places to the ____________,
so to divide by 10, I move the decimal point _____ places to the ____________.

b) To multiply by 100, I move the decimal point _____ places to the ____________,
so to divide by 100, I move the decimal point _____ places to the ____________.

3. Shift the decimal one or two places to the left by drawing an arrow, then write the answer in the blank. Hint: If there is no decimal, add one to the right of the number first.

a) 0.4 ÷ 10 = *0.04* b) 0.7 ÷ 10 = _____ c) 0.6 ÷ 10 = _____ d) 3.1 ÷ 10 = _____

e) 26.0 ÷ 10 = _____ f) 81 ÷ 10 = _____ g) 0.3 ÷ 10 = _____ h) 25.4 ÷ 10 = _____

i) 6.0 ÷ 100 = _____ j) 9.1 ÷ 100 = _____ k) 0.5 ÷ 100 = _____ l) 91.3 ÷ 100 = _____

4. Explain why 1.00 ÷ 100 = 0.01, using a dollar coin as a whole.

5. A wall 2.5 m wide is painted with 100 stripes of equal width. How wide is each stripe?

6. 5 × 3 = 15 and 15 ÷ 5 = 3 are in the same fact family. Write a division statement in the same fact family as 10 × 0.1 = 1.0.

NS7-48 Multiplying and Dividing by Powers of 10

1. a) To multiply by 10, I move the decimal ___1___ place(s) to the ___right___.

b) To multiply by 1 000, I move the decimal _____ place(s) to the _____________.

c) To divide by 100, I move the decimal _____ place(s) to the _____________.

d) To divide by 10, I move the decimal _____ place(s) to the _____________.

e) To _____________ by 1 000, I move the decimal _____ places to the left.

f) To _____________ by 10, I move the decimal _____ place to the left.

g) To _____________ by 100, I move the decimal _____ places to the right.

h) To divide by 10 000 000, I move the decimal _____ places to the _____________.

i) To multiply by 100 000, I move the decimal _____ places to the _____________.

2. Fill in the blanks. Next, draw arrows to show how you would shift the decimal. Then write your final answer in the grid.

a) 7.325 × 100

I move the decimal ___2___ places ___right___.

		7.	3	2	5			rough work
		7	3	2.	5			final answer

b) 5.3 ÷ 1 000

I move the decimal ___3___ places ___left___.

				5.	3			rough work
		.0	0	5	3			final answer

c) 247.567 × 1 000

I move the decimal _____ places _________.

		2	4	7.	5	6	7			rough work
										final answer

d) 100.45 ÷ 100

I move the decimal _____ places _________.

		1	0	0.	4	5				rough work
										final answer

e) 0.602 × 100 000

I move the decimal _____ places _________.

					.6	0	2			rough work
										final answer

f) 24.682 ÷ 10 000

I move the decimal _____ places _________.

			2	4.	6	8	2			rough work
										final answer

3. Copy the numbers onto grid paper. Show how you would shift the decimal in each case.

a) 2.65 × 1 000 b) 47.001 × 100 c) 0.043 × 10 d) 20.06 × 1 000 e) 0.07 × 10 000

f) 0.643 ÷ 10 g) 170.45 ÷ 100 h) 36.07 ÷ 1 000 i) 17.35 ÷ 10 000 j) 0.05 ÷ 1 000

NS7-49 Multiplying Decimals by Whole Numbers

The picture shows how to multiply a decimal by a whole number.

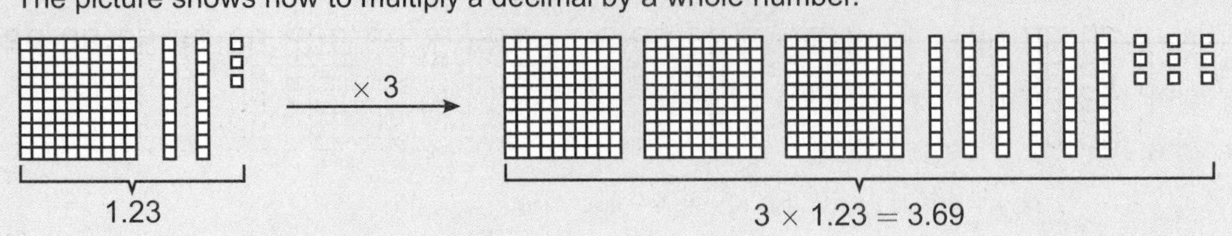

1. Multiply mentally. Multiply each digit separately.

   a) $3 \times 1.32 =$ ______ b) $2 \times 2.4 =$ ______ c) $6 \times 1.01 =$ ______ d) $3 \times 3.2 =$ ______

   e) $4 \times 2.12 =$ ______ f) $5 \times 3.1 =$ ______ g) $2 \times 4.21 =$ ______ h) $7 \times 4.11 =$ ______

2. Multiply by exchanging tenths for ones.

   a) $7 \times 1.3 =$ *7* ones + *21* tenths = *9* ones + *1* tenth = *9.1*

   b) $3 \times 3.4 =$ ______ ones + ______ tenths = ______ ones + ______ tenths = ______

   c) $4 \times 4.7 =$ ______ ones + ______ tenths = ______ ones + ______ tenths = ______

   d) $3 \times 2.9 =$ ______________________________

3. Multiply by exchanging tenths for ones or hundredths for tenths.

   a) $3 \times 3.51 =$ *9* ones + *15* tenths + *3* hundredths

   = ______ ones + ______ tenths + ______ hundredths = ______

   b) $4 \times 2.34 =$ ______ ones + ______ tenths + ______ hundredths

   = ______ ones + ______ tenths + ______ hundredths = ______

4. Multiply. In some questions you will have to regroup twice.

   a) 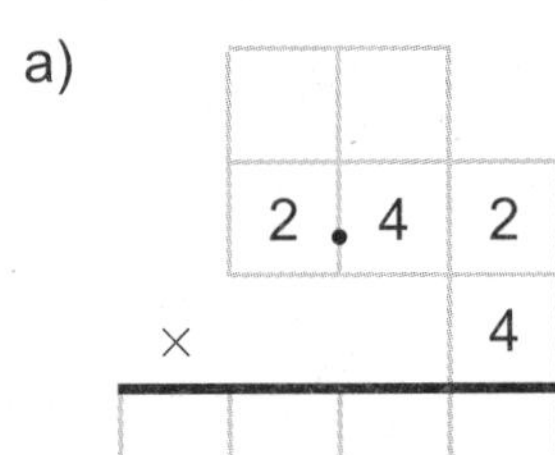

   b) 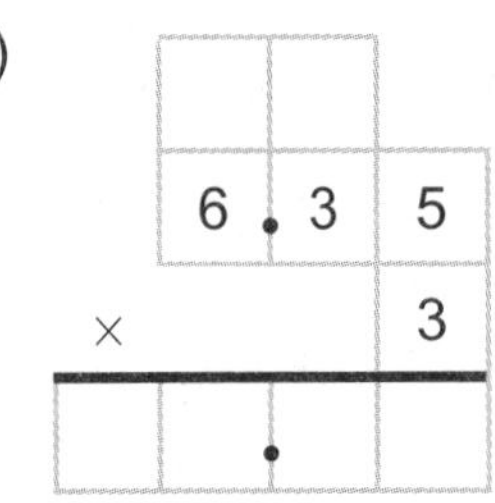

   c) 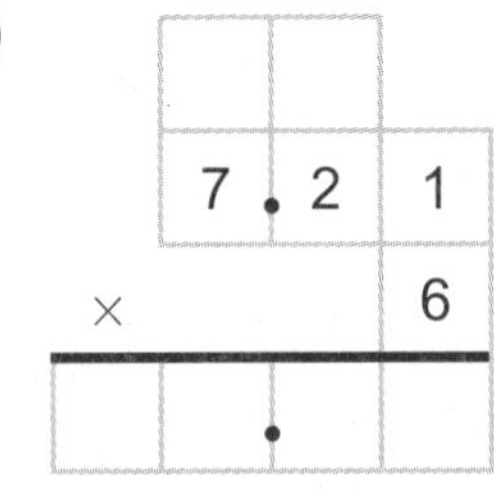

   d) 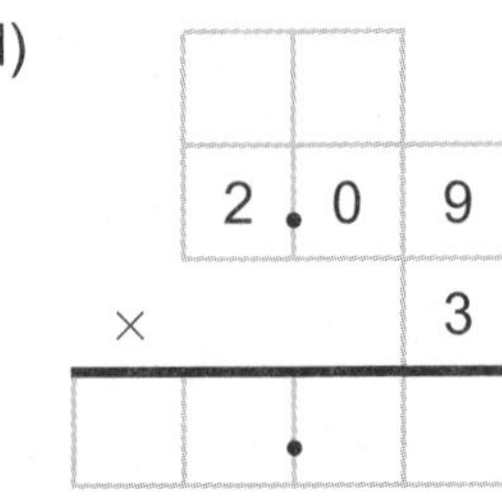

5. Find the products.

   a) 5×3.6 b) 3×0.4 c) 6×4.2 d) 9×2.27 e) 7×34.6 f) 8×4.3

   g) 4×2.7 h) 5×9.52 i) 7×5.98 j) 8×6.29 k) 3×46.92 l) 4×36.75

6. You can rewrite the product 80×3.6 as $10 \times 8 \times 3.6$. Use this method to find these products.

   a) 40×2.1 b) 60×0.7 c) 30×9.68 d) 200×7.5 e) 500×0.2

NS7-50 Multiplying Decimals Using Different Strategies

1. Use the base ten model to multiply the decimal.

a) 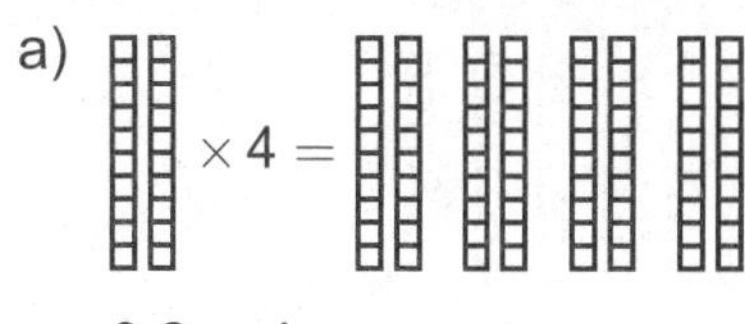

$0.2 \times 4 =$ __.__

b) 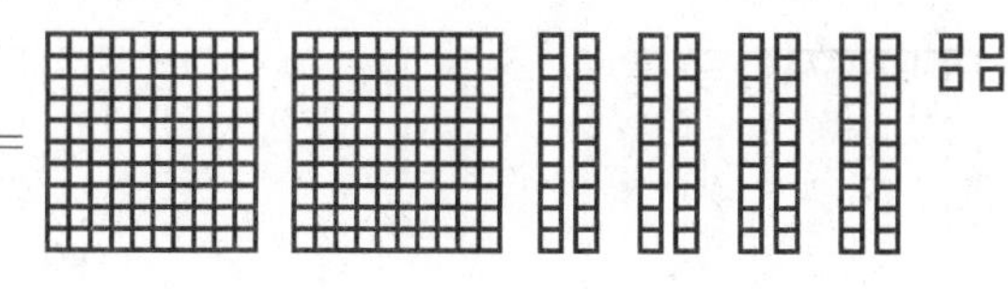

$1.42 \times 2 =$ __.__ __

2. Use repeated addition to multiply the decimal.

a) $0.5 \times 3 =$ _0.5 + 0.5 + 0.5_
$=$ ______

b) $2.4 \times 2 =$ ____ + ____
$=$ ______

c) $1.6 \times 4 =$ ______
______

3. Multiply.

a) 0.2×8
= _2_ tenths × 8
= _16_ tenths
= _1.6_

b) 0.47×5
= ____ hundredths × ____
= ____ hundredths
= 2.__ __

c) 0.132×3
= ____ thousandths × ____
= ____ thousandths
= __.__ __ __

d) 0.2×44
= ____ tenths × ____
= ____ tenths
= ____ ones + ____ tenths
= __.__

e) 1.2×4
= ____ tenths × 4
= ____ tenths
= ____ ones + ____ tenths
= __.__

f) 3.06×3
= ____ hundredths × 3
= ____ hundredths
= ____ ones + ____ hundredths
= __.__ __

4. Multiply each place value separately.

a) 0.73×2
= (____ tenths + ____ hundredths) × 2
= (___ tenths × 2) + (___ hundredths × 2)
= ____ tenths + ____ hundredths
= __.__ + __.__ __
= __.__ __

b) 0.063×3
= (____ hundredths + ____ thousandths) × 3
= (___ hundredths × 3) + (___ thousandths × 3)
= ____ hundredths + ____ thousandths
= __.__ __ + __.__ __ __
= __.__ __ __

5. Multiply by splitting the number you are multiplying into two numbers that are easier to multiply.

a) $4.35 \times 3 =$ (_4_ + _0.35_) × _3_
= (_4_ × ____) + (_0.35_ × ____)
= ____ + ____
= __.__ __

b) $6.021 \times 4 =$ (____ + ____) × 4
= (____ × ____) + (____ × ____)
= ____ + ____
= __.__ __ __

6. Multiply. Use the strategy of your choice.

a) 0.4×8 b) 1.5×7 c) 0.32×5 d) 2.9×4 e) 6.02×8 f) 0.047×2 g) 7.91×3

NS7-51 Dividing Decimals Using Different Strategies

1. What division statement does this model show? Fill in the blanks. 0.95 ÷ ____ = ____ R ____

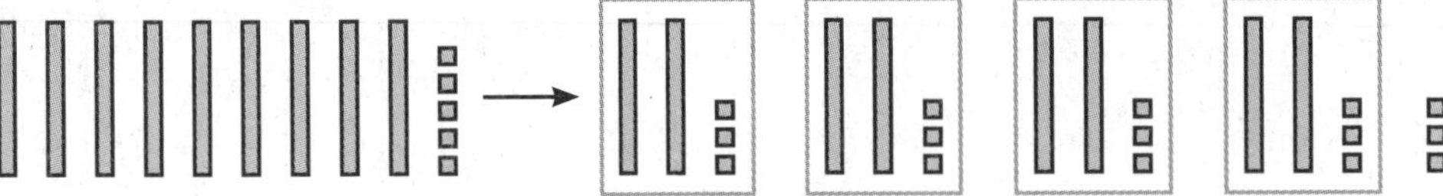

2. Divide.

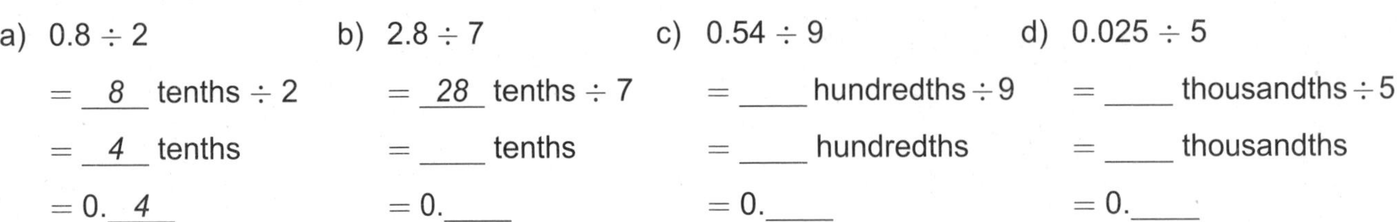

a) 0.8 ÷ 2
= 8 tenths ÷ 2
= 4 tenths
= 0.4

b) 2.8 ÷ 7
= 28 tenths ÷ 7
= ____ tenths
= 0.____

c) 0.54 ÷ 9
= ____ hundredths ÷ 9
= ____ hundredths
= 0.____

d) 0.025 ÷ 5
= ____ thousandths ÷ 5
= ____ thousandths
= 0.____

3. Regroup and then divide.

a) 0.3 ÷ 6
= 3 tenths ÷ 6
= 30 hundredths ÷ 6
= 5 hundredths
= 0.05

b) 0.04 ÷ 5
= ____ hundredths ÷ ____
= ____ thousandths ÷ ____
= ____ thousandths
= 0.____

c) 0.04 ÷ 8
= ____ hundredths ÷ ____
= ____ thousandths ÷ ____
= ____ thousandths
= 0.____

4. Divide one place value at a time.

a) 0.468 = 4 tenths + 6 hundredths + 8 thousandths

So 0.468 ÷ **2** = (4 tenths ÷ **2**) + (6 hundredths ÷ **2**) + (8 thousandths ÷ **2**)
= 2 tenths + 3 hundredths + 4 thousandths
= 0.234

The short way to write this is: $\begin{array}{r} 0.234 \\ 2\overline{)0.468} \end{array}$

b) $2\overline{)6.4}$ c) $3\overline{)3.9}$ d) $4\overline{)8.4}$ e) $6\overline{)12.6}$ f) $3\overline{)60.93}$ g) $3\overline{)0.396}$

5. Sometimes you can divide by splitting the dividend into two numbers that are easier to divide.

a) 7.2 ÷ 4
= (6.0 + 1.2) ÷ 4
= (6.0 ÷ 4) + (1.2 ÷ 4)
= 1.5 + .3
= 1.8

b) 4.8 ÷ 3
= (3.0 + 1.8) ÷ 3
= (3.0 ÷ 3) + (1.8 ÷ 3)
= ____ + ____
= ____

c) 15.6 ÷ 3
= (____ + ____) ÷ ____
= (____ ÷ ____) + (____ ÷ ____)
= ____ + ____
= ____

6. Divide. Use the strategy of your choice.

a) 0.8 ÷ 4 b) 4.8 ÷ 8 c) 0.54 ÷ 6 d) 0.393 ÷ 3 e) 0.08 ÷ 5 f) 0.7 ÷ 5

g) 7.2 ÷ 8 h) 5.6 ÷ 4 i) 0.54 ÷ 9 j) 27.9 ÷ 3 k) 1.64 ÷ 4 l) 20.4 ÷ 4

NS7-52 Long Division

Problem: Divide 95 objects into 4 groups (95 ÷ 4).

Here is a base ten model of the problem.

95 ÷ 4 → ? ? ? ?

95 = 9 tens + 5 ones

Solve the problem using **long division**.

Step 1: Write the numbers like this: $4\overline{)95}$

the number of groups ↗ ↖ the number you are dividing

Step 2: How can you divide 9 tens blocks equally into the 4 groups?

You can divide 8 of the 9 tens blocks into 4 equal groups of size 2:

There are 2 tens blocks in each group. → 2

There are 4 groups. $4\overline{)95}$

$$\begin{array}{r} 2 \\ 4\overline{)95} \\ 8 \end{array}$$

8 ← 2 × 4 = 8 tens blocks placed

1. How many groups are you going to make? How many tens blocks can you put in each group?

a) $4\overline{)91}$

groups _____

number of tens in each group _____

b) $3\overline{)84}$

groups _____

number of tens in each group _____

c) $6\overline{)75}$

groups _____

number of tens in each group _____

d) $2\overline{)93}$

groups _____

number of tens in each group _____

2. Find out how many tens can be placed in each group. Then multiply to find out how many tens have been placed.

a) $5\overline{)91}$ −

b) $3\overline{)82}$ −

c) $4\overline{)98}$ −

d) $5\overline{)99}$ −

e) $9\overline{)93}$ −

Step 3: How many tens blocks are left?

Subtract to find out. →

$$\begin{array}{r} 2 \\ 4\overline{)95} \\ -8 \\ \hline 1 \end{array}$$

There are 9 − 8 = 1 left over.

3. For each question, carry out the first **three** steps of long division.

a) $7\overline{)87}$ −

b) $3\overline{)84}$ −

c) $2\overline{)83}$ −

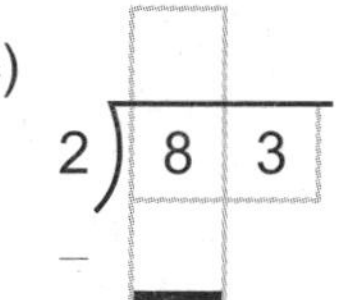

d) $4\overline{)63}$ −

e) $6\overline{)99}$ −

f) $5\overline{)94}$ −

Step 4: There is 1 tens block left over, and there are 5 ones in 95.

So there are 15 ones left in total. Write the 5 beside the 1 to show this.

There are still 15 ones to place in 4 groups.

$$\begin{array}{r|cc} & 2 & \\ 4) & 9 & 5 \\ - & 8 & \\ \hline & 1 & \end{array} \longrightarrow \begin{array}{r|cc} & 2 & \\ 4) & 9 & 5 \\ - & 8 & \downarrow \\ \hline & 1 & 5 \end{array}$$

← There are still this many ones to place.

4. Carry out the first four steps of long division.

a) 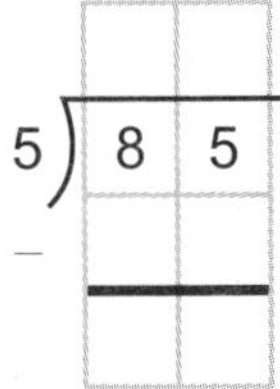
b) 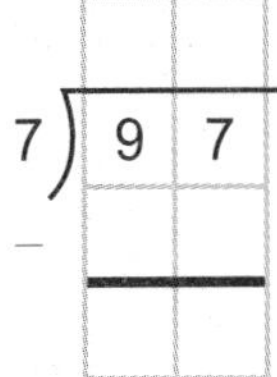
c) 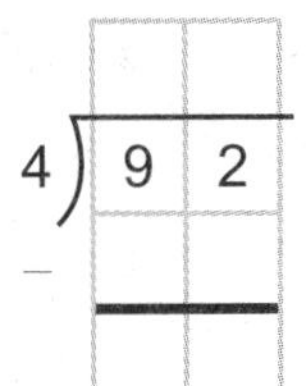
d) 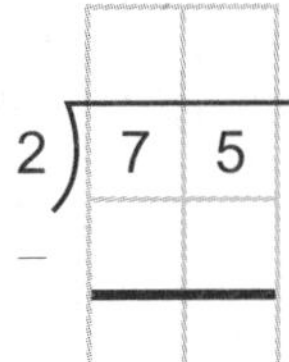
e) 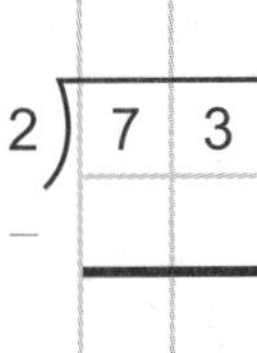

Step 5: How many ones can you put in each group?

Divide to find out:

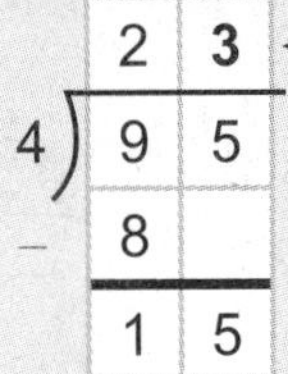

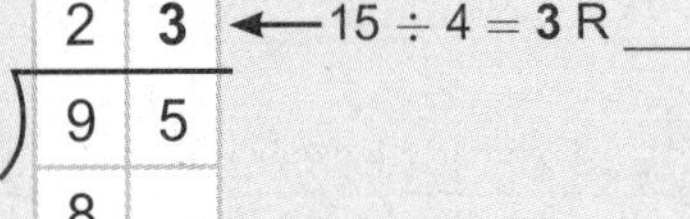

← $15 \div 4 =$ **3** R ____

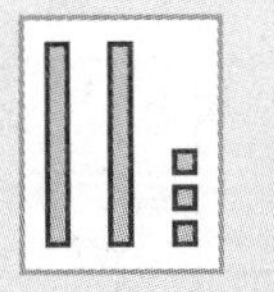

How many ones are left over?

5. Carry out the first five steps of long division.

a) 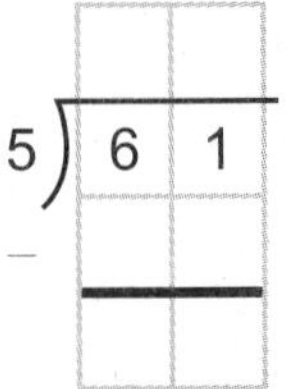
b) 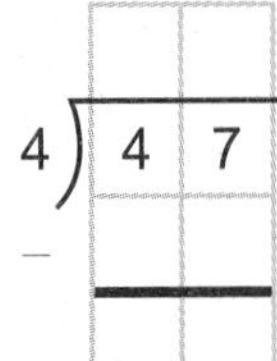
c) 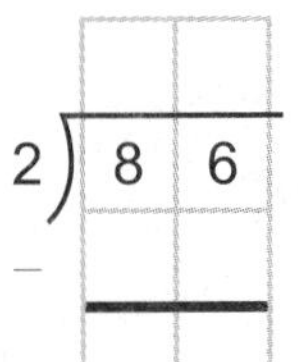
d) 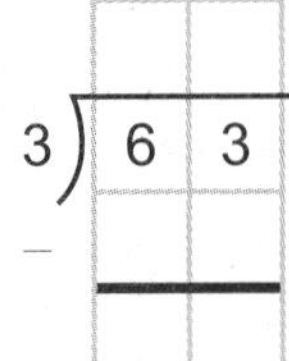
e) 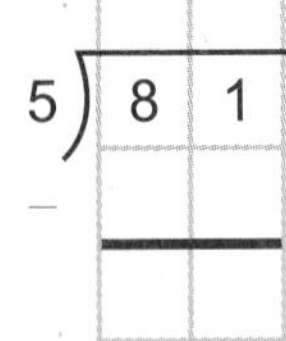

Steps 6 and 7: Find the number of ones left over.

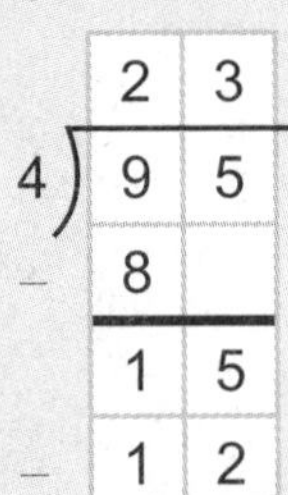

← There are $3 \times 4 = 12$ ones placed.

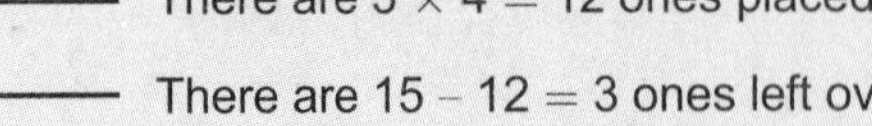

← There are $15 - 12 = 3$ ones left over.

Long division and the model both show that **95 ÷ 4 = 23 with 3 left over.**

6. Carry out all the steps of long division on grid paper.

a) $6\overline{)81}$ b) $4\overline{)52}$ c) $3\overline{)95}$ d) $3\overline{)82}$ e) $4\overline{)64}$ f) $7\overline{)87}$

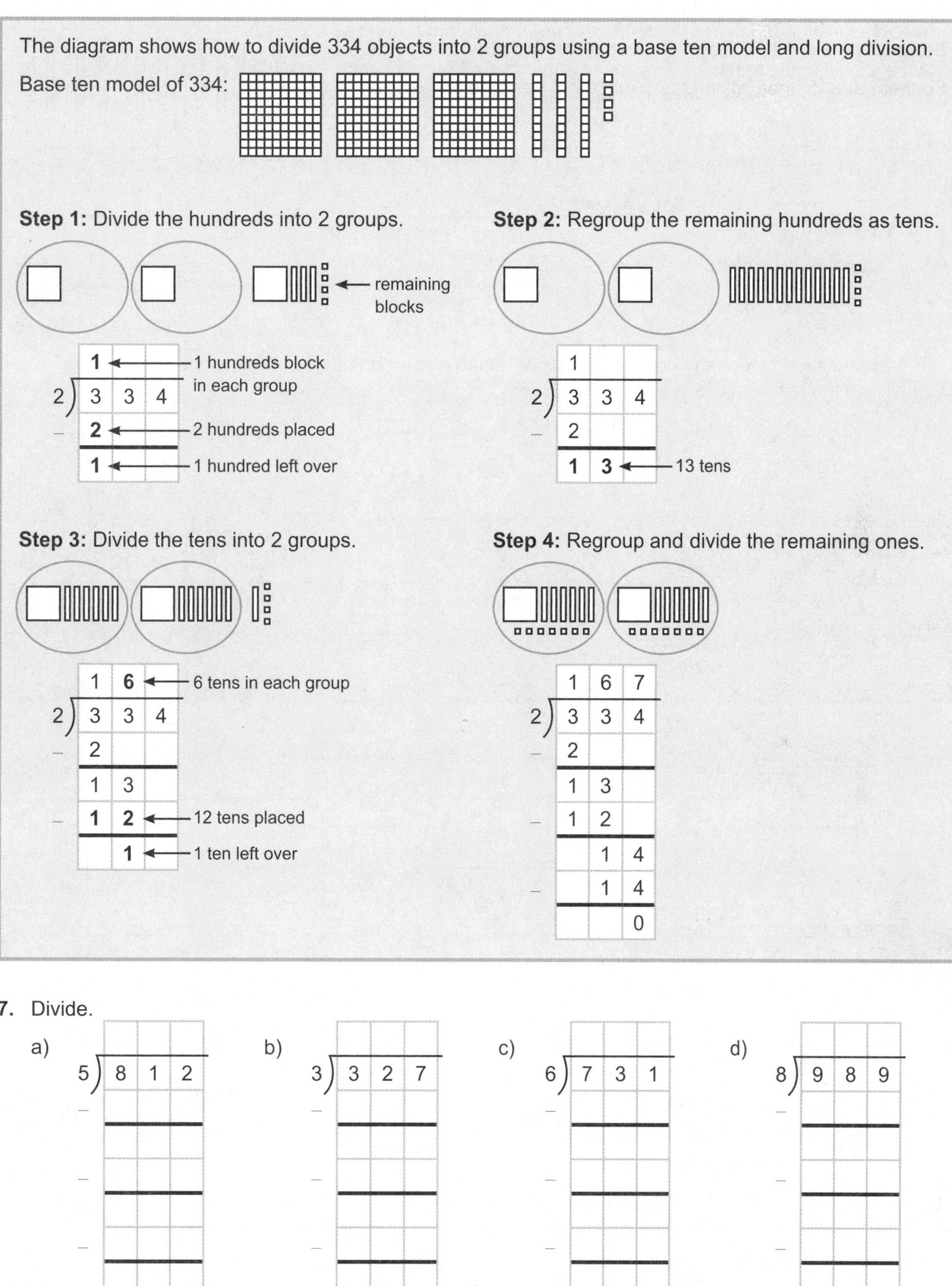
The diagram shows how to divide 334 objects into 2 groups using a base ten model and long division.
Base ten model of 334:
Step 1: Divide the hundreds into 2 groups.
remaining blocks
1 hundreds block in each group
2 hundreds placed
1 hundred left over
Step 2: Regroup the remaining hundreds as tens.
13 tens
Step 3: Divide the tens into 2 groups.
6 tens in each group
12 tens placed
1 ten left over
Step 4: Regroup and divide the remaining ones.
7. Divide.
a) 5) 8 1 2
b) 3) 3 2 7
c) 6) 7 3 1
d) 8) 9 8 9

8. In each question below, there are fewer hundreds than the number of groups.

Write a zero in the hundreds position to show that no hundreds can be placed in equal groups. Then perform the division as if the hundreds had automatically been exchanged for tens.

a) 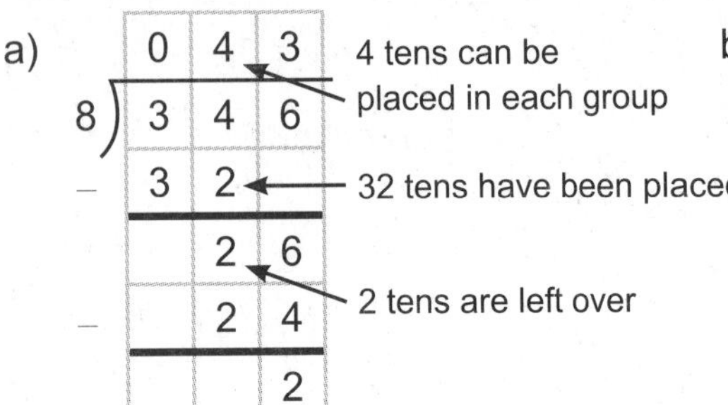
4 tens can be placed in each group
32 tens have been placed
2 tens are left over

b) 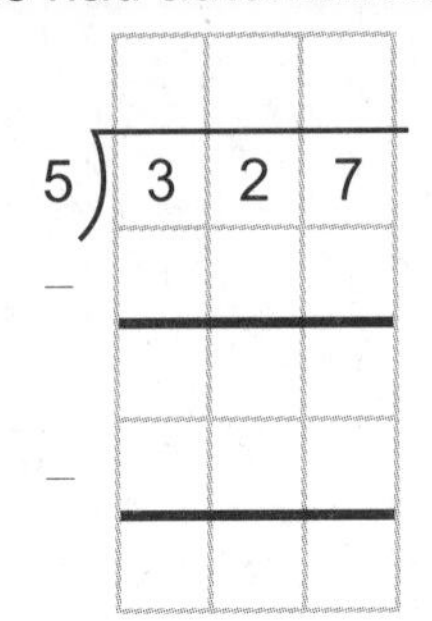

c) 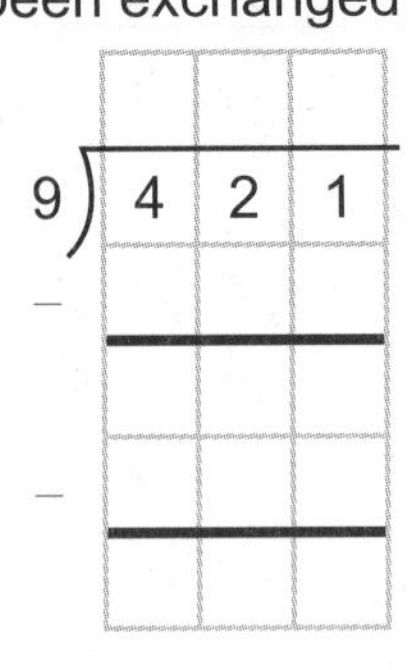

d) 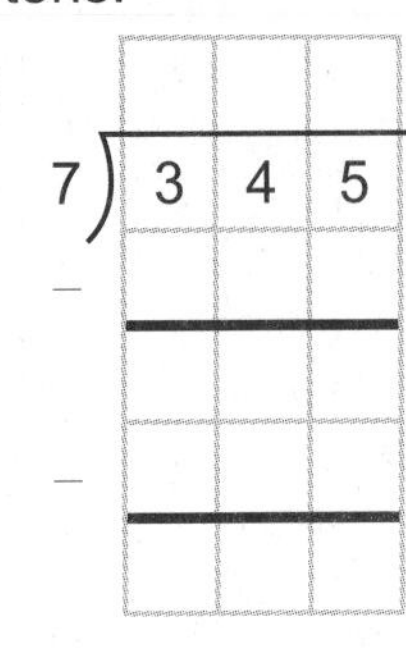

9. In each question below, say how many tens or hundreds can be placed in 5 groups. Underline the place values you will divide by 5.

a) $5\overline{)315}$ *31 tens*

b) $5\overline{)726}$ *7 hundreds*

c) $5\overline{)623}$ ______

d) $5\overline{)321}$ ______

e) $5\overline{)892}$ ______

f) $5\overline{)240}$ ______

g) $5\overline{)987}$ ______

h) $5\overline{)412}$ ______

10. Divide.

a) 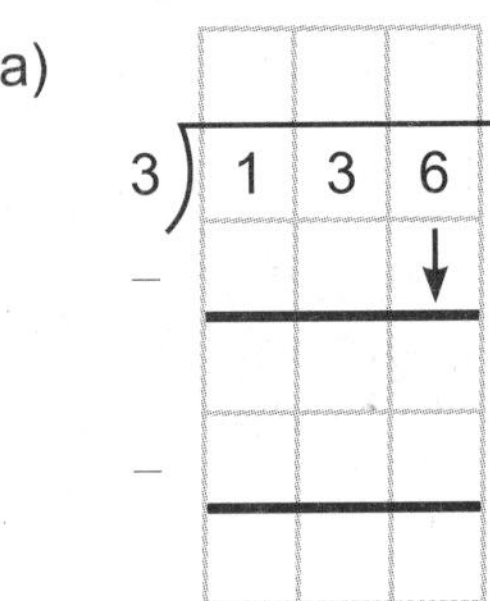

b) 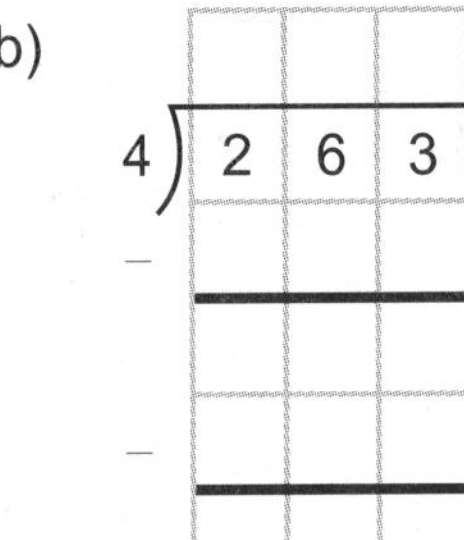

c) 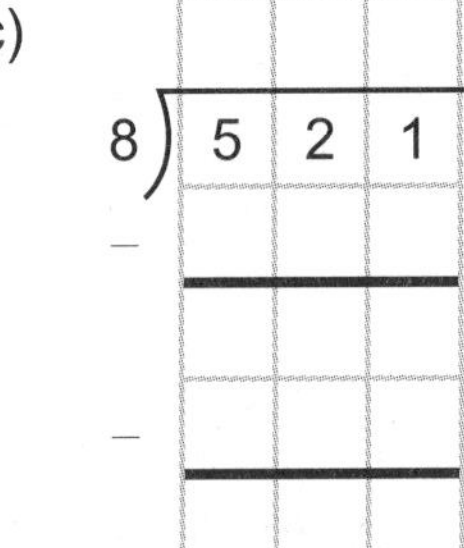

d) 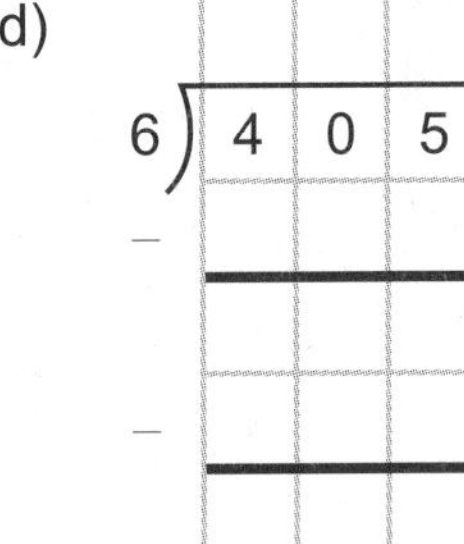

e) 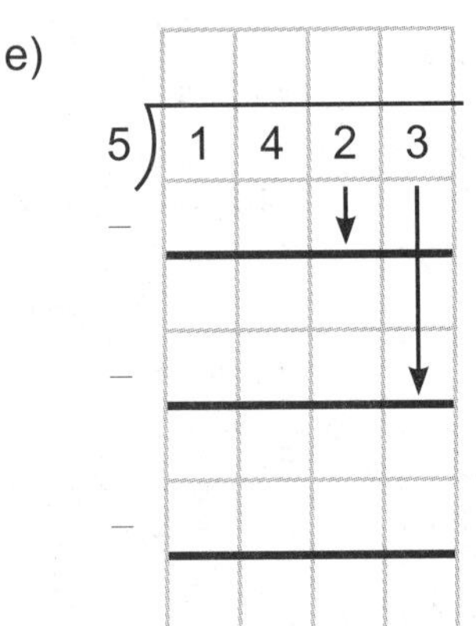

f) 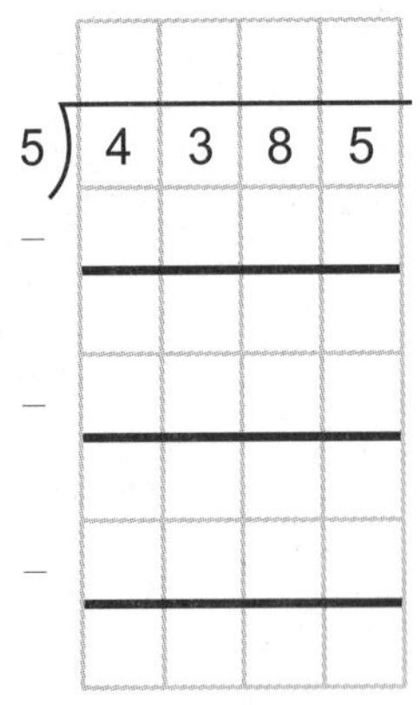

g) 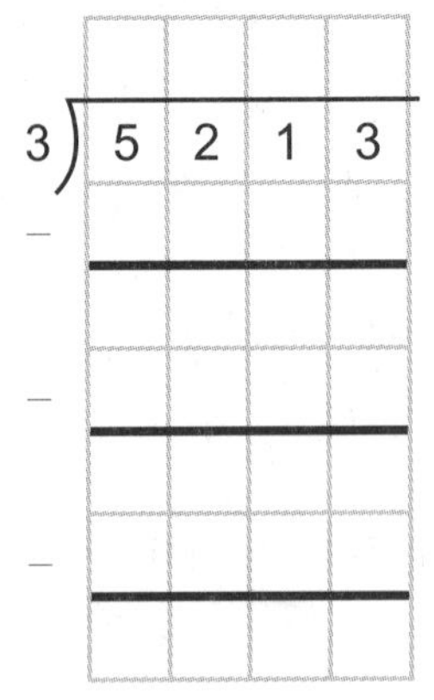

h) 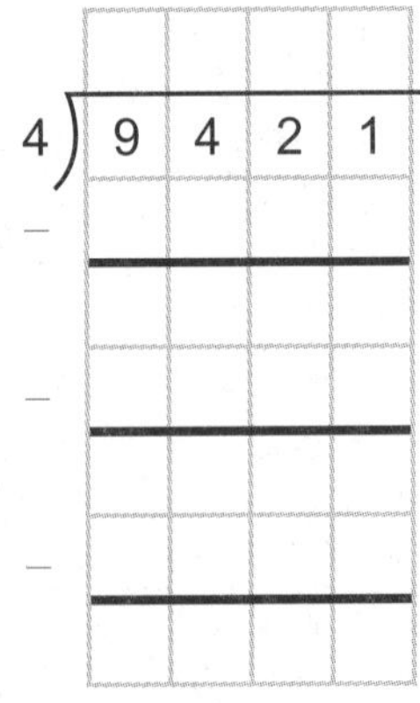

i) $9\overline{)684}$ j) $7\overline{)3\,512}$ k) $8\overline{)312}$ l) $6\overline{)4\,935}$ m) $2\overline{)7\,463}$

n) $3\overline{)7\,913}$ o) $5\overline{)1\,862}$ p) $5\overline{)2\,764}$ q) $4\overline{)9\,807}$ r) $4\overline{)1\,986}$

NS7-53 Dividing Decimals by Whole Numbers

You can divide a decimal by a whole number by making a base ten model. Here is what the blocks represent:

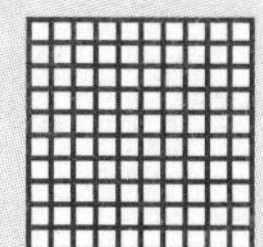 = **1 one** or **unit**

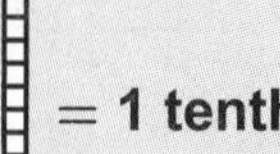 = **1 tenth**

□ = **1 hundredth**

Keep track of your work using long division.

1. Find **5.12 ÷ 2** by making a base ten model and by long division.

   Step 1: Draw a base ten model for 5.12.

   Draw your model here.

   Step 2: Divide the largest (unit) blocks into 2 equal groups.

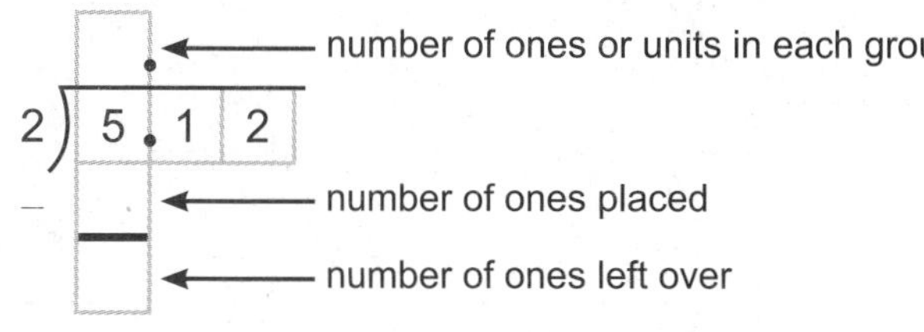

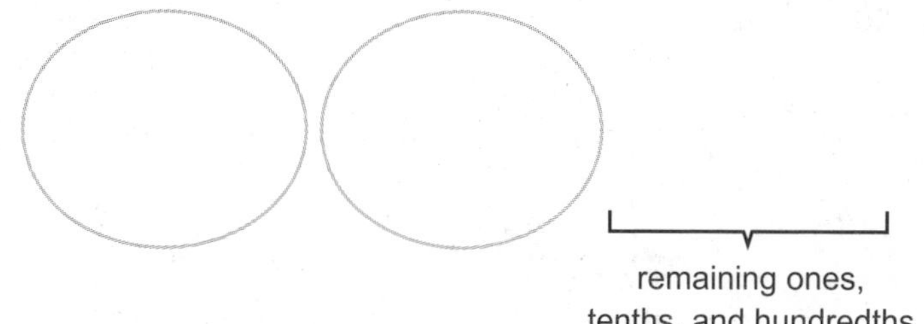

   Step 3: Exchange the leftover unit blocks for 10 tenths.

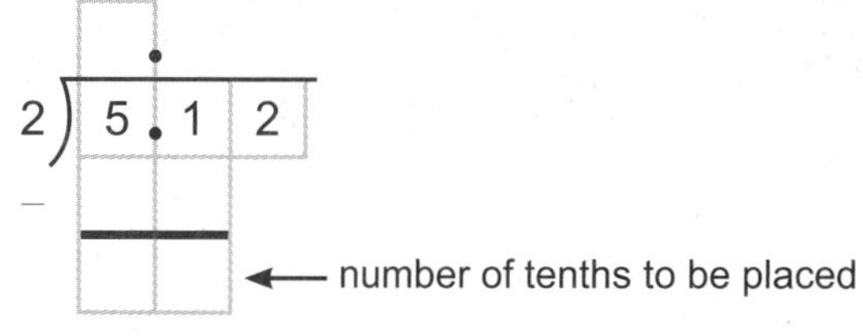

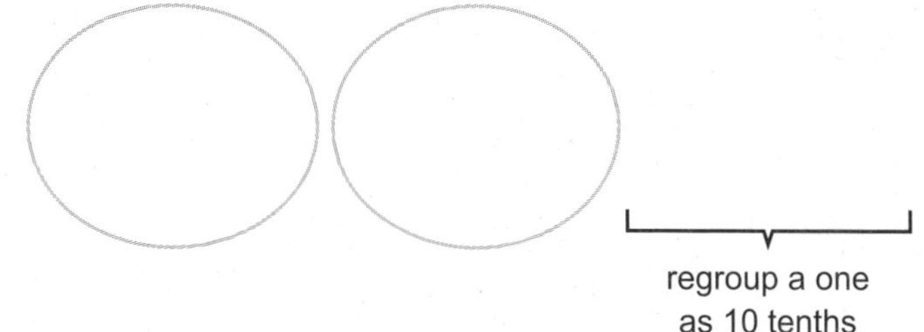

   Step 4: Divide the tenths blocks into 2 equal groups.

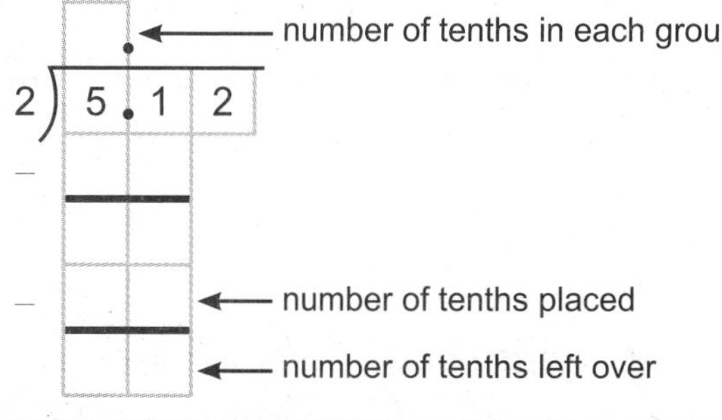

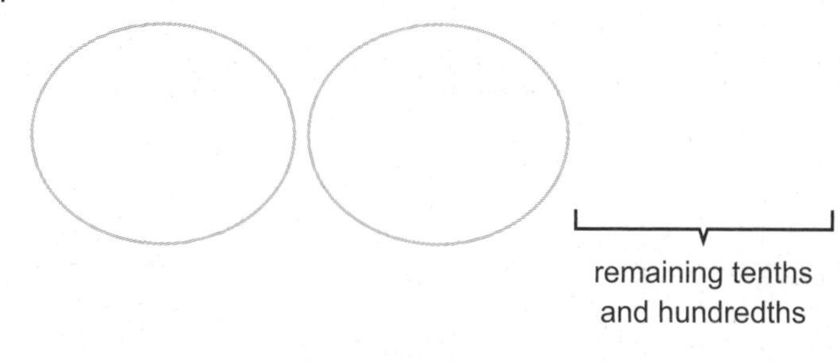

Step 5: Exchange the leftover tenth block for 10 hundredths.

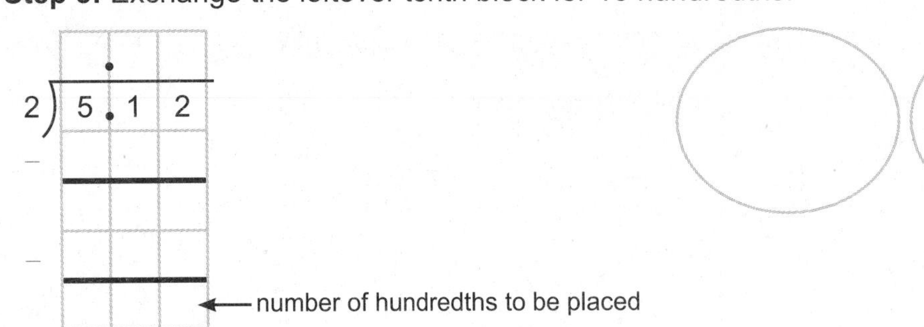

regroup a tenth as 10 hundredths

Steps 6 and 7: Divide the hundredths into 2 equal groups.

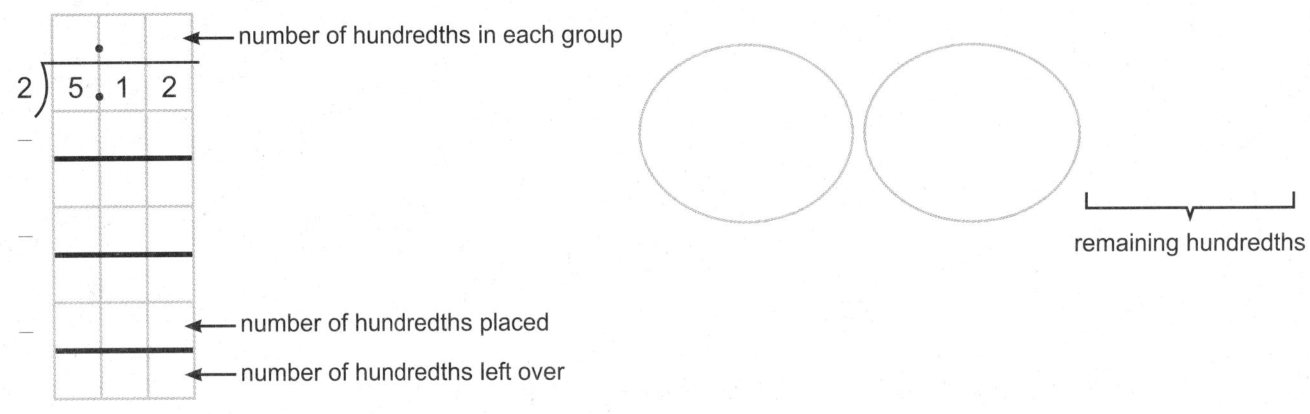

2. Divide.

a) 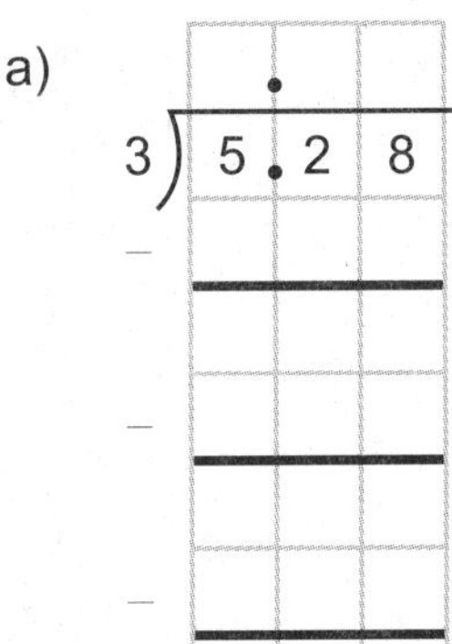

b) 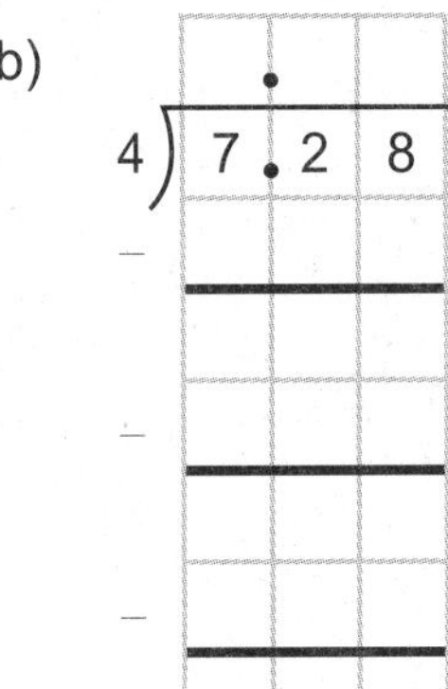

c) 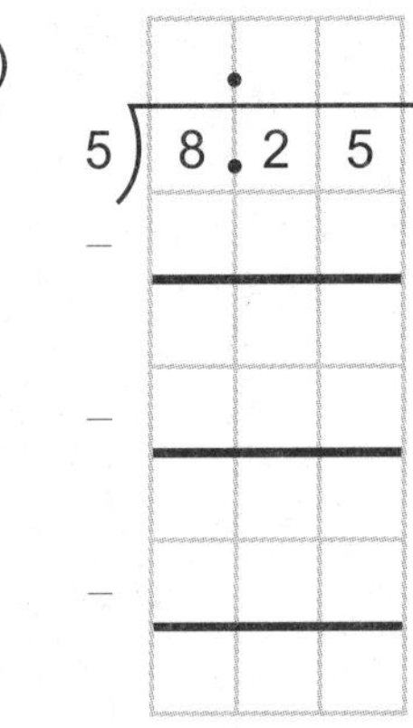

d) 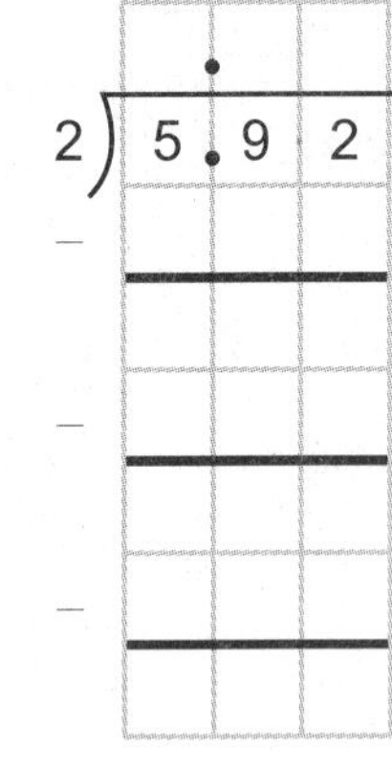

3. Divide.

a) $8\overline{)2.56}$ b) $7\overline{)5.6}$ c) $8\overline{)4.48}$ d) $9\overline{)6.21}$ e) $5\overline{)32.45}$

4. Five oranges cost \$3.65. How much does each orange cost?

5. An equilateral triangle has a perimeter of 3.12 m. How long is each side?

6. Philip cycled 58.4 km in 4 hours. How many kilometres did he cycle in an hour?

7. Ahmed earned \$97.36 in 8 hours. How much did he earn each hour?

8. Which is a better deal, 8 pens for \$6.16 or 7 pens for \$5.46?

NS7-54 Decimals Review

1. Write a decimal for each description. Some questions have more than one answer.

   a) Between 3.52 and 3.57: ☐.☐☐   b) Between 1.70 and 1.80: ☐.☐☐

   c) Between 12.65 and 12.7: ☐☐.☐☐   d) Between 2.6 and 2.7: ☐.☐☐

   e) One tenth greater than 5.23: ☐.☐☐   f) One hundredth less than 4.00: ☐.☐☐

2. Put a decimal in each number so that the digit **7** has the value $\frac{7}{10}$:

   a) 5 7 2   b) 1 0 7   c) 2 8 7 5 9   d) 7

3. Use the numerals 5, 6, 7, and 0 to write a number between the given numbers:

   a) 0.567 < ________________ < 0.576   b) 5.607 < ________________ < 5.760

4. Write the correct sign (−, +, ×, ÷) in the circle.

   a) 62.57 ◯ 10 = 72.57   b) 19.2 ◯ 10 = 192   c) 9 ◯ 10 = 0.9

5. Multiply or divide, then round your answer to the nearest whole number.

   a) 0.56 × 10   b) 0.34 × 10   c) 568.9 ÷ 100   d) 184.5 ÷ 9

6. a) The UN says women should get about 2.7 L of water a day, including about 0.54 L from food. How many litres will come from drinks?

   b) If one glass of liquid is 0.24 L, how many glasses should a woman drink each day? Hint: Use repeated addition.

7. The **water footprint** of a product is the total amount of freshwater used to produce the product.

   a) An apple has a water footprint of 70 L. The water footprint of a kilogram of beef is 221.43 times greater. Calculate the water footprint of a kilogram of beef. Round your answer to the nearest kilolitre (1 kL = 1 000 L).

   b) The water footprint of chicken is one quarter the water footprint of beef. Calculate the water footprint of chicken.

8. The chart shows how many times stronger (or weaker) gravity is on the given planets than on Earth. Example: Gravity on Jupiter is 2.34 times gravity on Earth, so you multiply your weight on Earth by 2.34 to find your weight on Jupiter.

Planet	**Saturn**	**Jupiter**	**Mars**	**Mercury**
Gravity factor	1.15	2.34	0.83	0.284

   a) On which planets is gravity weaker than on Earth?
   b) How much more would a 7-kg infant weigh on Jupiter than on Mars?

ME7-1 Changing Units

1. Fill in the blanks.

a) 2.32 × 1 000 = ________ b) 254 ÷ 1 000 = ________ c) .36 × 1 000 = ________

d) 5.07 ÷ 1 000 = ________ e) .043 × 1 000 = ________ f) .79 ÷ 1 000 = ________

Kilometres (km) and millimetres (mm) are measures of **length**.	Kilograms (kg) and milligrams (mg) are measures of **mass**.	Litres (L) and millilitres (mL) are measures of **capacity**.
1 km = 1 000 m 1 m = 1 000 mm 1 mm = .001 m	1 kg = 1 000 g 1 g = 1 000 mg 1 mg = .001 g	1 L = 1 000 mL 1 mL = .001 L

The prefix **kilo** means "1 000 times larger." The prefix **milli** means "1 000 times smaller."

2. a) Change 275 mg to g.

i) The new units are *1 000* times *bigger*.

ii) So I need *1 000* times *fewer* units.

iii) I *divide* by *1 000*.

275 mg = *.275* g

b) Change 3 700 mm to m.

i) The new units are ________ times ________.

ii) So I need ________ times ________ units.

iii) I ________ by ________.

3 700 mm = ________ m

c) Change 2 700 g to kg.

i) The new units are ________ times ________.

ii) So I need ________ times ________ units.

iii) I ________ by ________.

2 700 g = ________ kg

d) Change .3456 L to mL.

i) The new units are ________ times ________.

ii) So I need ________ times ________ units.

iii) I ________ by ________.

.3456 L = ________ mL

3. Change the units by following the steps in Question 2 in your head.

a) 700 m = ________ km b) .93 m = ________ mm c) 37 mm = ________ m

d) 2 340 mL = ________ L e) 15.4 L = ________ mL f) 0.05 mL = ________ L

g) 7.43 kg = ________ g h) .93 g = ________ mg i) 37 mg = ________ g

j) 2.34 m = ________ km k) 22.6 g = ________ mg l) 0.08 m = ________ km

m) 3 569 km = ________ m n) 6 789 kg = ________ g o) 0.02 km = ________ m

BONUS▶

p) 0.569 km = ________ m
= ____________ mm

q) 67 890 mg = ________ g
= ____________ kg

r) 90 875 mm = ________ m
= ____________ km

4. How many metres, centimetres, and millimetres are in 1 km?

1 km = _______ m = _________ cm = ___________ mm

REMINDER▸ 1 m = 100 cm
1 cm = 10 mm

Units increase in size as you go up the stairs. Each step is **10 times larger**.

m
cm
mm

5. a) Change 35 cm to m.

The new units are *100* times *bigger*,

so I need *100* times *fewer* units.

I *divide* by *100* : 35 cm = *.35* m.

b) Change 35 cm to mm.

The new units are _______ times _______ ,

so I need _______ times _______ units.

I _______ by _______ : 35 cm = _______ mm.

c) Change 35 mm to m.

The new units are _______ times _______ ,

so I need _______ times _______ units.

I _______ by _______ : 35 mm = _______ m.

d) 46 m = _____ cm e) .3 m = _____ cm

f) .8 mm = _____ cm g) 2.6 cm = _____ m

h) .03 m = _____ mm i) .23 mm = _____ cm

BONUS▸ j) 76.6 mm = _______ km k) .7 km = _______ cm l) .8 cm = _______ km

6. Is 5 m 28 cm equal to 5.28 m or 5.28 cm? Explain.

7. $1.72 stands for 1 dollar 7 dimes 2 pennies. In the measurement 1.72 m, are cm like dimes or like pennies? Explain.

8. Is 362 mm longer or shorter than 20 cm? How do you know?

9. Which is taller, a 2 350 cm tree or a 24 m building? Explain.

10. A fence is made of four parts, each 32 cm long. Is the fence longer or shorter than a metre?

11. 1 cm of ribbon costs 3¢. How much will 1.2 m cost?

12. Jack cycled 10 km in 1 hour. Jane cycled 44 000 m in 4 hours. Who rode faster?

13. Here are the masses of some primates.

• Gorilla: 175 kg • Baboon: 35 kg • Squirrel Monkey: 500 g • Pygmy Mouse Lemur: 30 g

a) How many grams does a gorilla weigh?
b) How many squirrel monkeys weigh 1 kg?
c) About how many times heavier than a mouse lemur is a baboon?

ME7-2 Changing Units to Divide Decimals

1. a) How many strings of length 2 mm fit into a string of length 14 mm? _______

   b) Convert the measurements to cm. 2 mm = _______ cm and 14 mm = _______ cm

   c) How many strings of length 0.2 cm fit into a string of length 1.4 cm? _______

   d) Explain why $14 \div 2$ and $1.4 \div 0.2$ have the same answer.

   e) Why is the quotient easier to find when the measurements are written in millimetres than in centimetres?

2. These decimal numbers represent the length of strings in centimetres. Convert the measurements to millimetres, then find the quotient.

   a) $1.8 \div 0.6$

   1.8 cm = _____ mm and 0.6 cm = _____ mm

   So $1.8 \div 0.6$ = _____ ÷ _____ = _____

   b) $4.2 \div 0.7$

   4.2 cm = _____ mm and 0.7 cm = _____ mm

   So $4.2 \div 0.7$ = _____ ÷ _____ = _____

   c) $7.2 \div 0.8$ d) $8 \div 0.4$ e) $8 \div 0.5$ f) $6.4 \div 0.4$ g) $9.1 \div 0.7$

3. Multiply both terms by 10 to find the quotient.

   a) $8.1 \div 0.3$
   = _____ ÷ _____
   = _____

   b) $72 \div 0.6$
   = _____ ÷ _____
   = _____

   c) $35 \div 0.7$
   = _____ ÷ _____
   = _____

4. These decimal numbers represent the length of strings in metres. Convert the measurements to centimetres, then find the quotient.

   a) $2.64 \div 0.02$
   = _____ ÷ _____
   = _____

   b) $8.9 \div 0.05$
   = _____ ÷ _____
   = _____

   c) $7.26 \div 0.03$
   = _____ ÷ _____
   = _____

5. These decimal numbers represent the length of strings in metres. Convert the measurements to millimetres, then find the quotient.

   a) $1.096 \div 0.008$ b) $1.778 \div 0.007$ c) $3.6 \div 0.009$ d) $5.16 \div 0.006$

6. Multiply both the dividend and divisor by 10, 100, or 1 000 to change them to whole numbers. (Be sure to multiply both by the same number!) Then divide.

   a) $12 \div 0.4$ = _____ ÷ _____
   = _____

   b) $51 \div 0.03$ = _____ ÷ _____
   = _____

   c) $16 \div 0.2$ d) $35 \div 0.07$ e) $640 \div 0.4$ f) $60 \div 0.005$ g) $9 \div 0.003$

   h) $2.5 \div 0.5$ i) $0.08 \div 0.4$ j) $0.42 \div 0.2$ k) $16.8 \div 0.2$ l) $3.3 \div 1.1$

ME7-3 Changing Units of Area

1. Fill in the blanks.

a) $2.7 \times 100 =$ _______ b) $29 \div 100 =$ _______ c) $.45 \times 100 =$ _______

d) $3.6 \div 100 =$ _______ e) $4.3 \times 10\,000 =$ _______ f) $37 \div 10\,000 =$ _______

g) $.18 \times 10\,000 =$ _______ h) $5.9 \div 10\,000 =$ _______ i) $6.253 \times 10\,000 =$ _______

j) $34.56 \div 10\,000 =$ _______ k) $41.31 \times 10\,000 =$ _______ l) $3278 \div 10\,000 =$ _______

2. a) Find the area of each square. (The diagrams are not to scale.)

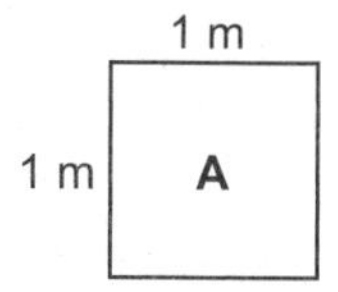

Area: _______

1 cm

1 cm **B**

Area: _______

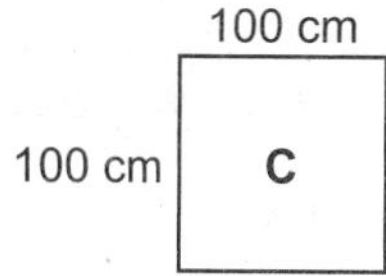

Area: _______

b) Which two squares have the same side length? _______ What is their area? _______

1 m^2 = _________ cm^2. A m^2 is _________ times larger than a cm^2.

1 m = _________ cm, so 1 m^2 = _________ × _________ cm^2 = _________ cm^2.

3. a) Change 270 000 cm^2 to m^2.

i) The new units are *10 000* times *larger*

ii) So I need *10 000* times *fewer* units

iii) so I *divide* by _______

270 000 cm^2 = *27* m^2

b) Change 3 700 cm^2 to m^2.

i) The new units are _______ times _______

ii) So I need _______ times _______ units

iii) so I _______ by _______

3 700 cm^2 = _______ m^2

c) Change 29 m^2 to cm^2.

i) The new units are _______ times _______

ii) So I need _______ times _______ units

iii) so I _______ by _______

29 m^2 = _______ cm^2

d) Change .4798 m^2 to cm^2.

i) The new units are _______ times _______

ii) So I need _______ times _______ units

iii) so I _______ by _______

.4798 m^2 = _______ cm^2

4. Change the units by following the steps in Question 3 in your head.

a) 500 m^2 = _______ cm^2 b) .9 m^2 = _______ cm^2 c) 3 cm^2 = _______ m^2

d) 1 950 cm^2 = _______ m^2 e) 15.4 cm^2 = _______ m^2 f) 0.05 m^2 = _______ cm^2

5. Fill in the correct units.

a) 2 cm × 2 cm = 4 _______ b) 2 cm + 2 cm = 4 _______ c) 4 cm^2 − 2 cm^2 = 2 _______

d) 2 _______ + 2 m = 4 m e) 2 _______ × 2 m = 4 m^2 f) 4 _______ − 2 mm = 2 mm

ME7-4 Area of Parallelograms

1. The rectangle below was made by moving the shaded triangle from one end of the parallelogram to the other.

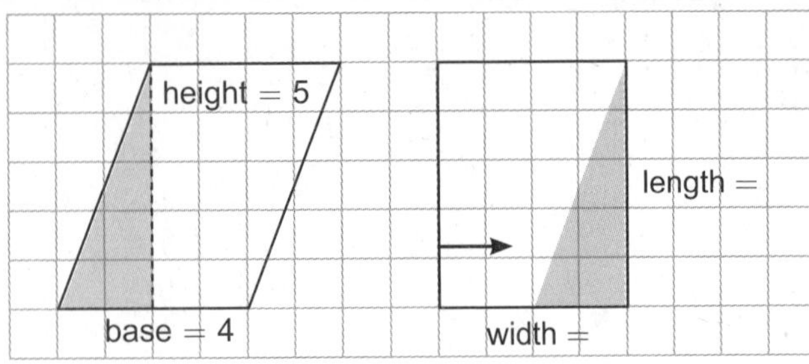

   a) Is the area of the rectangle the same as the area of the parallelogram? ______

   How do you know? ______

   b) Fill in the width of the rectangle.

   What do you notice about the base of the parallelogram and the width of the rectangle?

   ______

   c) Fill in the length of the rectangle.

   What do you notice about the height of the parallelogram and the length of the rectangle?

   ______

   d) Remember: For a rectangle, Area = (length) × (width).

   Write a formula for the area of a parallelogram using the base and height.

   Area =

2. In a parallelogram, height is always measured perpendicular to the base. Look at the lines in these parallelograms. Which one represents the height? Trace it.

a) 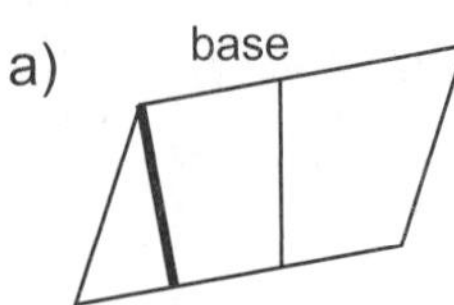

b) 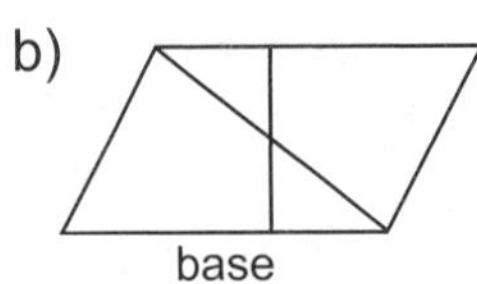

c) 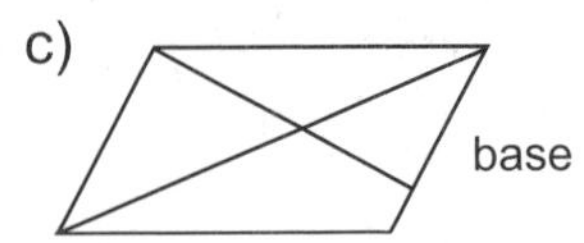

d) 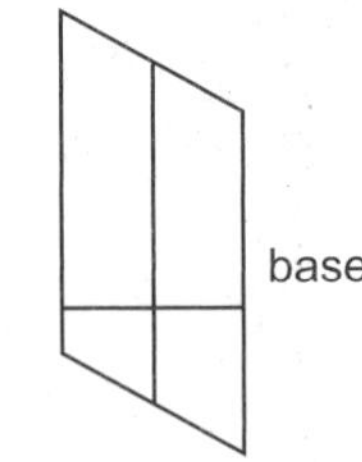

3. Find the area of the parallelograms with these dimensions.

a)	b)	c)	d)
Base = 5 cm	Base = 4 cm	Base = 8 cm	Base = 3.7 cm
Height = 7 cm	Height = 3 cm	Height = 6 cm	Height = 6 cm
Area = ______	Area = ______	Area = ______	Area = ______

4. Find the area in two ways, by using different sides as base. You will need a ruler.

a)

height: ______

base: ______

Area: ______

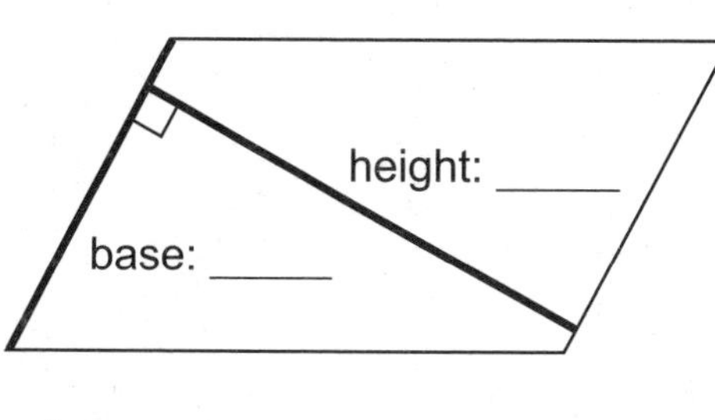

Area: ______

b)

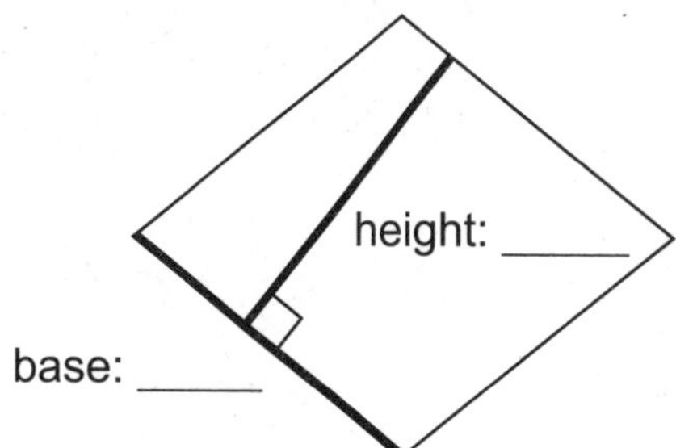

Area: ______

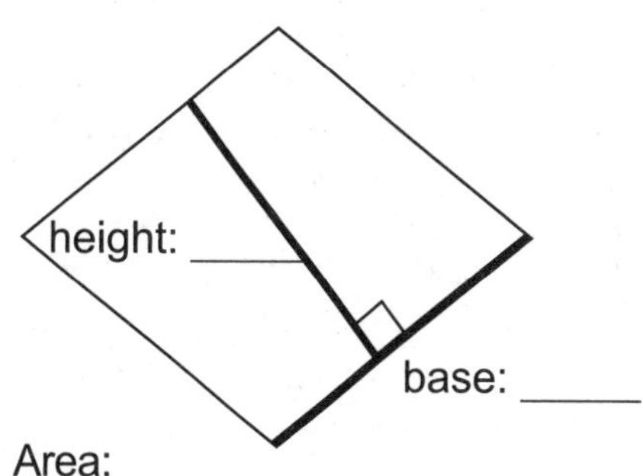

Area: ______

5. Draw a perpendicular to the base of the parallelograms using a protractor or a square corner. Measure the height and the base of the parallelograms using a ruler. Find the area of the parallelogram using your formula from Question 1d).

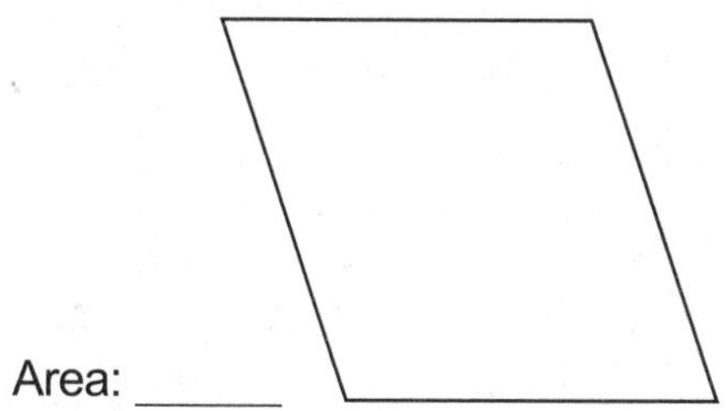

Area: ______

Area: ______

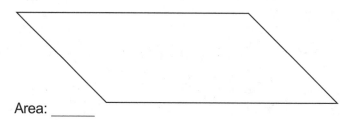

6. A parallelogram has height 80 cm and base 1.5 m.

a) Tom says: The area is 80 cm $\times$ 1.5 m $=$ 120 cm^2. Is he correct? Explain.
b) Find the area by converting both measurements to centimetres.
c) Find the area by converting both measurements to metres.
d) Are the answers in b) and c) the same? How do you know?

7. A bus has eight windows that are parallelograms with height of 1 m and base of 130 cm. The cost of the glass is $23.70 per m^2. How much will it cost to replace the glass in all the parallelogram-shaped windows?

8. a) Two parallelograms have the same height. One of the bases is three times longer than the other. Sketch the parallelograms. What can you say about the areas of these parallelograms?

b) Two parallelograms have bases of the same length. One of the parallelograms has a height three times longer than the height of the other. Sketch the parallelograms. What can you say about the areas of these parallelograms?

ME7-5 Area of Triangles

REMINDER▶ Area of triangle 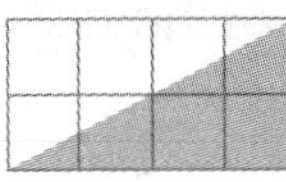 = Area of rectangle divided by 2 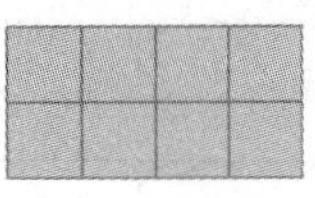

1. Find the area of the triangles in square units.

Area of A: ________ Area of B: ________

Area of C: ________ Area of D: ________

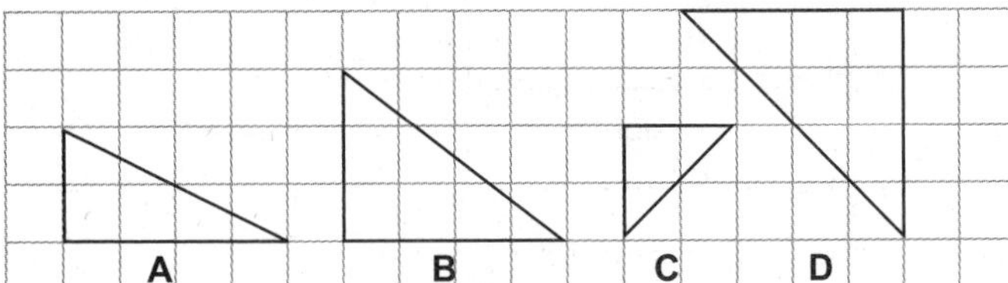

2. a) Draw a dotted line to show the height of each triangle. Then find the length of the height and base in square units.

b) Find the area of each triangle by adding the areas of 2 right triangles.

Area of A: ________ Area of B: ________

Area of C: ________ Area of D: ________

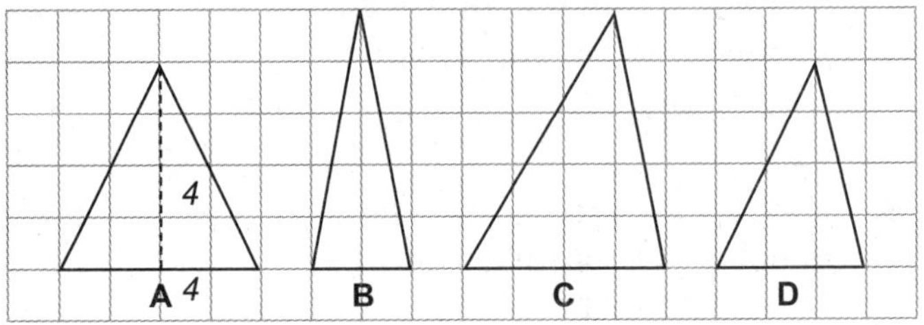

3. Yoram says: The area of triangle T is half of the area of the rectangle.

Is he correct? Explain. ______________________________

____

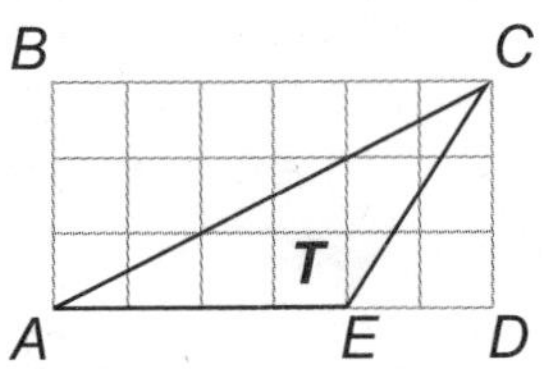

4. Follow these steps to find the area of the triangle T (ΔAEC) in Question 3.

a) Shade ΔADC in the first picture.

What fraction of the rectangle $ABCD$ is the triangle ΔADC? ________

What is the area of ΔADC? ________ $\times$ ________ $\div 2 =$ ________.

b) Shade ΔECD in the second picture. What is the area of ΔECD? ________

c) Shade ΔAEC in the third picture. Since area of $\Delta ACD =$ area of ΔAEC + area of ΔEDC, then area of $\Delta AEC =$ area of $\Delta ACD -$ ________

d) What is the area of ΔAEC? ________

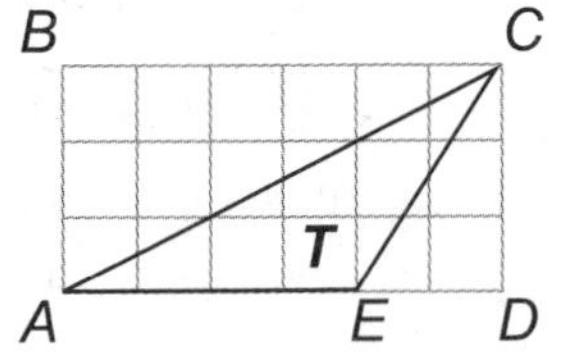
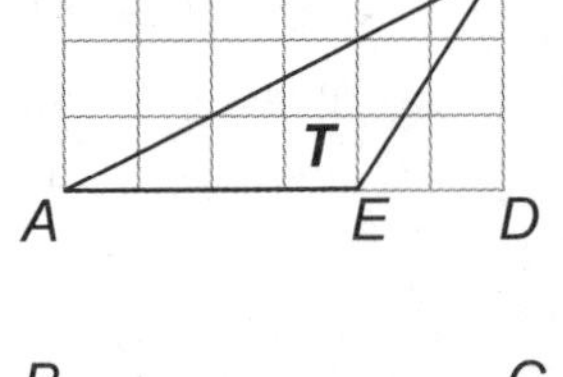

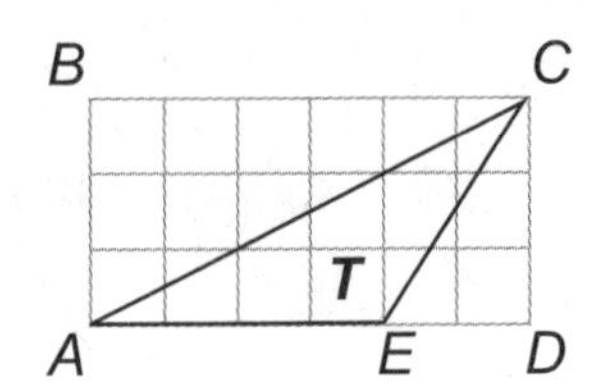

5. Use the method of Question 4 to find the area of the triangles.

B C
A E D

C B
D E A

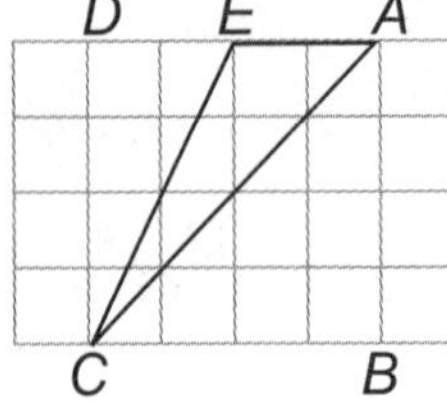

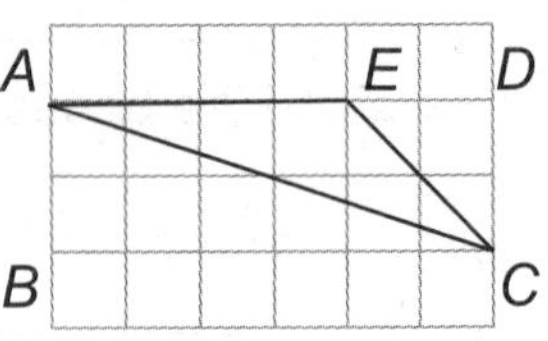

Area of ΔACD: ________ Area of ΔACD: ________ Area of ΔACD: ________ Area of ΔACD: ________

Area of ΔECD: ________ Area of ΔECD: ________ Area of ΔECD: ________ Area of ΔECD: ________

Area of ΔAEC: ________ Area of ΔAEC: ________ Area of ΔAEC: ________ Area of ΔAEC: ________

INVESTIGATION ▶

A. Jan wants to find the area of a triangle. She cuts the top of the triangle and rearranges the pieces as shown to form a rectangle.

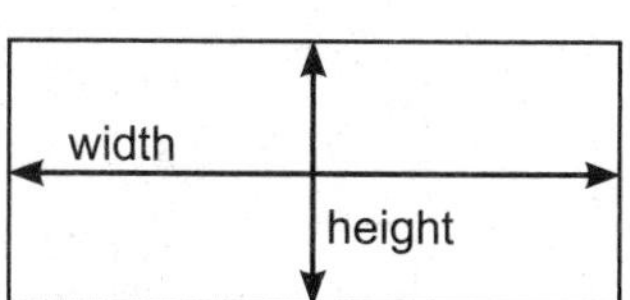

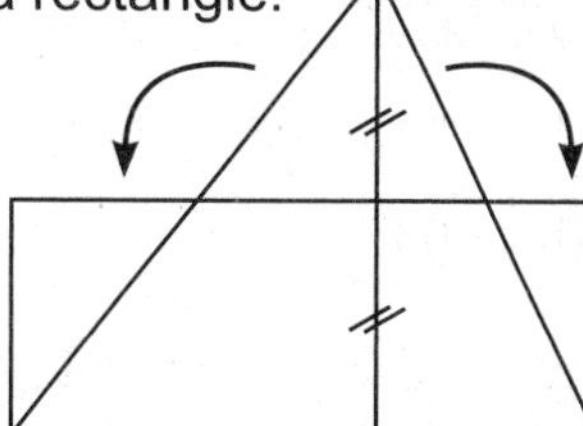

a) What is the width of her rectangle? How is it related to the base of the triangle? ______________

b) What is the height of her rectangle? How is it related to the height of the triangle? ______________

c) Write a formula for the area of the triangle using the base and the height of the triangle from Jan's method.

____

B. Ian finds the area of the same triangle a different way. He cuts the sides of the triangle and rearranges the pieces as shown to form a rectangle.

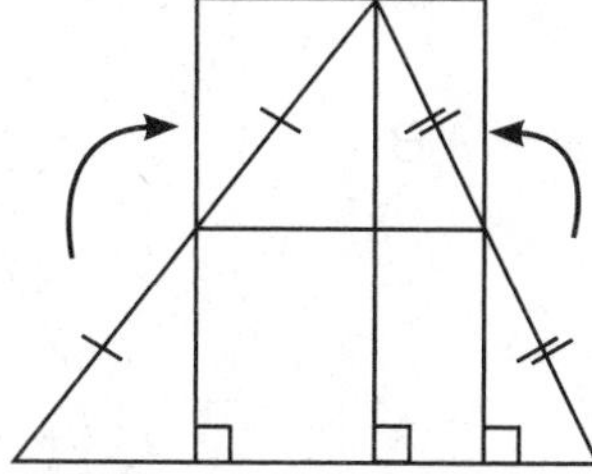

a) What is the width of his rectangle? How is it related to the base of the triangle? ______________

b) What is the height of his rectangle? How is it related to the height of the triangle? ______________

c) Write a formula for the area of the triangle using the base and the height of the triangle from Ian's method.

____

C. Jan and Ian start with a new triangle.

a) Draw how Jan and Ian would cut and rearrange the triangle.

Jan

Ian

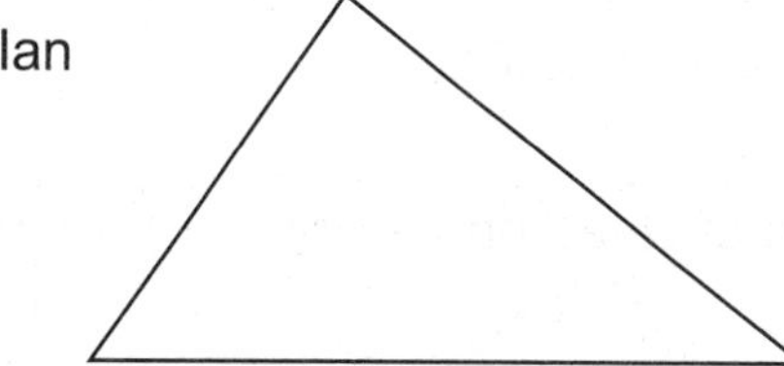

b) How are the bases and the heights of Jan's and Ian's triangles related?

____

____

c) Explain why they get the same area using the pictures and the formulas.

____

____

6. Measure the base and height of each triangle using a ruler. Then find the area of the triangle.

Area of a triangle = base × height ÷ 2

a)

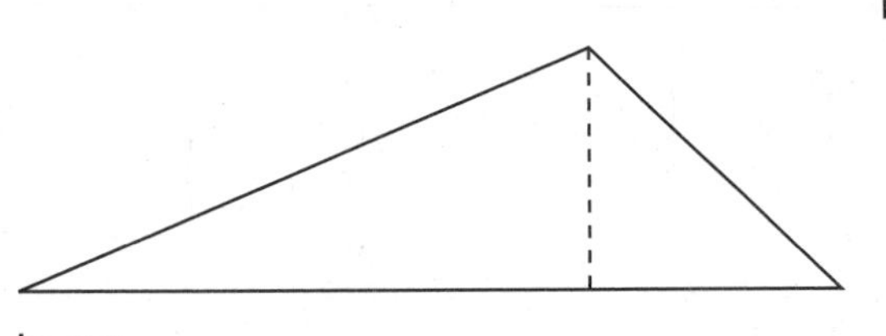

base: ________

height: ________

Area: ________

b)

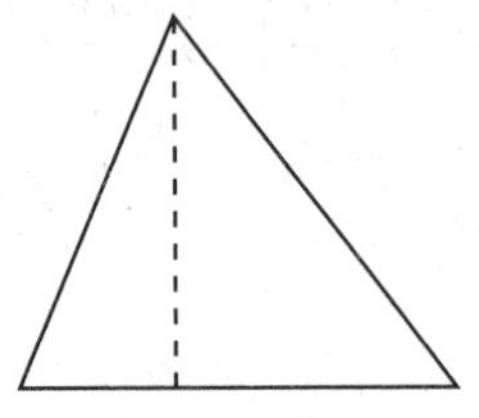

base: ________

height: ________

Area: ________

c)

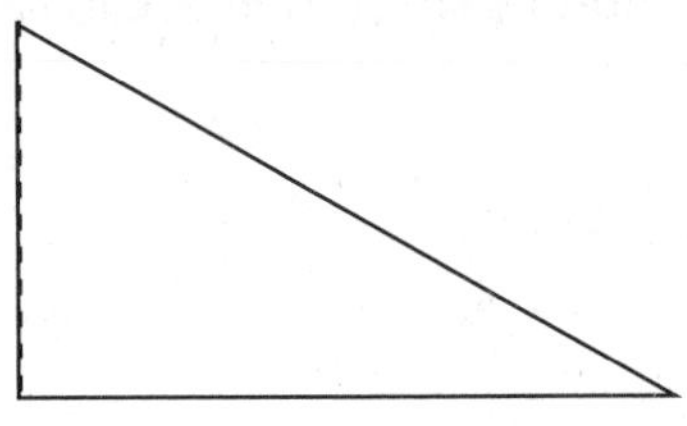

base: ________

height: ________

Area: ________

7. The base of each triangle is labelled. Draw the height.

a) b)

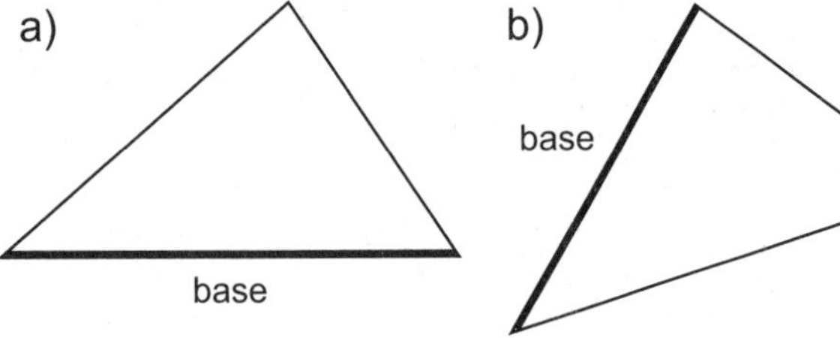

Sometimes the height is outside the triangle.

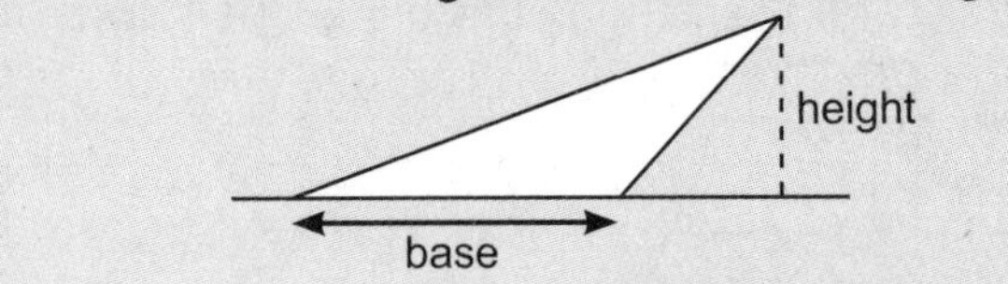

c)

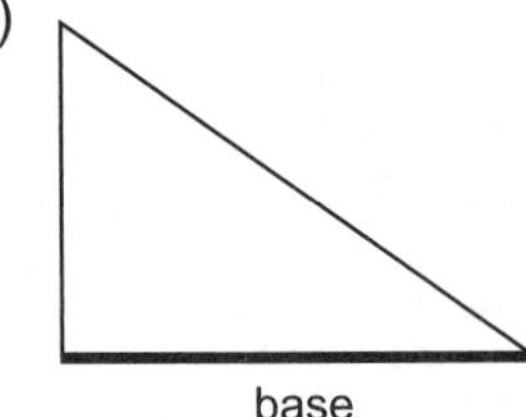

d)

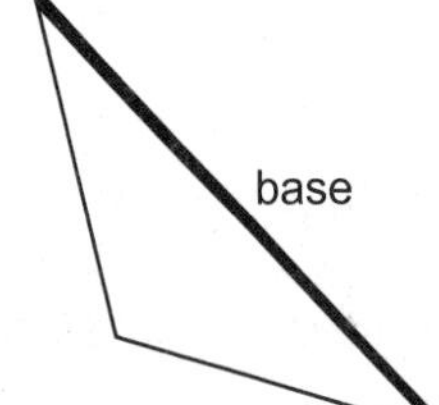

e)

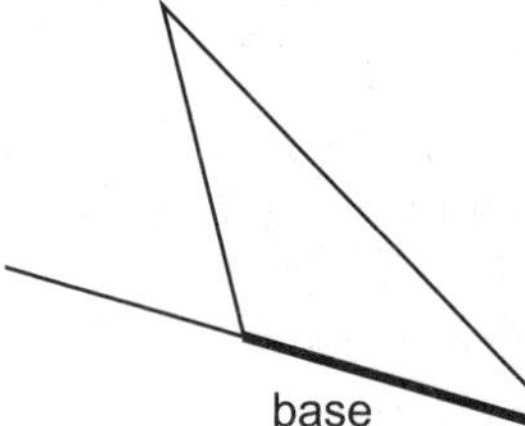

f)

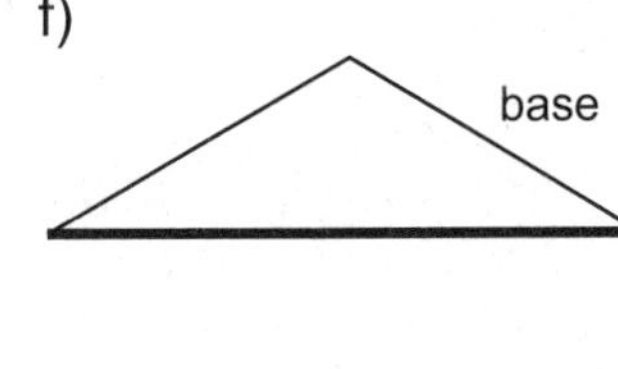

8. The height is given in each triangle. Label the base.

a)

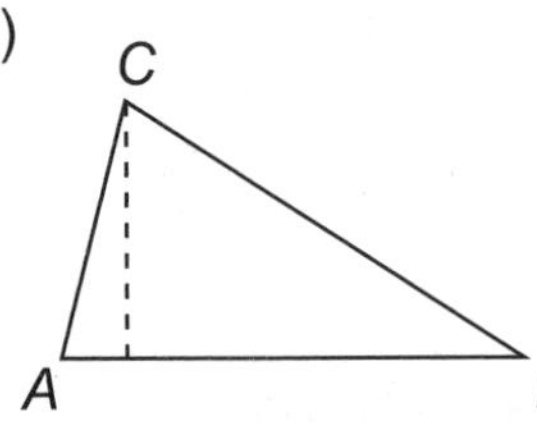

base: *AB*

b)

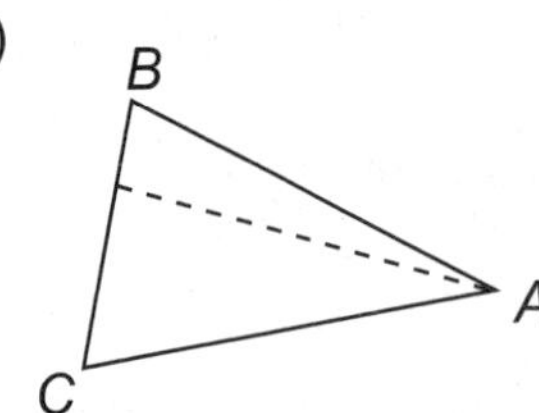

base: ________

c)

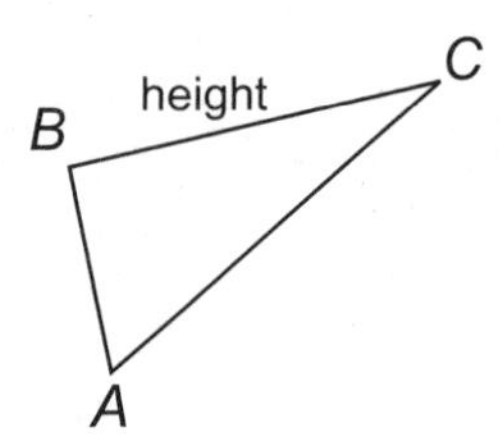

base: ________

d)

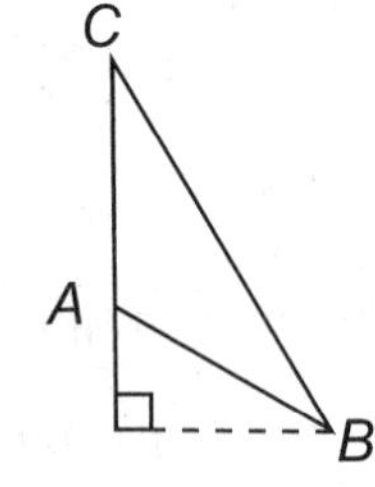

base: ________

9. a) Measure the lengths of the sides and the heights in this triangle. Mark the measurements on the diagram.

b) Find the area of the triangle three ways, each time using a different side as the base.

Did you get the same result? ________ Explain.

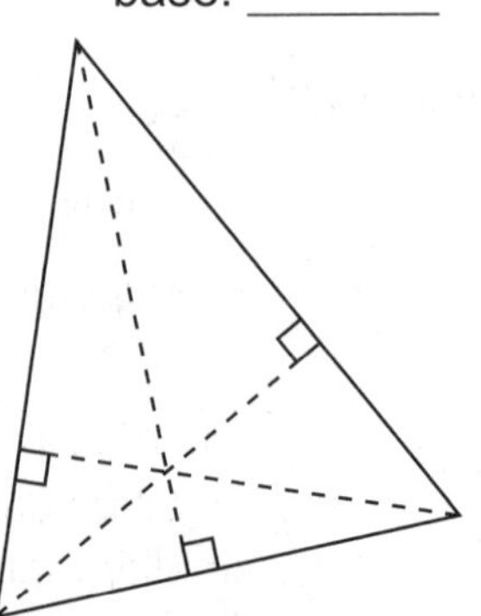

ME7-6 Area of Triangles and Parallelograms

1. Parallelogram B was made by joining two copies of triangle A together. How can you find the area of triangle A? Hint: Use what you know about the area of parallelograms.

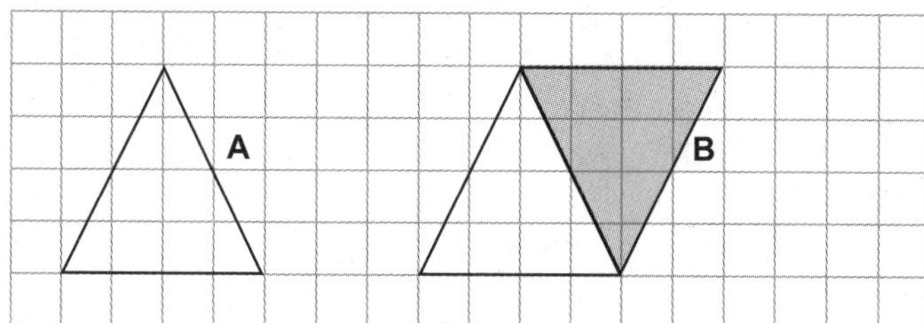

2. Find the area of triangle C by joining two copies together to form a parallelogram, as in Question 1.

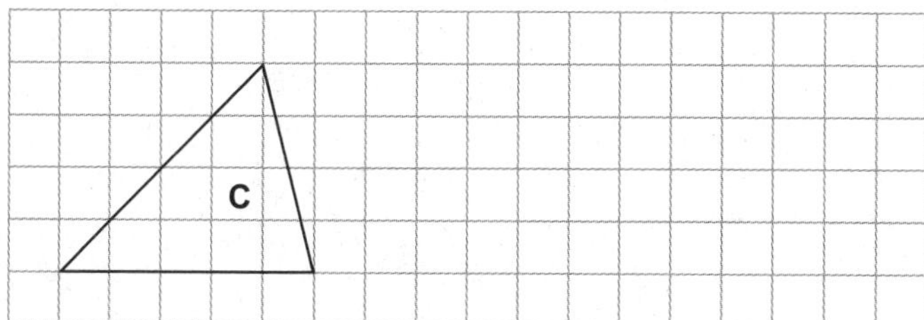

3. The base and height of the triangles above are **the same** as the base and height of the parallelograms! Write a formula for the area of a triangle using the base and the height of the triangle. Hint: How are the areas of the triangles in Questions 1 and 2 related to the areas of the parallelograms?

4. Show how you would calculate the area of triangle A in Question 1 using your formula.

5. Find the area of the triangles with these dimensions.

a) Base = 6 cm
Height = 2 cm

b) Base = 4 cm
Height = 3 cm

c) Base = 6 cm
Height = 4 cm

d) Base = 3.2 cm
Height = 8 cm

BONUS ▶

6. a) Draw a scalene triangle and find its area.

b) Find the midpoint of one of the sides and draw a median.

c) The median splits the triangle into two smaller triangles. What can you say about the areas of the smaller triangles? How do you know?

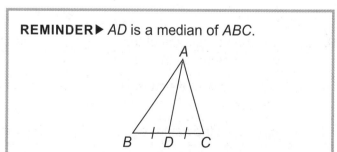

REMINDER ▶ *AD* is a median of *ABC*.

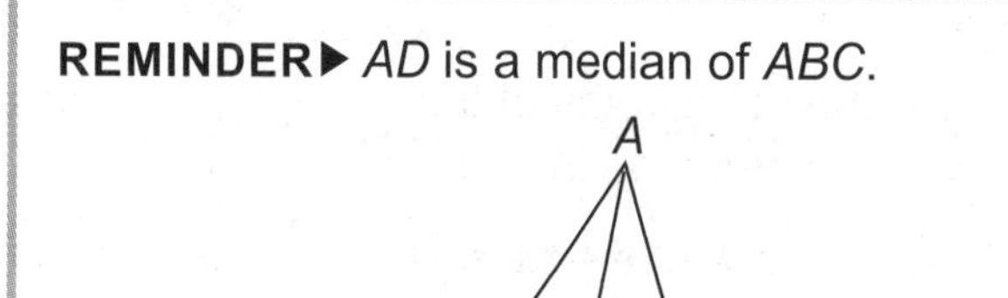

ME7-7 Problem-Solving — Using a Formula

When you read a word problem, identify **what you need to find** and **the information you are given**. If you can solve the problem using **a formula**, write the formula.

1. In each of the problems below, underline what you need to find and circle the measurements you are given. Then write the formula you would use.

a) A parallelogram has base 5 cm and height 35 mm. What is the area of the parallelogram?

Formula: *Area of parallelogram = base × height*

b) A book cover is 30 cm long and 20 cm wide. What is the area of the cover?

Formula: ____________________

c) Find the area of a triangle with base 2 m and height 75 cm.

Formula: ____________________

For geometric or measurement problems, it often helps to **make a sketch**. The sketch does not have to be perfect, but it should include all the information you know.

2. PROBLEM ▶ In a rectangle, two sides are each 3 cm long. The other two sides are each twice as long. What is the area of the rectangle?

a) Underline what you need to find and circle what you are given.

b) Which formula will you use? ____________________

c) Which of these sketches is the most helpful for solving the problem? Explain your choice.

A

3 cm

Twice as long as the short side

B

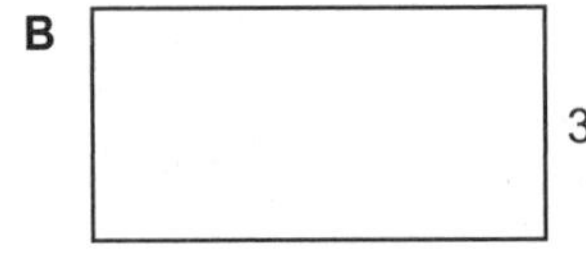

2 × 3 cm

C

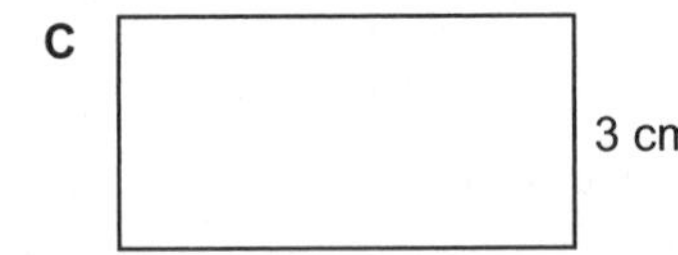

3. PROBLEM ▶ A parallelogram has a base that is 5 cm long. The height to this base is 2 cm shorter than the base. What is the area of the parallelogram?

a) Underline what you need to find and circle what you are given.

b) Which formula are you going to use? ____________________

c) Which of these sketches is the most helpful for solving the problem? Explain your choice.

A

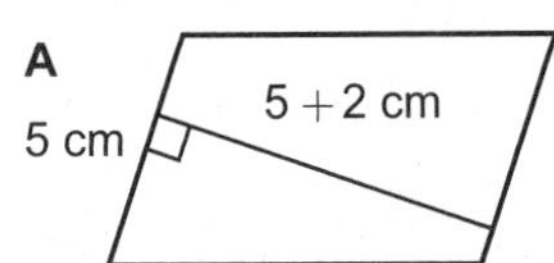

B

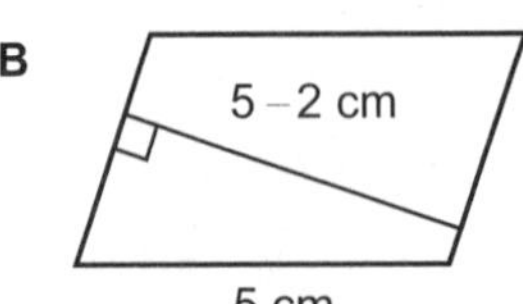

C

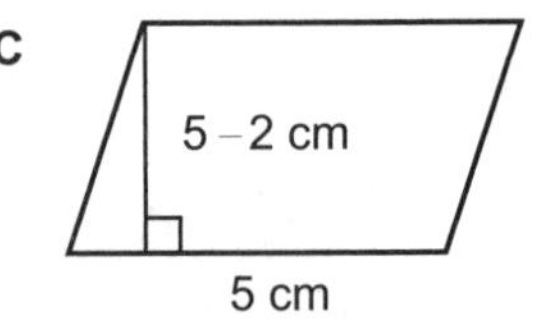

4. For each problem below:

- Underline **what you need to find**.
- Circle **the information you are given**.
- Write **the formula** you are going to use.
- Make **a sketch** to show the information that you know.

Do not solve the problems yet! The first sketch was started for you.

a) In a triangle *ABC*, *AD* is the height from *A* to the point *D* on side *BC*. $AD = 5$ cm, $BD = 3$ cm, and *CD* is as long as *AD* and *BD* together. What is the area of the triangle?

Formula:

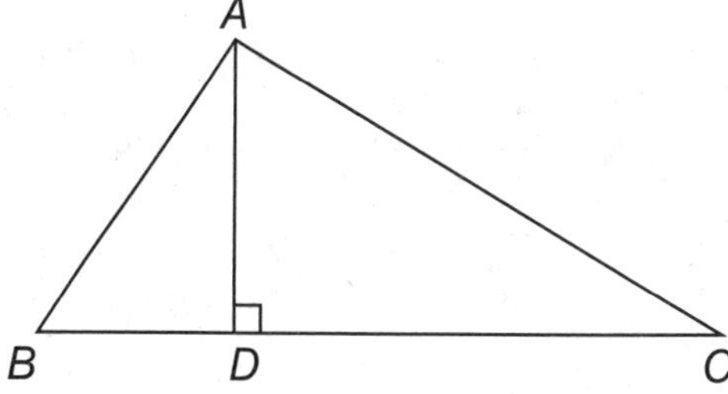

b) A parallelogram is long and thin. The height to a long side is 5 cm. The long sides of the parallelogram are three times as long as the height. What is the area of the parallelogram?

Formula:

c) In a rectangle, one of the sides is 3 m long. The perimeter of the rectangle is 10 m. What is the area of the rectangle?

Formula:

BONUS ▶ William cuts out a paper right trapezoid that is 10 cm high. When he folds his trapezoid, he sees that it makes a square and a right isosceles triangle. What is the area of the trapezoid?

Formula:

When you know what formula you are going to use, look for the values that you need in the word problem. Do you have all the measurements you need to use the formula? Sometimes you will need to do a calculation to **find a value that is not given**.

5. **PROBLEM ▶** A parallelogram can be cut into a square and two right triangles. The triangles are as high as the square. The base of each triangle is only half as wide as the square. The height of the square is 10 cm. What is the area of the parallelogram?

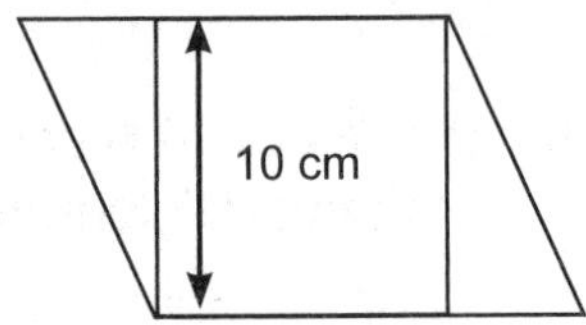

a) Judy decides to use the formulas for the area of a square and the area of a triangle to find the area of the parallelogram.

i) Judy uses these formulas:

Area of the square = width × height
= height × height

Area of a right triangle = base × height ÷ 2

Which information is not given directly in the problem? ______________________

ii) Fill in the values Judy needs and mark them on the sketch beside the problem.

The height of the square: ________ cm

The height of the triangle: ____________

The base of the triangle: ____________

iii) Area of the square = ________ cm²

Area of the triangle = ________ cm²

iv) Area of the parallelogram = area of the square + ________ × area of the triangle

= ________ + ________ = ________ cm²

b) Guy decides to use the formula for the area of a parallelogram to solve the same problem.

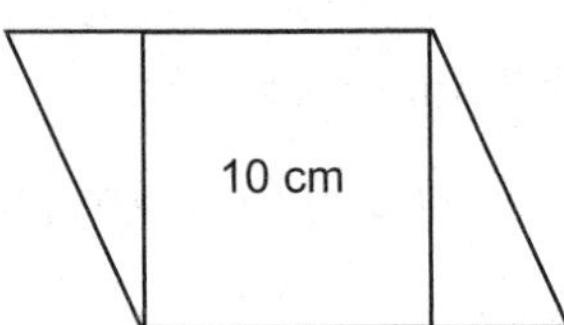

i) Write the formula Guy uses. ______________________

ii) Which value is not given directly in the problem? ______________________

iii) Fill in the information he needs and mark it on the sketch.

Base of parallelogram = ____________

Height of parallelogram = ________

iv) Find the area of the parallelogram. Is this answer the same as the answer in part a)?

When you substitute measurements into a formula or equation, **make sure that all the units are the same**! If they are not, convert them before you substitute. Do not forget to write the units in the answer.

Remember: cm $\times$ cm $=$ cm^2 and m $\times$ m $=$ m^2

You cannot multiply a measurement in metres by a measurement in centimetres!

6. **PROBLEM ▶** A parallelogram is 30 cm high. Its base is 1.2 m long. What is the area of the parallelogram?

   a) What units are more convenient, cm or m? _______

   Convert all measurements to the units you chose. base: _______ height: _______

   b) Solve the problem.

7. Find the areas of the shapes in Question 4.

8. The short sides of a right triangle are called **legs**. A right triangle has one leg 7 cm shorter than the other. The longer leg is 12 cm long. What is the area of the triangle?

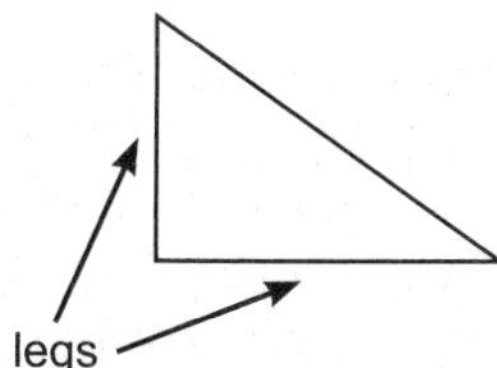

9. A **rhombus** (a parallelogram with equal sides) has sides 24 cm long. The height of the rhombus is three times shorter. What is the area of the rhombus in square metres? Hint: First find the area in cm^2, then convert the answer to m^2.

Sometimes you do not have a formula that will give you what you need to find right away.

What you need to find might be **part of a related formula**. Use a variable (such as x) to represent the piece of information you do not know in your formula.

10. **PROBLEM ▶** A rhombus has sides that are 5 cm long. Its area is 20 cm^2. What is the height of the rhombus?

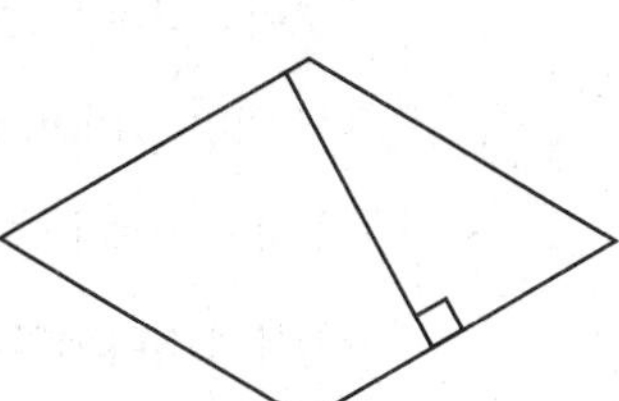

   a) Underline what you need to find. Circle the information you know.

   b) There is no formula for the height of a rhombus. But a rhombus is a parallelogram and there is a formula for the area of parallelograms.

   Area of parallelogram $=$

   c) Here is a sketch for the problem. Add the information you know. Mark the value you need to find with the letter x.

   d) Which value in the formula is x? _______

When you **substitute all the data and the variable** you chose into a formula, you get an equation. For example, in Question 10 above:

Area of parallelogram: 20 cm^2 base: 5 cm height: x cm

Equation: $20 = 5 \times x$, or $20 = 5x$

11. For each problem below, mark the information you know on the sketch. Mark x for the piece of information that you do not know. Then write an equation.

a) The area of a rectangle is 15 m^2. The short side is 3 m long. What is the long side of the rectangle?

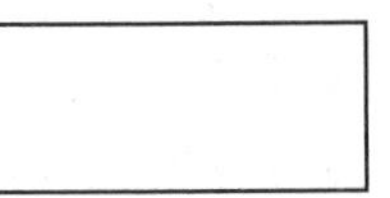

Equation: ______________________________

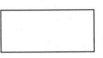

b) The area of a parallelogram is 3 m^2. The base is .5 m long. What is the height of the parallelogram?

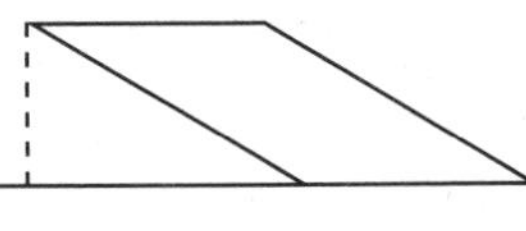

Equation: ______________________________

c) The area of a parallelogram is 24 cm^2. The height is 6 cm long. What is the base of the parallelogram?

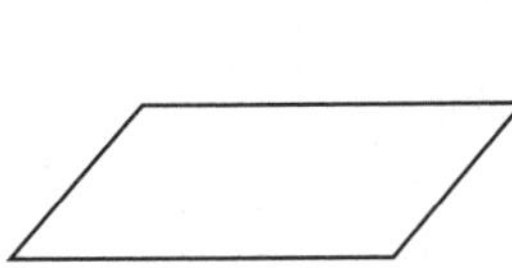

Equation: ______________________________

12. Compare these problems.

PROBLEM A ▶ A parallelogram has base 5 cm and area 30 cm^2. What is its height?

PROBLEM B ▶ A parallelogram has height 5 cm and area 30 cm^2. What is its base?

Do these problems produce different equations? Explain.

13. Fill in the correct units.

a) $3 \text{ cm} \times 3 \text{ cm} = 9$ _______

b) $9 \text{ cm}^2 \div 3 \text{ cm} = 3$ _______

c) 3 _______ $+ 3 \text{ m} = 6 \text{ m}$

d) 3 _______ $\times 3 \text{ m} = 9 \text{ m}^2$

e) 9 _______ $\div 3 \text{ mm} = 3 \text{ mm}$

f) 9 _______ $\div 3 \text{ m} = 3 \text{ m}$

14. PROBLEM ▶ The area of a parallelogram is 3 m^2. The height is 30 cm. What is the base of the parallelogram?

a) Would you convert the measurements for the problem into metres or centimetres? _______

b) Convert the measurements into the units you've chosen. area = _______ height = _______

c) Substitute the converted units into the formula for the area of a parallelogram. Use x for the base.

d) Now solve the equation. Do not forget the correct units in the answer!

15. Explain what is wrong with the following "solutions" of Question 14.

a) The equation is $3 \times x = 30$, so $x = 30 \div 3 = 10$ m.

b) The equation is $30 \times x = 3$, so $x = 3 \div 30 = .1$ m.

c) The equation is $30 \times x = 3$, so $x = 3 \div 30 = .1$ cm.

16. The area of a rectangle is 24 m². One of its sides is 4 m long. What is the length of the other side?

17. The area of a triangle is 2 m². Its longest side is 125 cm. What is the height to this side of the triangle?

For each of the following problems, decide whether what you need to find is given by a formula or is part of a related formula you could use. Write the formula, then use it to solve the problem.

18. Julie cuts a square into two congruent parts and rearranges the parts to make a rectangle. The short side of her new rectangle is 6 cm. What is the area of her rectangle?

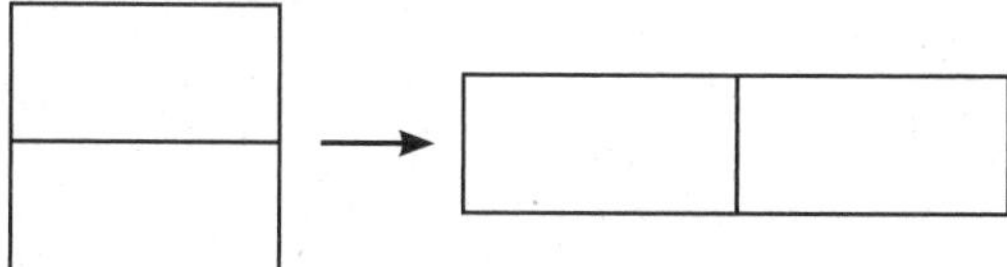

19. A park lawn has the shape of an isosceles triangle. The area of the lawn is 400 m². The shortest side of the lawn is 16 m long. How far is the opposite corner of the lawn from the shortest side of the lawn?

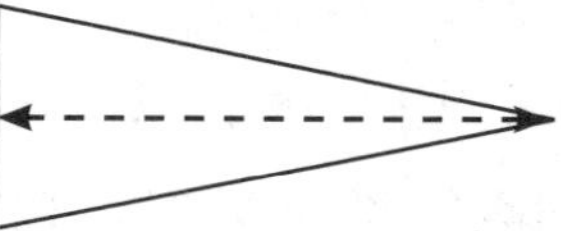

20. A bus window is 80 cm tall and has the shape of a parallelogram. The area of the window is .96 m². What is the length of the bottom side of the window?

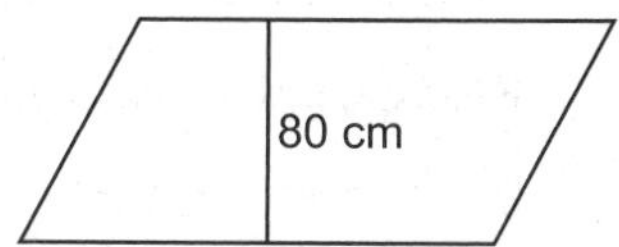

21. One of the sides in a triangle is four times shorter than the height to this side. The height is 3 cm. What is the area of the triangle?

22. A parallelogram is made from two right triangles joined along the longer leg. The legs of the triangles are 20 cm and 1.3 m. What is the area of the parallelogram?

23. Bilal says that he can draw a triangle with sides 5 cm, 12 cm, and 13 cm, and area 30 cm², so that one of the heights will be 10 cm. Is he correct? Explain.

24. A triangle has area 12 cm². Its base is 4 cm.

a) What is the height of the triangle?
b) On grid paper, draw three different triangles with area 12 cm² and base 4 cm.

BONUS ▶ The ancient Maya used units of length called **kaans**. An ancient Mayan field is rhombus-shaped. Its area is 30 square kaans. Each side of the field is 5 kaans long. What is the height of the rhombus-shaped field?

ME7-8 Area of Trapezoids

REMINDER ▸ A trapezoid is a quadrilateral with exactly one pair of parallel sides.

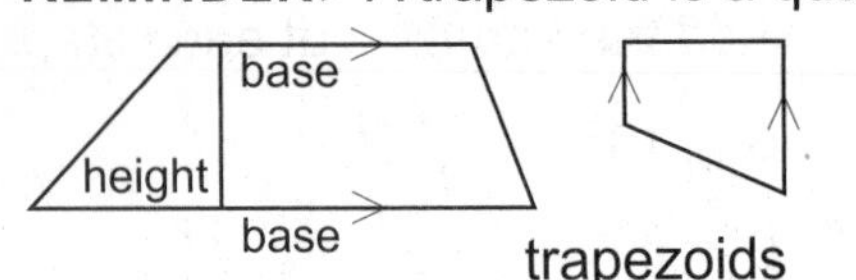

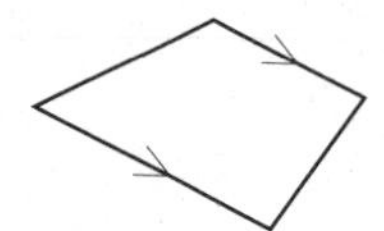

trapezoids

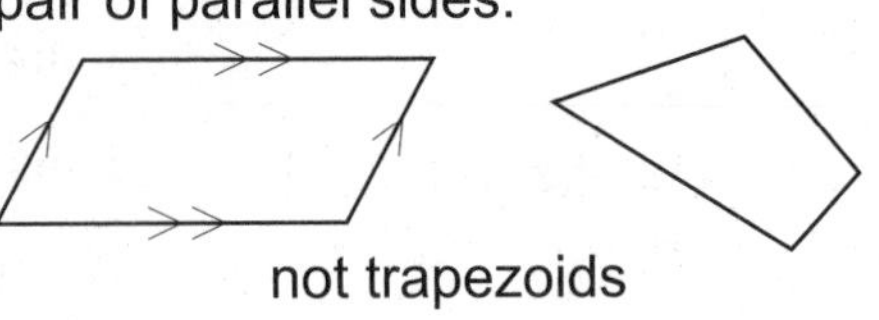

not trapezoids

1. Split each trapezoid into a triangle and a rectangle, then find the area of each shape in square units.

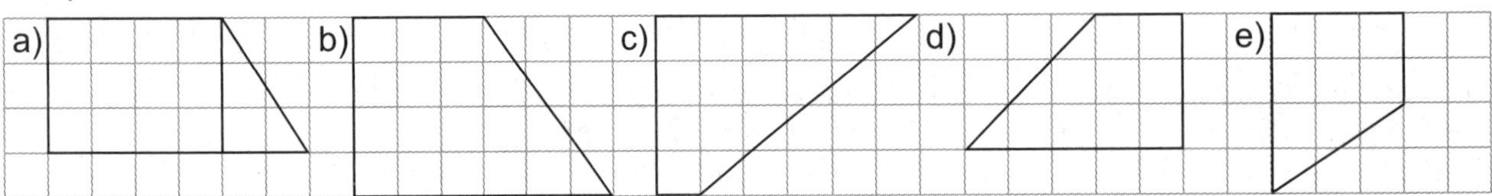

Area of…

a) rectangle *12* b) rectangle ____ c) rectangle ____ d) rectangle ____ e) rectangle ____

triangle *3* triangle ____ triangle ____ triangle ____ triangle ____

trapezoid *15* trapezoid ____ trapezoid ____ trapezoid ____ trapezoid ____

2. Split each trapezoid into two triangles and a rectangle, then find the area of each shape in square units.

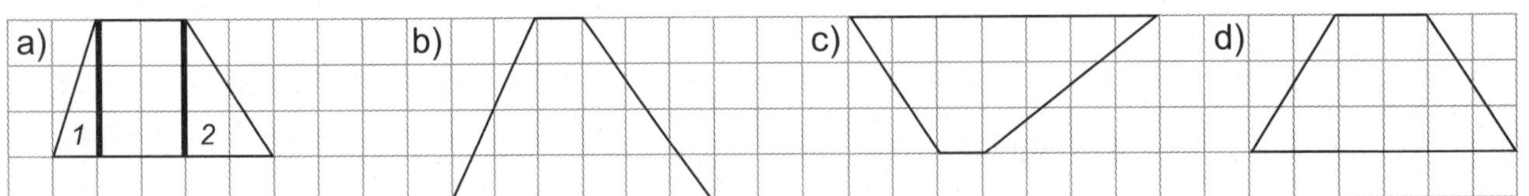

Area of…

a) rectangle *6* b) rectangle ____ c) rectangle ____ d) rectangle ____

triangle 1 *1.5* triangle 1 ____ triangle 1 ____ triangle 1 ____

triangle 2 *3* triangle 2 ____ triangle 2 ____ triangle 2 ____

trapezoid *10.5* trapezoid ____ trapezoid ____ trapezoid ____

3. **BONUS ▸** Find the area of this trapezoid.

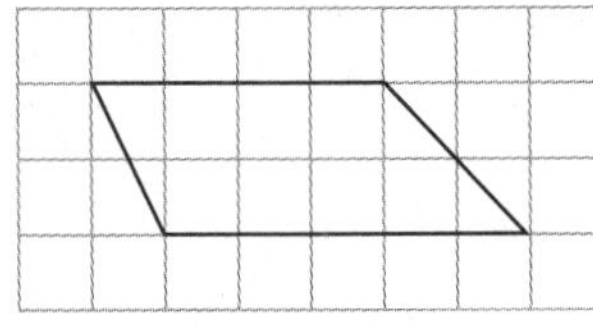

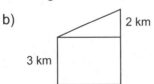

4. a) What is the base of the triangle?
   b) What is the area of the trapezoid?

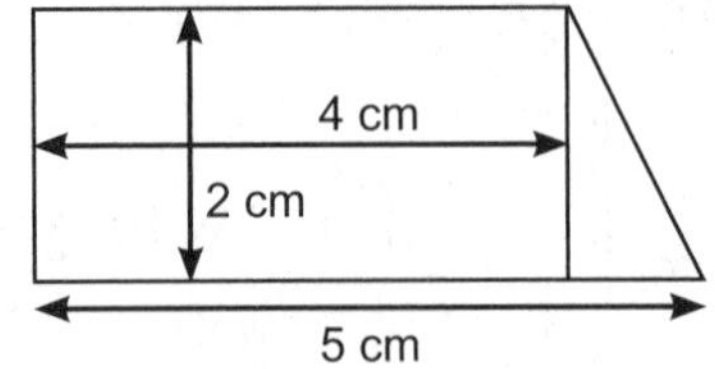

5. Find the area of these trapezoids. Do not forget to check the units!

a)

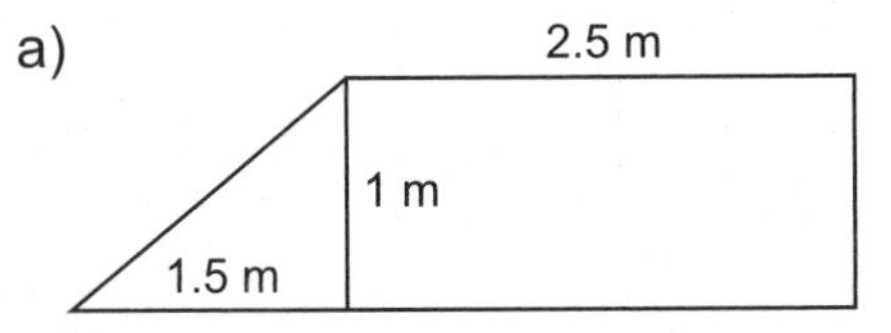

b)

c)

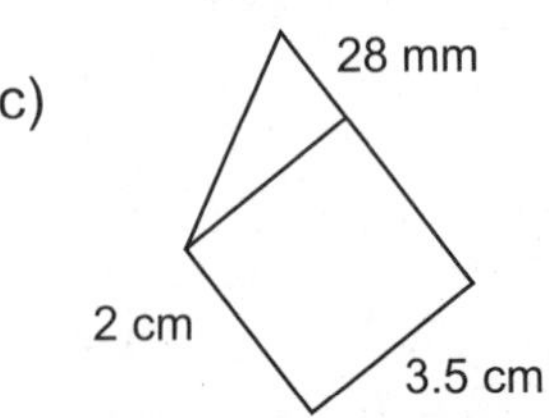

6. Carene finds the number that is halfway between 5 and 10 by using a number line. She takes steps of the same length towards the middle from both sides.

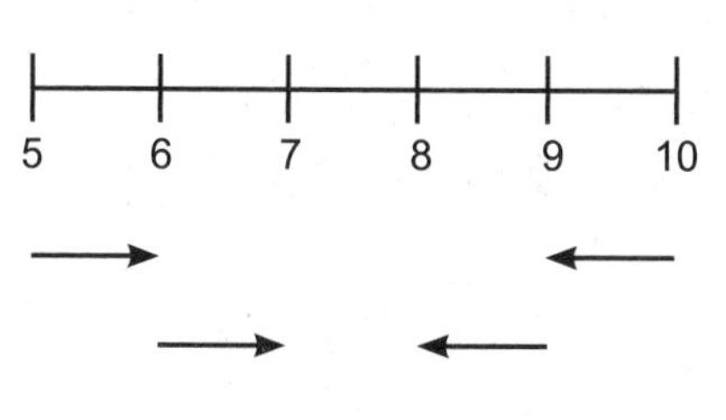

Carene's numbers	Add the numbers at each step:
5 and 10	$5 + 10 =$ _____
6 and 9	$6 + 9 =$ _____
7 and 8	$7 + 8 =$ _____
7.5 and 7.5	$7.5 + 7.5 =$ _____
7.5 is **halfway** between 5 and 10.	

Look at the sum of the numbers at each step. Does it change? _____

How is the number halfway between 5 and 10 related to the sum of the numbers at each step?

7. Use Carene's method to find the number that is halfway between the two given numbers.

a) 4 and 8: _____ b) 8 and 10: _____ c) 2 and 7: _____

5 and 7; $5 + 7 = 12$

6 and 6; $6 + 6 = 12$

The number is $12 \div 2 = 6$.

8. Find the number that is halfway between the two numbers using the sum of the numbers.

a) 3 and 5: b) 5 and 9 c) 6 and 7: d) a and b:

$(3 + 5) \div 2$

$= 8 \div 2 = 4$

9. Which of the following expressions represent the same number? Explain your thinking in your notebook.

$\frac{1}{2}$ of $(a + b)$ $(a + b) \div 2$ $(b + a) \div 2$ $(a + b) \times 2$ $\frac{(a + b)}{2}$

10. Draw a rectangle with the same area as the trapezoid. Then find the area of the trapezoid.

a)

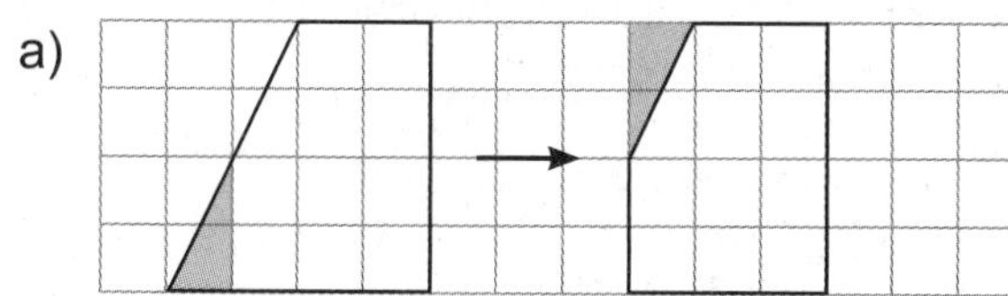

Area = *3* × *4* = *12*

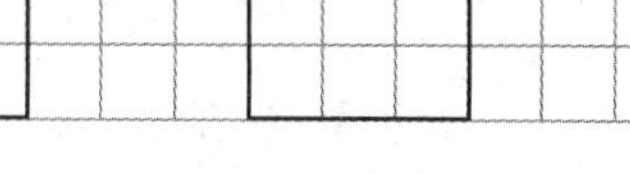

b)

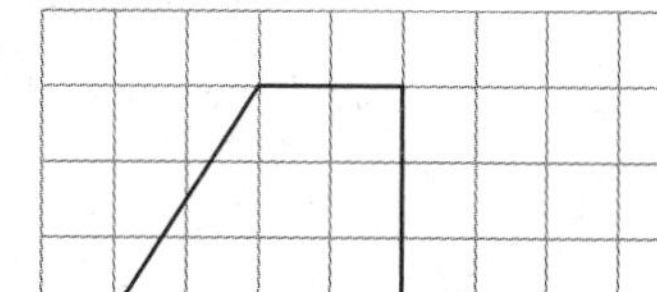

Area = _____ × _____ = _____

c)

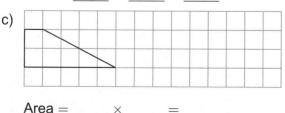

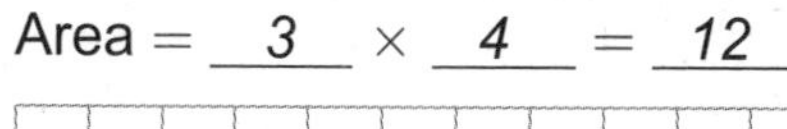

Area = _____ × _____ = _____

d)

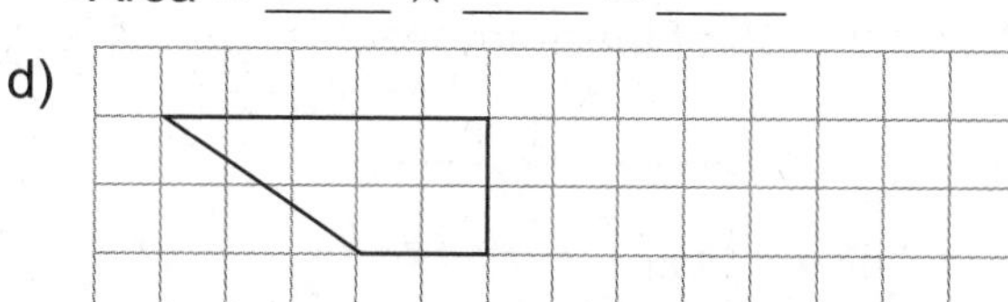

Area = _____ × _____ = _____

11. The length of the rectangle *BCFE* is halfway between the lengths of the bases of the trapezoid *ABCD*.

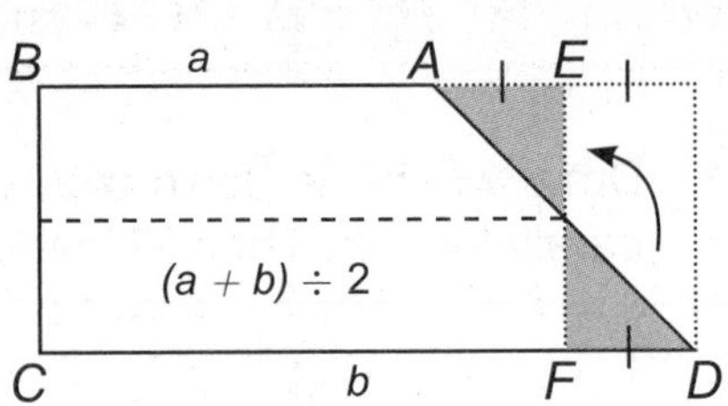

Find the length of the rectangle with the same area as the trapezoid.

a)
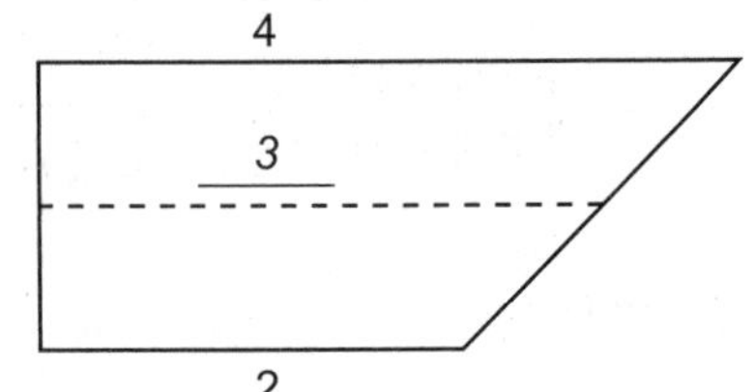

b)
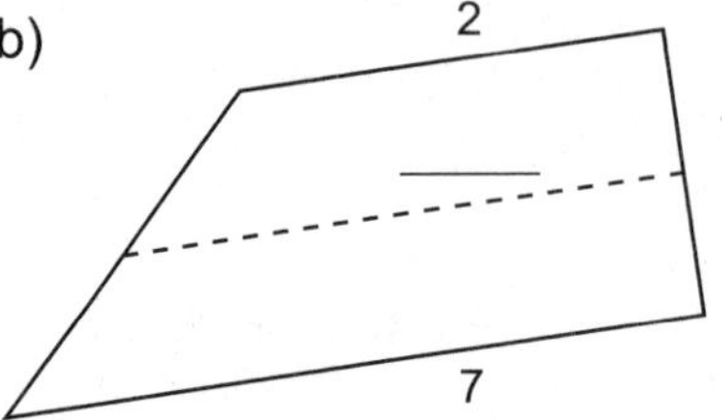

c)
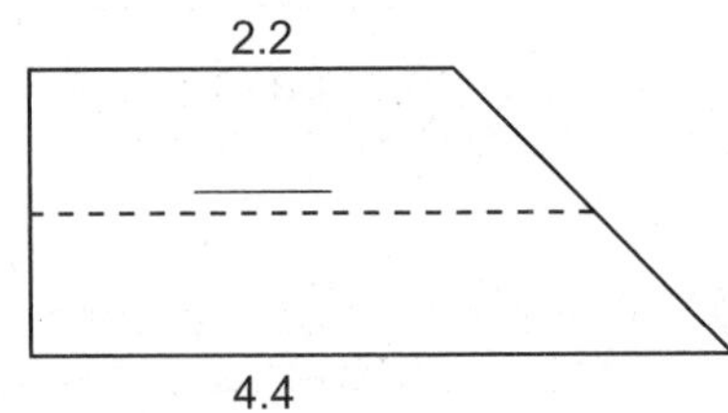

12. Find the area of these trapezoids by converting them to rectangles with the same length as the number halfway between the bases.

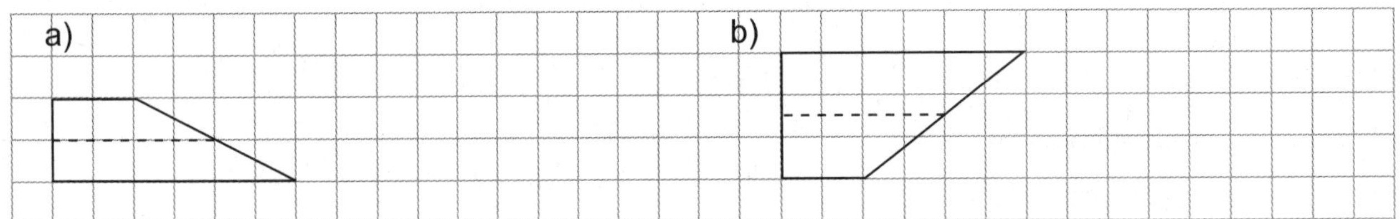

a)

bases: _____ and _____

number in the middle: _____

height: _____

area: _____

b)

bases: _____ and _____

number in the middle: _____

height: _____

area: _____

c)
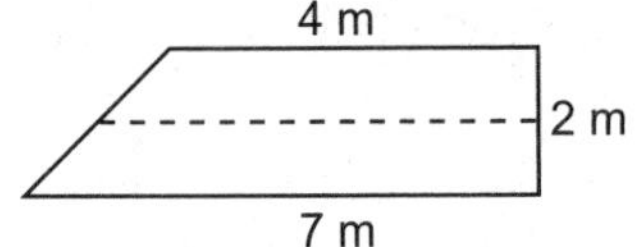

bases: _____ and _____

number in the middle: _____

height: _____

area: _____

d)

a

h

b

bases: _____ and _____

number in the middle: _____

height: _____

area: _____

13. Draw a trapezoid with two right angles, one base 6 cm, the other base 3 cm, and the height 4 cm. Then find the area of the trapezoid.

BONUS ▶

14. How can you find the area of this trapezoid? Use a sketch to explain.

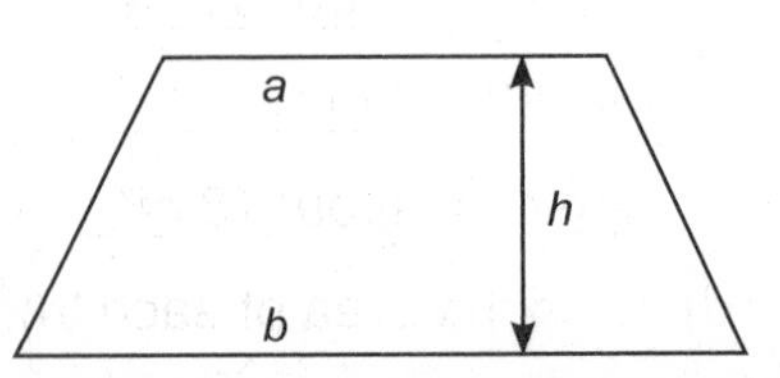

ME7-9 Area of Trapezoids and Parallelograms

1. Draw an upside-down copy of each trapezoid, as shown in a), to create a parallelogram. Then fill in the blanks for each parallelogram.

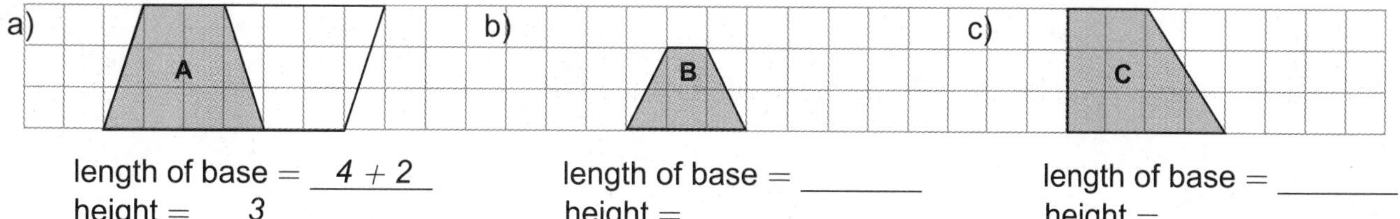

a)	b)	c)
length of base = *4 + 2*	length of base = _______	length of base = _______
height = *3*	height = _______	height = _______

2. A trapezoid has the bases given. If you make a parallelogram as in Question 1, what will the base of the parallelogram be?

   a) bases of trapezoid: 2 cm and 3 cm   base of a parallelogram = _____ cm

   b) bases of trapezoid: 5 m and 7 m   base of a parallelogram = _____

   c) bases of trapezoid: *a* and *b*   base of a parallelogram = _____

3. Find the areas of the parallelograms in Question 1.

   a) Area of parallelogram = _____

   b) Area of parallelogram = _____

   c) Area of parallelogram = _____

> **REMINDER▶**
>
> Area of parallelogram = (height) × (length of base)

4. a) How many trapezoids make up each parallelogram in Question 1? _____

   b) What would you divide the area of each parallelogram by to find the area of the trapezoid? _____

   c) Write a formula for the area of each trapezoid in Question 1.

Area of A:

sum of bases   height

$(4 + 2) \times 3 \div 2$

$= 6 \times 3 \div 2 =$ _____ cm²

Area of B:

(_____ + _____) × _____ ÷ 2

= _____ × _____ ÷ 2 = _____ cm²

Area of C:

5. Write a formula for the area of the trapezoid using *a*, *b*, and *h*. _______________

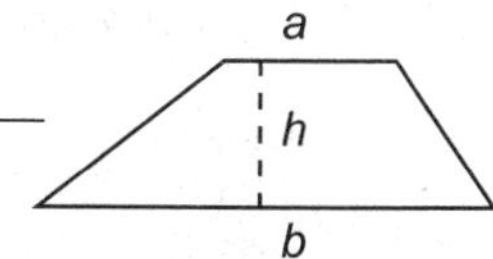

6. Estimate the area of the trapezoids.

a)

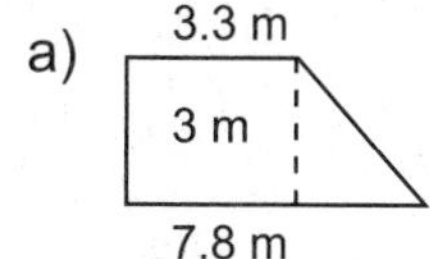

b)

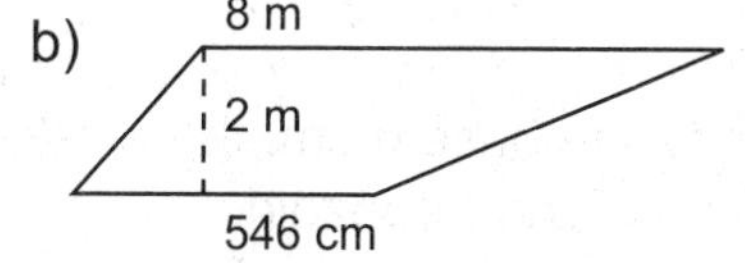

c)

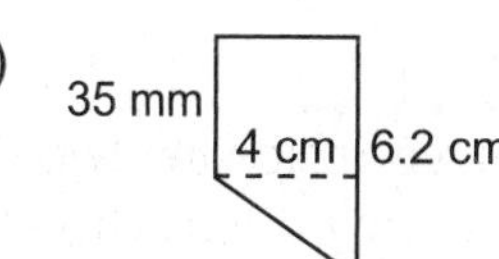

a)	b)	c)
bases: *about 3 m and 8 m*	bases: _______	bases: _______
height: *3 m*	height: _______	height: _______
area: *about 18 m²*	area: _______	area: _______

d) Find the area of each trapezoid.

ME7-10 Area of Composite Shapes

1. a) A B C

Area of A = ________

Area of B = ________

Area of C = ________

Draw a line to show how C can be divided into shapes A and B.

Write a formula for the area of C using the areas of A and B: Area of C = ____________

b) A

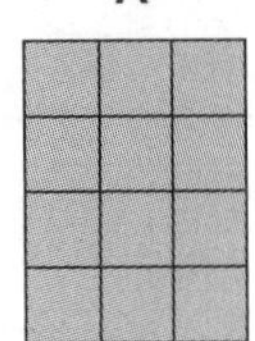

B

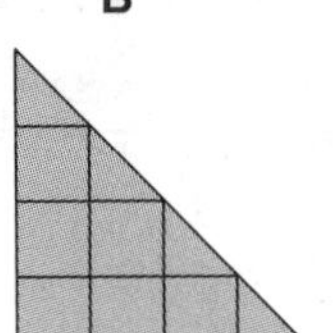

C

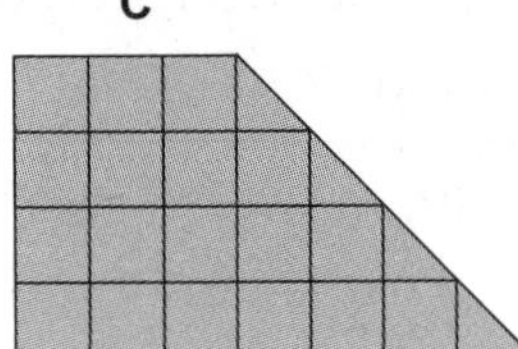

Area of A = ________

Area of B = ________

Area of C = ________

Draw a line to show how C can be divided into shapes A and B.

Write a formula for the area of C using the areas of A and B: Area of C = ____________

c) A B C

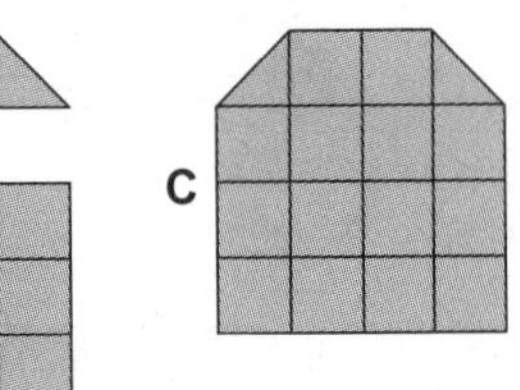

Area of A = ________

Area of B = ________

Area of C = ________

Draw a line to show how C can be divided into shapes A and B.

Write a formula for the area of C using the areas of A and B: Area of C = ____________

d) A B C

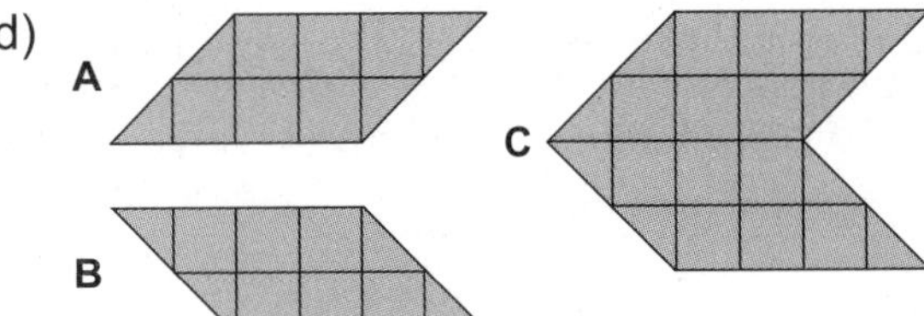

Area of A = ________

Area of B = ________

Area of C = ________

Draw a line to show how C can be divided into shapes A and B.

Write a formula for the area of C using the areas of A and B: Area of C = ____________

2. a) A

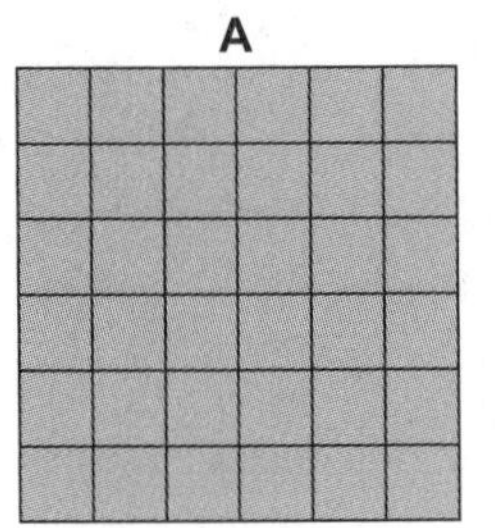

B

C

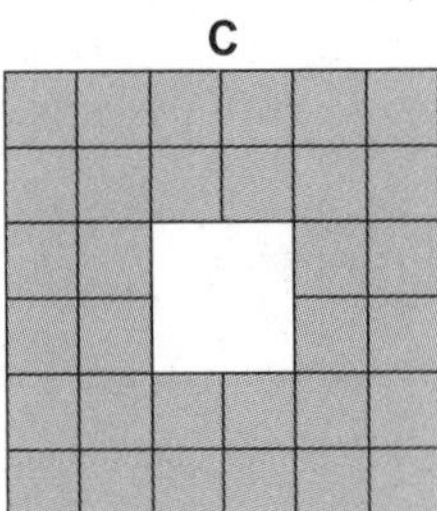

Area of A = ________

Area of B = ________

Write a formula for the area of C using the areas of A and B: Area of C = ____________

b) A

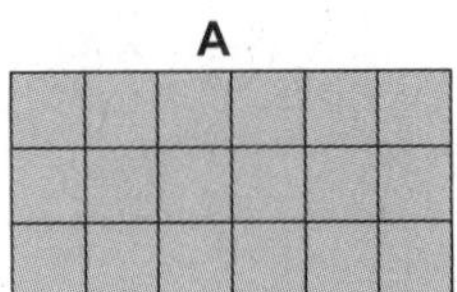

B

C

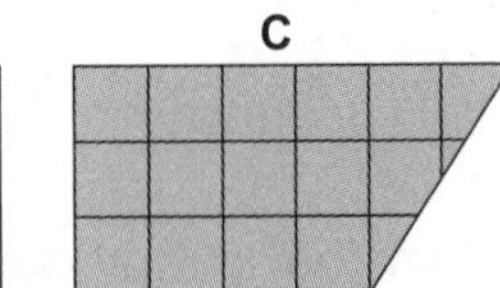

Copy the shapes onto grid paper. Calculate the area of trapezoid C in 3 ways:

i) by dividing the trapezoid into a rectangle and a triangle;

ii) by using the area of the large rectangle (A) and the unshaded triangle (B);

iii) by using the formula for the area of a trapezoid.

3. Draw a line to cut each figure into two rectangles. Use the areas of the rectangles to find the area of the figure.

a)

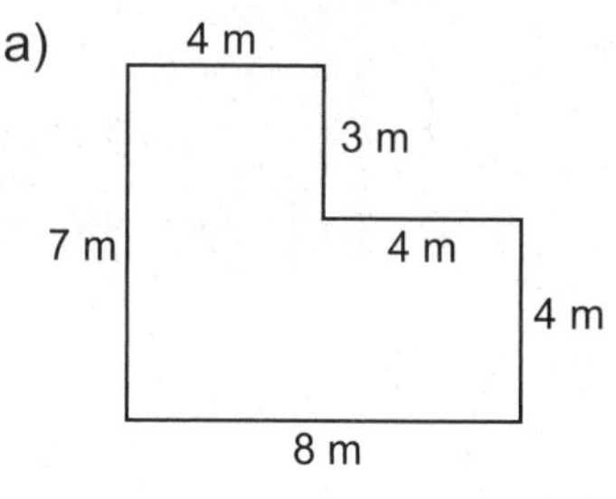

Area = ____________

b)

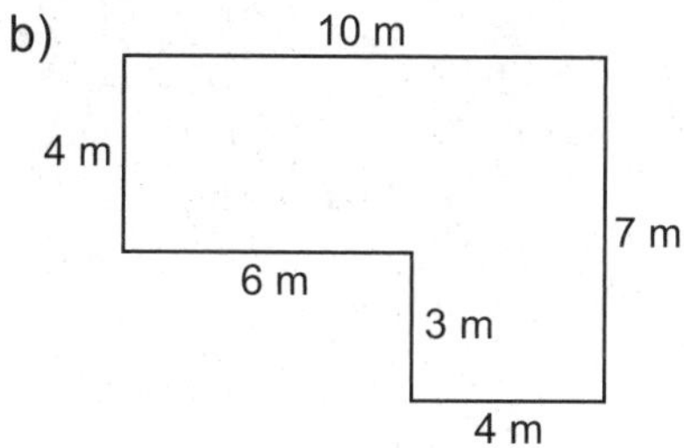

Area = ____________

c)

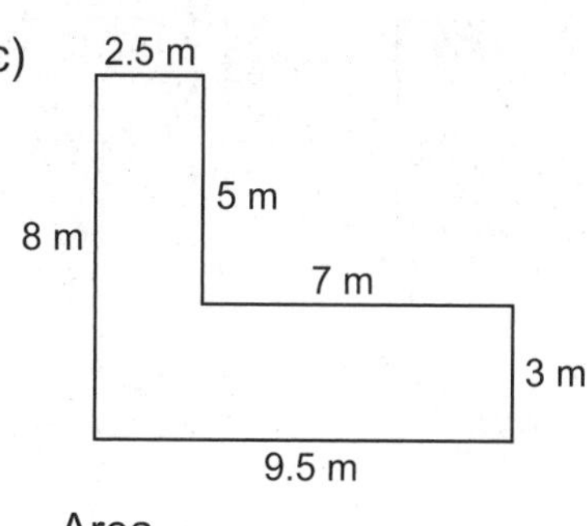

Area = ____________

4. a) A building is 8 stories high. The wing is 5 stories high. How many stories is the tower?

8 stories | tower | wing | 5 stories

The tower is _____ stories high.

b) The tower of a building is 10 m wide. The base is 50 m wide. How wide is the wing?

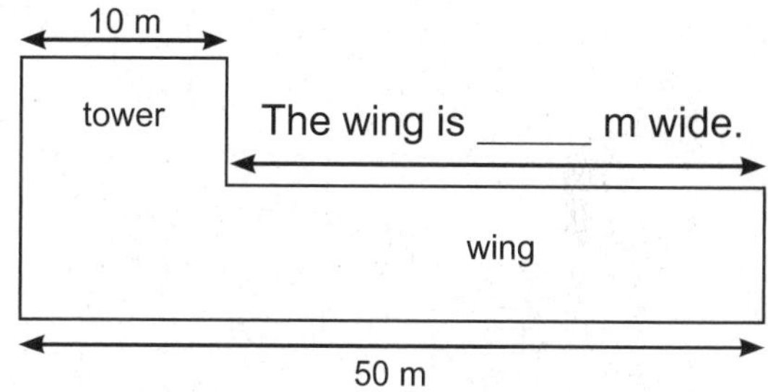

5. Find the measurements of the sides that have not been labelled. Then divide the figure into two rectangles and use the areas of the rectangles to find the area of the figure.

a)

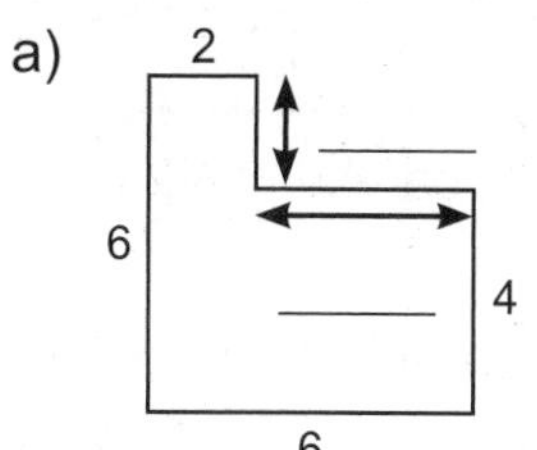

Area = ____________

b)

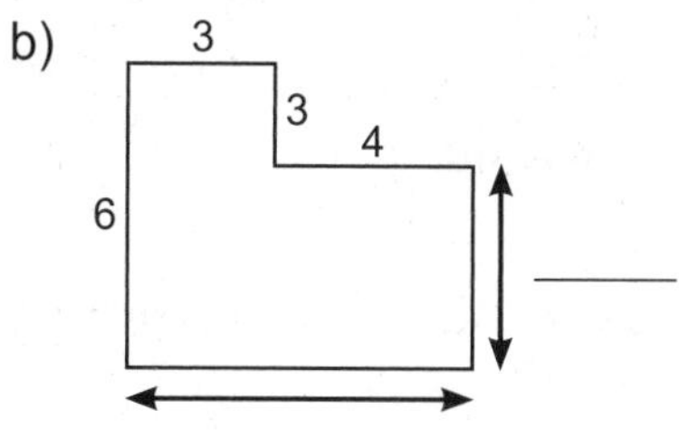

Area = ____________

c)

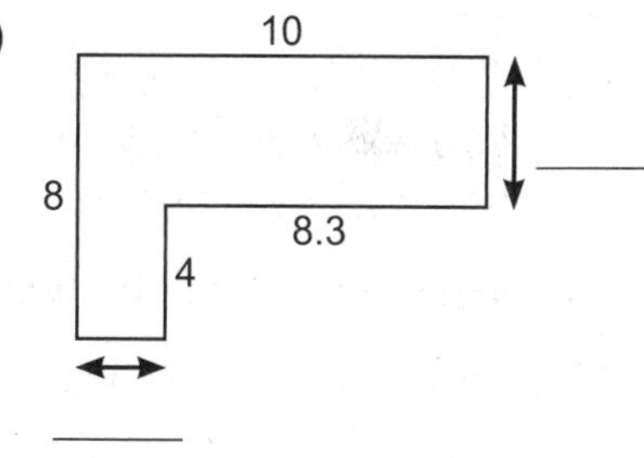

Area = ____________

6. Find the area of each figure. Include the units in your answer.

a)

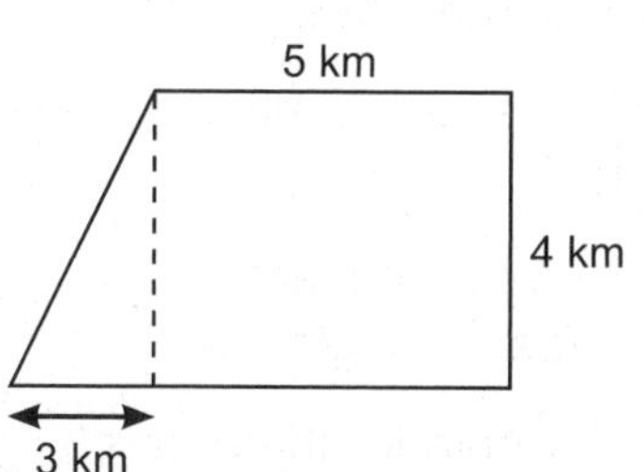

b)

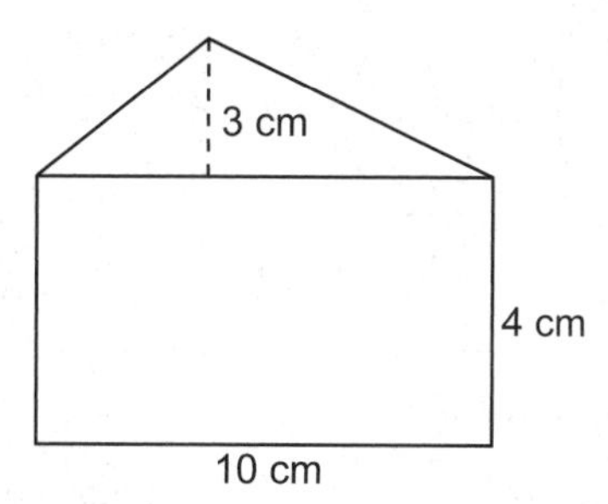

c)

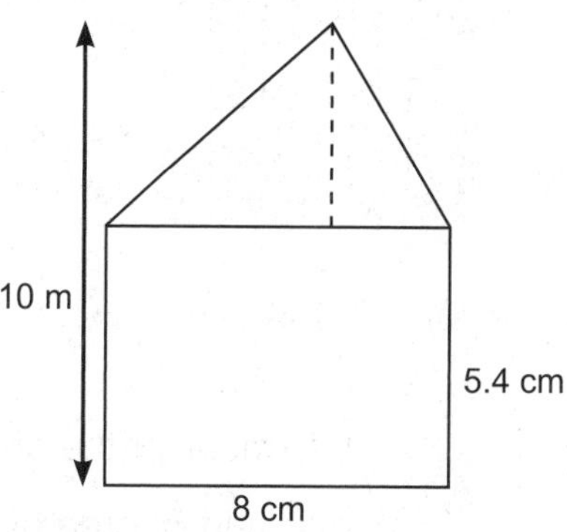

7. Find the area of each shaded shape.

a)

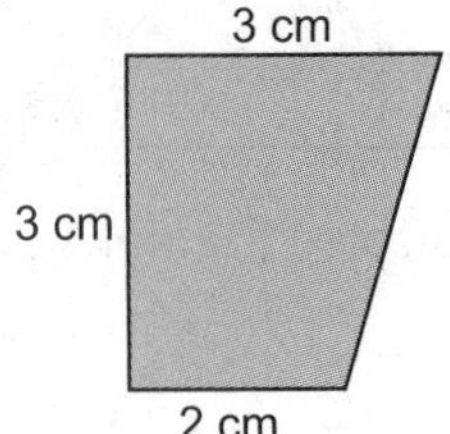

b)

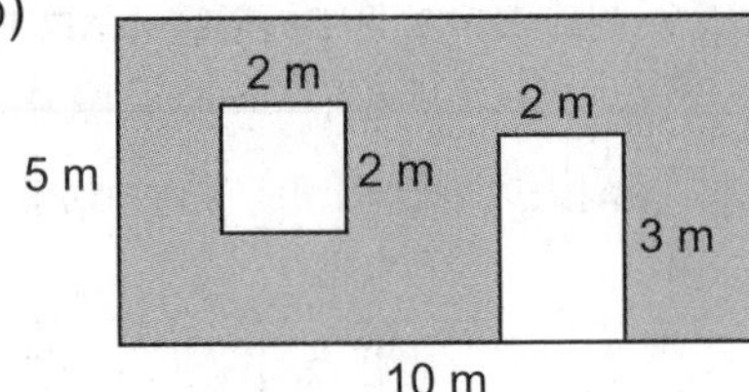

c)

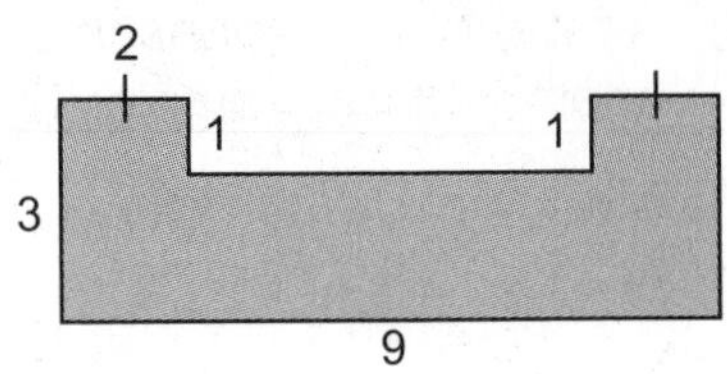

8. Estimate, then find, the area.

a)

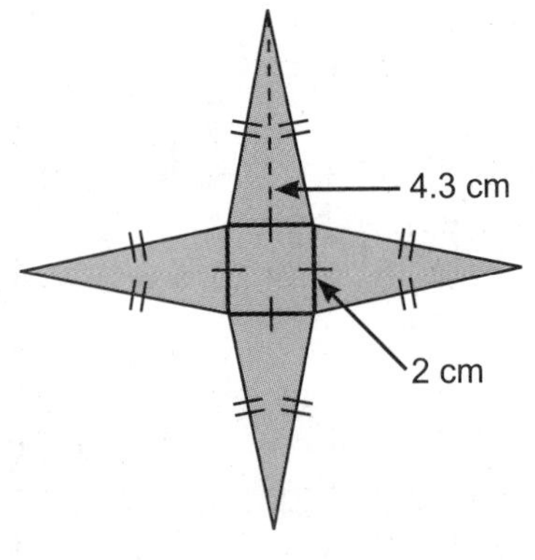

b)

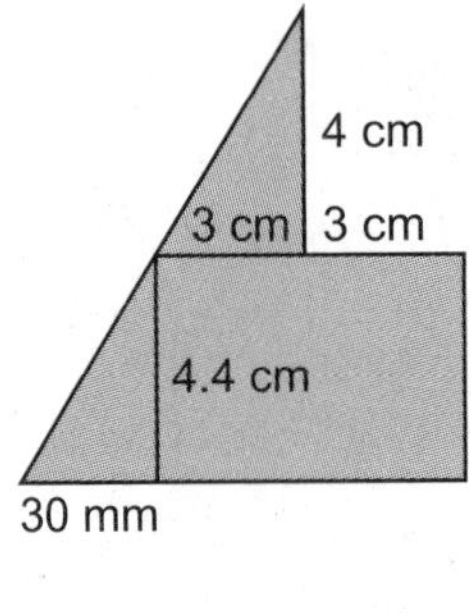

c)

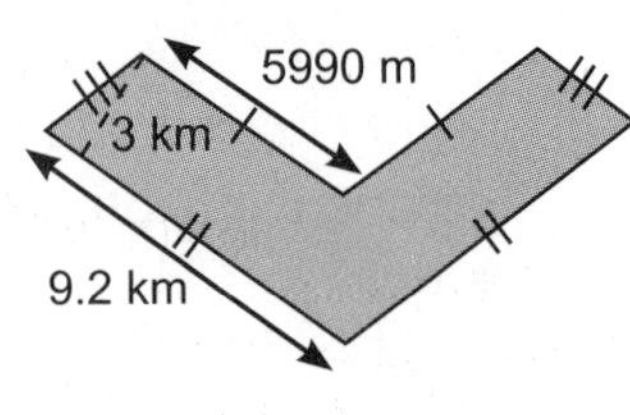

9. Find the area of the shaded part. Then say what fraction of the grid is shaded.
Hint: How can you use the area of the unshaded part and the area of the grid?

a)

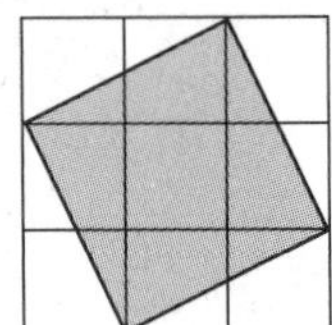

Area: ____________

Fraction: ____________

b)

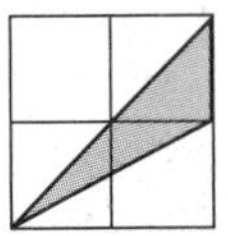

Area: ____________

Fraction: ____________

c)

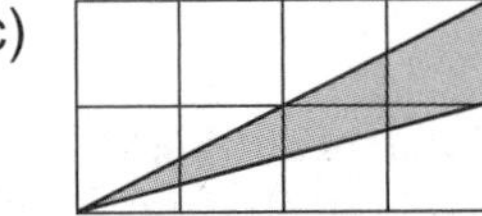

Area: ____________

Fraction: ____________

10. A garden has a path in the shape of a parallelogram. The shaded areas are flower beds.

a) What is the height of the path parallelogram?

b) The base of the path parallelogram is 1 m. What is the area of the path?

c) What is the total area of the flower beds? Show your work.

d) The path is covered in tiles. It cost $3 per square metre to lay the tiles. It cost $5 per square metre to plant the flowerbeds. How much did it cost to create the garden?

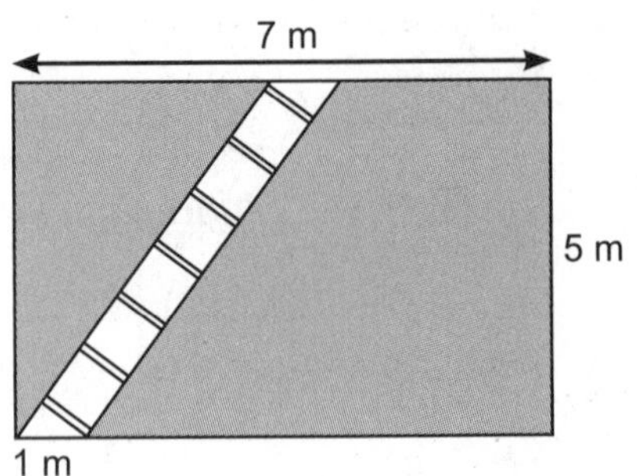

11. What is the area of the shaded part?

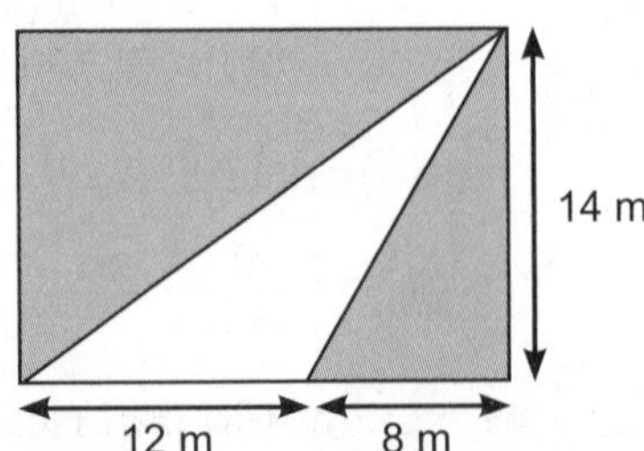

ME7-11 Introduction to Ratios

A **ratio** is a comparison of two or more numbers. A **part-to-part ratio** compares one part to another part. Example: The ratio of squares to triangles is 2 to 3, or 2 : 3.

A **part-to-whole ratio** compares one part to the whole. Example: The ratio of squares to total shapes is 2 to 7, or 2 : 7.

1. a) Write the part-to-part ratios for these shapes.

i) light circles to dark circles __2__ : __1__

ii) dark squares to light squares ____ : ____

iii) light circles to dark squares ____ : ____

iv) light squares to dark circles ____ : ____

b) Write the part-to-whole ratios in ratio form and as fractions.

i) squares to shapes __4__ : __7__

$\frac{4}{7}$ of the shapes are squares.

ii) light shapes to all shapes ____ : ____

____ of the shapes are light.

iii) light circles to circles ____ : ____

____ of the circles are light.

iv) dark squares to squares ____ : ____

____ of the squares are dark.

2. Some of these ratios are part-to-part ratios and some are part-to-whole ratios. Underline the parts and circle the wholes. Then write the ratio.

a) days in weekend : days in week __2__ : ____

b) days in January : days in June ____ : ____

c) vowels in **cat** : letters in **cat** ____ : ____

d) vowels in **dog** : consonants in **dog** ____ : ____

e) Atlantic provinces : all Canadian provinces ____ : ____

3. What does each ratio describe?

a) 2 : 3 *triangles : circles*

b) 5 : 10 ________________

c) 5 : 2 ________________

4. Which ratio in Question 3 is a part-to-whole ratio? ________

5. What does each ratio describe? There may be more than one answer!

a) 3 : 4 b) 3 : 5 c) 3 : 9 d) 6 : 9 e) 4 : 9 f) 1 : 4 g) 1 : 3

6. Use words or pictures to create your own part-to-part ratio and part-to-whole ratio.

There are 3 circles for every 2 squares. The **ratio** of circles to squares is 3 : 2, or 3 to 2.

7. Write the ratio of circles to squares.

a) There are 2 circles for every ____ square.

The ratio of circles to squares is ____ : ____.

b) There are 2 circles for every ____ squares.

The ratio of circles to squares is____ : ____.

c) There are 3 circles for every ____ squares.

The ratio of circles to squares is ____ : ____.

d) There are 2 circles for every ____ squares.

The ratio of circles to squares is____ : ____.

e) There are 4 circles for every ____ squares.

The ratio of circles to squares is ____ : ____.

f) There are 4 circles for every ____ squares.

The ratio of circles to squares is ____ : ____.

Each group has 3 circles and 2 squares.
So ○ : □ = 3 : 2.

Each group has the same number of shapes.
3 groups have circles and 2 groups have squares.

The ratio ○ : □ is 3 : 2.

The two sets have the same total number of circles and squares, so the ratios ○ : □ are the same!

g) There is 1 circle for every ____ squares.

The ratio of circles to squares is ____ : ____.

h) There are 3 circles for every ____ squares.

The ratio of circles to squares is ____ : ____.

ME7-12 Equivalent Ratios

We can write the same ratio in different ways. In each picture, there are 2 circles for every 1 square, so the ratio of circles to squares does not change.

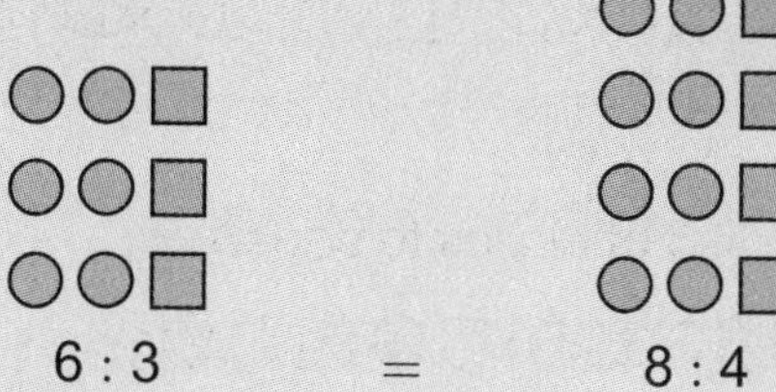

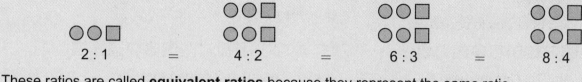

2 : 1 = 4 : 2 = 6 : 3 = 8 : 4

These ratios are called **equivalent ratios** because they represent the same ratio.

1. Write an equivalent ratio by multiplying each term by the same number.

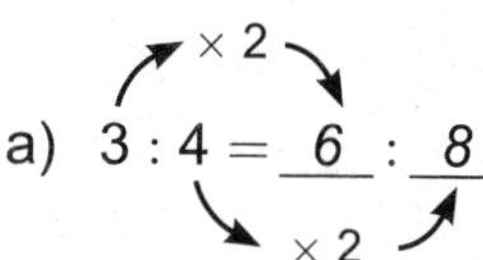

a) 3 : 4 = _6_ : _8_ b) 1 : 6 = ____ : ____ c) 2 : 7 = ____ : ____ d) 5 : 2 = ____ : ____

2. Write an equivalent ratio by dividing each term by the same number.

a) 20 : 15 = ____ : ____ b) 9 : 18 = ____ : ____ c) 12 : 15 = ____ : ____ d) 24 : 36 = ____ : ____

A ratio is in **lowest terms** when the numbers in the ratio are as small as they can be.

To write the ratio 30 : 36 in lowest terms:

Step 1: List the factors of 30 and 36:

30: 1, 2, 3, 5, **6**, 10, 15, 30

36: 1, 2, 3, 4, **6**, 9, 12, 18, 36

Step 2: Find the greatest common factor (GCF) of 30 and 36. The GCF is the greatest number that both lists have in common: 6.

Step 3: Divide each term in the ratio by the GCF.

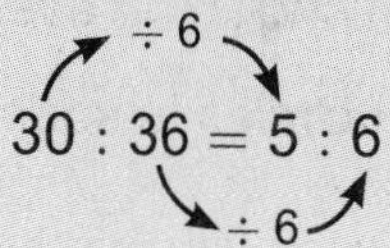

30 : 36 = 5 : 6

3. a) List the factors of each number. Do the rough work in your notebook.

i) 10: _1, 2, 5, 10_ ii) 12: ________ iii) 30: ________ iv) 75: ________

b) Find the GCF of each pair.

i) 10 and 12 ________ ii) 10 and 30 ________ iii) 10 and 75 ________ iv) 12 and 30 ________ v) 12 and 75 ________ vi) 30 and 75 ________

c) Write each ratio in lowest terms by dividing both terms by their GCF.

i) 30 : 12 ii) 10 : 30 iii) 12 : 75 iv) 12 : 10 v) 75 : 10 vi) 30 : 75

4. Write each ratio in lowest terms.

a) 25 : 35 b) 21 : 6 c) 20 : 12 d) 14 : 21 e) 84 : 27 f) 90 : 75

ME7-13 Solving Proportions

A **proportion** is an equation that shows two equivalent ratios. Example: 1 : 4 = 2 : 8

To solve a proportion, you need to find the number you multiply (or divide) each term in one ratio by to get the other ratio. Example: Solve 10 : 3 = 50 : □

Proportions are easier to solve if you write the proportions using fraction notation: $\frac{10}{3} = \frac{50}{\square}$.

1. Solve the following proportions. Draw arrows to show what you multiply by.

a) $\frac{4}{5} \overset{\times 4}{=} \frac{}{20}$ (×4)   b) $\frac{1}{5} = \frac{}{25}$ (×5)   c) $\frac{2}{5} \overset{\times 4}{=} \frac{8}{}$ d) $\frac{6}{7} = \frac{}{35}$

e) $\frac{3}{4} = \frac{18}{}$ f) $\frac{2}{3} = \frac{}{12}$ g) $\frac{5}{9} = \frac{}{45}$ h) $\frac{15}{25} = \frac{60}{}$

Note: Sometimes, the arrow may point from right to left.

i) $\frac{15}{} \overset{\times 5}{=} \frac{3}{4}$ (×4)   j) $\frac{10}{} = \frac{2}{5}$ k) $\frac{9}{} = \frac{3}{7}$ l) $\frac{}{35} = \frac{4}{7}$

m) $\frac{10}{15} = \frac{}{3}$ n) $\frac{30}{48} = \frac{5}{}$ o) $\frac{18}{22} = \frac{9}{}$ p) $\frac{63}{72} = \frac{}{8}$

2. Decide which way the arrow points. Then solve the proportions.

a) $\frac{}{10} = \frac{12}{40}$ b) $\frac{35}{} = \frac{7}{10}$ c) $\frac{3}{11} = \frac{9}{}$ d) $\frac{12}{42} = \frac{}{7}$

3. Solve the proportions by first writing the ratios using fraction notation.

a) 6 : 24 = □ : 8   b) □ : 15 = 2 : 5   c) 72 : 18 = □ : 3

4. Solve the proportions. Begin by writing the ratio that is complete in lowest terms.

a) $\frac{8}{10} = \frac{4}{5} = \frac{}{15}$ b) $\frac{4}{6} = \frac{}{} = \frac{}{9}$ c) $\frac{60}{100} = \frac{}{} = \frac{}{45}$

d) $\frac{}{30} = \frac{}{} = \frac{40}{50}$ e) $\frac{70}{100} = \frac{}{} = \frac{}{30}$ f) $\frac{}{24} = \frac{}{} = \frac{50}{75}$

5. Solve the proportions by first writing the ratios using fraction notation.

a) 6 : 24 = □ : 16   b) 11 : 22 = 5 : □   c) 26 : 12 = □ : 30

d) 30 : 9 = 50 : □   e) □ : 25 = 4 : 10   f) □ : 7 = 6 : 3

ME7-14 Word Problems

PROBLEM ▶ In a pet shop, there are 3 cats for every 4 dogs. If there are 12 dogs in the shop, how many cats are there?

SOLUTION ▶ Write the names of the two things being compared.
Write the quantities under the names, as a ratio.
Re-read the question to determine which quantity is given and which is unknown.
Write this information in a new row under the right names.
Solve the proportion.

	cats		dogs
	3	:	4
	?	:	12
3 : 4 =	?	:	12

? = 9, so there are 9 cats in the shop.

1. Mike can run 3 laps in 5 minutes. How many laps can he run in 20 minutes?

2. Jared can run 4 laps in 10 minutes. How long will it take Jared to run 6 laps?

3. The ratio of boys to girls in a class is 5 : 6. If there are 20 boys, how many girls are there?

4. If 9 bus tickets cost $19, how many bus tickets can you buy with $57?

5. Two out of every 5 students are wearing shorts. There are 300 students. How many are wearing shorts?

6. Four out of every 7 students like rap music. If 360 students like rap music, how many students are there altogether?

7. There are 2 rap songs for every 3 rock songs on Will's MP3 player. There are a total of 120 rock songs. How many rap songs are there?

8. Two out of every 12 students in a class say history is their favourite subject. There are 24 students in the class. How many students like history best?

9. The ratio of students in string band to students in brass band is 3 : 4. There are 36 students in the brass band. How many students are in the string band?

10. A basketball team won 2 out of every 3 games it played. The team played a total of 15 games. How many games did the team win?

11. There are 3 red fish for every 5 blue fish in an aquarium.

a) If there are 30 blue fish, how many red fish are there?
b) If there are 30 red fish, how many blue fish are there?

12. Sophia has 64 jazz CDs and 80 rock CDs. Is the ratio of jazz CDs to rock CDs 3 : 4 or 4 : 5?

ME7-15 Rates

A **rate** is a comparison of two quantities measured in different units. Rates are written with a slash or as a fraction.

Example: \$1 / 2 min (we read this as "\$1 **per** 2 minutes") or $\frac{\$1}{2 \text{ min}}$

1. Find the equivalent rate by first drawing arrows.

a) $\frac{10 \text{ km}}{2 \text{ h}} \xleftarrow{\times 2} = \xleftarrow[\times 2]{} \frac{5 \text{ km}}{1 \text{ h}}$ b) $\frac{18 \text{ km}}{3 \text{ h}} = \frac{\_\_\_ \text{ km}}{1 \text{ h}}$ c) $\frac{20 \text{ m}}{8 \text{ s}} = \frac{\_\_\_ \text{ m}}{2 \text{ s}}$ d) $\frac{42 \text{ km}}{3 \text{ L}} = \frac{\_\_\_ \text{ km}}{1 \text{ L}}$

e) $\frac{\$35}{7 \text{ kg}} = \frac{\$5}{\_\_\_ \text{ kg}}$ f) $\frac{\$96}{6 \text{ h}} = \frac{\$32}{\_\_\_ \text{ h}}$ g) $\frac{\$1.50}{10 \text{ min}} = \frac{\$\_\_\_}{2 \text{ min}}$ h) $\frac{6 \text{ m}^2}{0.5 \text{ L}} = \frac{\_\_\_ \text{ m}^2}{1 \text{ L}}$

In a unit rate, the second term is 1. The 1 is often left out. Example: 80 km / 1 h = 80 km/h

2. Find the unit rate by reducing the ratio to lowest terms. (Include the units.)

a) 20 km / 5 h = *4 km* / 1 h
b) \$5 / 2 boxes = ______ / 1 box
c) \$30 / 2 h = ______ / 1 h
d) 96 m / 12 s = ______ / 1 s
e) \$68 / 4 kg = ______ / 1 kg
f) \$80 / 16 jars = ______ / 1 jar

BONUS▶ \$1 / 6 min = ______ / 1 h

3. Solve each problem by first changing the rate to a unit rate.

a) Dana rode 100 kilometres in 5 hours. How far could she ride in 8 hours?
b) Cindy can type 60 words in 3 minutes. How many words can she type in 5 minutes?
c) A runner's heart beats 30 times in 10 seconds. How many times would it beat in a minute?

4. Change both prices to a unit rate to find out which offer is a better buy.

a) \$119 for 7 CDs or \$64 for 4 CDs
b) \$36.52 for 2 cans of paint or \$46.20 for 3 cans
c) 6 golf balls for \$10 or 12 golf balls for \$24

5. Clare can cycle at a speed of 23 km/h. Erin can cycle at a speed of 17 km/h. How much farther can Clare cycle in 3 hours than Erin?

6. a) A truck travels 40 km in half an hour. What is its average speed in km/h?
b) A car travels 30 km in 15 minutes. What is its average speed in km/h?

Hint: Convert the time given to minutes and find the number of kilometres per 60 minutes.

7. Estimate to the nearest half hour how long would it take to drive each distance at 100 km/h.

a) 254 km
b) 723 km
c) 1 426 km

ME7-16 Using Unit Rates

REMINDER▶ 100 km / 1 h = **100 km/h**

1. Use the unit rates in the chart to convert the measurements.

Example: To convert **25 mm to cm**, write and solve a proportion:

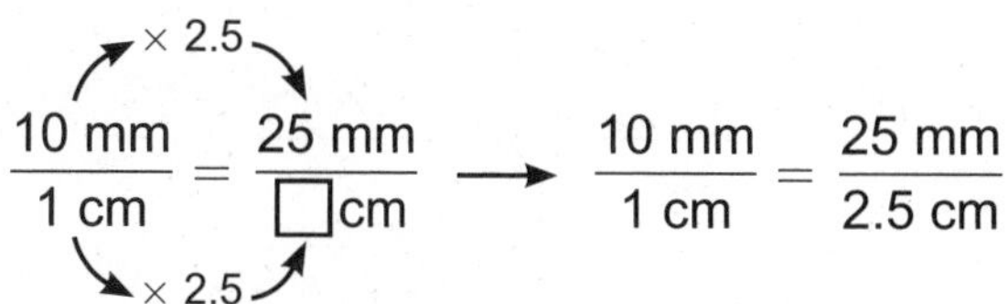

$$\frac{10 \text{ mm}}{1 \text{ cm}} = \frac{25 \text{ mm}}{\square \text{ cm}} \longrightarrow \frac{10 \text{ mm}}{1 \text{ cm}} = \frac{25 \text{ mm}}{2.5 \text{ cm}}$$

So, 25 mm = 2.5 cm.

Distance	Volume or Mass	Time
10 mm/cm	1 000 mL/L	60 sec/min
100 cm/m	1 000 mg/g	60 min/h
1 000 m/km	1 000 g/kg	24 h/day

a) 50 mm to cm b) 25 cm to m c) 3 200 m to km d) 4 500 mL to L

e) 6 900 mg to g f) 240 s to min g) 4 200 min to h h) 120 h to days

2. The scale on this map is 100 km / 1 cm. Measure the distance between Victoria and each other place on the map in centimetres. Use the scale to determine the distances in real life.

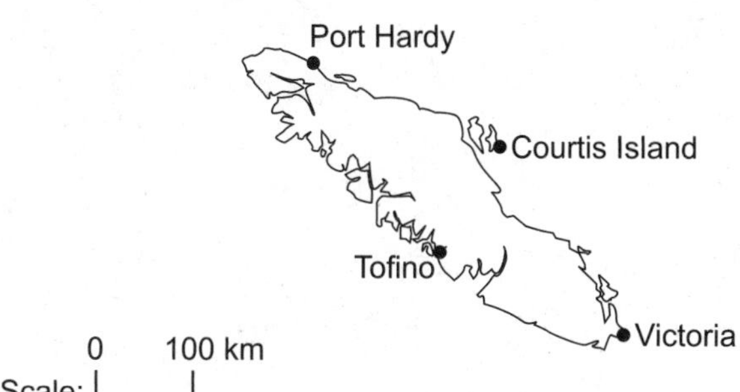

Cities	Distance on Map	Distance in Real Life
Victoria and Tofino		
Victoria and Cortes Island		
Victoria and Port Hardy		

3. On a map, 3 cm represents 15 km. How many kilometres do 19.5 cm on the map represent?

4. Cars are rated according to their fuel efficiency. David's car gets 11.45 km/L, Felicity's gets 12.76 km/L, and Jack's gets 38 km/L. How many kilometres can they each travel on 50 L of gas?

5. Connor is using paint that covers 12 m^2 per can of paint. He has to paint 160 m^2. How many cans of paint will he need?

6. Watermelon costs $1.50/kg and peaches cost $1.80/kg. Julie made a fruit salad with watermelon and peaches in a ratio of 2 : 3. She made 10 kg of fruit salad. How much did she spend on fruit?

BONUS▶ Al is paid $12.50/h. He works 4.5 h/day for 8 days/month. How much does he earn each month?

ME7-17 Ratios and Rates with Fractional Terms

PROBLEM ▶ A granola recipe uses $\frac{1}{2}$ cup of raisins for every 3 cups of oats. How many cups of oats are needed for 2 cups of raisins?

SOLUTION ▶ Write the names of the quantities being compared.

	cups of raisins		cups of oats
Write the given quantities under their names, as a ratio.	$\frac{1}{2}$	:	3
Find an equivalent ratio so that both terms are whole numbers.	1	:	6
Write the given and unknown quantities under their names.	2	:	?
Solve the proportion that consist of whole numbers only.	1 : 6 = 2 : ?		

? = 12, so 12 cups of oats are needed.

1. Write an equivalent ratio that uses only whole numbers. Hint: In parts d) and e), multiply each term by 10.

a) 2 km walked / $\frac{1}{2}$h =

b) 4 km rowed / $\frac{1}{3}$h =

c) $\frac{1}{4}$ cup of sugar : 3 cups of flour =

d) 0.9 km / 2 L of gas =

e) 1.9 mL of ginger ale : 0.4 mL of orange juice =

2. Multiply the numerator and denominator by 10. Then solve the proportion.

a) $\frac{2.4}{4} = \frac{24}{40} = \frac{\quad}{20}$

b) $\frac{5}{0.9} = \frac{\quad}{\quad} = \frac{\quad}{45}$

c) $\frac{3.8}{0.2} = \frac{\quad}{\quad} = \frac{\quad}{1}$

d) $\frac{6}{2.1} = \frac{\quad}{\quad} = \frac{20}{\quad}$

e) $\frac{7.2}{3.2} = \frac{\quad}{\quad} = \frac{\quad}{4}$

f) $\frac{5.4}{0.6} = \frac{\quad}{\quad} = \frac{18}{\quad}$

3. Solve each problem by first changing the ratio into a ratio of whole numbers.

a) Rhonda can ride her bike 6 km in $\frac{1}{4}$ of an hour. How far can she ride in 3 hours?

b) A plant grows 0.5 cm in 4 days. How many days will it take to grow 9 cm?

c) On a map, 0.4 cm equals 50 m. How many metres does 7 cm on the map represent?

d) A recipe uses $\frac{1}{3}$ cup milk to 2 cups flour. How much milk do you need if you use 3 cups of flour?

ME7-18 Circles

All points on a circle are the same distance from a point called the **centre**. This distance is called the **radius** of a circle. The plural of radius is **radii**.

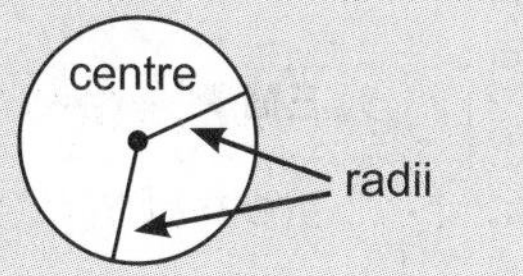

How to Construct a Circle Using a Compass Given the Centre and Radius

Step 1: Set the compass width to the given radius. 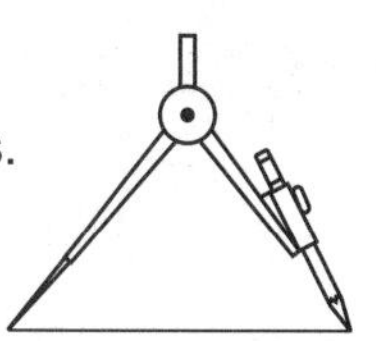	**Step 2:** Set the compass point on the centre point. 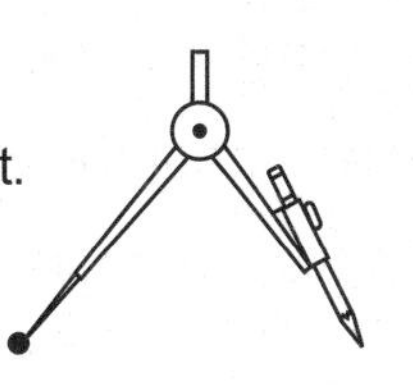	**Step 3:** Without changing the width of the compass, draw the circle. 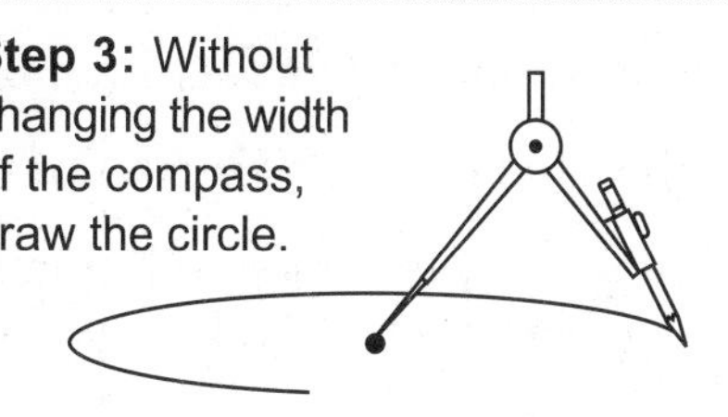

1. Construct a circle with centre O and radius AB.

a) A ——— B

O

b) A

B

O

2. a) Mark any two points on one of the circles above. Label the points C and D.

b) Construct the line segments OC and OD using a ruler. Measure them.
$OC =$ _____ $OD =$ _____

c) Explain why $OC = OD$.

The **diameter** of a circle is the distance across the circle. It is measured through the centre. The radius is half of the diameter.

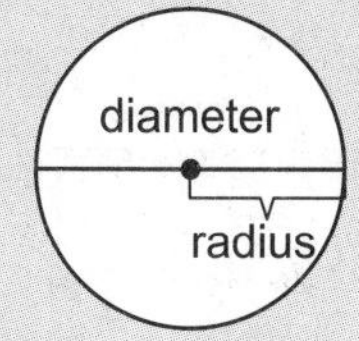

3. Find the radius. (Circles are not drawn to scale.)

a) 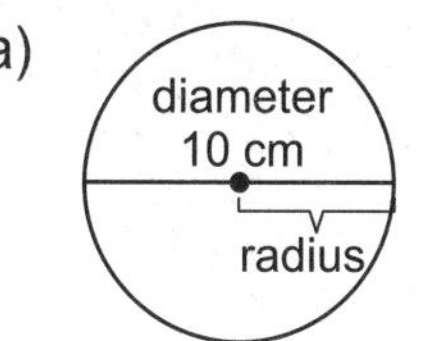

b) 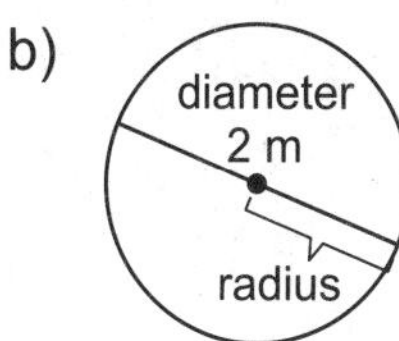

c) 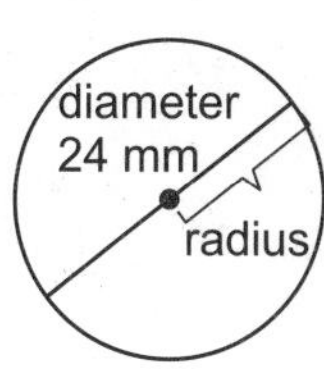

radius _____ radius _____ radius _____

4. Find the diameter. (Circles are not drawn to scale.)

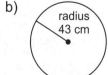

a) 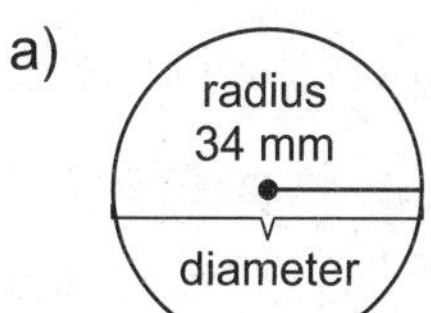

b) radius 43 cm

c) 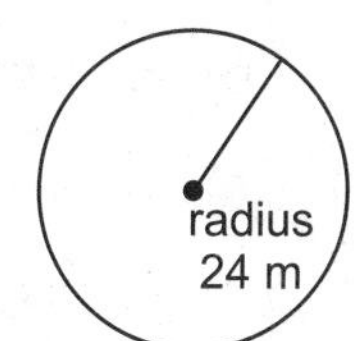

diameter _____ diameter _____ diameter _____

5. Fill in the missing radius or diameter for each circle.

Radius	3 cm	4 cm	12 cm			38 cm			r
Diameter	6 cm			4 mm	12 m		1 m	1.6 cm	

6. Draw and measure the diameter.

a)

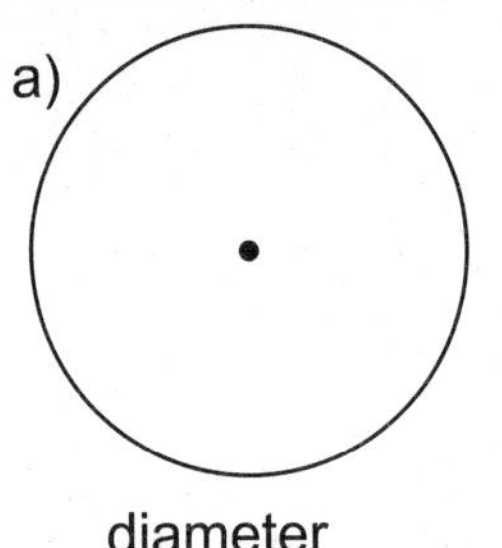

diameter _____

b)

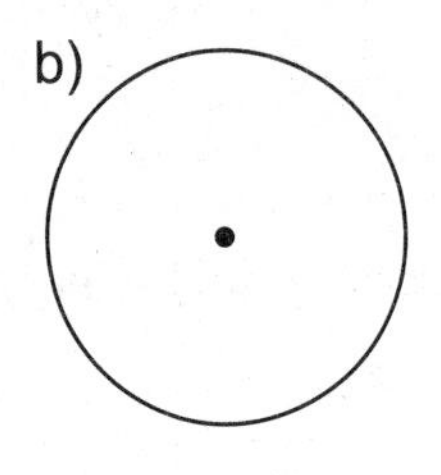

diameter _____

7. Draw and measure the radius.

a)

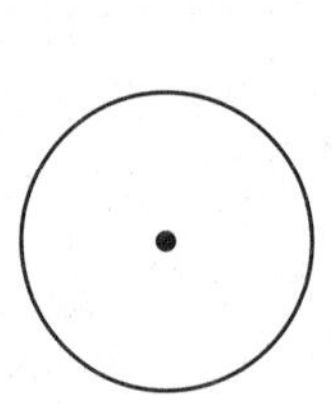

radius _____

b)

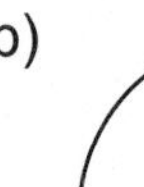

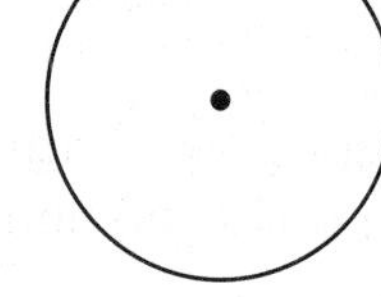

radius _____

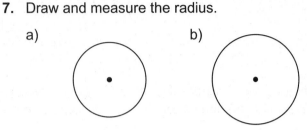

8. Construct a circle with…

a) radius 2 cm
b) diameter 6 cm
c) diameter 11 cm
d) radius 36 mm

9. The diameters in the circle at right are perpendicular.

a) Write the degree measures of all angles in the diagram.

b) What is the sum of the angles around the centre of the circle?_____

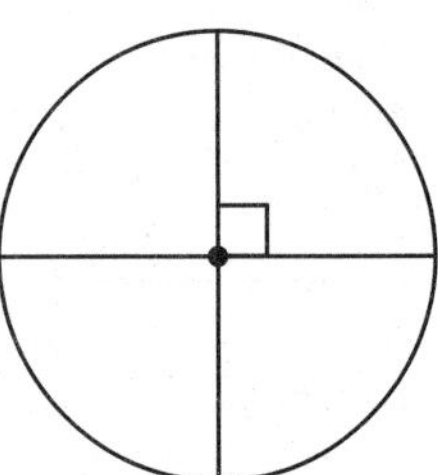

Angles that have vertices at the centre of a circle are called **central angles**. The sum of the central angles is _____.

10. a) Find these angles in the diagram, then circle the central angles.

(∠*BHD*) ∠*AHD* ∠*ACD* ∠*HAC* ∠*FEG*

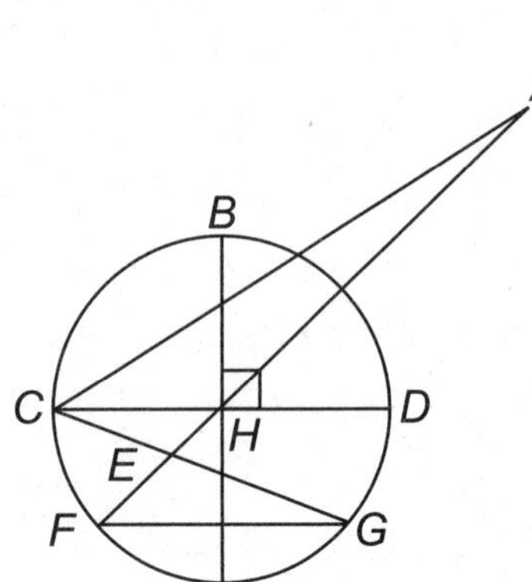

b) Name two more central angles in this diagram. _____________

c) $\angle AHD = \angle CHF = 45°$. What is the degree measure of these central angles?

$\angle AHD =$ _____ $\angle FHI =$ _____ $\angle FHD =$ _____ $\angle BHC =$ _____

d) To find the sum of the central angles, use angles that cover all the area around the centre of the circle but do not overlap. What is the sum of the central angles in this diagram?

$\angle BHC + \angle CHF + \angle FHD + \angle DHB =$ _____

e) Find the sum of the central angles using a different set of angles. Fill in the missing angle first.

$\angle AHC + \angle AHI + \angle$ _____ $=$ ________

f) Does the sum of the central angles depend on the angles used to find it? _____

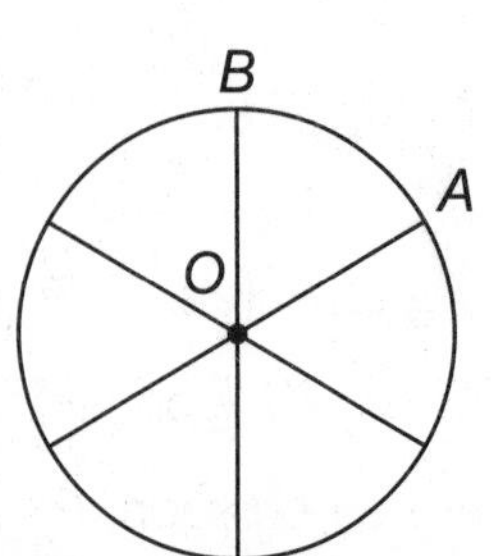

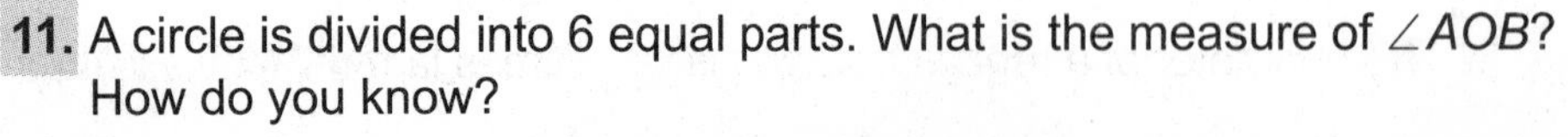

11. A circle is divided into 6 equal parts. What is the measure of $\angle AOB$? How do you know?

ME7-19 Circumference

The distance around a polygon is called **perimeter**.

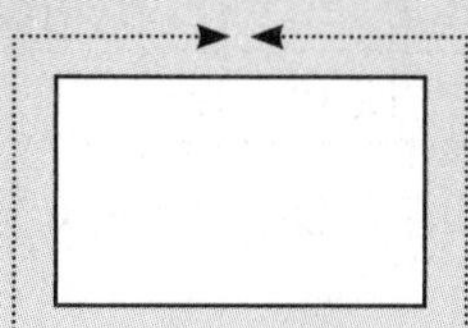

The distance around a circle is called **circumference**.

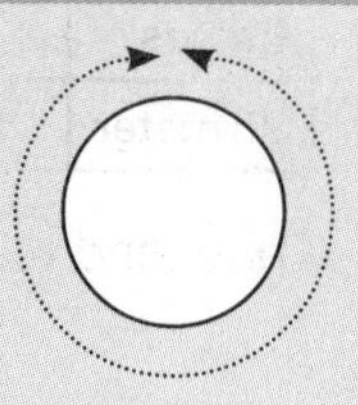

1. A polygon is **regular** if all its sides and all its angles are equal. This table gives the width (w) and side length (s) of different regular polygons.

   a) Find the perimeter (P) of each regular polygon.

   b) Find the ratio of the perimeter to the width, or $P : w$.

Squares 4 equal sides (w)	width (w) = 1 cm side length (s) = 1 cm Perimeter (P) = P = *1 cm × 4 = 4 cm* $P : w$ = ____	w = 2 cm s = 2 cm P = ________ $P : w$ = ____	w = 3 cm s = 3 cm P = ________ $P : w$ = ____
Hexagons 6 equal sides (w)	width (w) = 2 cm side length (s) = 1 cm Perimeter (P) = P = *1 cm × 6 = ___ cm* $P : w$ = ____	w = 4 cm s = 2 cm P = ________ $P : w$ = ____	w = 6 cm s = 3 cm P = ________ $P : w$ = ____
Octagons 8 equal sides (w)	width (w) = 8 cm side length (s) = 3 cm Perimeter (P) = P = ___ *× 8 = ___ cm* $P : w$ = ____	w = 4 cm s = 1.5 cm P = ________ $P : w$ = ____	w = 12 cm s = 4.5 cm P = ________ $P : w$ = ____

   c) What do you notice about the ratios $P : w$ in each row?

   d) For a square, $P : w$ = *4* : 1. The perimeter of a square is *4* times larger than its width.

   For a hexagon, $P : w$ = ____ : 1. The perimeter of a regular hexagon is ____ times larger than its width.

   For an octagon, $P : w$ = ____ : 1. The perimeter of a regular octagon is ____ times larger than its width.

INVESTIGATION ▶ What is the ratio of the circumference of the circle to its diameter (width)?

A. Measure the diameter (width) of the circles. Estimate the circumference of the circles by calculating the perimeters of the regular octagons.

a) 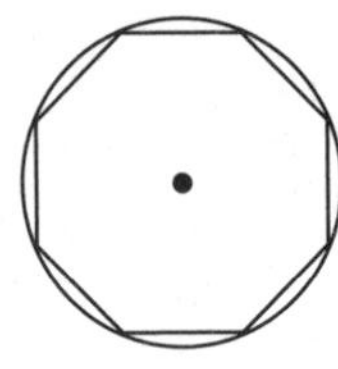

b) 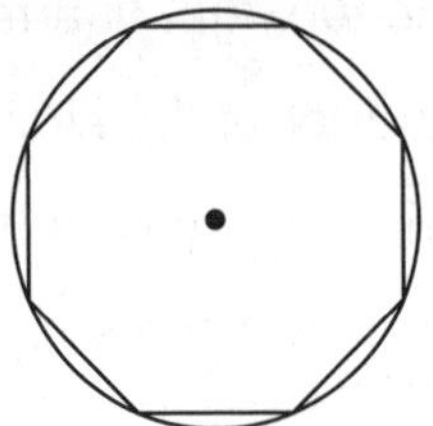

c) 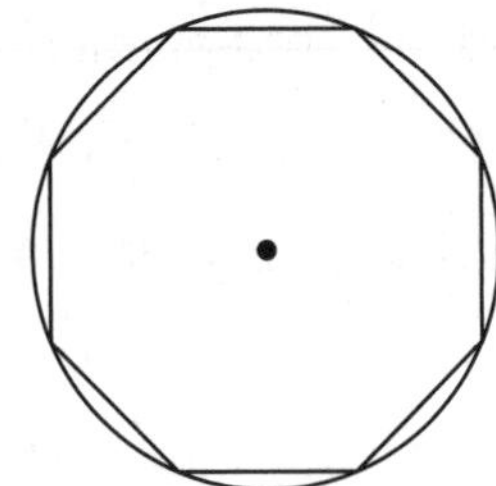

a)		b)		c)	
diameter (d)	*22 mm*	diameter (d)	____	diameter (d)	____
side of octagon	*8 mm*	side of octagon	____	side of octagon	____
perimeter of octagon	*64 mm*	perimeter of octagon	____	perimeter of octagon	____
circumference (C)	*about 64 mm*	circumference (C)	____	circumference (C)	____

B. Determine the ratio of the circumference to the diameter of each circle above.
Then divide the circumference by the diameter to write each ratio in the form ▢ : 1.

a) $C : d =$ ____ : ____ = ____ : 1 b) $C : d =$ ____ : ____ = ____ : 1 c) $C : d =$ ____ : ____ = ____ : 1

The ratio of the circumference to the diameter of the circles is about ________.

C. Here are the diameters and circumferences of some circles. Find the ratio of circumference to diameter for each circle. Write each ratio in the form ▢ : 1. What do you notice? ____________

Circle	Circumference (C)	Diameter (d)	Ratio (C : d)
A	15.7 cm	5 cm	*3.14 : 1*
B	31.4 cm	10 cm	
C	44 cm	14 cm	
D	62.8 cm	20 cm	

The ratio of circumference to diameter is **the same for all circles**. This number has an infinite number of digits after its decimal point. Mathematicians use the Greek letter π (pronounced "pie") to identify it.

$\pi \approx 3.14$

Circumference : diameter = π : 1, so circumference is π times larger than diameter.
Circumference $= \pi \times$ diameter $= \pi \times 2 \times$ radius $= 2\pi \times$ radius $= 2\pi r$

2. Find the approximate circumference of circles with the given measurements. Use 3.14 for π.

a) diameter = 7 m b) diameter = 10 m c) radius = 4 m d) radius = 2.5 cm

a) *circumference* $= \pi \times 7$ *m*
$\approx 3.14 \times 7$ *m*
= ________

ME7-20 Area of Circles

1. Estimate the area of the circle by finding the area of the shaded part.

   a) Find the area of each shaded shape in the top right quarter of the circle.

   b) Add the areas in a) to get the area of a quarter of the circle. Area of quarter circle ≈ ______

   c) Find the area of the shaded part of the grid using your answer in b). *Area of the circle* ≈ ______

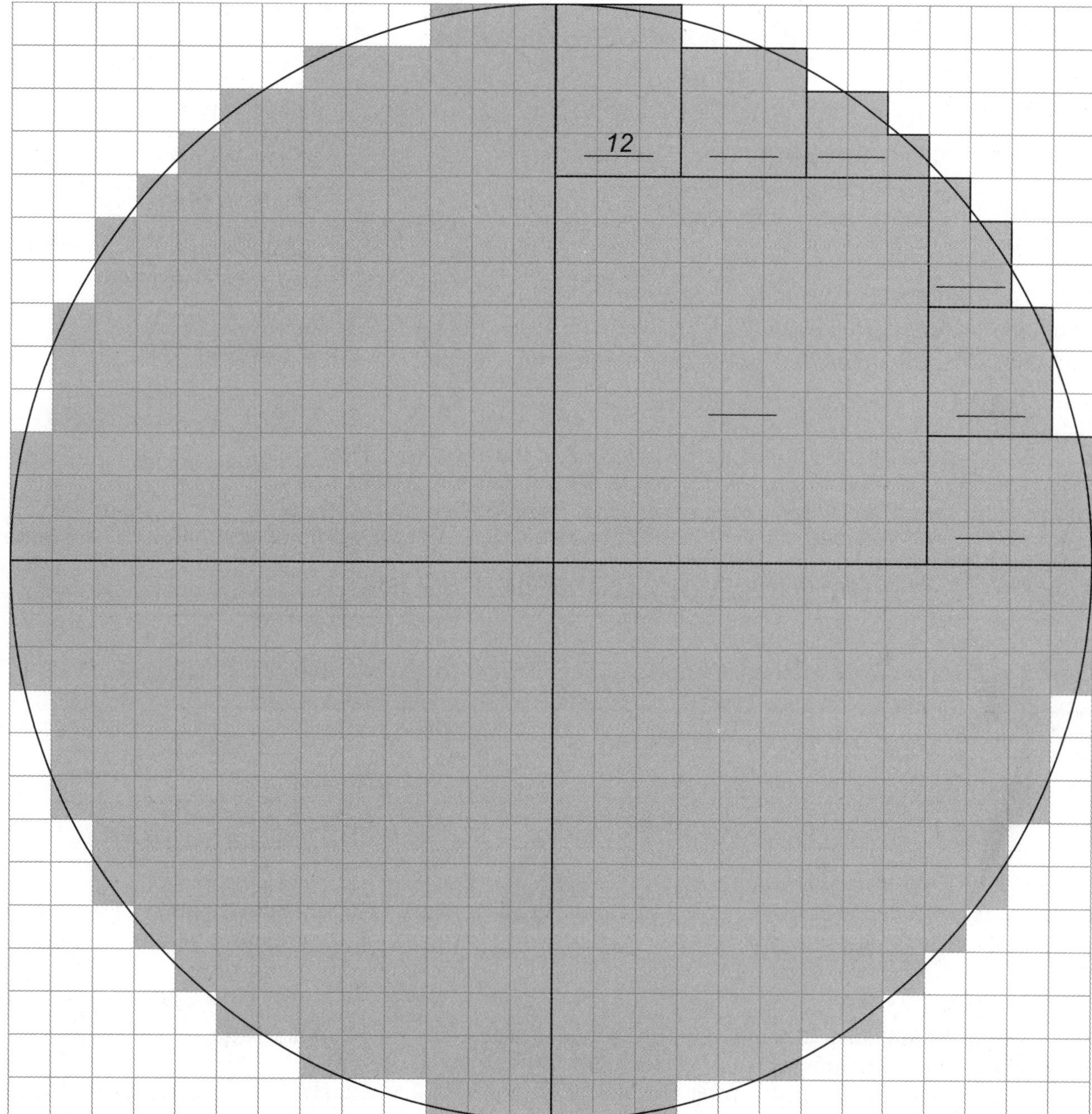

2. The radius of the circle above is $r =$ ____. Divide the area you found in Question 1c) by r^2.

   What do you notice? ________________________________

3. Explain why the area of the shaded part is a good estimate for the area of the circle.

INVESTIGATION ▶ What is the approximate relation between the radius of a circle and its area?

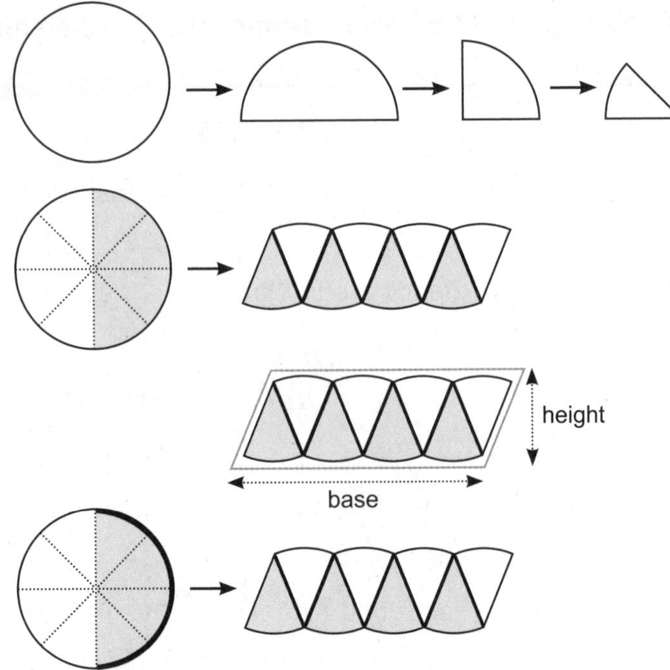

A. Draw a circle with a compass. Cut out the circle and fold it in half 3 times.

B. Unfold your circle and colour one half of it. Cut along the fold lines of the circle and rearrange the pieces, as shown, on top of a sheet of paper.

C. Draw a parallelogram around the pieces. The area of the parallelogram is **almost equal** to the area of circle.

D. Is the **height** of the parallelogram in C approximately equal to the radius or the diameter of the circle? How you know?

E. Which fraction of the circumference is the thick line? Where would this thick line be if you moved it to the parallelogram? Draw it.

F. How can you get the approximate length of the **base** of the parallelogram from the circumference of the circle?

G. The formula for the area of a parallelogram is **Area** $=$ **base** $\times$ **height**. Use your answers for parts D and F to give the approximate area of the parallelogram.

Area of parallelogram $=$ ____________ $\times$ ____________
(approximate height) (approximate base)

H. The correct answer for G is: Area of parallelogram $\approx$ radius of circle $\times$ the circumference of circle $\div$ 2.
Substitute r for the radius and C for the circumference: Area of parallelogram: ____ $\times$ ____ $\div$ 2.
The circumference (C) of a circle with radius r is $C = 2\pi r$, so

Area of parallelogram $\approx r \times$ ____ $\div 2 = r \times$ ____ $\times$ ____ $\times$ ____ $\div 2$

$=$ ____ $\times$ ____ $\times$ ____ $\times 2 \div 2$

$=$ ____ $\times r^2$

The area of the parallelogram is approximately equal to the area of the circle. Mathematicians have shown that the actual area (A) of a circle is given by the formula $A = \pi r^2$.

---

4. Find the area of the circles with the given radius. Use 3.14 for π.

a) radius $= 3$ m
Area $= \pi r^2 \approx 3.14 \times 3^2$
$= 3.14 \times 9 = 28.26$ m^2

b) radius $= 10$ cm
Area $\approx$ ________
____

c) radius $= 5$ km
Area $\approx$ ________
____

d) radius $= 7$ m
Area $\approx$ ________
____

5. What is the area of these circles? Hint: Find the radius from the diameter first.

a) diameter $= 12$ m b) diameter $= 34$ cm c) diameter $= 30$ dm d) diameter $= 1$ m

ME7-21 Area and Circumference

1. Half of a circle is called a **semicircle**. Find the area of the semicircles. Use 3.14 for π.

a) 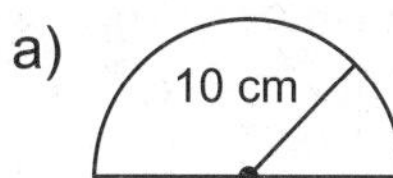

Area of circle $\approx$ *314 cm²*

Area of semicircle

$\approx$ *314 cm² ÷ 2 = 157 cm²*

b) 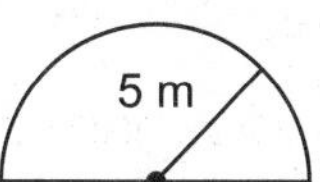

c) 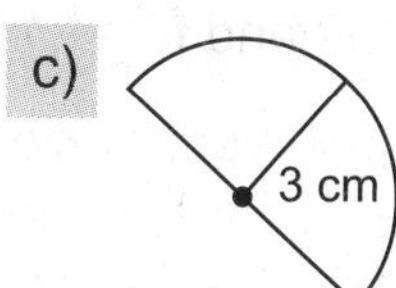

2. What is the distance around this semicircle?

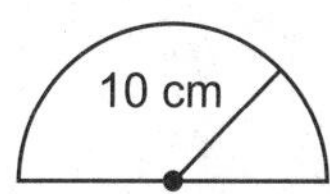

a) Circumference of whole circle $= C = 2\pi r \approx$ _______ cm

b) What fraction of C is the length of the curved side? _______

Length of the curved side = _______ $\approx$ _______ cm

c) Is the straight side of the semicircle the radius or the diameter of the circle? _______________

What is the length of the straight side in terms of r? _______ cm

d) The distance around the semicircle is _______ + _______ = _______ cm.

e) The area of a semicircle is half the area of the whole circle. Explain why the distance around the semicircle is not half the distance around the whole circle (circumference).

f) Find the distance around the semicircles in Questions 1 b) and c).

3. Find the area and the distance around each figure.

a) 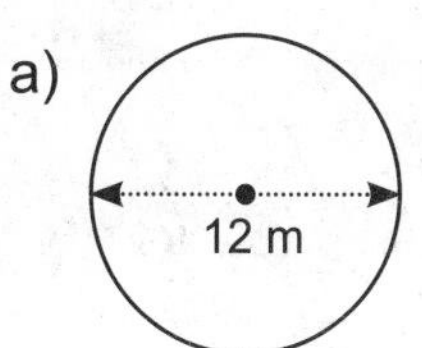

b) 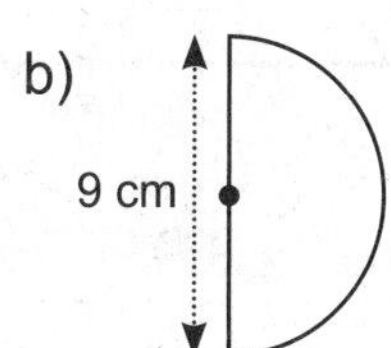

c) 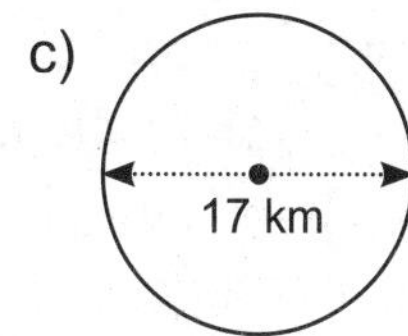

d) 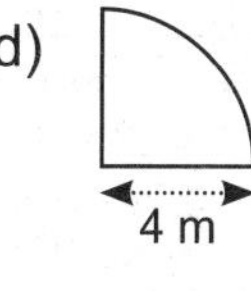

e) 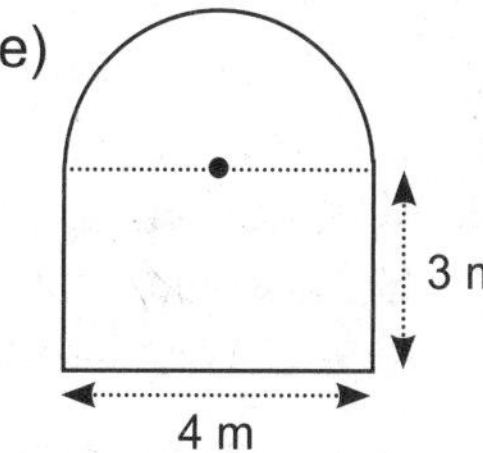

4. The rim of a bicycle tire has radius 30 cm. The tire is 5 cm thick.

a) What is the radius of the outer circle of the tire?

b) What is the circumference of the tire?

5. a) What is the sum of the central angles in a circle? _______

b) What fraction of this circle is shaded? _______ How do you know?

____

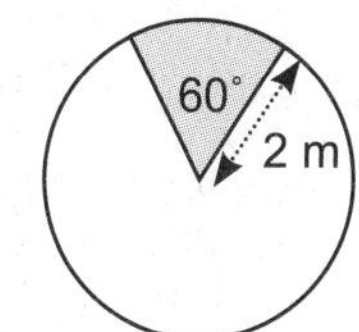

c) What is the area of the whole circle? _______

d) What is the area of the shaded part? _______

6. A rotating water sprinkler can spray water a distance of 20 m.
What area of grass can the sprinkler cover?

7. Fill in the blanks for the shape at right.

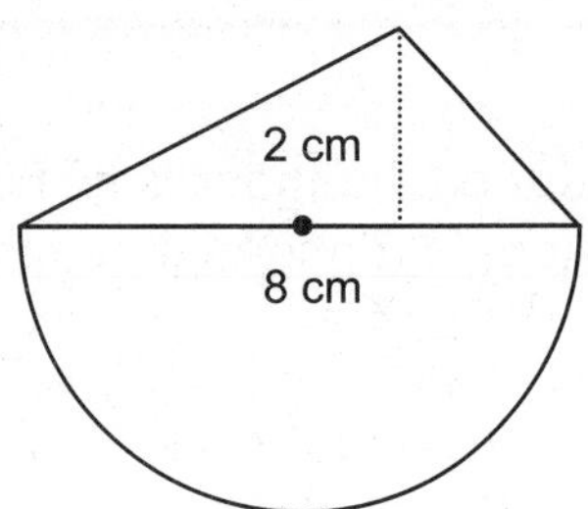

Area of the triangle: ______________

Radius of the semicircle: ______________

Area of the semicircle: ______________

Area of the whole shape: _______ + _______ = _______

8. These shapes were made from quarters or halves of circles and polygons. Find the area of the shapes.

a) 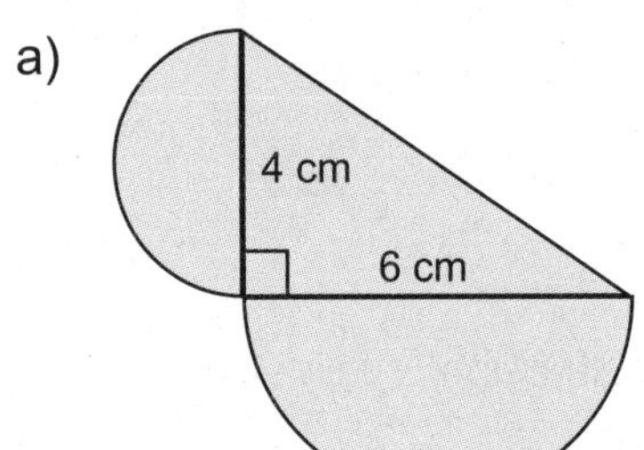

b) 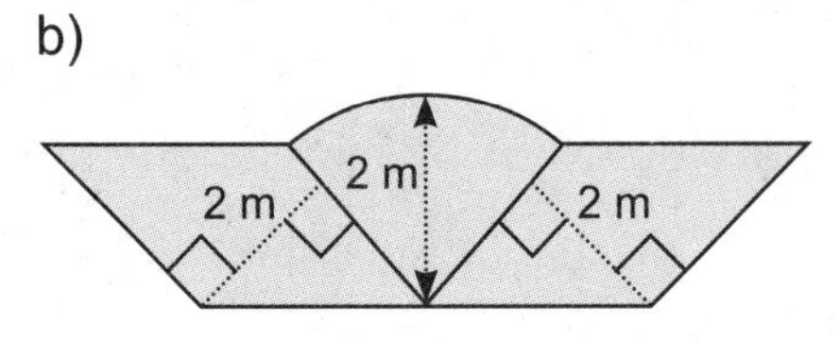

c) 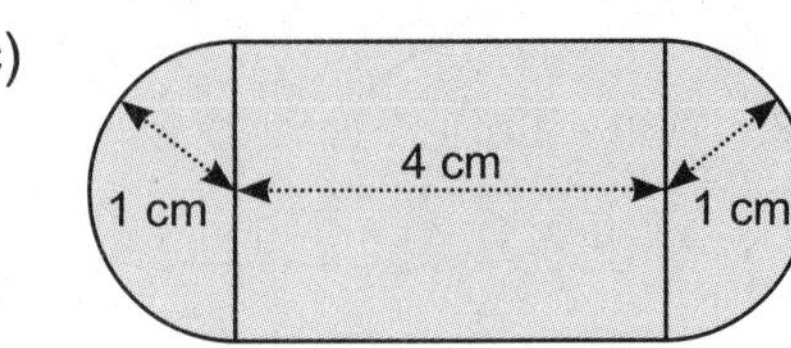

9. The London Eye is a giant Ferris wheel in downtown London, England.

a) The diameter of the wheel is about 135 m. What is the circumference of the wheel?

b) The wheel turns about 0.3 m every second. About how long does it take for the wheel to rotate once?

c) The Skywheel in Niagara Falls, Ontario, has a radius of 26.5 m. How many metres taller is the London Eye?

10. A tractor wheel has diameter of 1 m. About how many times would the wheel turn if the tractor drove 100 m?

11. This shape is made of an equilateral triangle with side 4 cm and three semicircles.

4 cm

a) How many curved edges does this shape have?

b) What is the radius of each circle?

c) What is the length of each curved edge?

d) What is the distance around the shape?

12. This shape was made from a regular pentagon with sides of 2 cm and five semicircles. Find the distance around the shape.

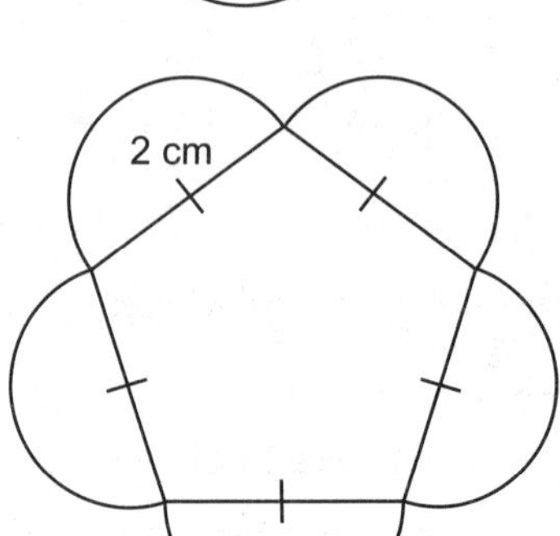

13. Use a calculator to find the diameter of each circle. Use 3.14 for π.

a) circumference = 118 mm   b) circumference = 1 m

PDM7-1 Stem and Leaf Plots

The **leaf** of a number is its right-most digit. The **stem** is all digits except the right-most digit. The stem of a one-digit number is 0, since there are no digits except the right-most one.

1. In each number, underline the leaf and circle the stem. The first one is done for you.

a) 1 2 3 b) 5 c) 7 4 d) 9 e) 2 3 f) 8 7 1 2 g) 3 4 5

2. Write a number with...

a) leaf 0. ________ b) stem 0. ________

3. Underline the numbers in each group that have the same stem. Hint: Circle each stem first, as you did in Question 1.

a) 7 8 7 9 5 9 b) 3 4 5 3 4 3 4 9 c) 5 7 8 2 5 7 8 5 7 4

d) 7 8 7 8 e) 4 5 6 7 4 5 6 4 5 6 6 f) 1 2 2 3 4 1 2 3 4 1 2 3 3

Build a **stem and leaf plot** for this data set: 45, 9, 23, 35, 29, 32.

Step 1: The stems are 4, 0, 2, and 3. Write the stems in a column, ordered from smallest to largest.

Stem	Leaf
0	
2	
3	
4	

Step 2: Write each leaf in the same row as its stem.

Stem	Leaf
0	9
2	3 9
3	5 2
4	5

Step 3: Put the leaves in each row in order.

Stem	Leaf
0	9
2	3 9
3	2 5
4	5

4. Put the leaves in the correct order. Then list the data from least to greatest.

a)

Stem	Leaf
2	1 4
3	8 5 6
5	3 2

rough work

→

Stem	Leaf
2	*1 4*
3	*5 6 8*
5	*2 3*

final answer

21 *24* *35* *36* *38* *52* *53*

b)

Stem	Leaf
0	5
8	7 3
2 3	4 9 6

rough work

→

Stem	Leaf

final answer

____ ____ ____ ____ ____ ____

5. Use the data sets to create stem and leaf plots.

a) 13 14 19 23 31

b) 5 19 23 39 217

c) 99 98 102 99 101

d) 2 37 88 2 104 39 87 3 43 100

e) 23 34 50 29 23 35 47 46 33 24

f) 3 417 4 312 3 210 3 219 3 412 4 312 4 314 3 821

What you can learn from a stem and leaf plot:

The **smallest number** is 981 and the **largest number** is 1 006. The range is:

the largest number − the smallest number

1006 − 981 = 25

Stem	Leaf
98	**1** 4 9
99	8 8 8
100	2 3 3 **6**

The number that occurs most often is called the **mode**. The mode here is 998, and it occurs three times.

Stem	Leaf
98	1 4 9
99	**8 8 8**
100	2 3 3 6

6. In each case, find the smallest value, the largest value, the range, and the mode.

a)

Stem	Leaf
2	3 6 7
3	0 1 1 2
5	2 3 3 3 8

Smallest: _______
Largest: _______
Range: _______
Mode: _______

b)

Stem	Leaf
31	0 5 5
33	1 6 9
37	8 8 8

Smallest: _______
Largest: _______
Range: _______
Mode: _______

7. Find the largest value, the smallest value, the range, and the mode of the sets in Question 5.

8. A gym class collected the results from their long-jump trials and ordered them in a stem and leaf plot.

Stem	Leaf
17	2 9
18	5 7 8 8
19	0 2 2 4
20	1 2 5 5 5
21	2 7 8
22	4 9

a) Circle the units of measurement that you think the class used.

mm cm m km

b) Riana's jump was recorded as 202. Underline the leaf for Riana's result in the plot.

c) What was the distance of the longest jump? (Include the units.) __________

d) What was the shortest jump? __________ What was the mode? __________

e) If the class were divided into two equal groups according to how they jumped, which group would Riana be in? Explain.

9. a) Write two numbers where the smaller number has the greater leaf.
b) Can you find two numbers where the smaller number has the greater stem? Explain.

10. Either explain why each statement is true or give a counter-example to show that it is false.

a) A one-digit number always has stem 0.
b) A one-digit number always has leaf 0.
c) Two numbers with the same stem always have the same number of digits.
d) Two numbers with the same leaf always have the same number of digits.
e) The stem is always a single digit.
f) The leaf is always a single digit.

PDM7-2 The Mean

1. Move enough beads so that all rods have the same number of beads. The **mean** is the number of beads on each rod.

a) 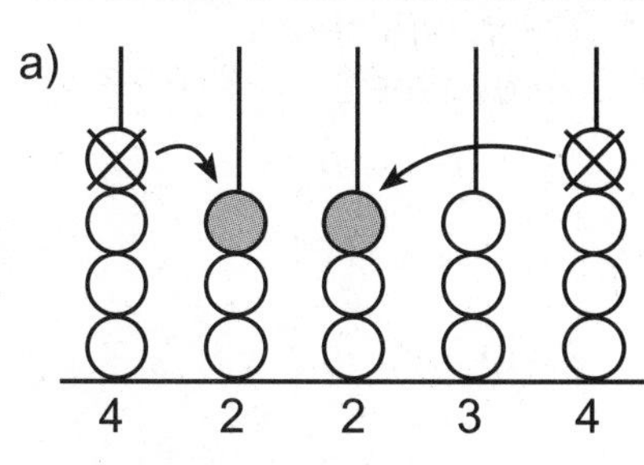

Mean: *3*

b) 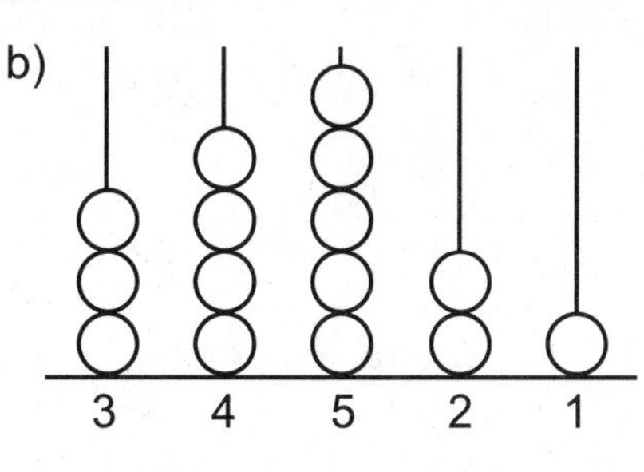

Mean: ________

c) 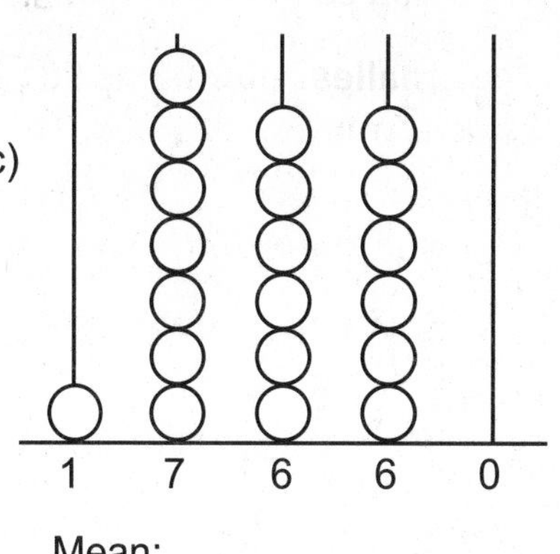

Mean: ________

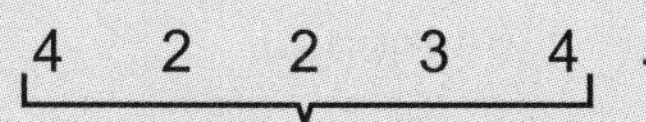

→ 3 3 3 3 3

Total number of beads = 4 + 2 + 2 + 3 + 4
= 15

Mean = number of beads on each rod
= total number of beads ÷ number of rods
= 15 ÷ 5

So **mean = sum of data values ÷ number of data values**.

2. Find the mean without using beads.

a) 0 3 4 6 7

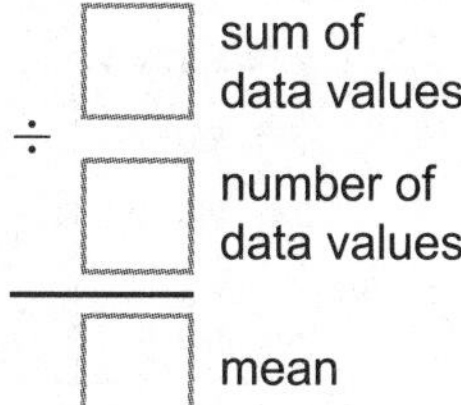

b) 1 4 5 7 8

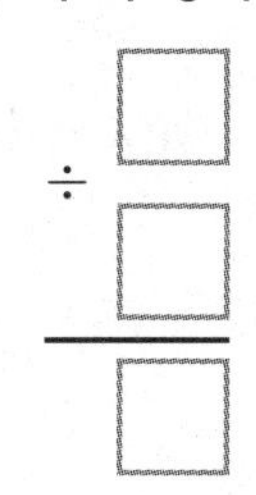

c) 2 5 6 8 9

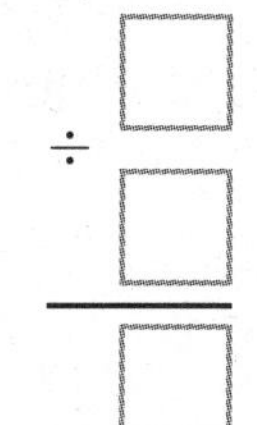

d) 3 6 7 9 10

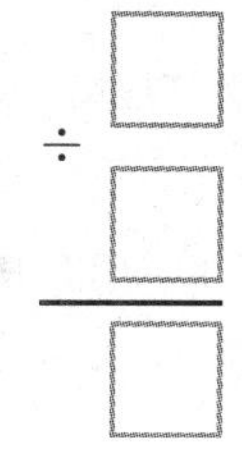

Compare the data values in the sets above — each one is 1 greater than the same value in the previous set. In your notebook, explain how the mean changes when you add 1 to each data value.

3. Find the mean.

a) 0 1 2 3 4 5

b) 24 25 27 29 21

c) 0 25 10 12

Explain why the beads model does not help to find the mean in a).

4. Find the mean and draw a horizontal line to show it.

a) 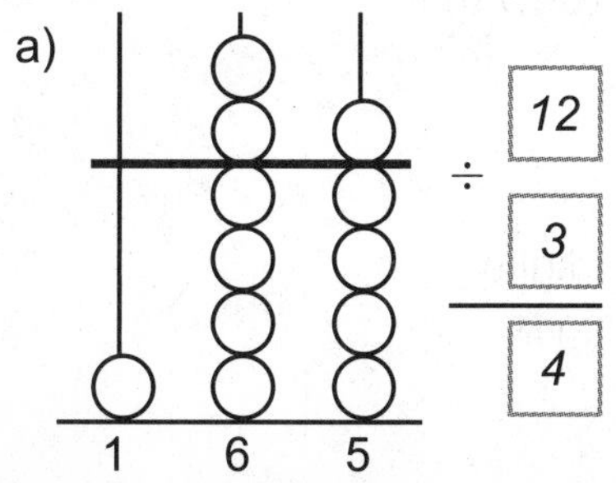

b) 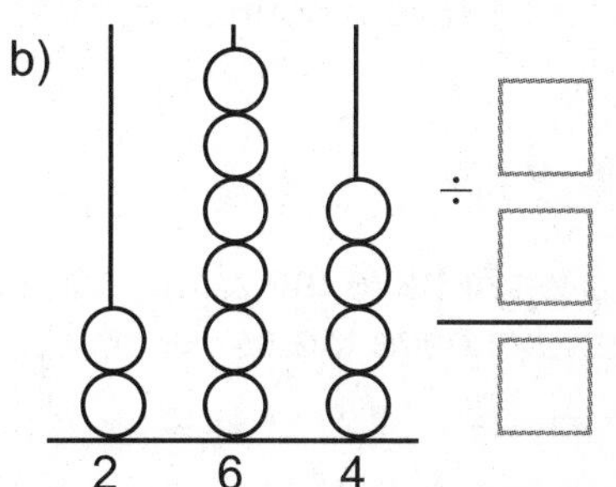

c) 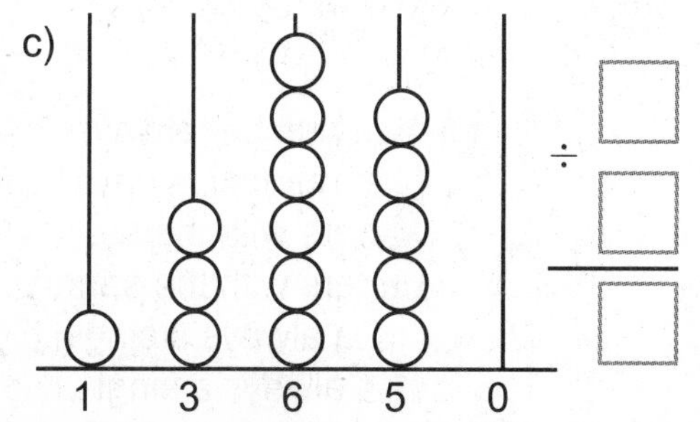

INVESTIGATION ▶ How does adding new data values to a set affect the mean?

A. The data set 1, 4, 10 has mean $15 \div 3 = 5$. Add the following data values to this set and decide if the mean increased, decreased, or stayed the same.

i) New data value: 3

New mean: *$18 \div 4 = 4.5$*

The mean *decreased*.

ii) New data value: 4

New mean: ______

The mean ______.

iii) New data value: 5

New mean: ______

The mean ______.

iv) New data value: 6

v) New data value: 7

vi) New data value: 8

B. Make a conjecture:

When the new data value is smaller than the mean, the mean ______________.

When the new data value is larger than the mean, the mean ______________.

C. Test your conjecture with a different set of data: 2, 3, 7. First find the mean, then add different new values above and below the mean and find the new mean. Did the mean increase, decrease, or stay the same?

D. If you add a value that is the same as the mean, would the mean change? Use this model to explain your thinking.

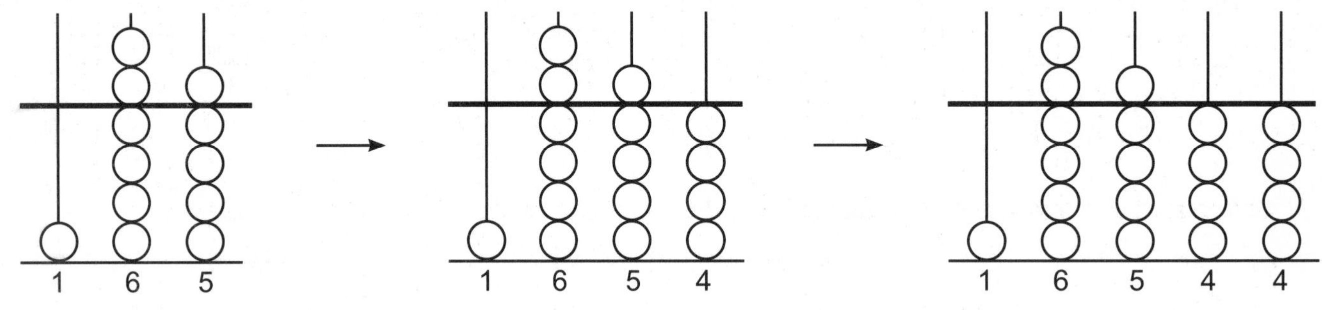

5. The data set is 3, 4, 7, 8, 8.

a) Find the mean.

b) Is the data value 7 above or below the mean?

c) Will removing 7 from the set of data increase or decrease the mean? Find the mean of the set 3, 4, 8, 8 to check your prediction.

6. Ten people work in an office. They get paid different salaries depending on their job.

Salesperson: $50 000 per year   Secretary: $35 000 per year   Clerk: $25 000 per year

There are 5 salespeople, 2 secretaries, and 3 clerks.

a) Find the mean salary in the office.
b) What is the mode (the most common value) of the salaries?
c) Will the mean salary increase or decrease if a secretary retires?
d) Will the mean salary increase or decrease if two new salespeople are hired?

7. Count the spaces below the mean and the blocks above the mean.

a)

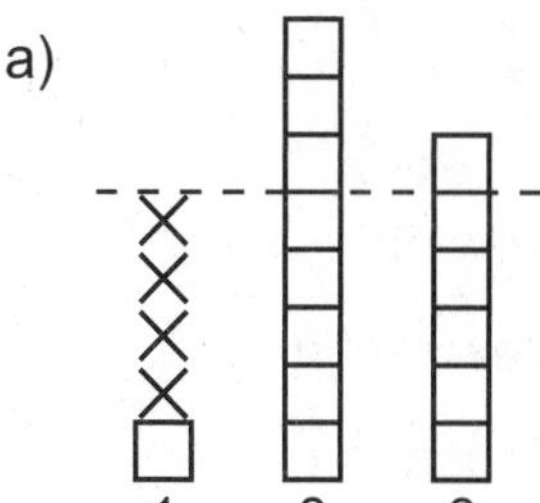

1 8 6

4 spaces *below* mean

4 blocks *above* mean

b)

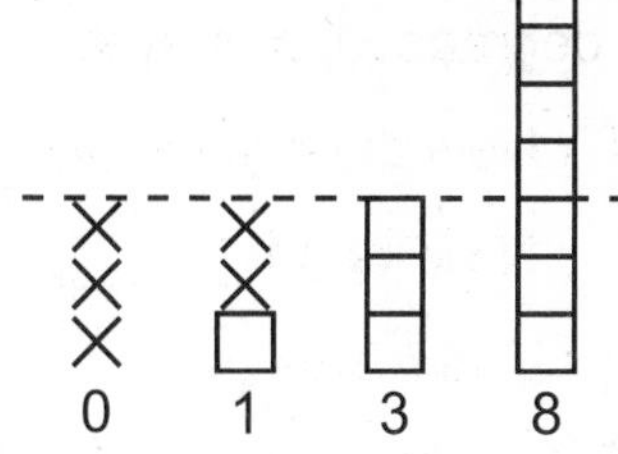

0 1 3 8

_____ spaces *below* mean

_____ blocks *above* mean

c)

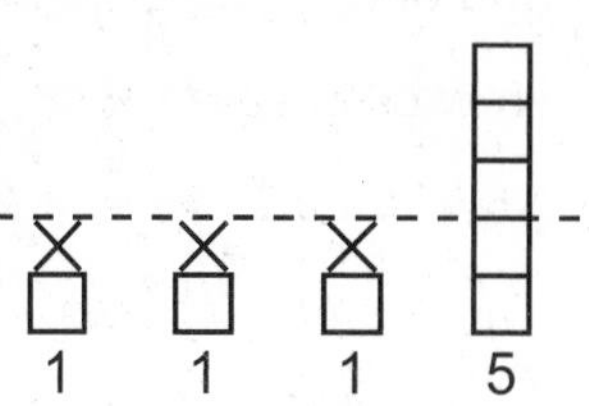

1 1 1 5

_____ spaces *below* mean

_____ blocks *above* mean

8. Look at your answers to Question 7. What do you notice? Explain.

9. The number of spaces below the mean is the same as the number of blocks above the mean. Write a number sentence to show this.

a)

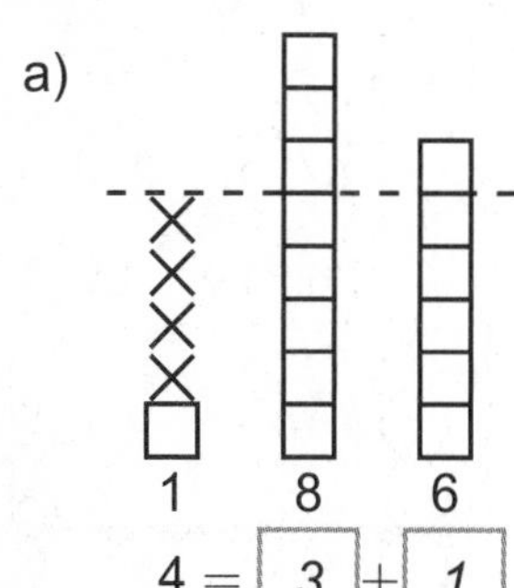

1 8 6

$4 = \boxed{3} + \boxed{1}$

b)

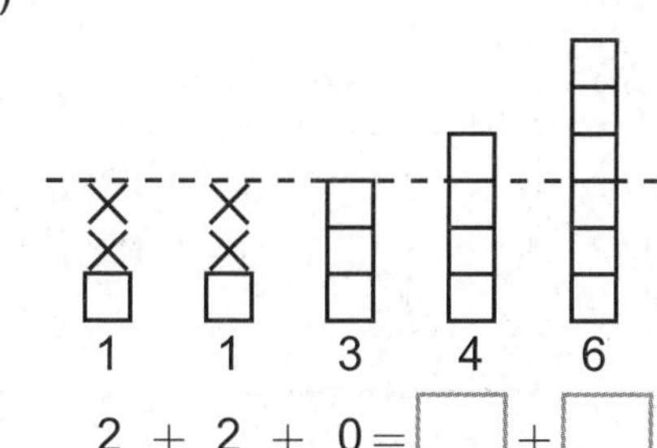

1 1 3 4 6

$2 + 2 + 0 = \square + \square$

c)

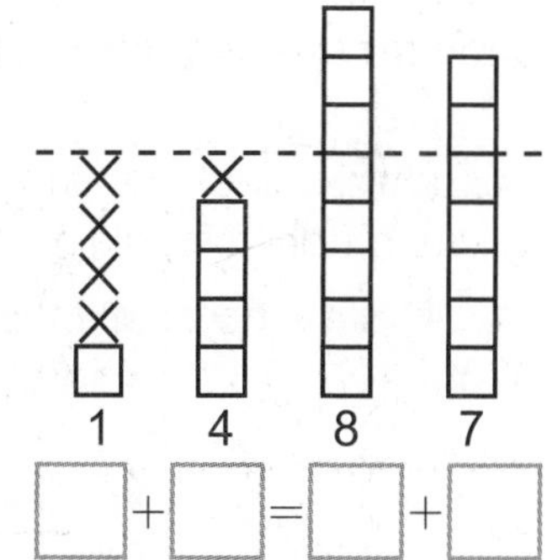

1 4 8 7

$\square + \square = \square + \square$

Do the remaining parts on grid paper. Draw the blocks and find the mean first.

d) 2 6 7

e) 3 4 8 6 9

f) 2 4 5 5

10. Find data sets with mean 4 using the number sentences. Draw beads to help you.

a)

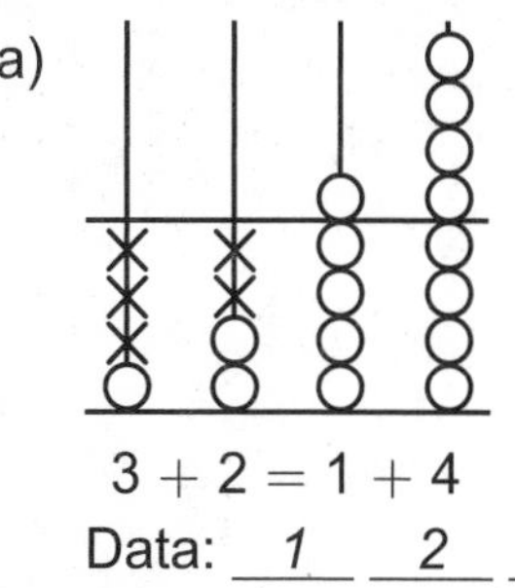

$3 + 2 = 1 + 4$

Data: 1 2 5 8

b)

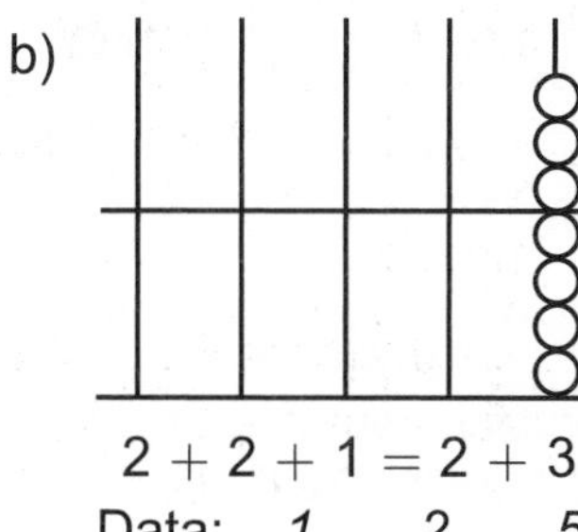

$2 + 2 + 1 = 2 + 3$

Data: 1 2 5 8

c)

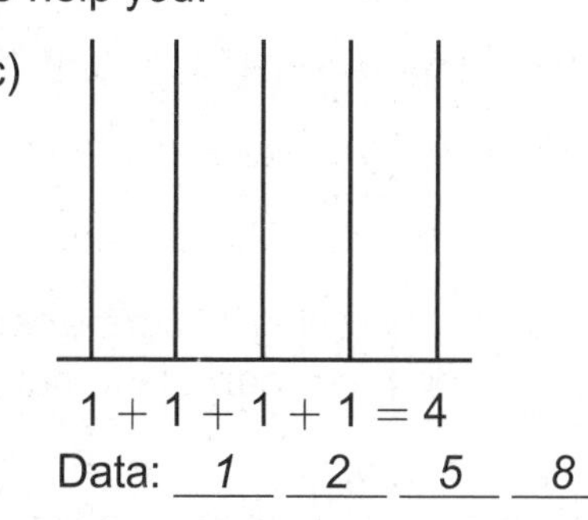

$1 + 1 + 1 + 1 = 4$

Data: 1 2 5 8

11. Create three different sets of data with mean 6.

12. **PROBLEM ▶** The mean of a set of data is 10. The data values are 2, 19, 7, 4, 15, and one other number. What is the other number? Solve the problem in two ways:

a) Use the beads model.

b) Let *x* represent the missing number, write the expression for the mean, and solve the equation.

PDM7-3 Mean, Median, Mode, and Range

To find the **median** of a data set, put the data in order. Count from either end until you reach the middle.

2 3 (6) 7 11

The median is 6.

2 3 (7 9) 11 15

The median is halfway between 7 and 9.
The median is 8.

1. Find the mean, the median, and the range.

a) 9 20 22

mean: $(9 + 20 + 22) \div 3 =$ $51 \div 3 = 17$

median: 20

range: $22 - 9 = 13$

b) 38 40 42

mean: ______

median: ______

range: ______

c) 10 15 20 25 30

mean: ______

median: ______

range: ______

Now order the numbers from smallest to largest first. Show your work in your notebook.

d) 15 18 40 32 25

e) 29 21 27 16 22 17 15

f) 40 25 10 15 20

2. When finding the median, does it matter whether you write the data list from lowest to highest, or from highest to lowest?

INVESTIGATION 1 ▶ When is the median the same as one of the data values?

A. Circle the middle number or numbers. Find the median.

a) 2 4 6 7 8 ______

b) 2 3 3 8 ______

c) 7 9 13 14 26 ______

d) 3 4 6 10 11 17 ______

B. In which of the sets is the median the same as one of the data values? ______

C. If there is an odd number of data values in the set, is the median always one of the numbers in the set? How do you know?

D. Create a set with an even number of data values and no mode. Find the median. Is the median a number in the set? Can you create a set that changes your answer?

E. The set 2, 3, 5, 5 has an even number of values and a mode. Find the median. Is the median a number in the set?

F. Create a set with 6 data values, a mode, and a median that is a number in the set. Are the median and the mode the same?

G. Is it possible to create a set with 6 data values so that the median is a number in the set, but the median is different from the mode? Explain.

BONUS ▶ Create a set with 8 data values so that the median is a number in the set, but the median is different from the mode.

3. Find the mean and the median of each set of two data values. Choose your own numbers in d).

a) 8 14 mean: _______ median: _______ b) 9 12 mean: _______ median: _______

c) 3 15 mean: _______ median: _______ d) ___ ___ mean: _______ median: _______

What do you notice about the mean and the median when there are only two data values?

____

INVESTIGATION 2 ▶ How does adding new data values affect the mean, median, mode, and range?

A. Find the range, mean, median, and mode of this set: 7, 7.

B. Add the data value 10 to the set. The new set is 7, 7, 10. Will the range, the mean, the median, and the mode increase, decrease, or stay the same as for the set 7, 7? Check your predictions.

Add 4 to the set instead of 10. Predict how the mean, the median, the mode, and the range change. Check the predictions again.

C. Look at the set 7, 7, x (where x represents any number). Can you find the mean, median, mode, and range for this set? Cross out the measures you cannot find.

mean _______ median _______ mode _______ range _______

D. What is the smallest number of values you have to add to the set 7, 7 so that 7 will not be the mode anymore? Give an example of such values.

E. What data value should you add to the set 7, 7 to make the mean 5? To make the mean 9?

F. How many data values should you add to the set 7, 7 to change the median? What could these values be?

4. A set of 4 data values has modes 7 and 5. What are the data values in the set?

5. a) Create two different sets of 4 values with mode 7 and median 6.

b) Is it possible to create a set of 4 data values with mode 7, median 6, and the largest number greater than 7? Explain why or why not.

c) Create a set of 4 data values with mode 7, median 6, and mean 5.

6. a) Use blocks to find a set of 5 test scores ranging from 2 to 7 with mean 5, median 5, and mode 7.

b) Add a test score of 12 to your data set from part a). Find the new mean, median, mode, and range and compare them to those in part a). How have they changed?

mean: _______ median: _______ mode: _______ range: _______

PDM7-4 Using the Mean, Median, and Mode

1. You are going on a trip during the March break. What kind of clothes should you pack? This chart shows the highest daily temperatures at your destination during March break last year:

Day	1	2	3	4	5	6	7	8	9	10	11	12	13	14	15
°C	23	22	20	21	22	23	23	10	2	2	5	7	8	12	17

a) Find the range, mean, median, and mode.

b) What does the range of temperatures tell you about what you should pack?

c) If you looked only at the mode of the temperatures, what mistake might you make in your packing?

2. In a company there are 20 employees. One person has a salary of \$ 200 000, two people have salaries of \$75 000, and all the rest have salaries of \$17 500.

a) What is the mean salary?

b) What is the median salary?

c) What is the mode of the salaries?

d) Which better reflects the salaries in the company, the mean or the mode? Explain.

3. In a company there are 20 employees. 1 person has a salary of \$300 000, two people earn \$70 000, another one earns \$45 000, and the rest have different salaries from \$17 000 to \$20 000, with no two salaries the same.

a) Is there enough information to find the mean salary? The median salary? The mode of the salaries? The range of salaries?

b) Which of the mean, the median, and the mode best reflects the salaries in the company? Explain.

4. You work at a clothing store, and your manager says that every week you need an average daily sales of at least \$500. What kind of average do you think your manager is talking about, a mean, a mode, or a median? Why?

5. This chart shows the class marks on a test.

76	78	69	76	73	76	74	66	69	85
74	66	71	76	87	96	66	98	91	73

a) Create a stem and leaf plot for the data.

b) Find the range, mode, median, and mean of the data. Which value is hardest to read or calculate from the stem and leaf plot? Explain.

c) Tom's mark was 76. Which of the following statements that he told his parents were true? Explain using the mean, mode, median, or range.

i) I did better than half of the class!
ii) My grade is higher than the average!
iii) A lot of students had the same grade as me.
iv) Only 6 students got a better mark than me!
v) 76 was the most common mark.

6. This table shows the price for the same pair of shoes at seven different stores.

Store	A	B	C	D	E	F	G
Price ($)	83	85	84	86	86	82	81

a) Find the mean, median, and mode of the prices.

mean: _______ median: _______ mode: _______

b) Store B claims that its prices are lower than average. Which "average" could they use to make this statement true: the mean, mode, or median? Do you think the claim is misleading? Why?

INVESTIGATION ▶

A. Consider the set 5, 5, 5, 5, 5. What are the mean, the median, and the mode of this set?

mean: _______ median: _______ mode: _______

Why are the mean, the median, and the mode the same? _______________

B. Consider the set 4, 5, 5, 5, 6. Find the mean, the median, and the mode. Compare your answers to the answers in part A.

mean: _______ median: _______ mode: _______

C. Use the bead or the block model to explain why the answers in A and B are the same.

D. Create another set of 5 numbers where the mean, the median, and the mode are 5.

E. Will the mean and median be the same or different in this set: 3, 4, 5, 6, 7? Is there a mode?

F. Use the bead or the block model to explain why the mean and the median are the same in the set 5, 5, 7, 8, 10.

---

7. Find a data set, not all numbers equal, where the mean, mode, and median are all the same.

8. a) Find the mean and the median of these sets.

Set A: 2, 3, 4 Set B: 2, 3, 4, 5, 6

b) Move one data value from set A to set B. Find the mean and the median of the new sets. Did the mean and the median of each set increase, decrease, or stay the same?

c) Explain why the mean and the median of set B cannot increase if a data value from set A is added.

9. When a soccer player moved from Team A to Team B, the mean age of **both** teams increased. Give an example of data to show how this could happen.

BONUS ▶ You have a set of 6 whole numbers (some of them can be 0). Find the lowest possible sum of all the numbers in the set if...

a) the median is 50. b) the mean is 500. c) the mode is 5 000.

PDM7-5 Outliers

INVESTIGATION 1 ▶ Which value in a set affects the range the most?

A. Find the range of the set 2, 3, 5, 202. Range: ______________

B. Remove one value from the set and find the range of the new set. Repeat with all other values.

New set: 3, 5, 202 New set: 2, 5, 202 New set: ____, ____, ____ New set: ____, ____, ____

Range: 202 − 3 = 199 Range: ____________ Range: ____________ Range: ____________

Which value affects the range the most?

C. Mark the data values on the number line below. Circle the value that affects the range the most.

0 10 20 30 40 50 60 70 80 90 100 110 120 130 140 150 160 170 180 190 200 210

D. Repeat parts B and C with this set: 2, 52, 102, 152, 202.

0 10 20 30 40 50 60 70 80 90 100 110 120 130 140 150 160 170 180 190 200 210

E. How does removing the value that most affects the range change the range?

An **outlier** is a data value that is far from the rest of the data values in the set. Removing an outlier changes the range of the set a lot. Examples:

In the set 2, 3, 4, 5, 90, the number 90 is an outlier.

0 10 20 30 40 50 60 70 80 90 100

In the set 2, 400, 406, 435, 470, 475, the number 2 is an outlier.

0 50 100 150 200 250 300 350 400 450 500

1. For each set below, create a stem and leaf plot of the data. Identify the outlier in each set.

a) 23, 25, 65, 25, 37, 761, 41 b) 789, 792, 770, 764, 200 c) 75, 77, 71, 90, 13, 86, 80

How can stem and leaf plot help you to identify the outlier?

2. This set does not have an outlier: 2, 3, 100, 201, 202. Explain why none of the values is an outlier.

INVESTIGATION 2 ▶ Does adding an outlier to a set affect the mode?

A. What is the mode of the set 110, 115, 110, 113, 114? ____ Does this set have an outlier? ________

B. Add the outlier 200. The new set is ____, ____, ____, ____, ____, 200. What is the mode? ____

C. Add the outlier 1. The new set is ____, ____, ____, ____, ____, ____, 200. What is the mode? ____

D. Does an outlier change the mode of the set? ________

INVESTIGATION 3 ▶ Consider the set 2, 3, 4, 5, 76.

A. Circle the outlier.

B. Find the mean and the median of the set.

C. Write the set without the outlier: ____, ____, ____, ____.

Find the mean and the median of the new set.

D. Which value was changed more by the removal of the outlier, the mean or the median?

E. Choose any other value in the set. Write the set without it: ____, ____, ____, 76.

Find the mean and the median of the new set.

F. Repeat the investigation with these sets.

i) 78, 77, 12, 69, 74

ii) 4, 4, 4, 4, 5, 6, 35.

G. What affects the mean and the median more, the removal of the outlier or the removal of another value?

---

3. The set 2, 3, 4, 5 does not have an outlier. If you add 100 as a new data value, what will be affected more, the mean or the median? Check your prediction.

4. a) Find the outlier in each set of data.

A: Ages of the members of the Bridge club in Golden Age Retirement Residence: 68, 76, 78, 89, 94, 69, 102, 69, 75, 7, 77

B: Yearly salaries of permanent employees in a company: $25 000, $35 000, $300, $45 000

C: Hourly rate of contract workers in a company: $25, $17.50, $300, $45

b) In which of the above situations is the outlier likely a mistake in the data? Explain.

5. Katie's math test scores (out of 20) are 16, 17, 17, 5, 19, 18, 17, 20, 19.

a) What is the outlier in this set?

b) When Katie's teacher finds the average for the report, should he include the outlier? Discuss with a partner.

6. One day a scene from a movie is filmed outside 10 Daffodil Street. At 8 Daffodil Street, there is a small coffee shop, and the daily sales at the coffee shop are 1 000 times larger than ever.

a) Does the set of the daily sales for the year contain an outlier?

b) To keep track of sales, the coffee shop finds the average daily sales for the year. Should the owner of the shop include the outlier in the calculation?

c) The owner decides to sell the store. She includes the average daily sales in an advertisement. Should she include the outlier in the calculation of the average?